CAPITAL THEORY AND THE DISTRIBUTION OF INCOME

ADVANCED TEXTBOOKS IN ECONOMICS

VOLUME 4

Editors:

C. J. BLISS

M. D. INTRILIGATOR

NORTH-HOLLAND PUBLISHING COMPANY
AMSTERDAM · OXFORD

AMERICAN ELSEVIER PUBLISHING CO., INC.
NEW YORK

CAPITAL THEORY AND THE DISTRIBUTION OF INCOME

C. J. BLISS
University of Essex

1975

NORTH-HOLLAND PUBLISHING COMPANY
AMSTERDAM · OXFORD
AMERICAN ELSEVIER PUBLISHING CO., INC.
NEW YORK

Library of Congress Catalog Card Number: 74-30938
North-Holland ISBN:
for the series: 0 7204 3600 1
for this volume: 0 7204 3604 4 (*clothbound*)
0 7204 3098 4 (*paperback*)

American Elsevier ISBN:
for this volume: 0 444 10782 7 (*clothbound*)
0 444 10865 3 (*paperback*)

PUBLISHERS:

NORTH-HOLLAND PUBLISHING COMPANY – AMSTERDAM
NORTH-HOLLAND PUBLISHING COMPANY LTD. – OXFORD

SOLE DISTRIBUTORS FOR THE U.S.A. AND CANADA:

AMERICAN ELSEVIER PUBLISHING COMPANY, INC.
52 VANDERBILT AVENUE, NEW YORK, N.Y. 10017

PRINTED IN THE UNITED KINGDOM

To my parents

Preface

When economists reach agreement on the theory of capital they will shortly reach agreement on everything else. Happily, for those who enjoy a diversity of views and beliefs, there is very little danger of this outcome. Indeed, there is at present not even agreement as to what the subject is about. This book aims at a systematic treatment of those topics which all would recognize to be central to the theory, and of some others besides. With the needs of students in mind the treatment of most topics has been made largely self-contained. Hence, it is hoped that the book will be useful for courses on the theory of capital and to those who study the subject on their own. In either case there may well be more in the book than teacher or student can cope with in a limited time. If so, parts I–IV and VI form a shorter book which is self-contained. More drastic pruning can be achieved by leaving out ch. 7 and all or some of part IV.

It is very difficult to know what background and prior knowledge to assume for a book like this. More students are interested in the theory of capital than in any other branch of economic theory and many want to get on with studying it before they have achieved a good grasp of microeconomic theory and general equilibrium theory. Furthermore, while the subject is naturally and inescapably a mathematical one, at least in part, it attracts students who are not specialists in mathematical economics. In this situation the author is propelled in opposing directions by conflicting needs to avoid obvious dangers. To pretend that a useful knowledge of the theory of capital is available to those without an adequate background in economic theory, or that what is needed can be learnt in passing, is to play the role of the charlatan. On the other hand, it is just as wrong to suppose that only a student highly trained in mathematics can master the subject. This makes for a presentation which is unnecessarily difficult and often needlessly obscure.

What has been done here is to eschew any pretensions to a tidy solution to the problem. In particular, there has been no attempt to make the mathematical level of different chapters even approximately comparable. Instead, the mathematical level in each case is that which I judge to be the minimum necessary for the accurate derivation of results and for the education of an intuition for what is true and what is not. As a consequence of this approach the mathematical difficulty varies greatly from one part to another, and from chapter to chapter. The most difficult mathematical arguments are to be found in the appendices, which may be missed out, particularly from a first reading, or in certain chapters, such as ch. 7, which again may be missed out without undue loss of continuity.

The majority of proofs employ no more than elementary algebra or matrix algebra, or linear programming theorems that will probably be familiar to the reader already. Beyond that there is a little calculus (far less than is usual in books on economic theory), some set theory and occasional use of basic concepts of mathematical analysis, such as a limit, continuity, differentiability, etc. Hence, the demands made on mathematical knowledge are only moderate ones. What is required, however, is a certain mathematical maturity and a familiarity with the mathematical mode of reasoning. This would normally be acquired from a course on analysis, linear algebra or mathematical economics. Therefore, one or more such courses might be regarded as a prerequisite.

Where economic theory is concerned the reader is assumed to have studied microeconomics to the level of a course for final-year undergraduate specialists, and to have acquired thereby, or otherwise, a sound grounding in the theory of general equilibrium. Nearly everything else that the reader will require is provided within the covers of the book.

This volume has been more time in the writing than I care to think about. For several years I have been working when time allowed on a book which has eventually turned out to be this one. Many papers that I have presented to seminars, much informal discussion with my fellow economists and a good deal of my advanced teaching, has been directly connected with the problem of sorting out one or other section of the book. As a consequence of this inordinately long gestation period I have accumulated more debts than I could begin to enumerate. Chief among them are those which I owe to students at the Universities of Cambridge and Essex. Whatever shortcomings are to be found in the following pages were at least as great, and sometimes much greater, in the earlier drafts which formed the basis of lectures. It has been my good fortune to have students who took a pride in detecting errors and obscurities in my arguments. When the reader finds that some of these still remain he should bear in mind that there would have been many more were it not for the beneficent effects of this attention to refutation.

My interest in the theory of capital I owe largely to Professor Joan Robinson, and in arguing with her at Cambridge I received my early education in the subject. The hours which she devoted to trying to convince me that I was taking a wrong view of the subject must have been totally unrewarding for her, but her interest and patience never abated. At the Massachusetts Institute of Technology, Professor R. M. Solow was likewise unstinting with his time. He taught me a great deal without seeming to teach, and he tempered his criticism with kindness and encouragement. In the case of each of these eminent economists I have departed, sometimes sharply, from views for which they are noted. But that does not diminish the debt that I owe to them. The simple fact is that my method of learning the theory of capital has been to evaluate critically the work which I judged to be most important. Hence, those I criticize are those from whom I have learnt.

I am grateful for valuable criticism and assistance to, among others, A. Dixit, F. H. Hahn, P. J. Hammond, M. C. Kemp, J. A. Mirrlees, D. M. G. Newbery and C. C. von Weizsäcker. Dr. D. Glycopantis rescued me from serious error in the first draft of the appendix to ch. 10. My co-editor, Michael Intriligator, gave me valuable advice and was endlessly patient regarding delays in the completion of the manuscript. Paul Hamelynck of the North-Holland Publishing Company has proved to be a friend as well as my publisher, this in spite of being terribly let down with regard to deadlines. The tedious chore of preparing the bibliography was undertaken cheerfully at different times by Mrs. Rachel Britton and Mrs. Joanne Davis. The manuscript was typed by Mrs. Phyllis Pattenden who was my secretary while I was chairman of the Department of Economics at Essex. More than anyone else she made it possible to bring this work to completion; not just by deciphering my scribbled drafts with wonderful inspiration, but also by lightening my load and leaving me time to write.

September, 1974 *C. J. Bliss*

Contents

PART V: INVESTMENT AND THE SHORT RUN

PART VI: CONCLUSION

Mathematical notation

Real numbers (scalars) will be denoted by roman or greek letters in normal type, upper or lower case, according to convenience. Thus a, v, α and λ are scalars while $U(v)$ is a real-valued function of the scalar v.

Integers will be denoted by roman letters in normal type, upper or lower case. The upper case is reserved for the highest value in a sequence of integers. Hence i is an integer variable which may take any of the values $1, 2, \ldots, I$. t is usually an integer-valued index of time, and T the largest number of time intervals considered.

Real vectors are denoted by roman letters in bold type. The scalars corresponding to individual components of vectors are denoted by subscripted versions of the same letters in normal type. Hence $\boldsymbol{x}$ is a vector and x_i is the ith component of that vector.

Matrices are denoted by upper-case roman letters in bold type and the individual components by doubly subscripted versions of the same letters in lower case and normal type. Thus $\boldsymbol{A}$ is a matrix and a_{ij} is the component of that matrix in the ith row and the jth column.

Sets of vectors are denoted by upper-case script letters, e.g. $\mathscr{T}$ and $\mathscr{S}$. The symbol $\in$ denotes set inclusion. Hence $\boldsymbol{x} \in \mathscr{T}$ means that the vector $\boldsymbol{x}$ belongs to the set $\mathscr{T}$. A set will be defined by enclosing between braces the notation for an element, followed by a vertical line and then the property or properties that must be satisfied for membership of the set. Thus $\{\boldsymbol{x} \mid \boldsymbol{x}$ has property $P\}$ is the set of all $\boldsymbol{x}$ such that $\boldsymbol{x}$ has property P.

Implication will be denoted by $\Rightarrow$. Thus, $A \Rightarrow B$ is to be read 'A implies B'.

The convention for denoting inequalities is the same for vectors and for matrices. Given two vectors $\boldsymbol{a}$ and $\boldsymbol{b}$:

- $\boldsymbol{a} > \boldsymbol{b}$ means that each component of $\boldsymbol{a}$ is larger than the corresponding component of $\boldsymbol{b}$;
- $\boldsymbol{a} \geqq \boldsymbol{b}$ means that each component of $\boldsymbol{a}$ is at least as large as the corresponding component of $\boldsymbol{b}$;

$\boldsymbol{a} \geqslant \boldsymbol{b}$ means that each component of $\boldsymbol{a}$ is at least as large as the corresponding component of $\boldsymbol{b}$ and at least one component is strictly larger (i.e. $\boldsymbol{a}$ and $\boldsymbol{b}$ are not the same vector).

Finally, the symbol $\cdot$ denotes the operation of forming the inner product of two vectors. Hence $\boldsymbol{a} \cdot \boldsymbol{b}$ is the inner product of the vectors $\boldsymbol{a}$ and $\boldsymbol{b}$.

Part I

INTRODUCTION

1

The problem of capital

This method, conclusion first, reasons afterwards, has always been in high favour with the human race: you write down at the outset the answer to the sum; then you proceed to fabricate, not for use but for exhibition to the public, the ciphering by which you can pretend to have arrived at it. The method has one obvious advantage – that you are thus quite sure of reaching the conclusion you want to reach: if you began with your reasons there is no telling where they might lead you, and like enough you will never get to the desired conclusion at all. But it has one drawback; that unanimity is thus unattainable: every man gives the answer which seems right in his own eyes.

A. E. HOUSMAN, *Introductory Lecture*

The subject matter of this book is the theory of capital. We should begin by explaining what that study concerns itself with; what are the distinctive problems which the theory attempts to elucidate; to what questions one can seek an answer in the following pages. Two kinds of definitions readily suggest themselves: on the one hand there are definitions so all-embracing that they take in the whole of economics while, on the other hand, there are definitions which insist on a narrow focus and are merely designed to impose the conclusions at which someone has already arrived long before framing a definition of the subject.

However, without making a fetish of precision, one can go a long way with the following definition. Capital theory is concerned with the implications for a market economy, for the theory of prices, for the theory of production and for the theory of distribution, of the existence of produced means of production. Among the various necessities to produce output by a particular method will usually be included the use of one or more inputs which themselves result from previous production. In other words, the typical cycle of production is not simply the application of human labour and things provided by nature to produce output, but it involves as well the use of man-made inputs which are themselves outputs from other production cycles. Or, to look at the matter from the point of income distribution, there are people who derive income from their ownership of produced goods. What determines how much income they will derive? How can the ownership of something which ultimately is not scarce, because augmentable by new production, command a rent?

As a starting point the focus on produced means of production is adequate. However, it will not escape notice that even this idea is imprecise[1]. Are there not cases where we would feel the need for concepts of capital theory and where yet it is hard to find any produced means of production to put a finger upon? Suppose, for example, the existence of a primitive community where an edible grain grows wild, as once upon a time presumably the grasses which are the ancestors of our wheats grew wild. Now imagine that men spend time and energy in pulling weeds and inedible grasses from amongst the desirable type, and that in this way the earth bears more grain, and their stomachs are better provided for. Are we to talk of capital in this case? If so, where are the produced means of production? We seem only to have the labour of mens' hands and the providence of the earth.

Why then think of capital at all in this case? Because there is a feature of this example which is closely related to the production of tools and other produced means of production. The labour which is applied while the grasses are growing is not applied for immediate reward, as when a man scales a coconut tree to bring down a coconut to eat. Rather, the benefits of that labour will accrue later when the grain is harvested. This aspect of the example, that there is a passage of time between the outlay and the return of that outlay, is almost necessarily involved where the production of tools is concerned. The man who stays behind to make himself a bow, while others hunt, is involved in delaying the arrival of the fruits of his labour so as to make them greater. The labour which he applies today to the manufacture of his bow yields him no immediate consumption, but later on he (or will it be someone else?) will be able to consume more because of the kills which can be made with a bow and arrow.

All this is suggestive of a different tack. The essential ingredient, it might be argued, is time. All outlays of labour or consumption foregone have a date and the benefits will accrue at different dates. What we must capture in our theory to have it encompass capital is this intertemporal aspect of production and consumption. In this view time is the essence of capital.

In the ultimate analysis there is no difference between the two approaches

[1] As an example which brings out the imprecision of the concept 'produced-means-of-production' consider the case of so-called 'human capital'. If a certain process requires a skilled craftsman to execute it he must first be trained. The taking of a workman from immediately productive labour to undergo training has all the features of tool construction, i.e. it is just like investment in capital. Are we then to regard the labour of skilled craftsmen as pure labour, the services of capital, or a bit of each?

which prohibits a reconciliation. If our model of capitalistic[2] production is sufficiently general it will take in both aspects of production with capital; that it involves the use of produced means of production and that the implications of a capitalistic production process are extended through time. In the following chapters we will introduce and work with a very general production model. We will not be concerned, except incidentally, with the special cases and the particular growth models which have accounted for so many printed pages. Hence it is not required of us to say whether it is produced means of production or time which is the essence of the matter – both will feature in our model.

However, generality is not a virtue in itself. Every scientific theory is a peculiarly special case. Indeed, one might say that the more we know the more special will be the cases that we consider. In brushing aside the view that time is the essence of capital we are rejecting a particular vision of capital, and one which it so happens is of great historical importance. The classical economists were not the first to notice the close relation between the passage of time and capitalistic production, but it was they who made it the centre of analysis. The relation in a way is a very obvious one if capital is considered with a market system in mind. The lender of 'capital' (meaning here finance) grants a loan to the borrower to be repaid later. If interest is charged more value must be provided later to service the loan. What the borrower gets is the dispensation to have some time elapse between receipt of the loan and the repayment of principle and interest. He can gain from that possibility if the passage of time can be put to productive use, if delaying the delivery of the product enables more product to be provided. This it plainly does do where the loan is used for the provision of working capital, the advance of wages or the purchase of raw materials, which is the case on which the classical economists concentrated their attention.

So far everything is unobjectionable, but it is now but a small step to an idea to which objection might very reasonably be taken. If capital is time, is not more capital more time? Thus we arrive at the distinctively Austrian vision of capital and capital accumulation. A capitalistic method of production is a 'roundabout' method and the roundabout routes to production yield more than the direct methods. Moreover, the most productive methods are the most roundabout; they involve most 'waiting', the longest 'periods of production'.

[2] 'Capitalistic' as we will use it is the adjective derived from the noun 'capital', not from the noun 'capitalism'. Thus capitalistic production processes are those which use capital. The organization of these processes may or may not be according to the social system of capitalism.

It is not a decisive objection to this view that it turns out on examination to be rather special, so that it is not difficult to invent examples where the most productive method does not take longer, but rather takes a shorter time. The Austrian vision would be much less interesting if there were no other logical possibility. It is not even clear that a few counter examples taken from reality would serve to discredit the vision. Economic theory pursues that clear-cut simplification which captures the essential features of reality. It is no merit of a model to cover every little case and each particular exception, if a simple scheme will take in the greater part of reality and reveal more clearly the grand structure.

The question is, does the Austrian vision do that? We think that it does not. Moreover, it carries with it a tendency to take the case of a single rate of interest, which is the case of simple examples, and to make it the only case which the theory recognizes. We hope to convince the reader in due course that this is an insidious tendency. The Austrian model is not alone in falling into this trap, but it cannot avoid falling into it. There is another objection: it is an impossible model to apply because its concepts do not correspond at all to those which are current in the thinking of the men who steer the economy and the firms and units which comprise it. Indeed, it is hard to make a connection. Now it is not an objection to a theoretical model that its concepts do not mirror the thought patterns of the men of whose behaviour it aims to give an account. On the other hand, it should be possible to forge a link between the two, and so far this has been done for the Austrian model only for cases which are clearly very special, so that exceptions to them must surely be legion. So it looks as though the Austrian route is a detour[3].

Although we will not follow the path of the Austrian model we will stay closer to it than to another vision of capital. According to this view capital is wealth, i.e. command over current output. Once again this view involves picking upon something which indeed is an aspect of capital and treating it as the essence. It is true, of course, that capital, meaning here the physical goods which are used in capitalistic production, is typically held by its owners as a store of wealth and a source of income. But it does not follow that the economic theorist should regard it exclusively in this light. Wherein lies the temptation to do so? It is to be found in a closely associated view; namely, that the rate of interest is the price of capital. The value which accrues from a sale is the product of price and quantity sold. Hence if the rate of interest

[3] Nonetheless, the reader would do well to look at the works of those modern writers who have tried to rehabilitate the Austrian model; see Hicks (1973) and von Weizsäcker (1971). For a critical review of the approach and a demonstration of how it is related to the model of this volume, see Burmeister (1974).

is the price of capital, the quantity of capital must be the wealth on which an interest yield is calculated. It will be shown shortly why this view is incorrect, but to cut a long story short, the conclusion may be announced at once. The rate of interest is not the price of capital.

The vision of capital which is embodied in the argument of the following chapters is that capital does spring from time and that the central problem of the theory is to show how economic analysis can deal with cases where we have to take into account the extension of production, consumption and planning through time. To go thus far with the idea that capital and time are closely associated is not to go all the way with the Austrians and accept that capital is time, and is to be measured as a quantity of time. In fact, our vision is one of the complexity and diversity of the productive processes of reality, so that we are not able to accept any particular simple production model as capturing the essence of capitalistic production.

So much for the essence of capitalistic production. We need only note that it is impossible to represent it without taking into account its extension through time. The main problem for the theory is to do just that. As for the essence of capital we think it best not to worry about that, because capital is many things to different men. To the *rentier* it is a claim on income now and in the future. To the entrepreneur it is some necessary inputs. To the accountant it is entries in a valuation account. To the theorist it is a source of production and a component of the explanation of the division of that production.

The desire to find something to be the essence of capital is closely associated with the feeling that capital must be aggregated. The path which we will follow when we come to consider capitalistic production as production extended through time leads to the consideration of capital inputs as a heterogeneous collection of goods. These are classed together according to their use, as we class 'farm animals' together, without any suggestion that there is any way of adding them up to reach a grand total. But many people will feel that we miss something if we treat capital as a mixed collection of capital goods.

Perhaps the feeling can be explained by a consideration of the following instance. No one who visits the USA can fail to be struck by the fact that it is a rich country and one very well endowed with capital goods. One could give expression to this view by explaining that the USA is very well endowed with highways, factories, steel plants and so on. But to offer this account of the matter is to miss an obvious point. In some sense the observations of the abundant endowment of the USA in various specific types of capital goods are not providing independent information. We expect a country well endowed with electrical generation capacity to be well endowed with power lines.

We do not expect a nation which generally eats very well to go about in rags. These expectations are governed precisely by our knowledge that capital goods are produced-means-of-production. If we were to talk of endowments with minerals or types of natural timber we might have to detail the endowment item by item, but is there not some sense in which we can say that the USA is well endowed with capital without having to detail all the particular items of capital with which it is well endowed?

These considerations serve to show that the aggregation problem is to some extent inescapable when we study the theory of capital. Hence the view that one sometimes meets according to which the problem can be avoided simply by not aggregating and treating only of specific types of capital goods separately is a little facile. Capital cries out to be aggregated – at least it does when we consider long-run equilibrium where the composition of the capital stock reflects the operation of conscious selection and is not merely the fortuitous result of history.

However, to say that capital invites aggregation is not to say that it will be aggregated. It is only to claim that the attempt is a reasonably motivated one. While common sense may insist that the USA is a capital-rich country, precise definitions of the quantity of capital, which would be in accord with the basic properties one would want of such a quantity, may prove elusive. We will see later that such is the case.

It remains to outline the path which the argument will follow through the book. In part II we develop the main idea, that the theory of capital can be treated as an extension of static equilibrium theory to take account of time. In ch. 2 we examine the static or timeless general equilibrium model. It is important to look it over because it is our point of departure. It is particularly important to detail what a static equilibrium theory can and cannot achieve, and to remove some misconceptions about this matter. Otherwise, certain features of the extended equilibrium model might be attributed to the extension of the model, when in fact they belong to all equilibrium models. In ch. 3 it is shown formally how a timeless equilibrium model can be extended to take account of time by extending the notion of a good to include date of delivery as one of the attributes. We call the equilibrium model thus extended the *intertemporal model*. We observe that this produces a rather formalistic model which is unlikely to mirror reality at all closely and we examine an alternative model, the *temporary-equilibrium model*, which perhaps is more applicable. In ch. 4 we examine a special case of the intertemporal equilibrium model where the plausibility of its assumptions is greater than is generally the case. This is the case of *semi-stationary growth* where the economy is the same at different times except for a change of scale. At this point the argument will connect with a large body of literature, since something like the assumption of semi-stationary growth is very frequently adopted. We pay particular attention to comparisons of semi-stationary paths and learn from this exercise, among other things, some important lessons concerning the aggregation of capital. An appendix proves an important theorem on the existence of a constant-rate-of-interest price system for a semi-stationary development. Ch. 5 is devoted to a very detailed examination of marginal productivity theory as it is affected by capitalistic production. Again some misconceptions must be cleared aside, but it is hoped that the result is a clarification of what marginal theory can and cannot achieve in the theory of capital. Ch. 6 is concerned with an examination of the so-called 'Cambridge model' regarded as a special case of the semi-stationary growth model.

In part III we turn our full attention to the problem of aggregation. Since it is very important not to discuss capital theory except from the perspective of an accurate understanding of the theory of the static economy, ch. 7 is devoted to a review of standard aggregation theory. This chapter may be of interest even to readers who know that theory since our methods of analysis are not the usual ones. Ch. 8 examines the case that is peculiar to capital theory and which standard aggregation theory does not cover, aggregation across long-run equilibria. Here we examine the aggregation procedure proposed by Champernowne, paying particular attention to the cases where it fails (such as the so-called double-switching case), since these have recently received a great deal of attention from theorists, following many years of neglect.

In part IV we are concerned less with the description of capital accumulation than with the extension to that area of certain basic concepts of static production theory such as efficiency. In ch. 9 we present a production model in detail which is the one used in the subsequent chapters. Ch. 10 and its appendix establish the fundamental property of an efficient development, that it is a kind of price equilibrium, and elucidate the connection between efficiency and the property of being a price equilibrium. The analytical method used is linear programming. Ch. 11 is concerned with a somewhat different question which is raised by the Cambridge model, namely under what conditions relative prices depend only upon the technology and the rate of interest. However, since the production model employed is that of part IV and the method used to answer the question is linear programming theory, the chapter is not out of place at this point. In ch. 12 we examine the implications for non-stationary developments through time of the comparative dynamic cases which were seen to interfere with aggregation by the Champernowne method.

Part V takes up some left-over questions concerned particularly with the short-run and temporary equilibrium. Ch. 13 is concerned with the theory of investment. The approach is to try to subsume investment into production theory rather than treating it as a separate theoretical problem. However, the importance of uncertainty must be recognized. Moreover, we are not able to follow other writers who apparently agree with this approach, notably Jorgenson. Ch. 14 is concerned with the theory of the term structure of interest rates.

Part VI is a single chapter, ch. 15, devoted to the issues of ideology and controversy in capital theory. Finally, some mathematical results to which reference is made in the text are collected together in the mathematical appendix.

Through this lengthy and wide-ranging discussion there runs one, possibly unifying, theme. At least there is an idea that turns up several times in seemingly unrelated contexts. Solow (1963)[4] has suggested that capital theory stands in need of being liberated from the concept of capital: in its place he proposes to put the rate of return. Our idea is nearly the exact antithesis of Solow's proposal. It is that capital theory should be liberated from the concept of the rate of interest, meaning by that one rate. In its place we will enthrone not the old king, capital; there can be no going back to days when his rule found unquestioned acceptance. Instead, we will find the concept of intertemporal prices to be fundamental and will see that working with the rate of interest is a clumsy groping for that concept.

This is a largish volume and the reader might hope to find all his interests catered for. If so he may be disappointed. There are many topics within the broad scope of the theory of capital which are not even broached in this volume. Two among them deserve mention. As has been noted already, we will not be much concerned with particular growth models. We have chosen for the most part to deal only with those results which are generally valid. As it happens there are not a few of these. It is appropriate that an introductory text should concern itself particularly with those results which are so fundamental that they do not depend upon the choice of a particular type of technology. Also, there is nothing more boring than a catalogue of growth models. However, it is obvious that the model that we work with is much too general to be applied and the study of it should be seen as a prelude to the study of special models which are manageable enough to permit quantification and estimation. But it is important to know that some properties are rather special and to be alerted to the possibility that they may fail to be realized if the conditions for them are not satisfied.

Some readers will come to this volume with a presumption that the theory of technical progress is the single most important topic in the theory of capital

---

[4] Full details of references are given in a list of references at the end of the book.

and will be amazed to find it scarcely discussed at all. However, there are good reasons why it finds so little mention. In part II we are eventually concerned with semi-stationary growth and any interesting technical progress is incompatible with the conditions of semi-stationary growth. Indeed, it is surely the case that technical progress requires us to recognize that imperfect foresight is what characterizes the actual progress of an economy through time. The study of semi-stationary growth is in part a device to put aside the analytical difficulties that flow from this fact. Hence, technical progress is scarcely compatible with that case, unless it be in the most simple and unconvincing form. Apart from the problem of perfect foresight there is an even more immovable difficulty. Normally, technical progress must fundamentally alter the structure of the economy so that there is no possibility of the pattern of previous events repeating themselves. Again there is a rather basic conflict with the assumptions of semi-stationary growth.

Turning now to part IV we have an altogether different situation. Here technical progress can easily be included. At least it creates no formal difficulties to put in the most general form of technical progress. So it will be included there, but then in such a general form that the type of results on technical progress which the literature might lead the reader to expect are not to be found.

Finally in part V, and more generally whenever we consider the short-run and temporary equilibrium, technical progress should surely be included. Yes, but we have not bothered to do so, although it might easily be done. The reason is that we have taken into account price uncertainty and this already carries with it all the complications implied by the uncertainties of technical progress. The addition of technical progress would be easily enough achieved, but it would bring with it no extra interest and we have thought it better to save the reader some trouble in terms of the exposition by leaving it out.

Much of the interest of the theory of capital lies in the fact that it holds the key to the theory of the distribution of income and this is a connection which we will explore. However, this is not a text on the theory of the distribution of income as such and there are several topics of great importance within the confines of that subject to which we will give no attention. It is the functional distribution of income, as represented by factor shares, that will figure in our argument. Recently, economists have rightly taken more interest in the personal distribution of income and the causes operating upon it through time. This, however, is not a subject that we will attempt to treat in the following pages. As has been remarked already, capital theory must somehow be defined so as to embrace something less than the whole of economics.

Part II

EQUILIBRIUM

2

Production without capital

Nevertheless, the above assumption of production without capital, or rather production in which capital is to be regarded as a free good, is logically conceivable and is, therefore, an abstraction which is permissible for purposes of exposition – in much the same way as it is permissible in Ricardo's theory of rent, of which we shall shortly speak, to regard cultivation as proceeding from 'better' to 'worse' land, even although, historically, the development may in many cases have been in the opposite direction.

KNUT WICKSELL, *Lectures on Political Economy* (1934, vol. I)

Whatever the merits of Wicksell's justification for excluding the consideration of capital from part of his work, some stronger justification must be needed for starting a book devoted explicitly to the theory of capital with a chapter from which any real consideration of capital will be rigorously excluded. Yet there are very good arguments for doing just that. Among the questions included in the theory of capital are these: What difference does the introduction of capital make to models of production and distribution and do the same methods and theories which are applied elsewhere prove adequate for the case of capital? This question cannot be answered without the clear identification of a point of reference, i.e. a model without capital but with another type of factor such as land, and the laws and conclusions which there apply. To be specific, it would be foolhardy to embark upon a discussion of whether marginal principles and marginal productivity conditions can be applied within the theory of capital without first being clear about the domain and interpretation of those principles in the most basic cases without the complications of capital. It might be held that there is no problem here, that the root meaning of marginal theory is clear and simple and everywhere understood, except perhaps by beginning students. That may be so, but there is some cause to doubt it.

Consider an economy in which no productive activities involve more than one period of time, called here a week, and in which no consumption good or production good can be stored. There will be factors of production, labour and land, which persist from one week to the next but the services that these provide, which is what matters here, will be provided in one particular week and cannot be stored until another. These stringent assumptions are necessary if we are to exclude all capital theoretic considerations at this stage: for only let the fertility of land be exhaustible according to use, and already the problem of the rate at which that fertility is to be exhausted presents itself, and we are involved with problems of capital theory.

So long as nothing can be stored[1], each week in the history of our economy is a separate and distinct interlude whose outcome can be determined independently of what has gone before and of what will follow. It is to the question of what will determine the equilibrium and the distribution of income between the owners of different factors of production of such an economy that we now turn. Because the passage of time is not involved we call this economy the *atemporal economy*. We suppose that there is some kind of organization which ensures that goods and factor services can be freely exchanged one for the other at prices which each actor[2] in the economy takes as given and independent of his own actions. In other words, we assume trading under conditions of 'perfect competition', using that term in the narrow sense to exclude the possibility that any actor might take account in formulating his decisions of his power to influence any price (see Robinson (1934)). It is not assumed, on the other hand, that there is 'free entry' of any firm to the area of operation of another, which assumption is not required here[3].

What is this organization which allows our actors to trade freely at what they take to be fixed prices? Who quotes these prices? Who 'makes the market'? What leads those who do it to act as they do? Is it public service, a traditional family role, or the same search for profit and material gain which drives those who play the role of producers? Economic theorists have been notably, if understandably, reticent on this point. As Koopmans has remarked (1957, p. 179), referring to the adjustment of prices in situations of market disequilibrium[4]:

> If, for instance, the net rate of increase in price is assumed to be proportional to the excess of demand over supply, whose behaviour is thereby expressed? And how is that

---

[1] We should include here paper assets or a monetary medium, for the existence of any such might serve to 'connect up' the economic activities of one week with those of another, even if no 'real' asset can be stored. The implications of paper assets in a world in which no real asset is storable can be far-reaching. Some of the possibilities have been discussed by Friedman (1969), Patinkin (1965) and Samuelson (1966), as well as elsewhere.

[2] The term 'actor' is used generically for any independent decision-making unit in the economy.

[3] Although it is used by Meade (1965, pp. 29–31) to indicate how something very like this state of affairs might be sustained in an economy with a small number of firms.

[4] For attempts to formulate a theory which is more explicit on these questions see, for example, Arrow and Hahn (1971, ch. 6) and Fisher (1972).

behaviour motivated? And is the alternative hypothesis, that the rate of increase of supply is proportional to the excess of demand price over supply price any more plausible, or any better traceable to behaviour motivation?

These are issues which do not arise only when we consider questions of a dynamic character of the form: how do prices change? For even to assume that prices come into being which can be treated by our actors as 'parameters' whose values are independent of their own actions is to assume some institutions which allow of this outcome.

There is a vague sketch to be found in one form or another in the writings of various neoclassical economists according to which a set of 'parametric' prices common to all buyers and sellers comes about through the competition of the various buyers and sellers of each commodity to carry out their desired transactions[5] (see Cournot (1897, ch. IV), Jevons (1911, ch. IV), Walras (1954, lesson 35) and Wicksell (1954, pp. 70–71)) but such 'parables' have misled few readers, and usually not even their authors, into thinking that economists have a rigorous theory of how a state of 'perfect competition' can be realized. They remain after all has been said just attractive ways of serving up what is no more than an assumption.

It is no part of our programme here to take these issues deeper, although we shall have occasion to mention them again. They are, of course, important issues, concerning as they do the mechanisms of price formation and the nature of competition. It seems very likely that Hicks' fear that a whole-hearted departure from the orthodox approach 'must have very destructive consequences for economic theory' (1946, p. 88) was well founded. However, if economic theory needs radical correction on account of its neglect of such problems, then it will not be only capital theory, or even capital theory particularly, that will be affected. Furthermore, these particular points are not apparently in contention in the debates of the leading 'schools'. There are, however, certain problems for the idea of 'perfect competition' and of 'parametric prices' which are peculiar to the context of capital-theoretic investigations. More discussion of these will follow in later chapters.

For the time being let it be assumed that our atemporal economy attains a state, called *equilibrium*, in which each actor of the economy has drawn up a plan of action, taking account of the prices ruling but taking them to be 'parameters', and such that the plans of all the actors taken together are consistent – they could all be brought to effect together. For it to be possible to bring to effect at the same time all the plans of all the actors these plans must satisfy the familiar conditions of supply and demand – every market must

[5] Marshall's conception of competition while not totally opposed to the above was in some ways more akin to later theories of imperfect competition.

'clear' – for otherwise not every actor could achieve his desired purchases and sales. But the assumption that the economy attains an equilibrium demands for its justification a demonstration that the concept makes sense and for that it must be shown that an equilibrium *exists.* Let us look at what is involved in such a demonstration without, however, aiming for a very full treatment, or for great generality, or for great rigour, since students desirous of these will do better to look at specialist texts on the theory of general equilibrium, for example, Debreu (1959), Arrow and Hahn (1971) or Quirk and Saposnik (1968).

To describe an equilibrium and show that one will exist it is necessary to describe how each actor will behave when confronted with a particular array of prices, or at the very least to assign to each actor a collection of actions which he would be willing to carry out. The most important influence on the actors' choices are prices, but there are other influences as well. In particular, firms may make profits, in which case the owners of these firms will benefit. The benefits take the forms of transfers of purchasing power, in this case from firms to households, and these will plainly influence the market behaviour of the households who enjoy the profit income.

To show that an equilibrium will exist it is necessary to establish three things. First, the trades of actors, their market sales and purchases, must be shown to exhibit some degree of determinacy in any particular price situation. If we can associate with each array of prices a unique choice of market action on the part of each actor, then we have this property of determinacy. But we may be able to make do with rather less. It might be that we could not state definitely what the choice of a particular actor would be, but we would yet be able to exclude certain possibilities, and narrow down the range of actions for the actor to a convex subset of the full set of feasible actions. An example, taken from the theory of household behaviour, will illustrate the point. Suppose that white and brown eggs cost the same. Some households prefer white, or brown as the case may be, and these will buy only their preferred type. But consider a household which is indifferent to the colour. Because some households discriminate between the two colours, white eggs and brown eggs must be treated as different goods in our model. But, at least where these two goods are concerned, we cannot say definitely how our household will act. It might buy a dozen white eggs but, by assumption, it would be equally content with six white and six brown eggs. However, what matters is not that one should be able to assign one and only one action to each actor. The important thing is to be able to delineate precisely, for each actor, a convex set of actions which are admissible for that actor in the circumstances concerned. For an action to be admissible it must be one of those which is consistent with the behaviour pattern of the actor. Clearly where there is only one admissible action in any particular circumstances, because the actor will do one and only one thing, we have a special case of determinacy and convexity.

We arrive at determinacy by recourse to the *principle of maximization*. That is, we assume that an action is admissible for an actor only if it cannot be improved upon, in the circumstances, in terms of the attainment of a specific objective. One does not have to proceed in this way: one could just assume determinacy as an axiom. But that would be felt by most people to be a somewhat unconvincing way of slipping into the model what is clearly a critical property.

The demonstration that each actor has a determinate set of best (and hence possible) actions in any particular circumstances is the first step towards a demonstration that an equilibrium exists. But it is only the first step. The second is to show that the set of possible actions varies *continuously* with prices. If, given an array of prices, there is only one action for each actor, it is not difficult to see what is entailed by continuity with respect to variations in prices. The trades of the various actors are functions of prices and they must be continuous functions. But the concept of continuity can be extended to cover even the case in which the set of admissible actions has more than one member, and thus extended it remains, not unnaturally, an essential property for the proof that an equilibrium exists. We will not pursue here the details of the argument which belong to the higher reaches of general equilibrium theory, but it is worth noting that one can dispense with functions and yet obtain similar results, because we will be dealing later with models in which, at least where firms are concerned, actions do not attach uniquely to prices.

The reason why continuity is an essential property, if we are to show that an equilibrium exists, can be understood intuitively. We want to choose an array of prices that will bring supply and demand into equality. If supplies or demands exhibit discontinuities this may prove to be impossible. Consider a very simple example. There is a subsistence wage measured, say, in terms of bread. If the wage is as high as the subsistence level or higher a large number of households want to sell labour time, and at the subsistence wage they strictly prefer the provision of certain hours of labour time to not selling any at all. However, this supply of labour time is more than the buyers of labour would like to take at the subsistence wage. They want some labour time at the subsistence wage but less than the households want to work at that wage. Clearly there can be no equilibrium in this case and there cannot be an equilibrium precisely because there is a discontinuity in the supply of labour. Plainly the example is not very convincing from the point of view of reality, because one naturally asks why say 10 hours of labour is strictly preferable to not working at all when an hour's wage buys one loaf, while selling no labour time is strictly preferable to selling any positive amount when the hourly wage is anything less than sufficient to buy one loaf.

We arrive at continuity by assumptions of *convexity*. The same assumptions guarantee that choices will take the form of convex sets where they are not unique. There are two kinds of actor, the *household* and the *firm*. According to the principle of maximization the behaviour of the actors is governed by the pursuit of certain objectives. In the case of a household it might be the maximization of utility, for a firm the objective will be the maximization of profit. In either case the actor is constrained in his choices in various ways. The firm can carry out production plans only if they are consistent with its technical possibilities. Similarly, a household can only consume according to a feasible plan of consumption for that household. If the household contains no water diviner it cannot sell the services of a water diviner. The household must also conform to a *budget condition* in that its expenditure must not exceed its income from all sources.

If the choices of actors are constrained to lie in *convex sets* and if they pursue what are called *quasi-concave objectives*, then their choices will vary continuously with prices. Leaving aside once again the detail and exactness which it is the job of the texts on general equilibrium theory to provide, we can understand intuitively why this should be so. In the absence of convexity from the sets of feasible actions, or a failure of the quasi-concavity property for objective functions, we may have discontinuities. This will be illustrated by means of examples.

Let there be n different 'goods' in the model, indexed by $i = 1, 2, \ldots, n$. We use the term 'good' in a very broad sense to include household goods such as bread and beer, producers' goods such as raw wool for spinning, and the services of factors of production, such as labour time or the use of land. The convention is to regard a positive value for a particular good as representing the supply or net production of that quantity and a negative value as representing demand for that good or net consumption of it. Thus if the bread value for a particular actor is -10 then he takes in 10 loaves; he is a consumer of 10 loaves. If the value were to be $+10$ he would be a net provider of 10 loaves; he must be a baker. Thus we may make use of an n vector to represent the trades which an actor carries out in the market, or some other aspect of his behaviour.

Consider the households. There are H of them, indexed by $h = 1, 2, \ldots, H$. At the outset the household has a non-negative vector of property *endowments* in which will be included such items as the ownership of land. The endowment vector for household h is denoted $\bar{\boldsymbol{x}}_h \geqq \mathbf{0}$. The transactions in which the hth household engages with the rest of the economy will be denoted by a vector

$\boldsymbol{x}_h$, the positive elements of which, following our convention, will represent sales to the rest of the economy and the negative components of which will represent purchases. It follows that what the *h*th household will eventually consume is $\bar{\boldsymbol{x}}_h - \boldsymbol{x}_h$, this being its initial endowment less the positive components of $\boldsymbol{x}_h$, its sales, and plus the absolute values of the negative components of $\boldsymbol{x}_h$, these corresponding to its purchases.

The households are interested in living the best life possible in the circumstances for the week concerned. They themselves evaluate what it is best to consume according to their *preferences.* The household has *quasi-concave preferences* if the set of all consumptions that are at least as good in its preference ordering as a specific consumption is a convex set[6]. In other words, the average of two consumptions, each of which is at least as good as a consumption $\boldsymbol{x}_0$, regardless of the weights used to form the average, and regardless of the value of $\boldsymbol{x}_0$, is at least as good as $\boldsymbol{x}_0$.

If we do not have the property of quasi-concave preferences then we may encounter discontinuities, as the following example shows. The household does not mind what colour its eggs are but it strongly prefers them to be all of one colour because it adheres to a superstition that mixed collections of eggs are unlucky and should be discarded. Then a basket of six white and six brown eggs is certainly not at least as good as a dozen of either colour, between which the household is indifferent, but in fact is useless. Imagine now that the price of white eggs is lower than the price of brown. The household buys white eggs. But now the price of white eggs increases. When white and brown cost the same the action of the household is no longer uniquely defined and the set of admissible actions is non-convex. Any further rise in the price of white eggs must take it completely into brown eggs. There is a jump in the consumption pattern, corresponding to a discontinuity in demand.

The household cannot choose any consumption that might take its fancy, not even if its budget would permit it to choose one. We have already mentioned that households that contain no water diviners cannot choose to supply the services of water diviners. Equally a household must eat to live, and it may need to eat more to work, and more still for certain types of labour, such as heavy manual work. These aspects of the problem are taken care of if we require that the choice of a consumption be confined to a *consumption set*, being a set of consumptions which are feasible for that particular household. The consumption set must be a convex set if we are to avoid discontinuities. An example very similar to the one given below for firms and production

---

[6] If the household's preferences can be represented by a utility function $U(\bar{\boldsymbol{x}}_h - \boldsymbol{x}_h)$ then this must be a quasi-concave function, i.e. $\{\boldsymbol{x} \mid U(\boldsymbol{x}) \geqslant U(\boldsymbol{x}_0)\}$ must be a convex set for all $\boldsymbol{x}_0$.

sets will illustrate the point. We leave it to the interested reader to construct such an example as an exercise.

There are F *firms* indexed by $f = 1, \ldots, F$. A firm differs from a household in two respects: it can carry out certain productive transformations of goods and factor services into different goods and factor services and its aim is a different one. The firm is interested in so operating that it will make the largest possible profit. There is no difficulty in constructing a mixed institution which is part firm part household; say a firm with a preference ordering over profits and the operations that it carries out, or a farming household which is able to carry out certain productive transformations within the household over which it may have preferences. However, there is no great gain to be had from going beyond our two pure types and we will not do so here.

The productive activity of the fth firm can be represented as a vector $\boldsymbol{y}_f$ of sales (positive components of $\boldsymbol{y}_f$) and purchases (negative components of $\boldsymbol{y}_f$) called the *production plan* of firm f. Notice that factor inputs will be represented by their services, which is all at present that the firm may purchase. The productive transformations to which firm f is capable of giving effect are represented by a set of vectors called its *production set* denoted $\mathscr{T}_f$. The profit realized by the firm f will be the value of its sales less the value of its purchases, that is $\boldsymbol{p}\cdot\boldsymbol{y}_f$, where $\boldsymbol{p}$ is the non-negative vector of goods prices. The firm chooses $\boldsymbol{y}_f$ from among the points of $\mathscr{T}_f$ so as to maximize $\boldsymbol{p}\cdot\boldsymbol{y}_f$.

For the firm's choice of production plan to depend continuously upon prices $\boldsymbol{p}$ we need to assume that $\mathscr{T}_f$ is a convex set. If it is not there may be discontinuities and again an example will illustrate the possibility. Suppose that the firm can produce eggs, which may be white or brown. Let b be the quantity of brown eggs produced and w the quantity of white eggs. Then the production (b, w) is feasible if

$$0 \leqslant b \leqslant 40, \qquad 0 \leqslant w \leqslant 40, \qquad (b-20)^2 + (w-20)^2 \geqslant 400. \tag{2.1}$$

The production possibility frontier is bowed in towards the origin and the production set defined by (2.1) is not a convex set. This may be confirmed by noting that (0, 40) satisfies (2.1), as does (40, 0). However, the average of these two plans, the convex combination with weights $(\frac{1}{2}, \frac{1}{2})$, (20, 20) does not satisfy (2.1) and thus is not feasible. As a possible interpretation of the example, suppose that it is inconvenient for the firm to produce a mixture of eggs of different colours so that the attempt to do so interferes with the total productivity of the firm measured simply by the number of eggs of either colour produced.

It may now be seen that a discontinuity will arise which is very similar to that which we encountered with the household that did not like eggs of mixed colours. If white eggs are priced below brown the most profitable action is to produce 40 units of brown. Now as the price of white eggs falls to equality with that of brown the firm will switch discontinuously to the production of brown when the prices cross over. The discontinuity arises because the production set of the firm is not convex[7].

To summarize the argument concerning the requirements for the existence of an equilibrium so far, we have listed two requirements. The first is that the actions of the actors be determinate and this is achieved by the principle of maximization. The second is that the actions of the actors should vary continuously with prices and this is achieved by assumptions of convexity.

There remain some further requirements that we will put together under the third heading. We need the property that the actions of the actors should depend only upon relative prices so that we may normalize prices by choosing a *numeraire* to have the value 1.0, when the price of a good will measure its value in terms of the *numeraire*. We have this requirement satisfied already, for it is an implication of the principle of maximization. This is most easily seen in the case of the firm. It is immediate that if $\boldsymbol{y}^0$ solves

$$\text{maximize } \boldsymbol{p}\cdot\boldsymbol{y} \quad \text{subject to } \boldsymbol{y} \in \mathscr{T}_f, \tag{2.2}$$

then the same $\boldsymbol{y}^0$ must solve

$$\text{maximize } \lambda\boldsymbol{p}\cdot\boldsymbol{y} \quad \text{subject to } \boldsymbol{y} \in \mathscr{T}_f. \tag{2.3}$$

Where households are concerned the matter is a little more complicated, because households are subject to more constraints than firms. The reason is that a household's choices are constrained by a budget condition as well as by a consumption set. When we formulate the budget condition we have to allow for the possibility that the household will receive *transfers* from other actors in the economy. It is important that we allow for this possibility because it is through such transfers that the profits of firms will be paid out to the households that own them. The budget condition of household h requires that

$$\boldsymbol{p}\cdot\boldsymbol{x}_h + I_h \geqslant 0, \qquad h = 1, 2, \ldots, H, \tag{2.4}$$

where I_h denotes the total purchasing power transferred to household h from other actors in the economy. We will only consider the case in which the transfers are accounted for by the profits distributed by firms. Clearly the choices of the household will be unaffected so long as the budget condition

---

[7] It needs the extended definition of continuity, of which mention was made above, to clarify why we have a discontinuity in this case but would not have one in the borderline case between convexity and non-convexity in which the production possibility frontier took the form of a straight line. It is left to the interested reader to pursue the point in one of the texts on general equilibrium theory cited above.

(which is the only route through which prices impinge on the constraints to which the household is subject) allows of the exact same possibilities. But this will not be the case if $\lambda \boldsymbol{p}$ is substituted for $\boldsymbol{p}$ and I_h remains unaltered. We will show, however, that I_h will vary proportionately with $\boldsymbol{p}$, so that the substitution of $\lambda \boldsymbol{p}$ for $\boldsymbol{p}$ is accompanied by the substitution of λI_h for I_h, so long as I_h is accounted for solely by the profits of firms.

For the sake of simplicity we assume that profits are distributed to households according to their proportionate shares in the 'equity' of the firm concerned. Thus household h will receive a proportion σ_{hf} of the profits of firm f. The values σ_{hf} give the pattern of the claims on the firms of the various households. To bear this interpretation the σ_{hf} values must satisfy two conditions:

$$\text{(i) } \sigma_{hf} \geqslant 0, \quad \text{all } h \text{ and all } f;$$
$$\text{(ii) } \sum_{h=1}^{H} \sigma_{hf} = 1, \quad \text{all } f. \tag{2.5}$$

Let the maximum profit that firm f can realize when prices are $\boldsymbol{p}$ be denoted by $\Pi_f(\boldsymbol{p})$. This value is a well-defined function of $\boldsymbol{p}$ even if the production plan of firm f is not uniquely determined by $\boldsymbol{p}$ because the value of $\Pi_f(\boldsymbol{p})$ is the maximum profit and this must be unique. Then

$$I_h = \sum_{f=1}^{F} \sigma_{hf} \Pi_f(\boldsymbol{p}), \qquad h = 1, 2, \ldots, H. \tag{2.6}$$

Hence, I_h is seen to be a function of $\boldsymbol{p}$ and since each $\Pi_f(\boldsymbol{p})$ function is homogeneous of degree one in $\boldsymbol{p}$, it follows that I_h varies proportionately with $\boldsymbol{p}$. We can now conclude that the actions of all actors, both firms and households, depend only upon relative prices. Hence if $\lambda \boldsymbol{p}$ is substituted for $\boldsymbol{p}$ it makes no difference to the actions of any actor.

We may take advantage of the property that has been established to normalize prices. It is important, however, to take care with the choice of a *numeraire*. It may be that some goods will turn out to be free goods in the equilibrium; they will have no value. If we try to measure relative prices in terms of a free good we produce nonsense. To avoid this difficulty choose as *numeraire* the composite good consisting of a basket which contains 1.0 unit of each of the n goods. This basket will have a positive value if anything is valuable and in this way we are able to avoid the difficulty that we do not know in advance which will be the free goods and which the valuable ones. The choice of our *numeraire* is equivalent to the normalization

$$\sum_{i=1}^{n} p_i = 1. \tag{2.7}$$

The last property which we require is that the sales of all actors taken together, and summing over the various goods, should cancel out. This is much less than the equilibrium conditions which require that demands should cancel out for each good taken alone. Hence it is not surprising that we have this property, which is called the *Walras identity*, by virtue of assumptions that we have already detailed and one extra fairly innocuous condition. The latter is the assumption that households are not *satiated*. This means that any household can reach a preferred consumption plan if it has more value at its disposal. It follows that the budget condition will be exactly satisfied, for if it were not, ~~in which case~~ there would have to be unspent purchasing power at the disposal of the household, the household's consumption plan could be improved upon and the household would not be maximizing.

Let the choice of firm f when facing prices $\boldsymbol{p}$ be $\boldsymbol{y}_f(\boldsymbol{p})$. Let the choice of household h when facing prices $\boldsymbol{p}$ and receiving transfers totalling I_h be $\boldsymbol{x}_h(\boldsymbol{p}, I_h)$. If there is more than one admissible decision for either household or firm then $\boldsymbol{y}_f(\boldsymbol{p})$ and $\boldsymbol{x}_h(\boldsymbol{p}, I_h)$ can denote for the time being any admissible choice for that actor. The net market supplies of all actors taken together are obtained by summing up the net sales to obtain

$$\sum_{f=1}^{F} \boldsymbol{y}_f(\boldsymbol{p}) + \sum_{h=1}^{H} \boldsymbol{x}_h\left[\boldsymbol{p}, \sum_{f=1}^{F} \sigma_{hf}\boldsymbol{p}\cdot\boldsymbol{y}_f(\boldsymbol{p})\right], \tag{2.8}$$

where, in (2.8) we have substituted for I_h using (2.6) and

$$\Pi_f(\boldsymbol{p}) = \boldsymbol{p}\cdot\boldsymbol{y}_f(\boldsymbol{p}). \tag{2.9}$$

Now compute the inner product of the aggregate net supply vector (2.8) and the price vector $\boldsymbol{p}$ to obtain

$$\sum_{f=1}^{F} \boldsymbol{p}\cdot\boldsymbol{y}_f(\boldsymbol{p}) + \sum_{h=1}^{H} \boldsymbol{p}\cdot\boldsymbol{x}_h\left[\boldsymbol{p}, \sum_{f=1}^{F} \sigma_{hf}\boldsymbol{p}\cdot\boldsymbol{y}_f(\boldsymbol{p})\right] = \sum_{f=1}^{F} \Pi_f(\boldsymbol{p}) - \sum_{h=1}^{H} I_h = 0. \tag{2.10}$$

This is the Walras identity, so called because (2.10) is true for all $\boldsymbol{p}$ and not just for $\boldsymbol{p}$ for which there is an equilibrium.

We have an equilibrium when there is no excess demand in aggregate for any good. We have to allow that there may be an excess supply, for there is always the possibility that one or more goods will be so abundant in supply that the glut will not dry up even when the price falls to zero. Hence, the condition for equilibrium is

$$\sum_{f=1}^{F} \boldsymbol{y}_f(\boldsymbol{p}) + \sum_{h=1}^{H} \boldsymbol{x}_h\left[\boldsymbol{p}, \sum_{f=1}^{F} \sigma_{hf}\boldsymbol{p}\cdot\boldsymbol{y}_f(\boldsymbol{p})\right] \geqq \boldsymbol{0}. \tag{2.11}$$

Clearly if (2.11) is satisfied as well as (2.10) then a good can be in excess supply only if the price of that good is zero. For, otherwise, taking the inner product of the price vector and the net excess supply vector we would obtain a positive term, and there could be no negative term to cancel it out. Hence, (2.10) would be contradicted.

Notice that (2.11) has been written as though the actors made unique choices at any particular prices, but if there is more than one admissible action then, for equilibrium to obtain, (2.11) must be satisfied for some admissible actions.

It is known that there will exist an equilibrium for our economy under the conditions that we have discussed, plus a few minor conditions[8]. For the proof the reader is once again referred to specialist texts on general equilibrium analysis. However, while the method of proof need not concern us here it is very important that we understand exactly what the result states. This is because we are going to appeal to the very same result later on, not to affirm again that the atemporal economy has at least one equilibrium: once the reader is satisfied of the validity of that claim he can presumably be relied upon not to forget it. What we are going to do is to show that the problem of existence of equilibrium for other models, apparently unlike the atemporal economy, is formally equivalent to the existence problem for the atemporal economy. To proceed in this way we need to know something about the mathematics of the proof of existence, even though we do not need to be able to rehearse the proofs ourselves.

From the mathematical point of view the problem of proving existence is the problem of showing that the system of inequalities (2.11) has a solution. On the left-hand side is a vector-valued function of $\boldsymbol{p}$ (or, more generally, there corresponds to each $\boldsymbol{p}$ a set of admissible vectors that may be assigned to the left-hand side). For the sake of brevity we will refer to the left-hand side of (2.11) for the time being simply as 'the vector'. To show that there exists a $\boldsymbol{p}$ for which the vector is non-negative the following mathematical conditions suffice:

(1) The vector is 'well defined' for each $\boldsymbol{p} \geqslant \mathbf{0}$. This means that we can assign

---

[8] One such condition to which no reference has yet been made deserves mention. The actions of the actors must be bounded. Were they to be unbounded we would have a failure of continuity, but one of a special kind which is not excluded by convexity assumptions. In the case of the atemporal economy the matter can be taken care of easily and not unreasonably by assuming that consumption and production sets are bounded. But when the existence argument is used later in new contexts we will encounter examples where the problem of unbounded actions is less easy to brush aside, and we will then refer again to this problem explicitly.

a unique value to the vector for each $\boldsymbol{p}$, or else we can assign a convex set of admissible values.

(2) The vector is homogeneous of degree zero in $\boldsymbol{p}$, meaning that it does (or can) take the same value if $\boldsymbol{p}$ is replaced by $\lambda \boldsymbol{p}$, for any $\lambda > 0$.

(3) The vector varies continuously with $\boldsymbol{p}$. This has the usual interpretation where the vector is single-valued. Otherwise a generalization of the notion of continuity is implied.

(4) For all $\boldsymbol{p}$ the inner product of the vector and $\boldsymbol{p}$ has the value zero.

Whenever we want to know whether a market clearing array of prices exists these are the main properties that we must look at. For the atemporal economy we have now sketched the assumptions that would give us these properties and provided some justification for the claim that the conditions will be satisfied. Let it be clear that the sketch was a rough one and that it dealt quite coarsely with the delicate and interesting problems of precise general equilibrium theory. But once again we are practising the division of labour, and precise general equilibrium analysis is not now our concern. We have concluded that the atemporal economy will have an equilibrium. Hence the assumption that the actors have arrived at consistent plans under the operation of a competitive price system does not involve us in any contradiction.

We have got as far then as establishing that there can be an equilibrium in the atemporal economy. But that does not mean that there will be equilibrium: it is one possibility, no more. Hence, the next question that asserts itself: will the equilibrium state be realized?

Broadly, there are two approaches that have been adopted with regard to economic equilibrium. On the one hand, equilibrium may be regarded as something which would be expected to be realized, because the dynamic forces which operate upon the economy operate in such a way, and sufficiently rapidly, to bring the economy to an equilibrium. In this case, equilibrium being something which is expected to occur, anything which can be shown to be a feature of equilibrium will itself be expected to occur. It should then be possible in principle to give to the relations of the economy a dynamic formulation of which the equilibrium solution would be one particular solution state, but a particular state which could be shown to be attained rather rapidly (see Samuelson (1947, pp. 260–263)). The study of the behaviour of the economy out of equilibrium will be called *disequilibrium dynamics*. Alternatively, we may regard the assumption that equilibrium obtains as no more than an analytical stepping stone, as a necessary simplification to render possible some progress in an otherwise hopelessly difficult analytical endeavour. Either approach is possible; both have been adopted fairly explicitly by those writers who have taken the trouble to make clear how they regard equilibrium; and both suffer from serious shortcomings between which, inescapably, the theorist must make his choice.

The disadvantage of regarding the equilibrium state as the culmination of disequilibrium dynamic adjustment is simply that the formulation of models of disequilibrium dynamics is hard and uncertain work. It is work which may turn out to be singularly unrewarding to a scholar who would like to arrive at the conclusion that the equilibrium of his model is a stable one which the economy will tend to approach. The investigations that have been undertaken into the stability of general equilibrium have admittedly been largely confined to investigating the stability of the Walrasian *tâtonnement* – the adjustment process under which no actual trades take place until the equilibrium prices have been attained. And it is known that the stability of the *tâtonnement* is sometimes more problematic than for some alternative processes[9]. Be that as it may, it remains true that it is only for the *tâtonnement* that any systematic investigations, including producers along with households, have been undertaken, and here the stability of equilibrium is known to be problematic – there is certainly no guarantee that every, or even any, economic equilibrium will be stable. Furthermore, even if equilibrium were to be stable there might not be enough time within the space of a 'week' for prices to adjust to an equilibrium, for firms to give effect to their production plans and for exchange to be affected.

In the face of all the foregoing problems it may seem more sensible to simply assume that equilibrium will prevail and to thus confine our investigations to the equilibrium state. We could regard the object of our investigations not as 'the economy' but as 'economic equilibrium' and we could attempt to justify this procedure as a useful starting point to what one might eventually hope to see realized in a complete account of the behaviour of the economy, including a full specification of its disequilibrium dynamics. This approach, while less ambitious than a full dynamic approach, may seem to be more attractive, if only because more tractable, than the Herculean programme of constructing a complete theory of the behaviour of the economy out of equilibrium. The awkwardness of proceeding in this manner is that we are introducing assumptions of a rather special, perhaps even a dubious, character.

Consider what a theoretical economic model does. It lays down some assumptions or postulates and from these it proceeds, by logical or mathematical deduction, to conclusions. We might say that a postulate of a theoretical model is a *primitive postulate* if the question of whether it is likely to be

[9] For a review of the known results, see Arrow and Hahn (1971).

valid or not is a question largely outside the domain of theoretical economics as such. This is no doubt a disconcertingly vague definition, but it seems to be hard to make it tighter, if only because the 'domain of economic theory' is itself an imprecise concept. Nonetheless, it probably conveys something and, without considering the inevitably difficult borderline cases, all economists would recognize a fundamental difference, for example, between the character of the following two assumptions:

(a) An improvement in the balance of trade will increase the wage rate of labour relative to the price of butter.

(b) The central bank does not intervene in the forward market for the home currency.

Assumption (a) is not a primitive assumption while assumption (b) is. Roughly speaking we are here distinguishing between the basic specification of a model and statements about how it will behave.

The trouble with including non-primitive postulates in an argument is simply that they inevitably throw a veil of obscurity over everything that follows. Such assumptions are by their nature obscure because their realism is difficult to evaluate. The natural question to ask is: what basic features would the economy have to exhibit for that postulate to be a valid one? It goes without saying that we would not have been presented with non-primitive postulates if that question were to admit of an easy answer[10]. It is in this light that one must view the assumption of economic equilibrium where it is not derived from a model of disequilibrium dynamics.

The reader may wonder why he has been subjected to this seemingly inconclusive digression into the methodology of economic model construction. The explanation is that the issues that have been touched upon by this digression are relevant to a question to which we shall give consideration later in this chapter and again in following chapters; namely, in what sense if any can certain quantities or variables be said to be 'determined' or 'caused' by particular influences or 'explained' by a particular theory? It is hoped that when

---

[10] The classic example of a non-primitive assumption employed in economic theory is the assumption that all goods are *gross substitutes* in demand. Here an assumption concerning the way in which aggregate demands will respond to changes in prices is imposed without an explanation of what properties of preferences, production sets, endowments, etc., would give rise to this property. On gross substitutability see Hicks (1946) and Arrow and Hahn (1971, 221–227). As it happens, the general equilibrium system can be shown to be dynamically stable under the *tâtonnement* if gross substitutability is assumed. Thus we can treat the attainment of equilibrium as a prediction of the model instead of a non-primitive assumption, but only by substituting another non-primitive assumption – that all goods are gross substitutes.

we do eventually confront this kind of question the digression will be seen to have been useful.

It is important to note that the existence proof shows that at least one equilibrium exists. It does not, and could not, show that only one equilibrium exists. The possibility that there will be multiple equilibria cannot be excluded. What should the economic theorist make of a multiplicity of distinct and perhaps highly contrasting equilibria? His response will depend upon how he has viewed equilibrium in terms of the earlier taxonomy. If he takes the view that equilibrium is a state which one would expect to be realized following adjustment of the dynamic disequilibrium system he will at once investigate the stability of each equilibrium price vector according to whatever dynamic adjustment system he favours. Alas, this promises no resolution of the problem of multiple solutions, for just as there may be many price equilibria, so there may be many stable price equilibria, although on the contrary there might be no stable price equilibrium at all. On the other hand, stability considerations may at least eliminate some possibilities so that the theorist who views the attainment of equilibrium as simply an assumption is even more 'embarrassed by riches' when there are multiple equilibria. Which one should then be examined? Lacking any means within the confines of equilibrium theory to distinguish one equilibrium from another, he must perforce examine them all.

The outlines of a theory of equilibrium for one 'week' in the life of the economy are now before us. The theory, it will be noticed, makes no particular distinction between the determination of the prices of consumption goods (such as bread, beer and haircuts) and the prices of factor services (such as labour time and the use of land). All these prices in one way or another exert their influence upon the decisions of various actors to supply or demand some or all of the various goods and factor services in the respective markets for these goods and services. On account of these multifarious influences on supply and demand it will emerge that some configurations of prices are inconsistent with the requirements of equilibrium while others are not. One of the things that will be embedded within any particular equilibrium solution will be what might be broadly called the *distribution of income*. As a specific equilibrium solution is nothing less than a complete description of what goes on in the economy as far as economic matters are concerned, it embodies, *a fortiori*, specifications of any particular aspects of the economy concerned of which one might enquire, such as the functional and personal distributions of income. And so it might be said that we have here a theory of income distribution, but so far only for the atemporal economy and for the atemporal economy in equilibrium at that.

Is the distribution of income in our atemporal economy now explained? Have we isolated the laws which determine the distribution of income? These questions are not easy to answer because the answers to them must depend upon what the questioner is seeking. The verbs that appeared in the two preceding questions – determine and explain – have different meanings and impose different demands. It is one thing to exhibit a mathematically determinate model, i.e. one whose relations correctly describe the economy and which together exclude all but one solution. It is another thing, and it is to achieve more, to isolate the actual causes which operate upon the distribution of income and the manner in which they influence it. This we have seen already with regard to the assumption that equilibrium obtains. Suppose that, as it happened, we did have economic equilibrium and suppose the equilibrium to be unique. Then if the other postulates of the theory were to be valid our model of equilibrium would give to us a unique configuration of prices, a unique description of economic events and a unique distribution of income. We might then say that the causes of this income distribution lay in the data of the model, the initial distribution of resources and ownership, the preference orderings of households, the production sets of the firms and more generally in behavioural assumptions such as profit maximization. Yet the equilibrium model does not explain why equilibrium obtains and it could not by its nature do so. The point is of great importance. There is no sense in asking whether or how any economic variable is determined without specifying closely within what context and under what postulated circumstances the said determination is required. The narrower the conditions within which we confine our investigations the easier it is to exhibit relations which will determine the values concerned and the less, in a basic and causal sense, we will have explained the values that will obtain.

Let it be further noted that even from the particular mathematical point of view no determinate equilibrium solution has yet been obtained for the atemporal model. The distribution of income emerges as a by-product of the equilibrium configuration of prices of goods and factor services and we have seen that there is no necessity for there to be only one equilibrium configuration. Suppose that there are two or many distinct equilibrium price vectors: what consideration will determine which of them will prevail, always supposing that some equilibrium vector will prevail? Presumably this is a matter of history where it is not a matter of chance, so that we may have to admit, even to a single week of our atemporal model, the direct influence of historical factors.

It should not be supposed that it is only as 'tie breakers' when there happens to exist a multiplicity of possible equilibria that historical or sociological influences will enter into the determination of the distribution of income. They are there anyway in the primitive postulates of the model, influencing as they do the preferences of the households, the technical possibilities of the firms and not least the distribution of the initial endowments of goods and the ownership claims on the profits of the firms. Economic theories that attempt to explain prices or distribution from the postulate of a general equilibrium of supply and demand have sometimes been criticized for neglecting the influence of sociological and historical factors as though the 'laws of supply and demand' embodied only the working out of purely economic forces. Plainly this is a misunderstanding. If there is a valid explanation of prices and distribution in terms of an equilibrium of supply and demand (always remembering that this may or may not be the correct theory – it is not a matter of logical necessity) then the influence of sociological and historical factors will be channelled through the excess supply functions of the various actors and in that sense the operation of these influences will be indirect. To say that many factors will operate indirectly is not to devalue their importance. It is, of course, largely 'non-economic' factors that will give to any particular case its peculiar character. The observation that it has proved possible to formulate the equilibrium of the atemporal model without an explicit reference to many important questions of a sociological character indicates only that the question of existence of equilibrium, to which we have given a good deal of attention, is not one whose solution is sensitive to the precise and detailed form taken by the sociological factors.

While the equilibrium model as formulated leaves many sociological influences in the background it contains also some explicit social theory in its designation of how the various actors of the economy behave. The assumption, for example, that the firms are maximizers of profit is by no means the only possible one. The possibilities for ringing changes are legion and, in so far as we are concerned with showing the existence of a solution, we have seen above that the indispensable requirements are not particularly onerous. So long as we stick to determinate behaviour, continuity and budget constraints, we know that an existence argument can go through. For example, the assumption that the preferences of households are independent of each other or of the form of the equilibrium solution can be dispensed with.

It is evident, however, that there is nothing to be gained by erecting models of greater and greater generality. The model may be over-general already in many respects. Perhaps what is needed is some drastic special assumptions in one direction and some new and more general features in another. We will examine such a case in ch. 6.

The reader may be wondering by now why so much time is being wasted on a model as notably uninteresting as the atemporal model. But the investigation of peculiar and special cases is not without its uses, especially when what the investigation reveals is that even without the intervention of capital there are a number of serious methodological issues to which attention must be directed. Also, we are already brought up against some significant features of general equilibrium models. Firstly, we have noted that the existence theorem does not guarantee a unique equilibrium. Secondly, one might add the observation that general equilibrium analysis tends to belie apparently obvious ideas based upon economic intuition. This is because the repercussions of any change in a general equilibrium system are so multifarious and widespread. One needs, for example, to impose strong restrictions on a general equilibrium model to reach even such a seemingly 'obvious' conclusion as the following. A shift of demand towards beef and away from mutton, in the sense that every actor would buy more beef and less mutton, and the same of other goods, at any prices, will raise the price of beef relatively to that of mutton[11].

These conclusions concerning the atemporal model are not without importance for the theory of income distribution in broader contexts and for the theory of capital. Not infrequently the writings and pronouncements of economic theorists on the theory of income distribution have given rise to the impression that everything would be simple and straightforward were it not for capital and time. Now the view that capital and time bring with them formidable theoretical problems is not to be disputed, but they do not explode into an analytical world which would otherwise be calm, clear and definite. There are no grounds for such a view of the field unless it be that the writer has in mind some radical specialization of the model that has been examined above.

To come at last to a type of enquiry which would be for many the beginning of their interest, a direct question is addressed to the atemporal model. What determines the price of the service of a particular factor? Or, more specifically, what determines the wage rate of a certain type of labour or the rent of a particular grade of land? This is the form that the enquiry usually takes, although in this form it is not evident exactly what it means and not all writers have taken the trouble to make it clear what they intend. Consider a statement of the form: 'Z is determined by A', where suitable terms are substituted for the variables A and Z. The verb 'to determine' could be taken at its weakest to mean no more than that, in some specified context, a knowledge of the determining term is sufficient to allow the determined term to be inferred. It is in this sense only that it is correct to claim, in the context of constant costs, that the equilibrium price of a good is determined by its cost of production.

[11] A sufficient condition is once again gross substitutability.

Notice that this implies neither that *A* 'causes' *Z*, nor that *A* explains in any but a superficial sense why *Z* is what it is. If there are only two factors of production the share of the first in total output might be said to 'determine' the share of the second. If we know that the share of labour in net income is 70% then we may assign the share of 30% to other factors – there is no disputing it. If, however, someone were to propose the theory that the share of labour in net income is determined by the share of other factors the claim would be a source of merriment, but only perhaps because this is a peculiarly unsubtle example of a theoretical method which in its more refined manifestations is sometimes received less jovially[12].

On one interpretation – which is at once weaker and stronger than the preceding one – *Z* may be said to be determined by any primitive feature of the system for which an alteration in its specification might necessitate an alteration of *Z*. Here is an idea which corresponds much more closely to the idea of an original cause. The separation of cause from effect in a complex interrelated system is no easy matter and should not be attempted without due awareness of the difficulties involved. More than once below we shall return again to this problem and it is desirable to establish some terminology once and for all. Throughout the following discourse a statement of the form: '*A* is determined by *X*, *Y* and *Z*' will carry no implication beyond the existence of a mathematical relation from which *A* may be inferred given *X*, *Y* and *Z*. Where the implication of a causal relation is intended we shall say that *X*, *Y* and *Z* are 'causes' of *A*.

To return to the original enquiry, how is that now to be interpreted? Let it be assumed, as seems to be most likely, that what the questioner is seeking is a list of primitive causes and that he will not be fobbed off with a formula from which, given some other values, he may calculate the answer. If the supposition be incorrect, then the task of responding is greatly lightened for it will surely not prove difficult to find some determining values for the price of a factor service, indeed there will probably be more than one such collection to hand.

According to a classic statement the price of a factor service is determined by the value of the marginal product of that factor service. The reader may have remarked that neither the concept of the marginal product of a factor service, nor indeed any marginal concept, has played a role in the presentation of the theory of equilibrium and price determination for the atemporal economy above. That is how it should be. Although they were historically prior to the kind of theory that we have examined, marginal concepts are,

---

12 For an argument which comes perilously close to the type of reasoning which we are considering here, see Ricardo (1953, ch. 6, 'On profits').

from the logical point of view, not prior concepts but highly derived ones. This is not to say that we may not sometimes gain from making use of them, but they are not something that we need to derive an equilibrium and this, as will be seen later, is fortunate because as usually understood they are not always valid concepts.

We shall examine carefully in ch. 5 the conditions that must obtain if the statement that the price of a factor service is determined by the value of the marginal product of that factor is to be valid. However, without now going into those detailed issues, let it be granted that there could easily be cases in which there was no difficulty in interpreting the notion of a marginal product, say of labour. Suppose that output in any productive process can always be increased, or decreased, by varying the amount of labour employed, and that the response of output to labour input is smooth, so that output is a differentiable function of the quantity of labour used. Then the wage rate must be equal to the value of the marginal product of labour, for if it were not at least one firm would be able to increase its profit by varying the amount of labour employed.

All this is elementary, it is just a trivial implication of the assumption that the firm is successful in choosing a maximizing plan in the conditions stated. From this elementary formula can we go on to say that the wage rate is determined by the value of the marginal product? Yes, we may do so, the usage proposed allows just that. Under the conditions specified a knowledge of the marginal product of labour allows a unique value to be assigned to the wage rate. But we may go further. The wage rate determines the marginal product of labour! It is so. Since the two values are equal one to the other a knowledge of one determines uniquely, and at once, the value of the other[13].

What of the causes of the wage rate of labour; what can be said about these? Well, it is immediate that the marginal product is no candidate to be a primitive cause of the wage rate. It is not a primitive fact, being itself something which economic theory is in duty bound to elucidate, and in part because of this it does not stand to the wage rate as effect to cause. A search for causes will take us inescapably to the primitive specifications of the atemporal model, because in general each of these will have played some part in influencing

---

[13] Cf. Robertson (1950, pp. 222–224). As Robertson's argument makes clear there is one point of view (which is not that of the economy as a whole viewed as an equilibrium system) according to which it does make sense to think of one of the quantities as causing the value of the other. In the theory of the competitive firm the wage rate is a datum and the marginal product, embodied in the plan chosen is, if one likes, a choice. But here, in this restricted context in which a direction of cause to effect is so easy to ascertain, it is not the marginal product which causes the wage but just the opposite.

the price of a particular factor service. As evidence that it is so we need only consider what would follow from a change in one of the primitive specifications, say a change in household preferences or an alteration in productive possibilities. Here we would conclude that usually among the effects of such changes would be an alteration in the equilibrium value of the price of the factor service.

Someone who demands of a model as complicated as the atemporal equilibrium model what causes a particular value to be what it is should normally expect to be told that everything, meaning all the primitive specifications of the model, have played a part in causing the variable concerned to take whatever value has arisen. It may be that some of the possible causes are not operative 'locally', meaning that in a certain case small variations in a specification that would sometimes influence the variable concerned do not here do so. Or there may be very special cases. It is trivial to construct models in which a price has but one cause, say a subsistence wage rate in an economy with unutilized land of uniform quality to which any worker would return did he not receive the subsistence wage. However, one can declare with confidence that, in any equilibrium model of sufficient generality to treat more than one very special type of economy, the causes of a particular factor-service price are bound to be numerous. And they may not exclude history or even chance.

It is a merit of general equilibrium analysis that it continually brings us back to the observation that causes are not simple things to tie down in economics. It is sometimes irritating to be reminded of the fact, but then the truth sometimes is irritating. The reminder is not out of place because all too often claims are advanced that the wage rate, or the rate of profit, is caused by this or that, where the cause suggested is not more than the very same wage or profit rate looked at from a different angle. As Wicksell (1958, p. 205) put it:

> Consider, for example, the important question of the distribution of the products between the owners of the different productive factors, especially the three main classes of them: labour, land and capital. If we assume that the value of the products P is equal to the sum of the costs of production, we can express this in symbols by the equation
>
> $$P = A + R + I,$$
>
> where A denotes wages, R rent and I profit on capital for the branch of production in question, or for the production of the whole country. As soon as this equation has been written down, it is clear as day that in order to solve it we must have three further independent relationships between the four quantities. But it is quite safe to declare that before Walras no economist had formulated this necessary condition clearly, although Ricardo and his followers came near to doing so. But there have been innumerable writers who have thought that they had contributed something to the solution, one might say, by moving one of the quantities from the right-hand side of the equation to the left, or vice versa.

The atemporal model as developed here is a model of a perfectly competitive economy. This assumption is more dispensable than might be imagined, although no attempt has been made here to dispense with it. The difficulty lies not so much in replacing competition but in knowing what to replace it with, that is how to formalize monopoly or oligopoly and what assumptions concerning the conduct of firms in these situations are appropriate, and this is no simple matter. In delivering us from the burden of such difficulties the assumption of competition is a cure for some headaches. But the relief, as has been seen, is in part illusory because in seeming to rescue us from the need to deal with some questions of an institutional character the assumption of competition has no clear institutional basis. In this respect it resembles to some extent the assumption of economic equilibrium and it is in fact related to this assumption since it makes little sense for the actors to assume that they may trade freely at parametric prices unless they are either in an economy where consistent plans have been formulated, or unless they are engaged in a *tâtonnement.* On economic equilibrium we are led to conclude that one such will always exist for the atemporal economy as specified and hence, supposing the economy to be in a state of equilibrium, involves no logical difficulties. But this leaves us a long way from explaining how equilibrium might be realized or predicting that it will occur. Furthermore, there may be two or many equilibria anyway and there may be many stable equilibria or none at all.

From the viewpoint of the theory of distribution, the study of the atemporal economy has proved valuable in more than one respect. It has highlighted the numerous problems, both technical and philosophical, that must be faced if a theory of distribution is to be constructed. It has shown that equilibrium does have implications for the distribution of income which must be accepted by anyone who wants to consider equilibrium states, but the implication is not necessarily a unique distribution. Another conclusion is that an interdependent market system is a very complicated construction in which all the primitive specifications will normally play a part in influencing any particular magnitude, so that it usually makes no sense to ask for the cause of a particular magnitude while expecting a brief answer. Finally, it has been shown that marginal concepts are not essentially involved in this theory; although where applicable, they cannot stand in contradiction to it. They are, one might say, 'optional extras'. In so far as equilibrium in the atemporal economy prevails it does have some implications for the 'causes' of the prices of the services of the various factors, but these 'causes' do not include the marginal products of the factor services.

3

Equilibrium, prices and time

Time is the primitive form of the stream of consciousness. It is a fact, however obscure and perplexing to our minds, that the contents of consciousness do not present themselves simply as being (such as conceptions, numbers, etc.) but as being now, *filling the form of the enduring present with a varying content. So that one does not say this* is *but this is* now, *yet now no more.*

HERMANN WEYL, *Space–Time–Matter*

One of the essential tasks of a theory of capital is to show how time enters into economic reality and to make clear why a purely static and timeless economic theory could not be adequate. The task is such a difficult one that there is everything to be said for undertaking it in several relatively easy stages and this is what will be done here.

The events which concern us – consumption of goods by individuals, supplies of inputs to production and productive activities themselves – take place at different moments of time. They also take place at various different points of space. There is an analogy here, which will soon be seen to be a partial one, between space as an aspect of reality which distinguishes one economic event, or one economic quantity, from another, and time which similarly distinguishes economic events and quantities. This analogy is worth pursuing for it is fairly easy to tackle the problems posed by spatial differentiation for economic theory, although it is nonetheless educational to do so. The methods that prove powerful for this case can then be applied to time. In this way we learn something about the problem of time and economic theory. What we learn in particular is that the analogy between space and time is ultimately a false one. For time differs from space in having a direction and it is this that makes capital theory a vastly more difficult subject than the disciplines that concern themselves with the economic implications of spatial location – transport economics and location theory. The capital theory that pretends that time is just like space is interesting and has something to teach us, but it is not the answer to the questions which are at once the most formidable and at the same time the most important.

At the outset the atemporal equilibrium model of ch. 2 presumed a list of goods, including factor services, which were distinguished within the model, although no attention was given to the principles to be applied in compiling such a list. As so often happens in economics this seemingly trivial matter turns out on examination to be less trivial than might at first be supposed. Two goods should obviously be distinguished and allotted separate reference numbers if they differ in some economically relevant manner. The test for this is whether or not there is any actor in the economy, household or firm, who would, in any circumstance, pay more for one unit of one good than for one unit of the other. The very idea of a competitive economy springs from the supposition that a list might be compiled such that the numbering of different goods would be independent of which firm produced them, or which household supplied them.

What would happen if the 'degree of delicacy' in distinguishing between different goods differed markedly from actor to actor? We would then have to allot separate reference numbers to several goods just on account of certain individuals although, for the majority, these different goods would be perfect substitutes. An immediate implication is that a household that does not distinguish between two goods cannot have a single-valued decision function $\mathbf{x}_h(\mathbf{p}, I_h)$ for all $\mathbf{p}$. For if these two goods have the same price it will matter not to the household how the total that it demands is made up as between the two, as it would have it, indistinguishable goods. By way of example, consider the case in which the technical conditions under which a certain good is produced give rise to 'good' and 'bad' specimens. In such a case organizational details become important in determining what will come about. If there is a grading organization this may organize the marketing of the different specimens in different markets. Buyers will shop in whichever market they prefer, given the prices ruling, and always in the cheapest market if all specimens are the same to them.

There is a lot involved in the notion of a 'good' but we are not at the moment concerned with all its ramifications. Our present concern is with location in space. Should one good be distinguished from another and allotted a separate reference number, just on account of the point in space that it occupies? Applying the critical test it may be seen that this is an appropriate basis for distinguishing one good from another because in the preference orderings of households and in the production sets of firms, spatial location is of consequence. This fact is reflected in a willingness to pay more for an identical good if it be delivered at one point rather than another. Households will pay more for milk delivered on their doorsteps than for the same milk available to them to dispose as they will but 100 miles away. Or, and this is merely another way of checking that we have two distinct goods, there are costly undertakings – transport activities – whose effect is to transform milk in one place to milk in another. It seems then that we do not need a separate theory of transport economics (not, that is, at the very abstract and general level of pure equilibrium theory) but we can simply treat position in space as one of the many properties which are taken into account in labelling and distinguishing between different goods. Thus we might assign the index 1157 to the good 'coal in London' and the index 1158 to another good 'coal in Newcastle'. As far as the logic of this approach to space is concerned these are different goods and so households in Newcastle may be willing to pay more for a ton of good 1158 than for a ton of good 1157. On account of this willingness to pay more for the former good it is not inconceivable that a costly activity might be employed by a firm in certain circumstances to transform a ton of good 1157 into good 1158. There might be such a productive activity, with an input of one ton of good 1157 plus the services of 274 ton-miles of truck service and an output of one ton of good 1158, called 'transporting coal to Newcastle'.

This does seem to be a most attractive approach, solving at one stroke, and subsuming into an existing theory, a whole field of economics and the mass of problems to which it gives rise, but nothing is quite that simple. It may need more than an elegant device to dispose of the problems posed by spatial differentiation and this for two reasons.

Firstly, the general equilibrium model of ch. 2 is notably general and abstract, and that is in many respects its strength. In particular, it abstracts from any special structures of preferences, production possibilities or knowledge. It also manifestly abstracts from institutional matters and specific divergences from the most basic model. These are all considerations which give body to specialized studies of international trade, transport economics and location theory. To say, therefore, that the introduction of position as a property of goods makes little difference to pure general equilibrium theory is not to say anything very earth-shaking. For the general equilibrium model is little concerned with specific structures and their possible consequences, but only with what can be said at an abstract level in terms of a very general framework.

Secondly, it is evident that any reinterpretation of the model, so as to extend its coverage, will put extra strain upon the assumptions and specifications which have been adopted – strain which they may prove unable to bear. Here is an illustration of this last point. It is one thing to assume that each actor knows of all the prices of goods located at the point in space which he himself occupies. It is to assume a lot more to suppose that he knows equally well prices ruling at all other points of space. If actors, be they firms or households, lack a complete knowledge of prices ruling at other points in space then the list of goods has a special structure, not well represented by a simple sequential list. We would want in such a case to index goods twice, once by physical type and once by position in space, so as to exhibit the two-dimensional differentiation of goods, which in this case would be basic to the structure of the theory that we would then have to construct.

It is evident now that the coverage of the equilibrium model of ch. 2 can be extended considerably by exploiting vigorously the wide scope which the simple concept of 'a good' offers to us. At the same time it should be no less evident that this method is a dangerous one to employ uncritically. The danger is always of lapsing into empty formalism. Yet, if used critically, the method has much to recommend it, not least when the models it produces turn out to be inadequate. If, for example, we treat space as just like any other quality which differentiates one good from another then we deal easily with those cases in which space does not introduce any considerations not already raised by colour[1] and we should also help ourselves to see clearly which problems this approach fails to illuminate. We should then understand better the nature of these problems.

Bearing in mind these points, we can now consider another extension of the concept of a good – perhaps the most radical and interesting of all. Goods can be distinguished according to the *time at which they become available*, as well as by other characteristics. Thus 'coal in Newcastle on 1 April, 1975' is a different good from 'coal in Newcastle on 2 April, 1975'. The point would be clear to anyone anxiously awaiting delivery. Clearly this distinction between goods is justified on the critical test. An anxious actor might well be willing to pay a premium to advance delivery of his coal and suppliers might then incur costs to speed the supply to him. In principle, therefore, it seems that time, like space, might be subsumed into our general grading and listing of goods by economically relevant characteristics and so disposed of, as does Debreu (1959, pp. 29–30). Let us see why we cannot properly do this.

Once again the analogy to space proves a useful one. A manager decides that a certain coal mine in Pennsylvania will produce 50 000 tons of coal. Where is the manager who makes this decision – what point of space does he occupy? A moment's consideration will convince the reader that this is a matter of no importance provided only that the manager has the relevant information, which might be transmitted to him in New York, Acapulco or

[1] This example, colour, is an interesting one in that it shows that there are cases where we could classify goods according to more than one property; yet there would be no case at all for so doing given our present concerns. From the point of view of economics the 'redness' which red objects share in common is most unlikely to carry with it a common place in preferences, production structures or channels of knowledge.

Bangkok. The same cannot be said of time. A decision is made at some moment of time and we wish to describe such decisions. Now two dates attach themselves to a decision, the date at which it is made, here called the *instruction date* and the date at which the actions defining the decisions are to be carried out, here called the *action date*. In the case where something is decided upon and at once put into effect the two dates coincide, otherwise they will differ. Similarly we might attach to decisions instruction positions and action positions, but we have already seen that this distinction is unlikely to prove important.

Now the difference between space and time is immediately evident. If the manager decides upon the output of coal somewhere else than the pit-head he might in principle be anywhere else – provided only that he can communicate his decision to his subordinates. He may be 'up the railway line' or 'down the railway line'; and if in some particular case he must be 'down the line' because the only train that will take his message travels up the line, we could equally well imagine a situation in which the train will travel in the opposite direction, in which case he would have to be up the line. In short, space has no direction independently of the objects that occupy it.

With time a new consideration enters in. The action date cannot precede the instruction date. To decide upon an action of yesterday is not to decide upon anything; it is either to mentally confirm an action or else it is day-dreaming. The instruction date determines for us, therefore, the sequence of action dates that have to be taken into account in our theory and it is necessarily then a matter of central importance to an economic theory which takes account of time. We may quite reasonably treat decision-makers as if they did not, for the purposes of the theory, occupy any particular point in space – although we might get a better theory if we took into account this feature and its possible consequences for tastes, knowledge and so forth. But we cannot meaningfully treat our decision-makers as so 'disembodied' that they do not occupy even a moment of time. Our description of the economy will start at a particular moment of time and this will be our first instruction date.

It would be tedious, and it will not be necessary, to rehearse all the differences between position and date as they affect the reinterpretation of the labelling goods according to the time at which they become available. The reader will readily note for himself the most obvious ones. The central difference resides in one point: *decisions about future action dates are important for the description of how the economy behaves at present only in so far as they lead to present actions*. We are not so interested in the resolutions which the actors may make[2]. If a coal producer decides to increase his production next year that is

[2] Except that it could happen that one actor's resolution would influence the action of another actor.

interesting, but not as such of vital importance – he may well change his mind. It is quite different if he decides to increase at once the production of mines that he owns in another town. But typically decisions to act in the future demand present actions of their progenitors: the coal producer, for example, may order more lift gear to raise the extra coal to the surface and once he has acted to do this there is no going back on that action – even if he is allowed to cancel orders he cannot return himself to a state where no order was ever placed. Again the problems differ from those posed by position. The dates of the future will eventually be upon each actor and at those dates he will choose to act in a particular way; yet long before they arrive future dates reach out and exert an influence upon present actions through planning and expectations.

Account must also be taken of the uncertainty of the future. There is no need to enter upon philosophical disquisitions about whether the future, including human actions, might in principle be predicted perfectly accurately, for we are so far from being able to do this in fact that the future must be regarded as highly uncertain. This means that the actors do not know for certain what will happen in future time periods. If, therefore, we reinterpret the basic equilibrium model of the atemporal economy by supposing that goods have been labelled according to the date at which they become available, as well as according to other properties, and if no other modification were to be made, we would place an impossible strain upon the assumption of perfect knowledge. Thus the appropriateness for an economy that persists through time of a model that is formally analogous to the perfect knowledge atemporal model is to be doubted. Nonetheless, this theory will be developed here and indeed taken quite a long way. This is in part for didactic reasons – the model has something to teach us and it represents a good starting point. Also, it is an astounding fact, and a disconcerting one too, that the proportion of received theory of any school that is definitely excluded if one confines oneself to this approach is rather small. Capital theory as we know it has scarcely begun to come to grips with the issues posed by time. Inadequate though a model is that treats time just as it treats space, economists have proved willing to work within the confines of such models for a long time.

There must be an explanation of such a notable fact and in this case there are probably two. One is that, just because it produces a theory closely analogous to the one that we already know, treating time like space makes for simplicity. Another explanation, and perhaps the more important one, is that economic theorists, as we shall see, have very frequently worked with models of the economy in a stationary state, or in a not very different state from the present point of view – balanced or 'golden-age' growth at a constant rate. In such an economy the future will be exactly like the past in every important respect, except only for the merest change of scale. All the magnitudes which directly concern an individual actor: prices, wage rates, interest rates, his initial endowment if any and his transfer income, will all be strictly invariant over time. In this context, then, it is not unnatural to assume that the actors will expect these selfsame prices and quantities, i.e. that they will have learnt to expect just these magnitudes. If the future is in every important respect exactly like the past it is not unreasonable to suppose that the future might be correctly predicted and predicted with a high degree of confidence. In this case one of the most irritating features of time, uncertainty about the future, is purged from the theory.

To look more closely now at the consequences for general equilibrium analysis of the extension of the concept of a good embodied in the notion of the date of delivery as a distinguishing characteristic, consider a construction that is the equilibrium of the atemporal economy except that we now think of the goods as characterized by dates of delivery along with their other properties. We call this edifice the equilibrium of the *intertemporal economy*. As with the atemporal model of ch. 2, to which we shall attempt to keep close wherever possible, we start from a parametric price vector: but now the prices apply to goods for delivery in more than one week. Similarly, the consumption plans that will be drawn up by the households will now span many weeks but, this being understood, there is no formal difficulty in the way of considering a preference ordering to cover as many weeks as one likes. Notice here, however, an assumption suddenly taking a great deal of extra strain as the coverage of the model is drastically extended. Can we accept the existence of a preference ordering for a long span of weeks, perhaps enough weeks to add up to many years? The fact that this is an implication of the simple extension of the atemporal equilibrium model does not guide us to an answer to the question. We call the plans drawn up by households in the intertemporal economy *intertemporal consumption plans*. One of these plans will again be most preferred among all plans available to the household given its consumption set (which will now dictate on the feasibility of connected sequences of week-by-week plans) and its budget condition which will now include transfer incomes for many weeks.

Firms will likewise draw up *intertemporal production plans* in the form of a net supply vector for each future week and will narrow down the range of choices to a convex subset consisting of elements each of which is a profit-maximizing plan. The firm's production set will now embody not just the possibilities for one week or another but also the interconnections between what is undertaken in one week and what can be undertaken in another. The transformation constraints will now include possibilities of transforming goods available in one period into goods available in another. One firm might be able, for example, to transform two man-weeks of bricklayer's time and inputs of various materials, bricks and a 52-week-old cement mixer, into a brick wall available one week later and a 53-week-old cement mixer again available one week later.

Naturally, an immediate implication of our going from the atemporal to the intertemporal economy is that capitalistic processes and durable capital goods, investment and depreciation, are now straightforwardly included: production with capital is now taken into account within the purview of the theory.

There is no need at all to rehearse again the definition of equilibrium, the question of existence and the question of free goods: for it is already done. All that is involved is a new interpretation of the old model which, from the formal point of view, makes no difference. Formally all is as before: there are prices and transfers; there are preferences and production sets, therefore decisions which have implications for trades with the rest of the economy; there is equilibrium and of course there is disequilibrium. The extension to the intertemporal model is in a sense no more than a greater licence to the imagination.

How many weeks should be taken into consideration in the analysis of the intertemporal economy? Here we are confronted by an issue that might undermine the very idea of considering time as just another property of goods. For our list of goods in the atemporal economy was a finite one, although the number might be a very large one. In treating only a finite list of goods we might there be grading according to a classification mesh which lumped together all goods not differing sufficiently to fall within separate classifications, notwithstanding the possibility of a continuously variable quality such as the alcoholic content of a wine. Similarly, by dividing time into blocks of 'weeks' and not concerning ourselves at all closely with what goes on inside a week, we have given to time, which comes to us as an unbroken continuum, a granular structure. There remains, however, a crucial difference: even after it has been chopped up into weeks time remains unbounded. No limit can be placed on the number of weeks during which the economy that concerns our actors might persist. This statement is probably not accurate from the viewpoint of cosmology from which one might hope to obtain, were cosmologists better able to agree than economists, at least an agreed outside limit. However, an agreed outside limit is no great help so long as no firm date is provided to the actors and firmly accepted by them. There is a problem then of bounding the number of goods to be considered in the intertemporal model and ever since Ramsey's (1928) famous paper a branch of the theory of capital has given serious consideration to the unbounded case. In the present volume that case will not be given much consideration and where it is considered it will only be in the context of the pure theory of efficient capital accumulation. This is the context in which Ramsey first posed the problem and the one that most economists ever since have felt to be the natural one for this particular assumption.

If an infinity of weeks is rejected there is but one other turn to be taken. The sequence of weeks must be chopped short at an *horizon*, being the last week to which any consideration is given by the analysis, or by any actor in the economy. This is what will be done here. Let the first week to be considered be numbered 1 and the last week T, and let the sequence of weeks be indexed by $t = 1, \ldots, T$. Regardless of whether this drastic method of doing away with infinity is justified, it can be stated definitely that it is only if this path is taken that a formal analogy to the atemporal example is available. Otherwise, the intertemporal model is fundamentally different, having no case that overlaps even formally with the atemporal model.

Just as in the atemporal model, so in the intertemporal model, every good must have a price. The logic of the close analogy to the atemporal economy dictates that every actor must be fully aware of, and treat as a parameter, each price that is ruling. Now there are nT goods: n goods in each week, T weeks in all. Just as before, these prices can be displayed as a sequence in whatever order we care to arrange them, say the following:

$$p_{11}, \ldots, p_{n1}; p_{12}, \ldots, p_{n2}; \ldots; p_{1t}, \ldots, p_{nt}; \ldots; p_{1T}, \ldots, p_{nT}. \tag{3.1}$$

The price of the ith good in week t is p_{it} $(i = 1, \ldots, n; t = 1, \ldots, T)$.

There is one thing that has not so far been made clear. What does it mean for a 'price to be ruling' for a good that is not a current good? The answer to this question, which springs from regarding the intertemporal model as an extension of the atemporal model by way of a reinterpretation of the concept of a good, would be in terms of *forward markets*. In the atemporal economy there were markets for every good, so likewise in the intertemporal economy every good should have its market and its competitive market price. Where the good or factor service transacted is not a current good but one to be delivered some number of weeks in the future, we speak of a forward market and the price of a good in such a market is to be interpreted as the *present quotation for future delivery*. The atemporal economy was an economy of complete certainty: prices, preferences, production possibilities and transfer incomes were known to the actors – there was no doubt about them. It follows that on crudely extending this model to a sequence of many weeks we arrive at an economy where again everything is known. Obviously, such a radical extension of the original model puts enormous strain on the assumption of certainty, so much so that the model is for many purposes not viable. But as an exercise in pure theory it is nonetheless worth pursuing. For while time undoubtedly brings with it uncertainty, time and uncertainty are by no means the same thing. By studying a model which includes the passage of time, but not for the moment the effects of uncertainty, we should take a step towards clarifying the issue of which problems arise from time and which from uncertainty, if any such separation is possible.

In relation to actual market economies the assumption of a complete system of forward markets is a very far-fetched representation. Forward markets do exist but they cover only a fraction of the goods for which there are active current markets. Also they seldom reach anything like as far into the future as the span covered by many planning calculations. In the absence of forward markets the actors must 'take a view' or make guesses as to what the levels of prices will be for current transactions in future weeks. If all actors always held their beliefs about these prices with complete certainty (this is a description of their subjective state of mind) and if the beliefs of each actor happened to coincide with those of every other, then it would be exactly 'as if' there were forward markets. To a certain extent this is what happens in the stationary-state economy where everyone views the future with a clear and firm belief that future prices will be the same as today's prices. In this case, forward markets would have no function to perform. There is no point in transacting in advance unless it be to reduce uncertainty about what the price will be. If all actors believe confidently that they know what prices will rule, which must involve a belief that supply and demand will match at those prices, for otherwise the prices would quickly change, then forward markets have nothing to offer them. Equally we can treat them 'as if' they transacted in advance in forward markets – it makes no difference either way.

As will often be the case, the stationary-state economy is a very special, and not very interesting, example. Normally, beliefs about the future, even if firmly held, might be inconsistent and in more than one way. Firstly, the actors may hold different expectations about prices. Secondly, even if they expect the same prices, the actors may plan to supply and demand at those prices quantities that will not match. A system of forward markets in equilibrium eliminates both these kinds of inconsistency. It is therefore the most straightforward extension of the atemporal equilibrium model to assume that forward markets exist and that they are cleared at the ruling prices.

The extension of the atemporal model has important consequences for the interpretation of the budget condition of a household. To take a very simple example, consider a household which will persist for 20 'weeks' and which has only its own labour to supply and which eats only bread. Let the present price of bread in week t be π_t ($t = 1, \ldots, 20$) and the present price of labour time be ω_t ($t = 1, \ldots, 20$). Let the household plan to consume β_t pounds of bread in week t and to work η_t hours ($t = 1, \ldots, 20$). The budget condition of this household now requires that

$$\sum_{t=1}^{20} \omega_t \eta_t - \sum_{t=1}^{20} \pi_t \beta_t \geqslant 0. \tag{3.2}$$

The budget condition is a single constraint involving the weighted sums of the consumptions of bread and the labour times. As such it says nothing about the timing of the individual credits and debits that will go to make up the total. In fact, all credits and debits occur simultaneously when the household commits itself to its complete plan of action in the future weeks. Thus, a household may satisfy its budget condition by planning to eat bread and not work for the first 10 weeks, provided that it commits itself to working hard enough in the subsequent weeks to feed itself, however frugally, and to 'pay off its debts'.

As the example makes clear, when one extends the coverage of markets to include forward markets the budget condition carries new implications. If actors are allowed to choose and act freely, subject only to budget conditions, then they are deemed, in effect, to be perfectly 'creditworthy'. This is a feature which does not arise in the atemporal economy where, if a transactor failed to 'deliver the goods', he could be denied the goods promised to him in the trading equilibrium – and these would be goods of equal value within that one trading period on account of the budget condition.

It is not clear what institutions could be imagined to ensure 'perfect creditworthiness', and this is not a problem to which those economists who have treated the subject of intertemporal economic equilibrium have given any attention. It must be supposed either that all men are too honourable to default on their obligations or that they can be forced to comply with them. The first assumption seems dubious and the second would require forced labour in certain cases. The point at issue here is not by any means an unimportant one. One of the basic and crucial problems that we must face when we leave behind the atemporal economy – when we embark upon capital theory – is that the intertemporal economy involves the institutions of trading present obligations for future obligations, or one future obligation for another. There is no escaping the desire of those who put themselves in a position where they are due to receive goods in the future to attend to the security of these 'loans'. This is a problem which is of particular importance in a world where the future is uncertain – for then a man may find himself unable to fulfil obligations he once expected to be able to discharge. But it is not only a problem of an uncertain world, for men who can discharge their obligations might choose not to do so.

When there is an intertemporal competitive equilibrium we have a set of nT equilibrium prices. Recalling that p_{it} denotes the price of the ith good in the tth week, the equilibrium prices can be arranged in a rectangular array, as shown in table 3.1. Although the stress is laid here on the intertemporal

Table 3.1.

	Weeks					
Goods	1	2	..	t	..	T
1	p_{11}	p_{12}	..	p_{1t}	..	p_{1T}
2	p_{21}	p_{22}	..	p_{2t}	..	p_{2T}
.	.	.	..	.	..	.
.	.	.	..	.	..	.
.	.	.	..	.	..	.
n	p_{n1}	p_{n2}	..	p_{nt}	..	p_{nT}

features of the model the analogy to the atemporal case is, by construction, still complete. By this analogy we know that if the above array is an equilibrium price configuration then so is the same array with each p_{it} replaced by λp_{it} where $\lambda > 0$. Once again only relative prices count. Note that there is still only one price configuration, regardless of the fact that any type of good is priced T times, once in each week; so we can still choose only one *numeraire*. For convenience, let us choose $\lambda = 1/p_{11}$, i.e. choose good 1 in week 1 as *numeraire*.

As before, this is only one *numeraire* and not necessarily the best one. Indeed we cannot divide by p_{11} if it is zero, as it would be if the first good were to be a free good in week 1. By analogy to the atemporal economy the composite good consisting of one unit of each good (which here means one unit of each good in each week) is perhaps a particularly suitable *numeraire* for general use. To express the prices in terms of this *numeraire* we would have to divide the array through by

$$\lambda = \sum_{i=1}^{n} \sum_{t=1}^{T} p_{it}. \tag{3.3}$$

However, our immediate concern here is not with analysis but rather with the exposition of certain ideas and for that purpose it is somewhat preferable to take the simplest of *numeraires*, a single good, which is here to be good 1 delivered in week 1. In fixing on this as the unit of account we implicitly suppose that it is not a free good.

Following upon adjustment to give to the *numeraire* the price 1, the array appears as shown in table 3.2. Here the prices are relative to the first good delivered in the first week.

Table 3.2.

	Weeks					
Goods	1	2	..	t	..	T
1	1	p_{12}	..	p_{1t}	..	p_{1T}
2	p_{21}	p_{22}	..	p_{2t}	..	p_{2T}
.	.	.	..	.	..	.
.	.	.	..	.	..	.
.	.	.	..	.	..	.
n	p_{n1}	p_{n2}	..	p_{nt}	..	p_{nT}

Now run the eye along the first row of the array of table 3.2. Assume that an actor holds one unit of good 1 in week 1. If he wished to use his command of that good to purchase good *i* for delivery in a later week, say week *t*, how much would he be able to purchase? Let the largest amount that he could purchase – the quantity whose purchase would just exhaust his revenue from the sale of one unit of good 1 – be x_{it}. The unit price of good i for delivery in week t is p_{it}, so that the cost will be $p_{it}x_{it} = 1$. Hence, $x_{it} = 1/p_{it}$. Thus a present-value price in the array of table 3.2 is to be interpreted as the inverse of the quantity of good *i* for delivery in period *t* which one unit of the *numeraire* will purchase. It makes very little difference to this interpretation if the *numeraire* is a composite of all the goods of week 1. Then $\sum_{i=1}^{n} p_{i1} = 1$ and p_{it} bears the interpretation of the inverse of the quantity of good i in week *t* that may be obtained in return for the surrender of one unit of the composite good[3].

Let

$$\rho_1(1,t) = (1/p_{1t}) - 1 = (1 - p_{1t})/p_{1t}. \tag{3.4}$$

Then $\rho_1(1,t)$ measures how much extra of good 1 may be obtained in week t per unit surrendered in week 1 by deferring delivery from week 1 to week t.

[3] Similarly with the composite *numeraire* $\sum_{i=1}^{n} \sum_{t=1}^{T} p_{it} = 1$, the inverse of a price would indicate the amount of the good concerned which could be purchased in return for the surrender of one unit of each good in each week.

Subscript 1 indicates that the good involved in the transaction is good 1 (this is an own-rate of interest of good 1) while the $(1,t)$ in parentheses indicates the weeks spanned by the transaction – from week 1 to week t. It is natural to call $\rho_1(1,t)$ the *t-week own-rate of interest for good 1 in week 1*, for it has the character of an interest rate. If, for example, $p_{1t}=\frac{2}{3}$ then $\rho_1(1,t)=0.5$ and the t-week own-rate of interest for good 1 in week 1 is 50%. By giving up one unit of good 1 for delivery in week 1 an actor may obtain 50% extra (i.e. 1.5 units) in week t. The own-rate of interest to deferring acceptance of good 1 from week 1 to week t is measured by the proportional rate of decrease of the price of that good over the weeks concerned.

The sign of $\rho_1(1,t)$ is not immediately evident: it will be positive if $p_{it}<1$, and negative if $p_{1t}>1$. The reader may feel less inclined to accept the possibility that $\rho_1(1,t)$ might be negative than to accept the possibility that it might be positive. Later we shall see that the former case will indeed usually be realized provided only that productive processes taken together are capable of expanding the stock of goods available; for then present-value prices must decline with time to eliminate pure profits. For the present, however, the possibility of present-value prices rising through time and negative own-rates of interest cannot be ruled out. It certainly has nothing to do with prices being negative which is a very different matter.

Now, more generally, let the delivery of one unit of good i be deferred from week t to week $t+s$. Denote the own-rate of interest to this deferment by $\rho_i(t,t+s)$. We have

$$p_{it}=x_{i,t+s}p_{i,t+s}, \tag{3.5}$$

where $x_{i,t+s}$ is the quantity obtained in week $t+s$. Then the proportionate gain in terms of good i is $x_{i,t+s}-1$ which is equal, by definition, to $\rho_i(t,t+s)$. Thus,

$$\rho_i(t,t+s)=x_{i,t+s}-1=\frac{p_{i,t}}{p_{i,t+s}}-1=\frac{p_{i,t}-p_{i,t+s}}{p_{i,t+s}}. \tag{3.6}$$

Here again the own-rate of interest is measured by the rate of decline of the present-value price expressed as a proportion of the price of the later period. Yet again it might, so far as any considerations so far advanced are concerned, be either positive or negative.

An examination of the definitions of own-rates of interest will reveal that the various own-rates of interest values are not independent of each other. Consider, for example, the value $\rho_i(t,t+s)$, defined as

$$(p_{i,t}/p_{i,t+s})-1. \tag{3.7}$$

Then we have

$$1+\rho_i(t,t+s)=\frac{p_{i,t}}{p_{i,t+s}}=\frac{p_{i,t}}{p_{i,t+1}}\frac{p_{i,t+1}}{p_{i,t+2}}\frac{p_{i,t+2}}{p_{i,t+3}}\cdots\frac{p_{i,t+s-1}}{p_{i,t+s}}$$
$$=[1+\rho_i(t,t+1)]\,[1+\rho_i(t+1,t+2)]$$
$$\times[1+\rho_i(t+2,t+3)]\ldots[1+\rho_i(t+s-1,t+s)]. \tag{3.8}$$

This is the familiar relationship between long and short rates of interest (or own-rates of interest) of Hicks' *Value and Capital* (1946, pp. 144–147). From this formula we may calculate all the own-rates of interest involving deferments for more than one week from the complete list of 'short' or one-week own-rates of interest. Equally, given all the own-rates of interest for deferments from week 1 to any later week, we may infer the short rates for later weeks. What we cannot do is to simultaneously and independently choose short and long own-rates of interest, for that would imply more than one intertemporal price system.

Let us now focus attention on the short or single-week own-rates of interest. Are the own-rates of interest on two goods the same in equilibrium for any given week? In general they are not equal. Let the two goods be i and j. Then

$$1+\rho_i(t,t+1)=\frac{p_{i,t}}{p_{i,t+1}} \quad\text{and}\quad 1+\rho_j(t,t+1)=\frac{p_{j,t}}{p_{j,t+1}}. \tag{3.9}$$

For these two gross rates of interest to be equal we must have

$$\frac{p_{i,t}}{p_{i,t+1}}=\frac{p_{j,t}}{p_{j,t+1}} \quad\text{or}\quad \frac{p_{i,t}}{p_{j,t}}=\frac{p_{i,t+1}}{p_{j,t+1}}. \tag{3.10}$$

Thus *the one-week own-rates of interest in week t of two goods are equal if and only if their relative prices are unchanged between week t and week t + 1*. Clearly the same result holds for any number of weeks.

It is now clear how something very like rates of interest enter into a model which started only with present-value prices. The equilibrium price system already contains a whole structure of own-rates of interest; one own-rate for each good and each pair of weeks. The own-rates for non-adjacent weeks are related to the rates for the succession of adjacent weeks that link them by the Hicksian condition (3.8). The short own-rates for different goods are linked by the condition

$$\frac{1+\rho_i(t,t+1)}{1+\rho_j(t,t+1)}=\frac{p_{i,t}/p_{j,t}}{p_{i,t+1}/p_{j,t+1}}, \tag{3.11}$$

which states that the gross own-rates of interest for two goods are in the same ratio to each other as the ratio of their relative prices in the two weeks.

By now it is clear that as one runs the eye across the array of prices from left to right prices are changing on account of what one may regard as two distinct influences. Firstly, because own-rates of interest will be positive (negative) prices will tend mostly to fall (increase) from left to right. Secondly, relative prices may alter and this will cause certain own-rates of interest to diverge from the average. We can show the separate effects of these influences by another rearrangement of the price array. Set the current price of the first good to unity in each week, or note equivalently that

$$p_{11} = [1 + \rho_1(1, t)]p_{1t} \tag{3.12}$$

so that when the array is divided through by p_{11}, so as to express all prices in terms of the first good in the first week, we obtain the price array in a new format.

Table 3.3.

Goods	Weeks 1	2		t		T
1	1	$\frac{1}{1+\rho_1(1,2)}$	...	$\frac{1}{1+\rho_1(1,t)}$	...	$\frac{1}{1+\rho_1(1,T)}$
2	$\frac{p_{21}}{p_{11}}$	$\frac{p_{22}}{p_{12}}\frac{1}{1+\rho_1(1,2)}$	...	$\frac{p_{2t}}{p_{1t}}\frac{1}{1+\rho_1(1,t)}$	...	$\frac{p_{2T}}{p_{1T}}\frac{1}{1+\rho_1(1,T)}$
⋮	⋮	⋮		⋮		⋮
i	$\frac{p_{i1}}{p_{11}}$	$\frac{p_{i2}}{p_{12}}\frac{1}{1+\rho_1(1,2)}$	...	$\frac{p_{it}}{p_{1t}}\frac{1}{1+\rho_1(1,t)}$	...	$\frac{p_{iT}}{p_{1T}}\frac{1}{1+\rho_1(1,T)}$
⋮	⋮	⋮		⋮		⋮
n	$\frac{p_{n1}}{p_{11}}$	$\frac{p_{n2}}{p_{12}}\frac{1}{1+\rho_1(1,2)}$	...	$\frac{p_{nt}}{p_{1t}}\frac{1}{1+\rho_1(1,t)}$	...	$\frac{p_{nT}}{p_{1T}}\frac{1}{1+\rho_1(1,T)}$

In table 3.3 each price has been expressed as the product of two terms: a relative price for the particular week concerned and a discount factor related to the t-week own-rate of interest for good 1. The general rule for computing an entry to table 3.3 is that p_{it} $(i = 1, \ldots, n; t = 1, \ldots, T)$ is replaced by

$$\frac{p_{it}}{p_{1t}}\frac{1}{1 + \rho_1(1, t)}. \tag{3.13}$$

From (3.13) one may confirm the somewhat obvious conclusion that the present value of the ith good in week t, in terms of good 1 in week 1, depends firstly upon how the present value of good 1 in week t stands in relation to its value in week 1, and secondly upon how the value of good i stands in week t in relation to that of good 1 in the same week.

If by chance relative prices were to be constant over time, each week would have the same p_{it}/p_{1t} entries. The tendency of prices to fall over time is shown by the terms of the form $1/[1+\rho_1(1,t)]$ and in this case all prices fall at the same rate, i.e. all own-rates of interest are equal in any week. We can then call the common value of these own-rates of interest the rate of interest for that week, without any qualification to indicate that we are referring to some particular good. Furthermore, if we can write

$$[1+\rho_1(1,t)] = [1+\rho_1(1,2)]^{t-1} \qquad (t=1,\ldots,T), \tag{3.14}$$

then the rate of decline of prices is equal for each week. We can then talk unambiguously of a *rate of interest.* Notice the special assumptions that are necessary for an intertemporal equilibrium to have associated with it a single constant rate of interest. In general, all that is known is that in any week there is a uniquely defined own-rate of interest for any good, but this may differ from the own-rates of interest for other goods in that week or from the own-rates of interest for that good in a different week.

It is hoped that the point has not already been too much laboured and that the reader will bear with yet another statement of it. According to equilibrium theory – according indeed to any theory of economic action which relates firms' decisions to prospective profit and households' decisions to budget-constrained searches for the most preferred combination of goods – it is prices which play the fundamental role. This is because prices provide the weights to be attached to the possible amendments to their net supply plans which the actors have implicitly rejected in deciding upon their choices. In an intertemporal economy it is then, naturally, present-value prices which play the fundamental role. Although this argument is mounted here on the basis of a consideration of an economy with forward markets in intertemporal equilibrium, it in no way depends upon this particular foundation. As has been remarked, if forward markets are not in operation the economic actors have no choice but to substitute their 'guesses' for the firm quotations of the forward markets. This will make a big difference, since full intertemporal equilibrium is not likely to be achieved unless there is a mechanism to check and correct for inconsistency in plans and expectations. But the forces that pull economic decisions one way or the other are present-value prices (present-value prices because weights relevant to present decisions) be they guesses or firm quotations. This is something of which we should never lose sight.

The reader might object that the above claim is the purest sophistry. Since the foregoing discussion has shown in some detail that there is an exact equivalence between a full system of present-value prices and a set of week 1 prices plus a full system of own-rates of interest of various durations, how can it now be claimed that one of these ways of arranging the price array, for it is no more than that, has primacy over the other?

Well, yes, that would have to be conceded. Ultimately it can make no difference which approach is used if the practitioner be ever so careful. It can make no difference because there is an exact translation to hand from one system to the other. True, as we shall see, the present-value prices spring immediately from the mathematical analysis of the production theory for an intertemporal economy – the mathematics prefers to speak the language of present-value prices – but that is not an immediate reason why, necessarily, searching for a grasp of the economic ideas, we should follow suit. We might instead follow what might be called the 'mainstream' of economic thought which has regarded the explanation of the determination of *the rate of interest* as the central problem of capital theory. The claim of this chapter, which can only be fully validated in later chapters, is that whatever the ultimate logical status of working with own-rates of interest as the vocabulary (or is it the grammar?) of capital theory, it is in fact a powerful source of confusion. The reason for this no doubt lies in the ever present temptation to simplify the whole price array down to just a few, or even one, rate of interest – a temptation which does not so easily overcome one who works with present-value prices. So it is after all perhaps not too extreme to claim that the primacy of present-value prices, while having no ultimate purely logical status, is, as it happens, a point of the utmost importance. It is one to which we shall return again in later chapters.

The major conclusion at which the investigation of intertemporal equilibrium has arrived is that no really new analytical issues arise when time is treated, as one might more plausibly treat space, as no more than a property of goods according to which they are indexed. Nothing is involved beyond a reinterpretation of the symbols which are already on paper before our eyes. So long as time is treated as if it were space we have already to hand the analysis that is needed. However, all the postulates of the atemporal model take extra strain as the model is so radically extended. In particular, the supposition that everything that concerns an actor is known with certainty by him is, as far as a description of the world is concerned, not an abstraction but a fantasy. So how should we proceed? Since for the moment we really are not concerning ourselves with the vagaries of technical progress and the development of household preferences through time, it is not inappropriate to hold to the assumption that preference orderings and production sets are known to the actors both as they concern the present week and reaching into the future.

Prices, however, are a different matter and we would take what is perhaps the crucial step towards a model of an economy in which time plays its own essential role by dropping the assumption that there exists a complete system of perfect forward markets. Of course, if we were to drop all forward markets and allow no trades of present goods for future goods, we would be prohibiting any consideration of a central issue of the theory of capital. We would be left with an economy in which firms and households would link up with future weeks only by storing various durable goods. It should not be supposed that the resulting economy would be a sequence of atemporal economies following one upon the other, but each one an independent *scenario*. It is not so, for to arrive at the atemporal economy it was necessary not merely to exclude forward markets but to exclude also durable goods which could be stored or not stored according to an actor's decision. If there were no forward markets at all the actors would look about for a good to store as a means of transferring to a future week not that particular good, which could be sold in the then current market, but purchasing power. In this case, various goods stored up according to convenience or for speculative reasons would link one week to another. It does not have to be money that provides an 'essential link between the present and the future' (Keynes, 1936, p. 293) although money, where it exists, may be particularly suitable for this purpose.

The most interesting case is intermediate between the pure types – the atemporal economy and the intertemporal economy. Hicks has provided an ingenious example of such an intermediate case in his discussion of what he has called *temporary equilibrium* (Hicks, 1946, p. 123; 1965, pp. 58–75)[4]. Suppose that the economy features perfect current markets for all goods. In general, forward trading is not possible since forward markets largely do not exist, but there is a set of perfect markets in 'cocoa futures' which any actor may enter and trade freely no matter whether he goes long or short. Let 'cocoa' be good 1. We do all our accounting in terms of current cocoa, and in terms of this *numeraire* the market system provides an array (table 3.4) which we may compare to table 3.3.

[4] See also the treatment provided by Arrow and Hahn (1971, pp. 136–151). Our temporary equilibrium construct is not exactly the same as that of Hicks, in that production is treated differently.

Table 3.4.

Goods	Weeks: 1	2		t		T
1	**1**	$\mathbf{\frac{1}{1+\rho_1(1,2)}}$	. . .	$\mathbf{\frac{1}{1+\rho_1(1,t)}}$	. . .	$\mathbf{\frac{1}{1+\rho_1(1,T)}}$
2	$\mathbf{\frac{p_{21}}{p_{11}}}$	$\frac{p_{22}}{p_{12}}\mathbf{\frac{1}{1+\rho_1(1,2)}}$	. . .	$\frac{p_{2t}}{p_{1t}}\mathbf{\frac{1}{1+\rho_1(1,t)}}$	. . .	$\frac{p_{2T}}{p_{1T}}\mathbf{\frac{1}{1+\rho_1(1,T)}}$
⋮	⋮	⋮		⋮		⋮
i	$\mathbf{\frac{p_{i1}}{p_{11}}}$	$\frac{p_{i2}}{p_{12}}\mathbf{\frac{1}{1+\rho_1(1,2)}}$	. . .	$\frac{p_{it}}{p_{1t}}\mathbf{\frac{1}{1+\rho_1(1,t)}}$	. . .	$\frac{p_{iT}}{p_{1T}}\mathbf{\frac{1}{1+\rho_1(1,T)}}$
⋮	⋮	⋮		⋮		⋮
b	$\mathbf{\frac{p_{n1}}{p_{11}}}$	$\frac{p_{n2}}{p_{12}}\mathbf{\frac{1}{1+\rho_1(1,2)}}$	. . .	$\frac{p_{nt}}{p_{1t}}\mathbf{\frac{1}{1+\rho_1(1,t)}}$	. . .	$\frac{p_{nT}}{p_{1T}}\mathbf{\frac{1}{1+\rho_1(1,T)}}$

The market system provides an actor with the entries to table 3.4 that are printed in bold type, but he wants to know the complete table including the relative prices for weeks 2–T. If he could know for certain what those relative prices would be he would not mind the lack of all the forward markets for he could simply provide enough cocoa to purchase whatever else he wanted. In other words, the link between the present and the future weeks, which a system of forward markets would normally provide, is provided just as efficaciously if future relative prices are known for certain.

We may proceed now to an assumption which is perfectly ridiculous as a serious proposition, but which is, nonetheless, analytically useful. Let each actor make a guess about the relative prices for current trades in future weeks and having made his guess let him proceed as if certain that just those relative prices would be realized in future weeks. Assume further that these expectations concerning relative prices are independent of movements in the futures markets for cocoa. Of course, this is an absurdity: we allow objective uncertainty (for the actors may make different guesses, in which case they cannot all be right) but abstract from subjective uncertainty (each actor feels certain that he knows the future). It is clear, however, that one could go beyond this case and allow in subjective uncertainty, or allow expectations concerning relative prices to react continuously to movements in the markets for cocoa futures, although this would make the analysis a little more complicated. The present assumption makes for a very manageable problem because each actor will now draw up a full intertemporal plan as if trading in a full system of forward markets. Suppose, for example, that an actor has guessed that the price of a grand piano in week 10 will be 130 tons of week 10 cocoa. Suppose further that the 10-week own-rate of interest for cocoa, which is a quoted market value about which there is no doubt, stands at 30%. Then the present value of a grand piano in week 10, in terms of week 1 cocoa, is 100 tons (the reader should confirm that he agrees). To our confident actor it is as good as a forward market in grand pianos. If he wants to buy forward a grand piano for delivery in week 10 he buys forward instead 130 tons of cocoa, which will cost him 100 tons of week 1 cocoa and that is as good as buying a grand piano. The clear implication is that week 1 prices and a sequence of forward prices for cocoa are to each actor as good as a complete system of forward markets.

A full analysis of temporary equilibrium throws up numerous problems and difficulties to be resolved. Without making any attempt to treat the subject fully a sketch will be provided from which the nature of some of the main issues will emerge. There is a problem concerning how the firm should be assumed to behave. It might follow its own price expectations, the expectations of its owners, or the expectations of those who might come to own it if it were to pursue a certain course of action. It seems most convincing to endow the firm with some independence regarding its plans and suppose it to be guided by its own price expectations. But will the profits that it announces it will distribute (which we must have if we are to give to the households clear guidance on the transfer incomes that they may expect to receive) be credited by households whose price expectations may not tally with those of the firm? There are so many unclear issues to be resolved.

Since our present interest is in obtaining a definite assumption to allow an exposition of a temporary equilibrium to be realized, let it be assumed that a household cannot directly evaluate the prospective profits of a firm. Let firms prepare plans on the basis of their own price expectations, maximizing the present value of profit and computing the consequent net supplies and demands in terms of cocoa for each future week: and let these figures be announced by the firm and accepted by each household. Much of this will appear to be artificial and dubious but at the same time a number of issues are brought to our attention even upon being crudely resolved. The household will now draw up a plan on the assumption that it knows for certain its future transfer incomes and these will be consistent with the expectations of firms.

It can be shown that a temporary equilibrium will exist for the kind of economy that has been described. Briefly, the method of demonstrating this proposition is to show that the model is equivalent to the atemporal model reinterpreted. There are $n+T-1$ 'goods' – n current goods plus $T-1$ claims to future cocoa. Since all actors mentally reduce future goods to cocoa, each in his own way, we can construct derived utility functions and derived production sets in which only current goods and cocoa futures appear. Every good that appears explicitly then has a market and an agreed price. It is then 'as if' we had an atemporal economy and were seeking an equilibrium. There is some detailed analysis necessary to show that we would have all the necessary conditions satisfied, but it is so, and perhaps not surprising.

There will be then some array of present prices and prices for cocoa futures which will call forth from the actors of the economy a set of intertemporal plans which will be consistent *in so far as they affect trading in current goods and trading in cocoa futures.* Of course, it is only in this particular sense that plans need be consistent. Price expectations may be completely incompatible. There may be an excess planned demand for some goods in week 2 and an excess planned supply of other goods. What there cannot be is a general excess demand or supply for the goods of one week as measured by the effect on the cocoa futures market for that particular week so long as that market is in equilibrium.

We shall not pursue further for the moment the detailed formulation and discussion of the model of temporary equilibrium. Suffice it to record that we have here a central attempt to give a precise form to an idea which has occurred to many economists and which must seem rather a compelling one. According to this view, market equilibrium would always be partial, even if it were to be realized. This is because not all, or even most, transactions are covered by markets so that the markets that do exist serve in part as 'proxies' for the markets that the actors would like to use. Equilibrium then, if attained, would only be a sham equilibrium which would not survive the passage to the next week but it would allow in the meantime a definite theoretical description of how the actors will behave. We have seen, however, even in a sketch that the analysis of temporary equilibrium throws up a fearsome mass of analytical problems. We are forced to face such issues as how our actors will respond to uncertainty, how the firm will pursue the profit that it desires, and more besides. For the most part, economists have shied away from all this, or sought at least to defend themselves against the worst of these problems by seeking refuge in an analytical haven. That refuge is the *semi-stationary economy* and the analysis of it is the subject of the next chapter.

4

Semi-stationary growth

Socrates: And let us see first what sort of existence the men and women of this society will have. They will make bread and wine and clothes and shoes. They will be builders of houses. And in summer they will do their work for the most part without clothes or shoes, but will put them on in winter; won't it be so? . . . A happy company not producing more than enough offspring for fear of getting into need or war.
Glaucon: But with nothing to give taste to their food!
Socrates: True, I was overlooking that. Well, let them have salt, olives, and cheese, and onions and greens, and the sorts of things they boil in a pot in the country, and nuts and berries. With such healthy meals, and keeping within measure in their drink, long may they go on living at peace, and hand on, at the end, the same existence to their offspring after them.

PLATO, *The Republic*

According to the argument of ch. 3 the most straightforward and natural extension of the static general equilibrium theory of the atemporal economy to take account of time involved treating goods delivered during different weeks as different goods, and supposing the existence of a complete set of competitive forward markets. From this approach came the idea of an *intertemporal equilibrium*; a construct to which time has been admitted but only after having been thoroughly sterilized. This was no real step towards a truly dynamic theory in which time would play its own peculiar and essential role. Although the model of intertemporal equilibrium is severely limited as a usable theory there are still one or two things to be learnt from it, as was evidenced by the insight which it can provide into the relation between present-value prices and own-rates of interest.

The fact that the intertemporal equilibrium model is highly abstracted from reality should not lead one to suppose that it is, as a consequence, a simple model. True, there is no reason to suppose that it will pose analytical problems notably more complex than those provided already by the atemporal equilibrium model. But even that model is already, as has been observed, extremely complicated. Experience with the analysis of even the elementary atemporal model has only served to underline the severe difficulty of reaching clear and definite conclusions on the basis of very general assumptions. Thus, while we were able in ch. 3 to contemplate the possibility of an intertemporal equilibrium and to arrive at certain conclusions concerning it, these conclusions were of a rather general character.

To proceed to more detailed conclusions some kind of simplified approach appears to be necessary. In this chapter a rather drastic simplification is imposed, namely, the development of the economy through time is assumed to exhibit a repetitive aspect so that what happens in each week is the same as what happens in every other week, except perhaps for a change of scale. We treat then of a system that reproduces just itself through time, perhaps expanding, perhaps contracting, but never changing in structure. Such a state of the economy, of which the classical stationary state is a special case, will be called a *semi-stationary state*[1], or where growth is taking place, we shall refer to to *semi-stationary growth.* What place does technical progress have in semi-stationary growth? Well, let it be admitted that it is largely excluded and that this is perhaps the severest limitation of the approach. There are odd exceptional examples which run counter to the claim. Certain special kinds of smooth continuous technical progress which have the effect of augmenting the efficiency of a factor service in all its uses; these may be accommodated within the state of semi-stationary growth, but that is neither here nor there. However, technical progress of an uneven or biased kind, technical progress which is erratic or unexpected, or technical progress which effects the efficiency of a factor service more in one use than in another (in other words, technical progress which exhibits any of the features which makes technical progress what it is) can find no place in the semi-stationary state.

The feature of an economy developing through time which makes the analysis of that development complicated is that normally each week is significantly different from the previous one so that a complete account of what happens must detail the events of each week separately. However, it is not this alone which accounts for the difficulties which beset us when we leave behind semi-stationary growth. If each week can be different from the last then some account must be taken of the implications of this fact for the expectations and the behaviour of the actors. Outside the semi-stationary state past experience cannot be a perfect guide to likely developments. In the semi-stationary state, even in a state of semi-stationary growth, the magnitudes which directly influence an actor, in particular the relative prices that he faces,

[1] This felicitous term is borrowed from Goodwin (1970, p. 88). The idea is the same as the one conveyed by the popular term 'balanced growth' and is related to Robinson's (1956) 'golden age'. However, Robinson's concept is not exactly the one of the text. It has to do with technical progress taking place smoothly as it affects the whole economy and is less concerned with the detailed developments for individual outputs and prices. For further discussion of this point. see ch. 6.

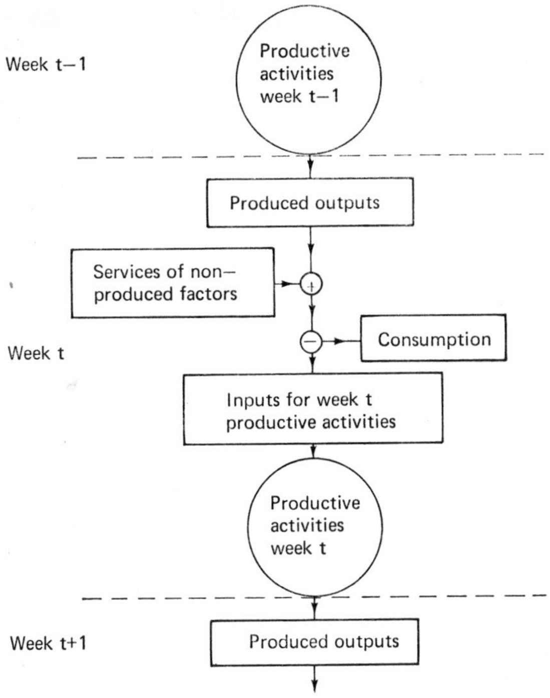

Fig. 4.1.

are all strictly invariant over time. It is then perhaps reasonable, as it probably never is otherwise, to assume that what will happen is foreseen accurately and confidently by every actor.

The outline of what occurs in one week of growth is illustrated in fig. 4.1. At the beginning of a week the productive activities of the previous week will have run their course and as a result all kinds of produced goods will be available. These goods comprise the contents of the uppermost rectangular box of fig. 4.1. The inventory of goods which are to be regarded as outputs of the productive activities of week $t-1$ is to be the most exhaustive possible, going far beyond the listing of items which would be commonly regarded as 'outputs' to include every good which remains extant at the end of the week. One might think of the inventory that would be prepared by a liquidator if economic activity were suddenly to cease at the end of week $t-1$ and the economy 'wound up'. Included in this list would be part-finished goods (where the production period exceeds one week) and those durable capital goods, such as a lathe, which retained some prospect of a useful life or which might be used as scrap. To the all-inclusive parcel of produced goods is added now the services of non-produced factors which will be provided during week t. And from it is subtracted that collection of goods and factor services which will comprise the consumption of households during week t. There remains now the parcel of goods that are available for use as input to the productive activities which will take place in week t. The effect of these productive activities is to transform the parcel of inputs into a different parcel of produced outputs. These are now ready in the rectangular box at the foot of fig. 4.1: but week t is over now and week $t+1$ will commence, as did week t, with a 'newly produced' parcel of goods.

One link in what may be conceived as an endless chain is completed and every following week will conform to the same general pattern. The reader will not fail to notice that this arrangement, of what is no more than a very detailed description of everything that occurs inside one week, allows a great variety of economic activities to be included without in any way complicating the scheme. In particular, there is no need to include an explicit distinction between goods that are present during production and goods that are used up in production. All goods are conceived as if 'swallowed up' by the productive engine, but some may be 'regurgitated' unchanged or 'regurgitated' in an altered form. In this way perfectly durable capital goods and the depreciation in use of capital goods are all features which are perfectly compatible with fig. 4.1.

Now fig. 4.1 makes no statement about how the economy will develop over time and in this respect it is completely general. Once we confine attention to semi-stationary growth, however, then the figure admits of a new interpretation: we may see it as representing not just one week but the whole development of the economy. The structure of a week's activity is already represented and every subsequent week will be the same, except for a change of scale. So, in particular, the productive activities will take place on a larger or smaller scale but without any change in their structure, i.e. so as to retain all ratios of inputs and outputs the same in every week. We must suppose, of course, that production possibilities are such as to allow that development. Let the rate of growth of the economy be γ, meaning by this that the events of one week are scaled up (or down) by a factor $1+\gamma$ in the following week ($\gamma > -1$). Let the productive activities initiated in week t transform a parcel of goods $\boldsymbol{u}_t$ into a parcel of outputs $\boldsymbol{v}_{t+1}$ available at the start of week $t+1$; then $[\boldsymbol{u}_t, \boldsymbol{v}_{t+1}]$ represents the effect of the productive transformations. $\mathscr{T}_{\mathrm{E}}(t)$ is the set of all transformations feasible at t. Subscript E reminds us that it concerns the complete economy. It has the same broad interpretation as the production set $\mathscr{T}_f$ of firm f in ch. 2, but with two differences. In the first place it refers to what is possible for the whole economy (i.e. all firms taken together) and thus comprises the sum[2] of the production sets of all firms in week t. Secondly, we must distinguish now between inputs and outputs and not take account only of the net effect of production. So we ask whether $(\boldsymbol{u}_t, \boldsymbol{v}_{t+1})$ is a possible plan and not merely whether $(\boldsymbol{v}_{t+1} - \boldsymbol{u}_t)$ is possible. If semi-stationary growth at rate γ is to be possible with a number of different possible structures then we need something like the following condition to be satisfied by the sequence of sets $\mathscr{T}_{\mathrm{E}}(t)$.

Condition 4.1. If $[\boldsymbol{u}_t, \boldsymbol{v}_{t+1}] \in \mathscr{T}_{\mathrm{E}}(t)$, *then* $[(1+\gamma)\,\boldsymbol{u}_t, (1+\gamma)\,\boldsymbol{v}_{t+1}] \in \mathscr{T}_{\mathrm{E}}(t+1)$, *all* t.

The expansion in the scale of productive transformations which semi-stationary growth implies, if $\gamma > 0$, must be permitted by the production possibilities.

It is very often assumed that $\mathscr{T}_{\mathrm{E}}(t)$ is the same for all t, whereupon condition 4.1 reduces to a condition on the common transformation possibilities of all weeks: namely, that these should satisfy a linearity, or constant-returns-to-scale, property. However, this is not necessary or even desirable; for to assume that the production set $\mathscr{T}_{\mathrm{E}}(t)$ allows indefinite proportionate expansion in the scale of a feasible transformation at any t implies either that at least one firm is capable of indefinitely expanding the scale of its operations, or that the number of firms may be indefinitely expanded inside one week. And these are not assumptions to which we would want to commit ourselves lightly. As it happens we have no need of them, but only of condition 4.1 as it stands which is consistent, for example, with the expansion at rate γ of the number of firms, each firm being capable only of a bounded set of transformations. If condition 4.1 is adopted, then care must be taken to count as technical progress not any change in a production set from one week to another but only a change which involves more than an expansion in the scale of a previously feasible transformation.

Let the vector of produced goods available at the start of week t be $\boldsymbol{q}_t$; let consumption in week t be a vector $\boldsymbol{c}_t$; let the services of non-produced factors be a vector z_t in week t; and let $\boldsymbol{y}_t$ be the vector of inputs to production in week t. These values may now be filled into the appropriate positions in an

---

[2] Let $\mathscr{T}_f$ be the production set of firm $f\,(f=1, \ldots, F)$. The *sum* of all the production sets, denoted $\sum_f \mathscr{T}_f$, is defined as follows. $\boldsymbol{y}_{\mathrm{E}}$ is included in $\sum_f \mathscr{T}_f$ if there exist vectors $\boldsymbol{y}_1, \boldsymbol{y}_2, \ldots, \boldsymbol{y}_F$ such that

$$\text{(i)} \sum_{f=1}^{F} \boldsymbol{y}_f = \boldsymbol{y}_{\mathrm{E}} \quad \text{and} \quad \text{(ii)}\ \boldsymbol{y}_f \in \mathscr{T}_f (f=1, \ldots, F).$$

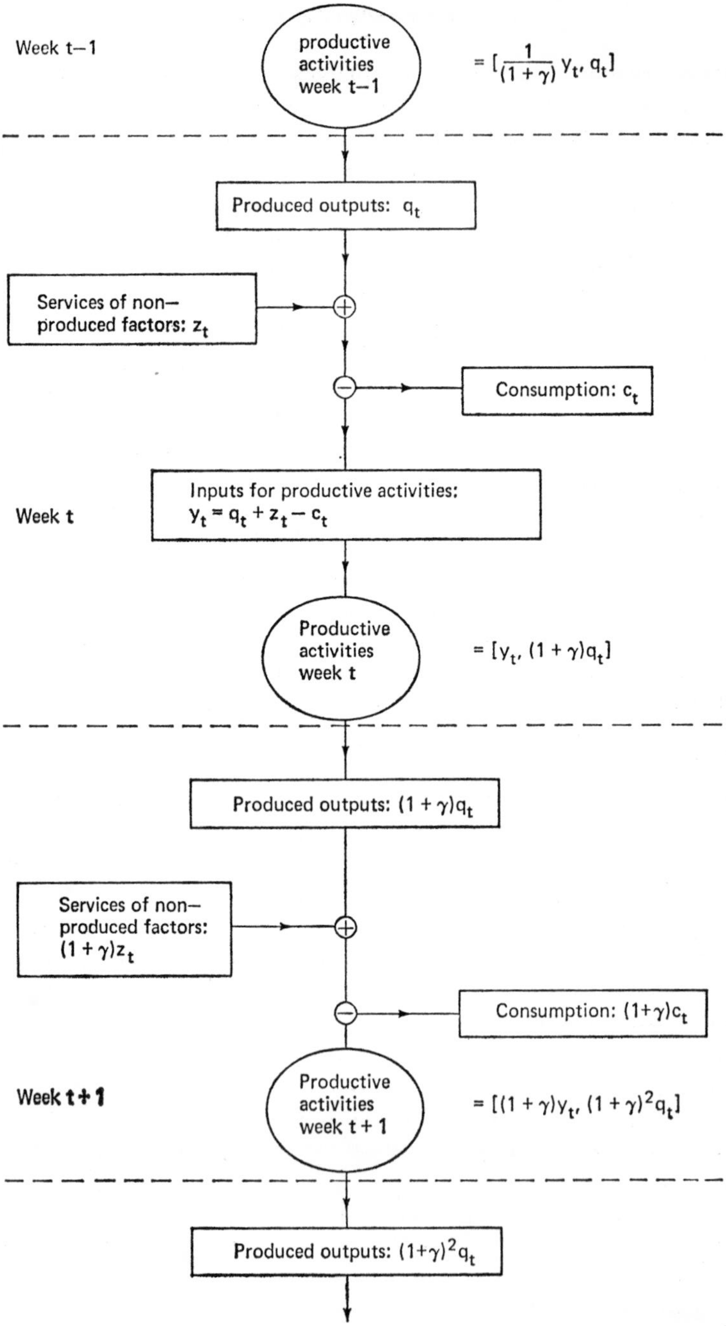
Week t–1
productive activities week t–1
$= [\frac{1}{(1+\gamma)} y_t, q_t]$
Produced outputs: q_t
Services of non–produced factors: z_t
Consumption: c_t
Inputs for productive activities: $y_t = q_t + z_t - c_t$
Week t
Productive activities week t
$= [y_t, (1+\gamma)q_t]$
Produced outputs: $(1+\gamma)q_t$
Services of non–produced factors: $(1+\gamma)z_t$
Consumption: $(1+\gamma)c_t$
Week t+1
Productive activities week t + 1
$= [(1+\gamma)y_t, (1+\gamma)^2 q_t]$
Produced outputs: $(1+\gamma)^2 q_t$

Fig. 4.2.

extended version of fig. 4.1 to obtain a detailed representation of semi-stationary growth.

Figure 4.2 illustrates the special characteristic of a semi-stationary growth path. The vector of produced goods which is available at the start of each week is proportional to the vector that was available at the start of the previous week and to the one which production will make available for the start of the next week. Equally, the consumption vectors of each week are proportional, as are the vectors of productive inputs. Note in particular that there must be proportional growth in the supply of the services of the non-produced factors z_t. Imagine various different types of labour, each of which accounts for a constant share of a population which is growing at proportional rate γ. Then the services of these types of labour will be represented by positive components of a vector z_0, the ratios of these components representing the relative incidence in the population of the different types of labour. The increase of the population will be reflected in the growth, but not a change in proportions, of the factor-supply vector. Thus,

$$z_t = (1 + \gamma)^t z_0. \tag{4.1}$$

If a good is only a produced good and is never supplied as the service of a non-produced factor, then the component of z_0 corresponding to the supply of that good will be zero, whereupon the same component of z_t will be zero for all t, as may be seen from (4.1).

There remains an issue which will not be evaded. What of supplies of inputs that are at the same time the services of non-produced factors and not augmented by the growth of human population? Obvious examples are the services of all kinds of land, including mineral deposits. The assumption of semi-stationary growth demands either that none such should be included in the model or that, being included, the supply of each and every such factor service should expand at rate γ. Of course, if $\gamma = 0$ our semi-stationary state is stationary and the problem is not so acute. But how are we to conceive of a smooth proportionate expansion of an economy in which is included an expansion of labour without labour becoming more plentiful relative to the supplies of the various services of different grades of land? One suggestion is that technical progress might be invoked to augment the efficiency of land services in every use, which would have the same effect as an augmentation of the supply. However, this suggestion is not to be taken seriously. Apart from being patently an artifice in the present context, it fails even to provide a reasonable idealization of land-augmenting technical progress, which almost always has the effect of changing the mix of inputs that it is optimal to employ along with land.

So it must be admitted that a theory founded in the semi-stationary state is seriously handicapped when it comes to dealing with some of the most important implications of capital accumulation. What point is there then to continuing with an investigation of the semi-stationary state, allowing γ to be positive? There is the usual didactic justification: one may learn something from a theoretical construct notwithstanding the fact that its applicability may be very limited. More importantly, the semi-stationary state has, for better or worse, become the major reference model in contemporary discussion of theoretical issues in the area of growth and distribution. So whether we like it or not we must treat of it.

The manner of reporting what happens in a week of semi-stationary growth which is embodied in figs. 4.1 and 4.2 gives no indication of the working out of the affairs of an individual firm. The firms are all lumped together, their combined possibilities recorded in $\mathscr{T}_{\mathrm{E}}$, and the combined effect of their operations is the transformation $[\boldsymbol{y}_t, (1+\gamma)\boldsymbol{q}_t]$ in week t. Naturally, one particular firm will not usually be carrying out a miniature version of the total productive transformation of the economy. However, in competitive conditions there is a justification for treating a collection of price-taking firms as if they were a single price-taking maximizing unit. The justification is as follows. Let the present-value prices ruling in week t and week $t+1$ be $\boldsymbol{p}_t$ and $\boldsymbol{p}_{t+1}$ respectively. Let $[\boldsymbol{u}^*_{t,\mathrm{E}}, \boldsymbol{v}^*_{t+1,\mathrm{E}}]$ be an element of $\mathscr{T}_{\mathrm{E}}(t)$ which is profit-maximizing at these prices, i.e. this production plan might be chosen by a master maximizer who controlled all the firms. Formally,

$$[\boldsymbol{u}_{t,\mathrm{E}}, \boldsymbol{v}_{t+1,\mathrm{E}}] \in \mathscr{T}_{\mathrm{E}}(t) \Rightarrow \boldsymbol{p}_{t+1}\cdot\boldsymbol{v}_{t+1,\mathrm{E}} - \boldsymbol{p}_t\cdot\boldsymbol{u}_{t,\mathrm{E}} \leqslant \boldsymbol{p}_{t+1}\cdot\boldsymbol{v}^*_{t+1,\mathrm{E}} - \boldsymbol{p}_t\cdot\boldsymbol{u}^*_{t,\mathrm{E}}. \quad (4.2)$$

Now $\mathscr{T}_{\mathrm{E}}(t)$ is the sum over all firms of the individual production sets $\mathscr{T}_h (h = 1, \ldots, H)$. Hence, there exists a collection of production plans, each one feasible for a firm, which add up to $[\boldsymbol{u}^*_{t,\mathrm{E}}, \boldsymbol{v}^*_{t+1,\mathrm{E}}]$. Let the plan for firm $h\ (h = 1, \ldots, H)$ be $[\boldsymbol{u}^*_{t,h}, \boldsymbol{v}^*_{t+1,h}]$, where

$$\sum_{h=1}^{H} \boldsymbol{u}^*_{t,h} = \boldsymbol{u}^*_{t,\mathrm{E}} \quad \text{and} \quad \sum_{h=1}^{H} \boldsymbol{v}^*_{t+1,h} = \boldsymbol{v}^*_{t+1,\mathrm{E}}. \quad (4.3)$$

Suppose that for some firm h' the plan is not profit-maximizing, i.e. there exists $[\hat{\boldsymbol{u}}_{t,h'}, \hat{\boldsymbol{v}}_{t+1,h'}] \in \mathscr{T}_{h'}(t)$ such that

$$\boldsymbol{p}_{t+1}\cdot\hat{\boldsymbol{v}}_{t+1,h'} - \boldsymbol{p}_t\cdot\hat{\boldsymbol{u}}_{t,h'} > \boldsymbol{p}_{t+1}\cdot\boldsymbol{v}^*_{t+1,h'} - \boldsymbol{p}_t\cdot\boldsymbol{u}^*_{t,h'}. \quad (4.4)$$

Now a point of $\mathscr{T}_{\mathrm{E}}(t)$ is obtained by summing feasible points of the firms' production sets at t. Hence,

$$\sum_{\substack{h=1\\ h\neq h'}}^{H} [\boldsymbol{u}^*_{t,h}, \boldsymbol{v}^*_{t+1,h}] + [\hat{\boldsymbol{u}}_{t,h'}, \hat{\boldsymbol{v}}_{t+1,h'}] \in \mathscr{T}_{\mathrm{E}}(t). \quad (4.5)$$

The profit associated with this point is

$$\sum_{\substack{h=1\\h\neq h'}}^{H} (\boldsymbol{p}_{t+1}\cdot\boldsymbol{v}^*_{t+1,h} - \boldsymbol{p}_t\cdot\boldsymbol{u}^*_{t,h}) + \boldsymbol{p}_{t+1}\cdot\hat{\boldsymbol{v}}_{t+1,h'} - \boldsymbol{p}_t\cdot\hat{\boldsymbol{u}}_{t,h}$$

$$> \sum_{\substack{h=1\\h\neq h'}}^{H} (\boldsymbol{p}_{t+1}\cdot\boldsymbol{v}^*_{t+1,h} - \boldsymbol{p}_t\cdot\boldsymbol{u}^*_{t,h}) + \boldsymbol{p}_{t+1}\cdot\boldsymbol{v}^*_{t+1,h'} - \boldsymbol{p}_t\cdot\boldsymbol{u}^*_{t,h'}$$

$$= \boldsymbol{p}_{t+1}\cdot\boldsymbol{v}^*_{t+1,\mathrm{E}} - \boldsymbol{p}_t\cdot\boldsymbol{u}^*_{t,\mathrm{E}}, \tag{4.6}$$

from (4.3) and (4.4). It follows that $[\boldsymbol{u}^*_{t,\mathrm{E}}, \boldsymbol{v}^*_{t+1,\mathrm{E}}]$ was not a profit-maximizing choice from $\mathscr{T}_{\mathrm{E}}(t)$, contrary to assumption. The consequence of this line of argument is that we may legitimately assume that a point is chosen from $\mathscr{T}_{\mathrm{E}}(t)$ to maximize $\boldsymbol{p}_{t+1}\cdot\boldsymbol{v}_{t+1,\mathrm{E}} - \boldsymbol{p}_t\cdot\boldsymbol{u}_{t,\mathrm{E}}$ knowing that this involves no conflict with the assumption that decisions are made separately and independently by different firms.

What of the prices that will rule in a semi-stationary state? These are assumed to exhibit a stationary property too, each vector being proportional to another price vector for any other week. There is, in general, no immediate implication from the fact of stationary growth of outputs and consumption that a growth path will have associated with it what one might call a *semi-stationary price system*, i.e. all present-value price vectors proportional to each other and all own-rates of interest equal. Yet the reader may feel, knowing that production activities essentially repeat themselves week by week, that perhaps prices might also repeat themselves, except again for a change of scale. This intuition would be correct, at least in so far as it asserts a possibility. It is possible to associate with any semi-stationary growth of outputs a constant-rate-of-interest price system, and by taking advantage of this fact we may simplify the analysis to a particular kind of growth path which is stationary both with respect to quantities of goods and activity levels and also with respect to prices. This is in fact our concept of semi-stationary growth.

Recall, however, the argument of ch. 3. A constant-rate-of-interest price system has no priority either from the point of view of logic or realism. If we demand nonetheless that the semi-stationary state has a constant rate of interest then we are making a somewhat arbitrary assumption and one that is additional to the assumptions already undertaken with respect to real magnitudes and embodied in fig. 4.2. We should at least be very clear about the logical relation of one group of assumptions to another. We might, of course, advance in defence of the stationarity assumption on prices similar justifications to those advanced already with reference to quantities of goods and factor services. Stationarity of prices makes sometimes for analytical convenience and it increases the plausibility of the assumption of correct and confident foresight. Moreover, it is well established in the literature – indeed not all writers seem to be aware that it is an extra and independent postulate on top of the assumption of semi-stationary growth of outputs and consumption. The explanation of this state of affairs resides undoubtedly in the fact that in a model of the traditional neoclassical kind, where relations and constraints are all specified by differentiable functions, it is the case that only a constant-rate-of-interest price system will be consistent with semi-stationary growth[3]. Let us by all means adopt the assumption that there is 'a rate of interest', but let us be very clear about what we are doing. It is an assumption adopted as an analytical convenience and if later, as will happen, it ceases to be an analytical convenience, it should be scuttled without further ado. The reader who would like to see a proof that a semi-stationary state is an equilibrium at a constant-rate-of-interest price system will find a proof in the appendix to this chapter along with a fuller discussion of the whole issue[4].

For the sake of exposition it is useful to divide the list of goods sharply into three categories and to assume that any particular good belongs to one of these categories and to one only. The categories are consumption goods, services of non-produced factors and producer goods. There is in fact no loss of generality in carving up the list of goods in this way, for if a good were to appear in more than one category we may treat it notionally as two goods for present purposes. In table 4.1 the productive transformations of one week of semi-stationary growth are arranged according to this scheme.

Table 4.1.

	Inputs (week 1)			Outputs (week 2)		
	consumption goods	producer goods	factor services	consumption goods	producer goods	factor services
Goods	–	k	z	$c(1+\gamma)$	$k(1+\gamma)$	–
Prices	$p_c(1+\rho)$	$p_k(1+\rho)$	$w(1+\rho)$	p_s	p_k	w

↓ this should be p_c

[3] Even if the production set is not differentiable households may not accept the same consumption vector each week except at constant relative prices. However, in the light of two recent developments – a growth of interest in linear production models and a concentration on producer equilibrium – earlier suppositions need to be reassessed.

[4] The proof depends on the supposition that the semi-stationary state concerned could not provide extra consumption during some week without diverging permanently from its original course. This property is satisfied by a semi-stationary state which is an equilibrium at any price system. It is therefore perfectly in order to assume it to show the existence of a particular kind of intertemporal price system.

We consider any pair of adjacent weeks, calling them weeks 1 and 2. Consumption goods are not used as productive inputs. The vector of productive inputs, previously denoted $\boldsymbol{y}_t$, is now partitioned into produced and non-produced inputs $(\boldsymbol{k}, \boldsymbol{z})$ in week 1, with prices $(\boldsymbol{p}_k, \boldsymbol{w})$ in week 2. Factor services are not outputs of production. The vector of outputs, previously denoted $\boldsymbol{q}_{t+1}$, is now partitioned into consumption and producer goods as $(\boldsymbol{c}, \boldsymbol{k})$ week 1, with prices $(\boldsymbol{p}_c, \boldsymbol{p}_k)$ in week 2. The balanced or stationary character of the transformations that take place is indicated by the fact that quantities in week 2 stand in the ratio $(1 + \gamma)$ to the quantities of week 1 (consumption in week 1 was $\boldsymbol{c}$ and the factor services provided in week 2 will be $(1 + \gamma)\boldsymbol{z}$), while prices similarly stand in a simple ratio, $1 + \rho$ being the ratio of any week 1 price to the corresponding price in week 2.

Consider now two distinct and independent economies, each subject to the same production constraints, each in semi-stationary growth at rate γ, and each using factor services $\boldsymbol{z}$ in a particular week. Suppose that both economies are in price equilibrium and both have constant-interest-rate price systems. However, their interest rates are different, as are possibly their consumption vectors, inputs of producer goods and relative prices in any week.

We may now enquire how these two economies will compare in detail and we shall call a study aimed at answering such an enquiry *comparative statics of semi-stationary growth*, or more briefly, where there is no danger of misunderstanding, *comparative statics*[5]. The reference is, of course, to the comparative statics of, for example, standard price theory in which something is altered in the specification of an equilibrium model and the new equilibrium compared to the old. The word 'static' reminds us that there is no implication of an actual move from one equilibrium to another through time. However, it is important to take note of a difference between the present enquiry and the usual comparative static exercise. Here we compare two growth paths one of which differs from the other, but the difference is not explicitly attributed to a difference in the specification of the primitive postulates of the model, as it would be, for example, were we engaged in examining the effect of a change in preferences on prices. Rather, a difference in interest rates between the two paths is our point of departure. Now there will usually exist changes in the primitive postulates of the growth model which would have the effect of bringing about an alteration in the interest rate ruling on a semi-stationary growth path. Indeed, most substantial changes would have this effect, so the procedure is in order. The implication for the interpretation of our results is clear: no significance is to be attached to the fact that the argument proceeds

---

[5] The foundation of the present study is a paper by Malinvaud (1960–1961).

→ An interesting sentence, which no doubt, is a good translation of the proposition $\exists x, y, \forall x, y, \in S_{G.P}$ where S_{GP} is the set of growth paths. Then if $x \neq y$, x, y, is a possible choice set from $S_{G.P}$

But most of us, would have just put "different" between "two" and "growth". Is mathematics necessary? PTO

from a postulated difference in interest rates to a certain conclusion. In fact, both the difference in interest rates and any other differences are together consequential upon some implicit change in the primitive postulates.

Let a superscript 1 denote values pertaining to growth path 1 with interest rate ρ^1, and a superscript 2 denote values of growth path 2 with interest rate ρ^2. The growth rate γ will carry no superscript being common to both paths, as are the factor services supplied z, also carrying no superscript. Thus, for example, $\boldsymbol{k}^1$ (the capital stock) will denote the total input of produced goods to production of week 1 on growth path 1. Growth path 1 will be our point of reference and changes will be regarded as from growth path 1 to 2, but there is, of course, no loss of generality in so viewing matters. In accordance with this convention, $\Delta \boldsymbol{x}$ is defined as $\boldsymbol{x}^2 - \boldsymbol{x}^1$, where $\boldsymbol{x}$ is any vector of values pertaining to a growth path.

Examine now growth path 1 as production in week 1 is about to be commenced. The economy has available inputs $(\boldsymbol{k}^1, \boldsymbol{z})$ so the production that takes place will have to make do with these inputs. But this is not a constraint that is perceived by a collection of price-taking firms; as far as they are concerned they could obtain any input vector at the prices ruling. If then they choose to carry out the transformation of growth path 1, $[(\boldsymbol{0}, \boldsymbol{k}^1, \boldsymbol{z}), (\boldsymbol{c}^1(1+\gamma), \boldsymbol{k}^1(1+\gamma), \boldsymbol{0})]$, it is because this is not less profitable than any other feasible transformation in $\mathscr{T}_{\mathrm{E}}(1)$ at the prices ruling on growth path 1. In particular, a transformation which we know to be allowed by $\mathscr{T}_{\mathrm{E}}(1)$ is the one actually carried out on growth path 2, $[(\boldsymbol{0}, \boldsymbol{k}^2, \boldsymbol{z}), (\boldsymbol{c}^2(1+\gamma), \boldsymbol{k}^2(1+\gamma), \boldsymbol{0})]$. The profitability of the actual decision of growth path 1 is Π^1, where

$$\Pi^1 = \boldsymbol{p}_c^1 \cdot \boldsymbol{c}^1(1+\gamma) + \boldsymbol{p}_k^1 \cdot \boldsymbol{k}^1(1+\gamma) - \boldsymbol{p}_k^1 \cdot \boldsymbol{k}^1(1+\rho^1) - \boldsymbol{w}^1 \cdot \boldsymbol{z}(1+\rho^1). \tag{4.7}$$

Or, simplifying and rearranging gives

$$\boldsymbol{p}_c^1 \cdot \boldsymbol{c}^1(1+\gamma) + (\gamma - \rho^1)\boldsymbol{p}_k^1 \cdot \boldsymbol{k}^1 - \boldsymbol{w}^1 \cdot \boldsymbol{z}(1+\rho^1) = \Pi^1. \tag{4.8}$$

Now the condition that the transformation of growth path 2 should not be more profit than Π^1 takes the form

$$\boldsymbol{p}_c^1 \cdot \boldsymbol{c}^2(1+\gamma) + (\gamma - \rho^1)\boldsymbol{p}_k^1 \cdot \boldsymbol{k}^2 - \boldsymbol{w}^1 \cdot \boldsymbol{z}(1+\rho^1) \leqslant \Pi^1. \tag{4.9}$$

Subtracting (4.8) from (4.9) one obtains

$$\boldsymbol{p}_c^1 \cdot \Delta \boldsymbol{c}(1+\gamma) + (\gamma - \rho^1)\boldsymbol{p}_k^1 \cdot \Delta \boldsymbol{k} \leqslant 0. \tag{4.10}$$

It may help to provide here an indication of the power of the approach adopted by making use of (4.10) to prove a well-known result in the theory of semi-stationary growth.

Language, after all, is an immensely more complicated symbolic device. And often it's clearer.

Theorem 4.1 ('the golden rule'). If a semi-stationary growth path with rate of growth γ could be an equilibrium at rate of interest $\rho = \gamma$, then no other semi-stationary growth path feasible under the same production sets, and with rate of growth γ, provides a consumption vector of greater value at any equilibrium prices for this path. In particular, if only one good is consumed, the amount of consumption attained is the largest consistent with semi-stationary growth.

Proof. Let the path for which $\rho = \gamma$ be growth path 1 and let $\boldsymbol{p}_c^1$ and $\boldsymbol{p}_k^1$ be any equilibrium price vectors. Substituting $\gamma = \rho^1$ in (4.10), the second term vanishes and there remains

$$\boldsymbol{p}_c^1 \cdot \Delta \boldsymbol{c}(1+\gamma) \leqslant 0. \tag{4.11}$$

Hence, for any feasible alternative growth path 2, we have $\boldsymbol{p}_c^1 \cdot \Delta \boldsymbol{c} \leqslant 0$, as required.

It is satisfying to obtain a result so quickly and easily. Unfortunately there seem to be no more comparable results for the present model of semi-stationary growth, except for some further implications of (4.10) which will be examined in ch. 5. This may seem surprising; the intertemporal equilibrium model is simplified drastically to semi-stationary growth and still no general results of the comparative static variety are forthcoming. Yet it is so: the model is still too rich in possibilities to yield definite results. The known further results are obtained by various specializations of the model to which we now turn.

In explaining the first specialization of the semi-stationary growth model it may be helpful to subject the profit terms Π^1 and Π^2 to a closer scrutiny than has so far been undertaken. It is evident that they are not the total of 'profits' in every usual sense of that term[6]. Along the semi-stationary growth path there is a 'going rate of return' to capital measured by ρ. There is a capital stock $\boldsymbol{k}$, growing at rate γ, which is in effect permanently present as if it were perfectly durable. As a matter of fact, $\boldsymbol{k}$ comprises raw materials, all kinds of circulating capital, and durables depreciating at various rates and in various ways, and so forth. But the fact that everything is replaced, and proportionally

---

[6] There are many usages in the literature concerning the terms 'interest' and 'profit'. These differences reflect different analytical conceptions of the roles of these two items. Let it suffice to say here that, as far as the present discussion is concerned, interest is just one of the forms in which surplus (total value added less factor service payments) presents itself. Firms desire to maximize the present value of surplus (i.e. surplus less interest charges at the ruling rate, here called profit).

augmented, along the semi-stationary path nullifies the importance of these distinctions. We may rearrange (4.8) to obtain

$$\underbrace{\mathbf{p}_c^1\cdot\mathbf{c}^1\cdot(1+\gamma)+\gamma\cdot\mathbf{p}_k^1\cdot\mathbf{k}^1}_{\text{net product of week 1}}-\underbrace{\mathbf{w}^1\cdot\mathbf{z}(1+\rho^1)}_{\substack{\text{cost of non-}\\ \text{produced}\\ \text{factors}}}=\underbrace{\rho^1\cdot\mathbf{p}_k^1\cdot\mathbf{k}^1}_{\substack{\text{return on}\\ \text{value of}\\ \text{stock at}\\ \text{rate of}\\ \text{interest 1}}}+\underbrace{\qquad\Pi^1\qquad}_{\substack{\text{surplus not}\\ \text{accounted for}\\ \text{by standard}\\ \text{interest return}}} \tag{4.12}$$

This arrangement makes it clear that the Π^1 term is that part of total surplus which is not accounted for by the rate of interest ρ^1. The possibility that Π^1 might not be zero arises precisely because we have not so far restricted $\mathscr{T}_{\mathrm{E}}(t)$ to satisfy the *linearity assumption* (constant returns to scale):

$$[\mathbf{u}_t, \mathbf{v}_{t+1}] \in \mathscr{T}_{\mathrm{E}}(t) \Rightarrow [\lambda\mathbf{u}_t, \lambda\mathbf{v}_{t+1}] \in \mathscr{T}_{\mathrm{E}}(t) \quad \text{for all } \lambda,\ 0 \leqslant \lambda. \tag{4.13}$$

Notice, recalling that Π^1 is the value that the firms aim to maximize, that if condition (4.13) is satisfied then Π^1 can only be maximized at zero. For if it were to take a negative value then $[\mathbf{0}, \mathbf{0}]$, which is known to be in $\mathscr{T}_{\mathrm{E}}(t)$ since $\lambda = 0$ is admitted by (4.13), would yield a larger profit $\Pi^1 = 0$. If, on the other hand, Π^1 were to take a positive value then a doubling of the input and output vectors, which is technically feasible according to (4.13), would yield twice as much profit, so that again profit would not be maximized, contrary to assumption.

In brief, the possibility that profit will be something over and above a return on the value of capital present, at the rate of interest ρ^1, arises because firms may not enjoy constant returns to scale and may be unable to expand their production levels indefinitely inside one week. In that case, production possibilities are, as it were, scarce and will command 'rents' even under competition. The Π^1 and Π^2 values are simply these rents.

It would be tedious to go into all the arguments over whether there will, or will not be, constant returns to scale in the production set $\mathscr{T}_{\mathrm{E}}(t)$ of one week, for most of the issues are well known and much discussed[7]. For the time being let it be understood that it is not a problem of obtaining inputs that inhibits the firm from expanding, for the production set details what a firm, or the economy, might do given various input vectors. Furthermore, it is not strictly the 'dynamic' factors that have been invoked by some writers to explain why production may be subject to diminishing returns in the 'short-

[7] Some of them will be taken up, where they belong most naturally in this volume, in ch. 9.

run' but not perhaps in the long-run, for these could only find expression in a model which allowed the production possibilities of week t to depend on the production plan actually carried through in week $t-1$ and this is inconsistent with the 'recursive' formulation of production that has been adopted here[8]. One possibility which is consistent with the postulates of the model is embodied in the classic idea of 'entrepreneurship' as a limiting factor on production. Or more generally, there might be certain inputs, not taken into account explicitly in the analysis, and not marketed (perhaps they are indivisible), the availability of which constitutes a firm. Perhaps the production possibilities do not allow linear expansion of a feasible plan because of the limited supply of these 'shadow inputs'. However, along a semi-stationary path the shadow inputs may be expanding at rate γ and with them the productive power of all the firms.

If, setting aside all these considerations, we accept (4.13), then we obtain a notable simplification of the maximum profit conditions of the type (4.8) and (4.9), which now reduce to

$$\boldsymbol{p}_c^1 \cdot \boldsymbol{c}^1(1+\gamma) + (\gamma - \rho^1)\boldsymbol{p}_k^1 \cdot \boldsymbol{k}^1 - \boldsymbol{w}^1 \cdot \boldsymbol{z}(1+\rho^1) = 0 \tag{4.14}$$

and

$$\boldsymbol{p}_c^1 \cdot \boldsymbol{c}^2(1+\gamma) + (\gamma - \rho^1)\boldsymbol{p}_k^1 \cdot \boldsymbol{k}^2 - \boldsymbol{w}^1 \cdot \boldsymbol{z}(1+\rho^1) \leqslant 0. \tag{4.15}$$

There are similar conditions involving the prices of growth path 2; namely,

$$\boldsymbol{p}_c^2 \cdot \boldsymbol{c}^2(1+\gamma) + (\gamma - \rho^2)\boldsymbol{p}_k^2 \cdot \boldsymbol{k}^2 - \boldsymbol{w}^2 \cdot \boldsymbol{z}(1+\rho^2) = 0 \tag{4.16}$$

and

$$\boldsymbol{p}_c^2 \cdot \boldsymbol{c}^1(1+\gamma) + (\gamma - \rho^2)\boldsymbol{p}_k^2 \cdot \boldsymbol{k}^1 - \boldsymbol{w}^2 \cdot \boldsymbol{z}(1+\rho^2) \leqslant 0. \tag{4.17}$$

The next step in distilling out special cases is to assume that the composition of the consumption vector is the same on every growth path. In other words, $\boldsymbol{c}^1$ is proportional to $\boldsymbol{c}^2$. Naturally, unless only one good is consumed, this is an absurd assumption, for consumption per unit of non-produced factor will not be the same on every path and to suppose that an increase in consumption might take the form of an equi-proportionate increase in each and every item consumed is to propose something wholly contrary to expectation and experience. Moreover, it is not just the unrealism of this assumption that renders it very dubious: it is also associated with a pernicious view, which we shall examine in detail in chs. 7 and 8, according to which aggregation of consumption goods raises no serious problems and may be treated rather lightly.

---

[8] For further discussion of this point see below, ch. 13.

For, of course, to assume all consumption vectors proportional is to assume in effect that there is only one, albeit composite, consumption good. The literature is full of papers making this assumption from the pens of writers who would recoil in horror from the assumption that there is only one, albeit composite, capital good.

In fact, we have to hand immediate evidence that the assumption of proportionate consumption vectors is no small matter: for there are several results on the comparative statics of semi-stationary growth which follow upon this assumption but which are not otherwise obtainable. Once consumption vectors are proportional to each other we may adopt, as we could not before, a basket of consumption goods of the composition common to all growth paths as the *numeraire*[9]. Eqs. (4.14)–(4.17) then appear as

$$C^1(1+\gamma)+(\gamma-\rho^1)\boldsymbol{p}_k^1\cdot\boldsymbol{k}^1-\boldsymbol{w}^1\cdot\boldsymbol{z}(1+\rho^1)=0, \tag{4.18}$$

$$C^2(1+\gamma)+(\gamma-\rho^1)\boldsymbol{p}_k^1\cdot\boldsymbol{k}^2-\boldsymbol{w}^1\cdot\boldsymbol{z}(1+\rho^1)\leqslant 0, \tag{4.19}$$

$$C^2(1+\gamma)+(\gamma-\rho^2)\boldsymbol{p}_k^2\cdot\boldsymbol{k}^2-\boldsymbol{w}^2\cdot\boldsymbol{z}(1+\rho^2)=0 \tag{4.20}$$

and

$$C^1(1+\gamma)+(\gamma-\rho^2)\boldsymbol{p}_k^2\cdot\boldsymbol{k}^1-\boldsymbol{w}^2\cdot\boldsymbol{z}(1+\rho^2)\leqslant 0, \tag{4.21}$$

where C is a scalar measuring the level of consumption of the composite consumption good.

Now, upon subtracting (4.18) from (4.21) one obtains

$$\gamma\Delta\boldsymbol{p}_k\cdot\boldsymbol{k}^1-\Delta\{\rho\boldsymbol{p}_k\}\cdot\boldsymbol{k}^1-\boldsymbol{z}\cdot\Delta\{\boldsymbol{w}(1+\rho)\}\leqslant 0. \tag{4.22}$$

This result may be interpreted and in so doing it is helpful to consider first the simplest case of the stationary state ($\gamma=0$). In that instance, the first term of (4.22) vanishes and we may rearrange what remains to obtain

$$\Delta\{\rho\boldsymbol{p}_k\}\cdot\boldsymbol{k}^1+\boldsymbol{z}\cdot\Delta\{\boldsymbol{w}(1+\rho)\}\geqslant 0. \tag{4.23}$$

Now $\boldsymbol{w}(1+\rho)$ is simply the vector of prices for the services of non-produced factors as may be seen from table 4.1. Thus the second term on the left-hand side of (4.23) is the change in the earnings of the non-produced factors in terms of the consumption good. The first term records the change in an index of the cost of the services of capital goods. The components of the vector $\rho\boldsymbol{p}_k$ are sometimes referred to as 'capital rentals' since these are the sums which an

[9] The only composite *numeraire* previously available was the vector of non-produced factor services $\boldsymbol{z}$. This could be given the value 1 to scale price systems of all paths to a common unit but there is no analytical gain from doing this.

owner of a capital good could obtain in a competitive market for allowing the use of that good during the production period of one week, on the understanding that all depreciation would be made good by the hirer. We may thus refer to $\rho \boldsymbol{p}_k$ equally appropriately as 'the cost of capital services'. It follows from (4.23) that if $\boldsymbol{z} \cdot \Delta\{\boldsymbol{w}(1 + \rho)\}$ is negative then $\Delta\{\rho \boldsymbol{p}_k\} \cdot \boldsymbol{k}^1$ must be positive. This may be translated into the following statement. *A growth path on which non-produced factor services earn less in terms of the consumption good than on growth path 1 will have a higher cost of capital services according to an index based on* $\boldsymbol{k}^2$.

No one could call this an earthshaking conclusion and it is indeed a very natural one, but even this somewhat unimpressive result is only valid for comparisons of stationary states. Let γ, for example, be positive and we have an extra term in (4.22) and we may no longer draw the same conclusions with regard to signs of changes as were previously obtainable. We will examine an example below to confirm that this is the case.

The next assumption to be considered is the most radical of all and one which might be thought to brush all difficulties out of the way. Consider the vector $\boldsymbol{k}$: it represents the stock of capital goods used by all firms together in week 1. Normally if two growth paths have different capital stocks the composition of their stocks will be totally different. This might be embarrassing for someone who wanted to investigate, or even justify, comparative static statements of the form: the growth path with the larger quantity of capital will feature a lower value of something (say the rate of interest). It is perfectly possible however, and surely highly probable, that two capital stocks belonging to two growth paths with different interest rates will neither one dominate the other, in the sense of including more of every kind of capital good, let alone having more or less of each good in exactly similar proportion. This is why $\boldsymbol{k}$ is represented by a vector: we specify the capital stock by a complete inventory of the items that comprise it. The question of whether the 'size' of two capital vectors can meaningfully be compared concerns the possibility of capital aggregation, which will be the subject matter of a later part. However, it is interesting from the analytical point of view to examine the consequence of assuming that capital stocks may be compared as two numbers are compared. This is achieved by the following drastic assumption. *Every pair of semi-stationary states have proportional capital vectors.*

The assumption is exactly parallel to the assumption that has already been adopted with respect to consumption vectors and it must be regarded as most implausible, if indeed there is more than one producer good, for closely parallel reasons. However, let it be understood that we are not going so far as to assume that there is only one capital good. As far as the whole economy is concerned our assumption has the same effect as, and it may well be no more plausible than, assuming only one capital good; but where economic analysis is concerned the assumptions are different. If there is strictly only one capital good then not only does every possible semi-stationary growth path use just that good in aggregate, but so does every separate production department or sector – the machine tool industry or the leather industry – use just this good. There are results in the theory of two-sector economic models that are obtainable only when the capital stock of every sector has the same composition and we will not go so far as to come within reach of those results. If the assumption is satisfied we may measure by K the quantity of the capital composite present and by π the price of the composite capital good in terms of the consumption good[10]. We then obtain a further simplification of eqs. (4.18)–(4.21) which now appear as

$$C^1(1+\gamma)+(\gamma-\rho^1)\,\pi^1 K^1 - \mathbf{w}^1\cdot\mathbf{z}(1+\rho^1)=0, \tag{4.24}$$

$$C^2(1+\gamma)+(\gamma-\rho^1)\,\pi^1 K^2 - \mathbf{w}^1\cdot\mathbf{z}(1+\rho^1)\leqslant 0, \tag{4.25}$$

$$C^2(1+\gamma)+(\gamma-\rho^2)\,\pi^2 K^2 - \mathbf{w}^2\cdot\mathbf{z}(1+\rho^2)=0 \tag{4.26}$$

and

$$C^1(1+\gamma)+(\gamma-\rho^2)\,\pi^2 K^1 - \mathbf{w}^2\cdot\mathbf{z}(1+\rho^2)\leqslant 0. \tag{4.27}$$

Now subtracting (4.24) from (4.27) one obtains

$$\gamma\Delta\pi(K^1)-\Delta\{\rho\pi\}K^1-\mathbf{z}\cdot\Delta\{\mathbf{w}(1+\rho)\}\leqslant 0. \tag{4.28}$$

Upon subtracting (4.26) from (4.25), and taking account of the general relation $\mathbf{x}^2=\Delta\mathbf{x}+\mathbf{x}^1$, one obtains

$$-\gamma\Delta\pi(\Delta K+K^1)+\Delta\{\rho\pi\}(\Delta K+K^1)+\mathbf{z}\cdot\Delta\{\mathbf{w}(1+\rho)\}\leqslant 0. \tag{4.29}$$

Now, upon multiplying both sides of (4.28) by $\Delta K+K^1$, both sides of (4.3) by K^1 and adding, one obtains

$$-\Delta K\mathbf{z}\cdot\Delta\{\mathbf{w}(1+\rho)\}\leqslant 0. \tag{4.30}$$

Recall that $\mathbf{w}(1+\rho)$ is simply the vector of the prices of factor services (see table 4.1). *The growth path with the higher level of capital relative to non-produced services cannot have lower total factor earnings in terms of the consumption good.* Where there is only one non-produced factor, say labour, this

---

[10] Let a vector in the common proportions of all capital vectors be $\mathbf{k}_0$. Then any capital vector may be specified as $K\mathbf{k}_0$. Let $\mathbf{p}_k$ be the price vector of capital goods in terms of the consumption good (itself a composite). Then $\pi=\mathbf{p}_k\cdot\mathbf{k}_0$.

result would dictate that the growth path with the higher level of capital per head could not have a lower wage rate. This result is perhaps somewhat satisfying in terms of simple intuition: the path where capital is plentiful has the other group of inputs highly priced. Can one say that the capital inputs will be cheap on the path where they are more abundant? This turns out to be not such a simple matter.

The addition of (4.28) and (4.29) yields

$$\gamma \Delta\pi \Delta K - \Delta\{\rho\pi\} \Delta K \geqslant 0. \tag{4.31}$$

Even this condition is a little obscure, so let us first examine the stationary state. Setting $\gamma = 0$ one obtains

$$\Delta\{\rho\pi\} \Delta K \leqslant 0. \tag{4.32}$$

Here is a second, thoroughly satisfying, comparative static result: *the stationary state with a higher level of capital relative to non-produced factor services cannot have a higher rental of the composite capital good in terms of the composite consumption good.*

Let us look back at the specializations of the original model of semi-stationary growth, the model for which the 'golden rule' was so simple to establish, that have been undertaken to achieve the above results:

(i) linearity of the aggregate production set;

(ii) homogeneous consumption vectors on all growth paths;

(iii) homogeneous capital vectors on all growth paths; and for the second result

(iv) stationary state conditions ($\gamma = 0$).

Let us recall also that even the semi-stationary growth model is a very considerable specialization of the general intertemporal equilibrium model. Surely a result founded in all this is not to be taken seriously?

Before commenting on the results let us confirm that all the above conditions really are needed; in particular let us enquire what happens when 'growth' takes place ($\gamma \neq 0$). Inspection of (4.31) now suggests that $\Delta\{\rho\pi\}$ cannot be signed just from knowing that ΔK is positive and this gives rise to the idea that a growth path with a higher level of capital might have a higher capital rental as well. This suggestion may seem strange and unlikely to a reader who has made a study of the literature on two-sector growth models in which no such possibility is encountered[11]. However, special as it is, our model is not as yet as special as the two-sector models to be found in the literature. In particular, we allow joint production of the capital good and the consumption good which the two-sector model excludes, we have not assumed that

[11] For a survey of the literature on two-sector growth models and derivations of the main results see Hahn and Matthews (1964, pp. 812–821).

non-produced factor services are perfectly homogeneous, and the capital stock of different sectors of the economy (with which we have not had to concern ourselves in the present discourse) may not be of identical composition. The following examples will help to elucidate the consequences of some of these departures from the established models as well as justifying some earlier claims.

Example 4.1. The production possibility set is specified by just two linear activities and all convex combinations of them. As this is an example we work with a very sparse production set for the sake of convenience, but obviously extra activities may be added so long as they do not make a positive profit at the two price systems given below. The only non-produced input is labour; the growth rate is $\gamma = 1$; and the two linear activities, numbered I and II, are as follows[12].

$$\begin{aligned} &\text{I: 1 unit of labour time} \oplus \text{1 unit of the capital good} \\ &\quad \ominus\!\!\rightarrow \text{1 unit of the consumption good} \oplus \text{2 units of the capital good,} \\ &\text{II: 1 unit of labour time} \oplus \text{4 units of the capital good} \\ &\quad \ominus\!\!\rightarrow \text{3 units of the consumption good} \oplus \text{8 units of the capital good.} \end{aligned} \tag{4.33}$$

In table 4.2 two feasible semi-stationary growth paths for this economy, each with growth rate $\gamma = 1$, are presented in the format of table 4.1.

Table 4.2.

I	Inputs (week 1)			Outputs (week 2)			
	consumption good	capital good	factor service (labour)	consumption good	capital good	labour	
$\gamma = 1$	–	1	1	1	2	–	Goods
$\rho = 4$	5	1.25	0.25	1	0.25	0.05	Prices
II	**Inputs**			**Outputs**			
	consumption good	capital good	factor service (labour)	consumption good	capital good	labour	
$\gamma = 1$	–	4	1	3	8	–	Goods
$\rho = \frac{4}{3}$	$\frac{7}{3}$	3.5	1	1	1.5	$\frac{3}{7}$	Prices

[12] The symbol $\ominus\!\!\rightarrow$ is to be interpreted as '. . . give rise in the following week to . . .'. Thus the goods listed preceding the arrow are inputs to production in a week and the goods following the arrow are outputs accruing at the start of the following week. Naturally, the symbol $\oplus$ means '. . . together with . . .'.

The reader may confirm that path I is an intertemporal equilibrium at its own price system as far as production is concerned and that the activity of growth path II would show a loss in terms of the present-value prices of path I. Similarly, growth path II is an intertemporal equilibrium at its own prices, while the activity of growth path I would show a loss at these prices. The actual magnitudes involved in the example are scarcely credible but that, of course, does not matter for present purposes.

Comparing the two growth paths and defining $\Delta \boldsymbol{x}$ as equal to $\boldsymbol{x}^{\mathrm{II}} - \boldsymbol{x}^{\mathrm{I}}$, one may compute

$$\Delta K = 3, \qquad \Delta\{\pi\rho\} = 1, \qquad \Delta\pi = 1.25. \tag{4.34}$$

Hence,

$$\gamma \Delta\pi \Delta K - \Delta\{\rho\pi\} \Delta K = 3.75 - 3 > 0, \tag{4.35}$$

in conformity with (4.31). However, the growth path with the higher level of capital (growth path II) also has a higher rental for the capital good.

The example is useful in indicating why it is only in a stationary state that we are able to declare definitely that the growth path with a higher level of capital will not have a higher rental for the use of capital. The example clearly establishes a possibility and in so doing it pronounces that an attempt to show that a plentiful endowment of even homogeneous capital carries any necessary implication that the rental per unit of capital will not be larger is doomed to failure, unless yet more assumptions are to be heaped on to the pile. The example has the character of a counter example, which is why its contrived character in no way mitigates against it. As a matter of fact, the technology specified carries no implication that the price of the capital service $\rho\pi$ will always be higher on a capital-rich growth path[13], but it may be higher, and that is the end of any contrary intuition.

It is in fact not difficult to understand why the possibility displayed in table 4.2 may arise. If anyone has a feeling that capital should command a lower rental in a state in which it is more abundant as compared to alternative inputs he is probably giving his consideration only to the influence of the cost of the capital service on demand for it as an input. But in semi-stationary growth the more capital abundant path produces capital more abundantly, as well as using it more freely, and the price of the capital good π must be

---

[13] See the example presented in table 4.3 where the growth path using activity I has a capital-service price of 1.5, while the growth path using activity II has the price of the capital service equal to 0.75.

such as to make it profitable to do so. There are then two forces, finding their quantitative expression in the two terms that make up the left-hand side of (4.31), pulling in opposite directions. A large production of the capital good relative to the producer good makes for a high value of π which in turn exerts an upward influence on $\rho\pi$. The use of a large volume of the capital service relative to labour time makes for a low value of $\rho\pi$. From these considerations it may be seen at once why the stationary state is a special case for which a strong result is obtainable: for the stationary state is not a net producer of the capital good so that the first influence is moribund.

The technology of the present example may be made the basis of another illustration, this time embodied in table 4.3. Here the output and consumption

Table 4.3.

I	Inputs			Outputs			
	consumption good	capital good	labour	consumption good	capital good	labour	
$\gamma=1$	–	1	1	1	2	–	Goods
$\rho=2$	3	2.25	0.25	1	0.75	$\frac{1}{12}$	Prices

II	Inputs			Outputs			
	consumption good	capital good	labour	consumption good	capital good	labour	
$\gamma=1$	–	4	1	3	8	–	Goods
$\rho=3$	4	1	1	1	0.25	0.25	Prices

levels are the same as in table 4.2, but there is a different price system. Now growth path II which has more of the capital good relative to the labour supply has a lower rental for the capital good (0.75 as against 1.5 on growth path I) but now the capital-rich path has a higher rate of interest.

The result for the stationary state is very valuable in indicating what exactly is the implication for the price system of more abundant capital when there is any simple implication to be drawn. The implication is the natural one: the cost to the firm of using capital is lower and that cost is the rental of the capital good $\rho\pi$. *The rate of interest is not the cost of using capital and even in a stationary state there is no implication that a capital-rich economy will not have a higher rate of interest than a path with less of the capital good.* There is nothing mysterious about this. An increase in π with ρ unchanged increases the cost of using the capital good in production. It follows immediately that any meaningful measure of the cost of using the capital good – the price which will stand in the same relation to capital as the wage rate does to labour – must include both the influence of the interest rate and the influence of the price of the capital good. The next example justifies the above claim.

Example 4.2. The production set is based upon three linear activities:

$$\begin{aligned} \text{I: } & 1 \text{ unit of labour time} \oplus 1 \text{ unit of the capital good} \\ & \ominus 1 \text{ unit of the consumption good} \oplus 1 \text{ unit of the capital good,} \\ \text{II: } & 1 \text{ unit of labour time} \oplus 12 \text{ units of the capital good} \\ & \ominus 2 \text{ units of the consumption good} \oplus 12 \text{ units of the capital good,} \\ \text{III: } & 1 \text{ unit of labour time} \oplus 41 \text{ units of the capital good} \\ & \ominus 4 \text{ units of the consumption good} \oplus 42 \text{ units of the capital good.} \end{aligned} \tag{4.36}$$

Here we have distinct production sectors but the composition of the capital stock is, in the case of this example, the same in each sector. We compare two stationary states in one of which activity I is used to produce the consumption good while in the other activity II is used. Neither state uses activity III, which is the only feasible method of augmenting the supply of the capital good since in neither state is the stock of the capital good increasing from week to week and there is no depreciation of the capital good in use[14]. However, in both the price systems of the stationary states activity III just breaks even, so that the capital good could be produced at a cost equal to its price, and it thus retains its character as a produced input. The two stationary states are displayed in table 4.4.

The reader may confirm that stationary state I is a production equilibrium at its own price system, at which prices activity II will show a loss. Likewise, stationary state II is a production equilibrium at its own price system, at which prices activity I will show a loss. Activity III just breaks even at each price system. Stationary state II is the capital-rich state, the level of consumption is twice as high as in stationary state I and the wage rate of labour in terms of the consumption good is slightly larger ($\frac{5}{6} > \frac{9}{11}$). The rate of interest, however, is twice as high in the capital-scarce state as it is in the capital-rich state. Naturally the capital-rich stationary state has the lower rental for the capital good ($\frac{1}{12}$ as against $\frac{1}{10}$) in conformity with (4.32).

There remains to be considered the most drastic simplification of all. The model of semi-stationary stationary growth has been reduced to one in which

---

[14] The example could easily be modified to allow for some depreciation of capital in use but as it stands it serves its present purpose.

Table 4.4.

I	Inputs			Outputs			
	consump- tion good	capital good	labour time	consump- tion good	capital good	labour time	
$\gamma=0$	–	1	1	1	1	–	Goods
$\rho=\frac{1}{10}$	1.1	1.1	0.9	1	1	$\frac{9}{11}$	Prices
II	**Inputs**			**Outputs**			
	consump- tion good	capital good	labour time	consump- tion good	capital good	labour time	
$\gamma=0$	–	12	1	2	12	–	Goods
$\rho=\frac{1}{5}$	1.2	0.5	1	1	$\frac{5}{12}$	$\frac{5}{6}$	Prices

there is only one consumption basket, and which features only one collection of goods as the aggregate of capital inputs. In short, all types of good are treated as homogeneous in aggregate so that quantities may be compared directly between two semi-stationary growth paths, as are the services of non-produced factors. However, one may go further and let there be only one basket of goods produced on any semi-stationary growth path. In this case the aggregate consumption vectors are proportional to the aggregate capital vectors with the immediate consequence that π is identically equal to 1 and $\Delta\pi$ is identically zero. Substituting these values into (4.31) one obtains

$$\Delta\rho\Delta K \leqslant 0. \tag{4.37}$$

The semi-stationary growth path with the higher level of capital relative to non-produced factor services cannot be the path with the higher rate of interest.

And so at last we arrive at a result which for many is the beginning, and for some the end, of the theory of capital. What is this result? It is a special case of a special case. In general, the price of the use of capital in semi-stationary growth is the product of the interest rate and the price of capital in terms of the *numeraire*. In general the price of the use of capital is not necessarily lower on a semi-stationary growth path which is better endowed with capital, although for the stationary state it is so. Now it is surely important to understand that there is no general presumption from the theory so far developed that more capital means a lower rate of interest, but what is really important is to understand why no such presumption exists. Unfortunately there are widespread misconceptions concerning this question. It is supposed to be because there is more than one kind of capital good that the 'paradox' of a capital-rich high-interest-rate growth path can arise and economists who fail to take account of this possibility have been accused of failing to take note that capital is not a homogeneous input all of a kind. There is not the slightest foundation for this claim as our investigation of various special cases has made clear.

The reason why it would be extremely rash to suppose that a capital-rich semi-stationary growth will not have a high rate of interest is not that there is more than one kind of capital good; it is that there is more than one kind of output. So long as there is more than one kind of output the 'paradox' of a low rate of interest ruling where capital is scarce can arise even in a stationary state (example 4.2). On the other hand, where there is only one produced input in aggregate which has the same composition as the aggregate of production then, and only then, is there any sense in supposing that the price of the use of capital might be the rate of interest. In that case as it happens that price, the rate of interest, will indeed be no higher on a capital-rich growth path than on a capital-scarce one.

The conclusions of our investigations into the comparative statics of semi-stationary growth have been more negative than positive, but to retain a sense of perspective on this observation it must be remembered that the same was true of the general equilibrium model of ch. 2 and the intertemporal equilibrium model derived from it. True, of course, the semi-stationary growth model is a very special case of the intertemporal equilibrium model and true, also, we have been taking a rather partial view of equilibrium, concentrating upon equilibrium of production; but these particular features of our approach while powerful aids to asking questions are not so helpful when it comes to answering them. The model remains reticent on comparative static questions except that it gives to us the golden rule, for which we require almost no assumptions beyond those necessary to allow of semi-stationary growth. Beyond that there is a paucity of general results.

Even people who have made no study of economic theory are familiar with the idea that when something is more plentiful its price will be lower, and introductory courses on economic theory reinforce this common presumption with various examples. However, there is no support from the theory of general equilibrium for the proposition that an input to production will be cheaper in an economy where more of it is available. All that the theory declares is that the price of the use of an input which is more plentiful cannot be higher if all other inputs, all other outputs and all other input prices are in constant proportions to each other.

Let $\mathscr{T}$ be a production possibility set satisfying the linearity assumption (4.13) in terms of input–output combination $(\boldsymbol{u}, \boldsymbol{v})$. Let $(\boldsymbol{u}^1, \boldsymbol{v}^1)$ be maximizing in $\mathscr{T}$ at prices $(\boldsymbol{p}_u^1, \boldsymbol{p}_v^1)$ and $(\boldsymbol{u}^2, \boldsymbol{v}^2)$ be maximizing in $\mathscr{T}$ at prices $(\boldsymbol{p}_u^2, \boldsymbol{p}_v^2)$. Then

$$\boldsymbol{p}_v^1 \cdot \boldsymbol{v}^1 - \boldsymbol{p}_u^1 \cdot \boldsymbol{u}^1 \geqslant \boldsymbol{p}_v^1 \cdot \boldsymbol{v}^2 - \boldsymbol{p}_u^1 \cdot \boldsymbol{u}^2, \qquad \boldsymbol{p}_v^2 \cdot \boldsymbol{v}^2 - \boldsymbol{p}_u^2 \cdot \boldsymbol{u}^2 \geqslant \boldsymbol{p}_v^2 \cdot \boldsymbol{v}^1 - \boldsymbol{p}_u^2 \cdot \boldsymbol{u}^1. \quad (4.38)$$

Hence,

$$\boldsymbol{p}_v^1 \cdot \Delta \boldsymbol{v} - \boldsymbol{p}_u^1 \cdot \Delta \boldsymbol{u} \leqslant 0, \qquad \boldsymbol{p}_v^2 \cdot \Delta \boldsymbol{v} - \boldsymbol{p}_u^2 \cdot \Delta \boldsymbol{u} \geqslant 0. \tag{4.39}$$

Thus,

$$\Delta \boldsymbol{p}_v \cdot \Delta \boldsymbol{v} - \Delta \boldsymbol{p}_u \cdot \Delta \boldsymbol{u} \geqslant 0. \tag{4.40}$$

If $\boldsymbol{v}^2$ is proportional to $\boldsymbol{v}^1$ we may choose these two vectors equal, by the linearity property, so that $\Delta \boldsymbol{v} = \boldsymbol{0}$. Then

$$\Delta \boldsymbol{p}_u \cdot \Delta \boldsymbol{u} \leqslant 0. \tag{4.41}$$

Now if all input ratios, except say those involving the ith input, are unchanged and if the use of the ith input has increased (remembering that output is unchanged) then $\Delta \boldsymbol{u}$ must have one positive component, the ith, and all others non-positive. Similarly, all price changes may be chosen to have the same sign, opposite to the sign of Δp_{ui}. It follows at once that $\Delta p_{ui} \leqslant 0$.

This is not a very useful result and it is particularly useless where capital is concerned, because appearing as it does as both an input and an output (the input being the service of the capital good and the output the good itself) capital plays a kind of dual role in comparisons of production equilibria. Where we discover then that a semi-stationary growth path may have more capital than another and yet that capital commands a higher rental in terms of output we should temper our surprise with due consideration of the fact that an atemporal economy might have more land than another, all other factor service inputs the same, and yet land commands a higher rent. In general it is not immediately clear what 'more' or 'less' capital means when we are confronted with a heterogeneous collection of capital goods. Hence a useful reference case, but of course a very special one, is where all capital vectors are proportional. If someone then asks whether it is not the case that a growth path with more of the capital composite will have a lower rate of interest, he is the victim of two serious misconceptions. In the first place, he is wrong to suppose that there is any presumption from economic theory that the price of the use of capital will be low in a state where more is used. There is no such presumption for any other input when, as with a pair of semi-stationary states, there are many differences in prices and relative inputs and outputs, so why should there be for capital? But furthermore even if there were to be a presumption that the use of capital will cost less where more is in use (as there is in a stationary state) this would not concern the rate of interest unless it is further assumed that all output is homogeneous with the capital input, which is of course just a special case where $\pi = 1$.

As an analytical construct the semi-stationary state is mainly of interest because it allows comparative-static comparisons of different paths where it is sufficient just to compare the events of two adjacent weeks, as was done above. In this chapter we have pursued a particular method of enquiry which has been very fashionable of recent years to see what it will yield. We have simply taken two semi-stationary states from the air, assumed them to differ, and then compared them to see what can be deduced about one difference from another. Naturally, this approach cannot elucidate the causes of differences because we are not here confronting directly the primitive postulates of semi-stationary growth. If two semi-stationary growth paths differ, notwithstanding identical technologies, then it will usually be because the households have different intertemporal preference orderings[15]. Hence, to build a theory of distribution in semi-stationary growth one must eventually examine the primitive postulates including the intertemporal preferences of households. Until this has been done we are in no position to talk of cause and effect. Take a simple example, the one good growth model. Here we know that (4.37) holds, i.e.

$$\Delta\rho\Delta K \leqslant 0. \tag{4.37}$$

Consider two semi-stationary growth paths for which $\Delta\rho > 0$ and suppose that $\Delta K < 0$. Is $K^2 < K^1$ because growth path 2 has a higher rate of interest; or does ρ^2 exceed ρ^1 because growth path 1 has more capital? The question is otiose. All that we can say is that whatever in the primitive specifications of these economies makes them different (and it might just be different histories) has caused both these differences but, so long as (4.37) holds, a set of causes of a higher interest rate cannot be simultaneously a set of causes of a higher level of capital in this particular case.

The semi-stationary growth path is a full-employment path for non-produced factors provided that these are not super-abundant in the classical sense. Thus 'involuntary unemployment' (Keynes, 1936, ch. 2) of factor services is no more consistent with equilibrium semi-stationary growth than it was with atemporal equilibrium. In reality there is no automatic tendency towards full employment but it is extremely doubtful whether the causes of a failure to attain the 'classical' full-employment solution would be operative on a semi-stationary growth path *were that state ever to be achieved.* Thus, while it is perfectly possible to construct an economy in a regularly progressing state but with unending *involuntary unemployment*, it is far from clear that the construct is a convincing one[16]. It follows that the most probable implication

[15] This is not necessary: there may be multiple semi-stationary equilibria for one set of primitive specifications.

[16] For a fuller discussion of these questions see below, ch. 6, pp. 129–130.

for the present discussion of the forces to which the writings of Keynes and his successors have drawn our attention is to throw doubt on whether the equilibrium exhibited in the semi-stationary state would ever be attained, and whether if attained it would sustain itself.

These are questions of the greatest importance but they are not, of course, questions that lie within the domain of the theory of intertemporal equilibrium. That theory commences from the assumption that an equilibrium is attained and this limits most severely the possibility of the theory throwing light on the question of whether equilibrium will be realized or not. To repeat what has been said before, the assumption that equilibrium is attained is an assumption of great force whose importance is in no way diminished because it is sometimes not stated explicitly. Moreover, it is not a primitive assumption so that our theoretical explorations will be incomplete so long as it remains.

Appendix: Existence of constant-rate-of-interest price systems

It is to be shown that a price system may be associated with any efficient semi-stationary state having the property that, for all t,

$$\boldsymbol{p}_t = (1+\rho)\,\boldsymbol{p}_{t+1}, \tag{A4.1}$$

for some scalar ρ, $\rho > -1$.

It is enough to establish that a semi-stationary development of outputs can be made a profit-maximizing development with a stationary price system. For full equilibrium to obtain the households must be willing to accept the consumption vector $\boldsymbol{c}_t$ at the prices ruling: of course, they may not do so, but if they will do so at all then they will do so with a stationary price system, so long as preferences are invariant from week to week.

Firstly some notation is established. Let $\mathscr{S}_1, \mathscr{S}_2, \ldots, \mathscr{S}_m$ be subsets of a vector space. Then the *convex sum* of these sets, denoted $(\mathscr{S}_1 \oplus \mathscr{S}_2 \oplus \ldots \oplus \mathscr{S}_m)$, is defined as

$$\left\{\boldsymbol{x} \,\middle|\, \boldsymbol{x} = \sum_{i=1}^{m} \theta_i \boldsymbol{x}_i;\ \sum_{i=1}^{m} \theta_i = 1;\ \theta_i \geqslant 0,\ i = 1,\ldots m;\ \boldsymbol{x}_i \in \mathscr{S}_i,\ i = 1,\ldots,m\right\}. \tag{A4.2}$$

We define two sets as follows:

$$\begin{aligned} \mathscr{V}_t &= \left\{\boldsymbol{k} \,\middle|\, \left[\frac{1}{1+\gamma}\boldsymbol{y}_t, \boldsymbol{k}\right] \in \mathscr{T}_{\mathrm{E}}(t-1)\right\}, \\ \mathscr{U}_t &= \{\boldsymbol{k} \,|\, [\boldsymbol{k} + \boldsymbol{z}_t - \boldsymbol{c}_t, (1+\gamma)\,\boldsymbol{k}_t] \in \mathscr{T}_{\mathrm{E}}(t)\}. \end{aligned} \tag{A4.3}$$

$\mathscr{V}_t$ is to be interpreted as 'the set of initial stock vectors that may be attained at the beginning of week t given the input vector that the semi-stationary path provides in week $t-1$'. $\mathscr{U}_t$ is to be interpreted as 'the set of initial stock vectors for week t from which it is feasible to provide consumption $\boldsymbol{c}_t$, take in non-produced factor services $\boldsymbol{z}_t$, and thence attain at the beginning of week $t+1$ the capital stock vector of the semistationary path'. The following are rather obvious results which the reader may confirm for himself:

(i) $\mathscr{V}_t$ and $\mathscr{U}_t$ are both convex sets, all t, so long as $\mathscr{T}_{\mathrm{E}}(t)$ is convex for all t.

(ii) If a semi-stationary path is feasible, $\boldsymbol{k}_t$ must be an element of $\mathscr{V}_t$ and also an element of $\mathscr{U}_t$.

(iii) If a semi-stationary path is efficient (delivers a consumption vector that cannot be dominated) then Int $\mathscr{V}_t \cap$ Int $\mathscr{U}_t$ is empty.

Figure A4.1 illustrates the efficient case. From its state in week $t-1$ the economy may arrive at the beginning of week t anywhere in the set $\mathscr{V}_t$. It may deliver $(\boldsymbol{c}_t - \boldsymbol{z}_t)$ and then proceed to its state at the beginning of week $t+1$ from anywhere in the set $\mathscr{U}_t$. If the two sets were to overlap, then a larger consumption vector could be substituted for $\boldsymbol{c}_t$, which would have the effect of shrinking the set $\mathscr{U}_t$ upwards to the right until no overlap would remain. If there were to be no common element at all, then the proposed semi-stationary path would be infeasible. If $\boldsymbol{k}_t$ were not a common element, then no feasible semi-stationary path with the specified consumption would have output vectors proportional to $\boldsymbol{k}_t$.

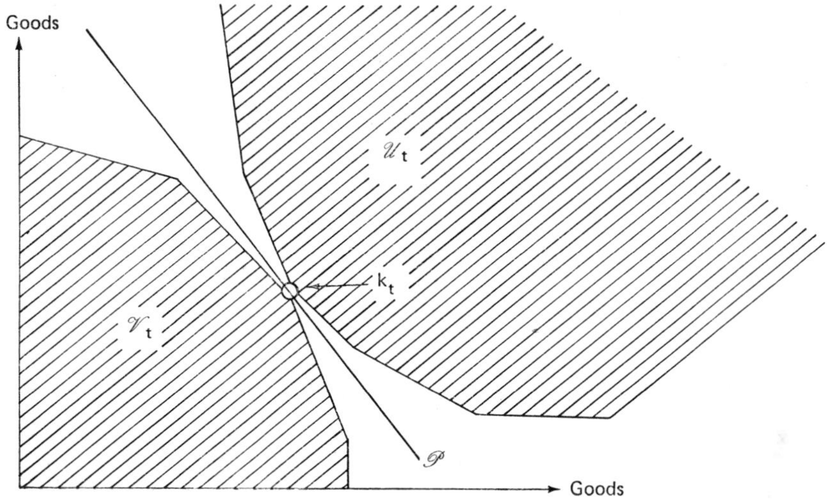

Fig. A4.1.

The sets $\mathscr{V}_t$ and $\mathscr{U}_t$ satisfy the conditions of the separating hyperplane theorem[17] so that we may obtain a hyperplane $\boldsymbol{p}_0 \cdot \boldsymbol{k} = k$ such that

$$\boldsymbol{k} \in \mathscr{V}_t \Rightarrow \boldsymbol{p}_0 \cdot \boldsymbol{k} \leqslant k, \qquad \boldsymbol{k} \in \mathscr{U}_t \Rightarrow \boldsymbol{p}_0 \cdot \boldsymbol{k} \geqslant k. \tag{A4.4}$$

Since $\boldsymbol{k}_t \in \mathscr{V}_t \cap \mathscr{U}_t$ it follows that $k = \boldsymbol{p}_0 \cdot \boldsymbol{k}_t$. Since $\mathscr{U}_t$ contains arbitrarily large positive vectors it is immediate that the vector $\boldsymbol{p}_0 \geqslant 0$. Let

$$\begin{aligned} \mathscr{P}_1(t) &= \{(\boldsymbol{k}, \boldsymbol{0}) \mid (\boldsymbol{p}_0, \boldsymbol{p}_0) \cdot (\boldsymbol{k}, \boldsymbol{0}) = \boldsymbol{p}_0 \cdot \boldsymbol{k}_t\}, \\ \mathscr{P}_2(t) &= \{(\boldsymbol{0}, \boldsymbol{k}) \mid (\boldsymbol{p}_0, \boldsymbol{p}_0) \cdot (\boldsymbol{0}, \boldsymbol{k}) = \boldsymbol{p}_0 \cdot \boldsymbol{k}_t\}. \end{aligned} \tag{A4.5}$$

Now replace $\mathscr{T}_{\mathrm{E}}(t)$ by $\bar{\mathscr{T}}_{\mathrm{E}}(t) = (\mathscr{T}_{\mathrm{E}}(t) \oplus \mathscr{P}_1(t) \oplus \mathscr{P}_2(t))$. The effect of this substitution is to allow inputs or outputs to be freely substituted one for the other along a hyperplane with slope coefficients $\boldsymbol{p}_0$ from $\boldsymbol{k}_t$. It is as if we added to the transformation possibilities an opportunity to trade freely, either outputs or inputs, on 'foreign markets' at prices $\boldsymbol{p}_0$. The reader may confirm for himself the following results:

(i) Following the proposed modification to $\mathscr{T}_{\mathrm{E}}(t)$ the new production possibility set is convex, as are the modified derived sets $\mathscr{V}_t$ and $\mathscr{U}_t$.

(ii) The modified sets $\mathscr{V}_t$ and $\mathscr{U}_t$ remain with disjoint interiors and $\boldsymbol{k}_t$ remains a common point.

(iii) The hyperplane $\boldsymbol{p}_0 \cdot \boldsymbol{k} = \boldsymbol{p}_0 \cdot \boldsymbol{k}_t$ still separates the modified $\mathscr{V}_t$ and $\mathscr{U}_t$.

The reader will probably sense already how the argument is going to run. We have expanded the transformation possibilities of a semi-stationary path, but so as to retain convexity in order that a price system will still be obtainable, and so as to leave the particular path on which our interest is focused only just feasible. We will now obtain a price system for the semi-stationary path with the expanded production sets. Now if a price system is an equilibrium price system from the point of view of production it means that no other feasible production decision would yield a greater present value of profit at the equilibrium prices. Hence, a price system that implies equilibrium with expanded production sets implies equilibrium *a fortiori* for a smaller production set so long as the particular decision vector of the equilibrium path remains feasible. Thus to obtain equilibrium prices for the economy with expanded production sets, since the expansion leaves $\boldsymbol{k}_t$ a common boundary point of $\mathscr{V}_t$ and $\mathscr{U}_t$, is to obtain a set of prices that will satisfy our requirements.

Let $(\ldots \boldsymbol{p}_1, \boldsymbol{p}_2, \ldots, \boldsymbol{p}_t, \ldots)$ be an equilibrium price sequence for the semi-stationary state with expanded production sets. Then we have

$$(\boldsymbol{u}_t, \boldsymbol{v}_{t+1}) \in \bar{\mathscr{T}}_{\mathrm{E}}(t) \Rightarrow \boldsymbol{p}_{t+1} \cdot \boldsymbol{v}_{t+1} - \boldsymbol{p}_t \cdot \boldsymbol{u}_t \leqslant \boldsymbol{p}_{t+1} \cdot \boldsymbol{k}_{t+1} - \boldsymbol{p}_t \cdot \boldsymbol{y}_t. \tag{A4.6}$$

[17] See the mathematical appendix, p. 354.

In other words, $(\boldsymbol{p}_t, \boldsymbol{p}_{t+1})$ defines a supporting hyperplane to $\mathscr{T}_{\mathrm{E}}$ at $(\boldsymbol{y}_t, \boldsymbol{k}_{t+1})$. It is immediately evident, however, by construction, that no vector $(\boldsymbol{p}_t, \boldsymbol{p}_{t+1})$ can define a supporting hyperplane to $\mathscr{T}_{\mathrm{E}}$ unless $\boldsymbol{p}_t$ and $\boldsymbol{p}_{t+1}$ are each proportional to $\boldsymbol{p}_0$, and this must be true for all t. We have thus obtained a price system with invariant relative prices, as required.

To demonstrate that (A4.1) holds it remains to show that the factor of proportionality between the price vectors of adjacent weeks can be chosen the same for each pair of adjacent weeks. However, this is a straightforward implication of condition 4.1. For once a factor of proportionality has been chosen that will do for two adjacent weeks it will do for any other pair of adjacent weeks, since the only difference is a change of scale, and when condition 4.1 obtains a difference of scale is of no consequence for the separation property.

5

Marginal products and capital

Generalizing from the work of a particular machine to that of machinery of a given aggregate value, we may suppose that in a certain factory an extra £100 worth of machinery can be applied so as not to involve any other extra expense, and so as to add annually £4 worth to the net output of the factory, after allowing for its own wear and tear. If the investors of capital push it into every occupation in which it seems likely to gain a high reward; and if, after this has been done and equilibrium has been found, it still pays and only just pays to employ this machinery, we can infer from this fact that the yearly rate of interest is 4 per cent. But illustrations of this kind merely indicate part of the action of the great causes which govern value. They cannot be made into a theory of interest, anymore than into a theory of wages, without reasoning in a circle.

ALFRED MARSHALL, *Principles of Economics* (1920, VI.1)

As was remarked in ch. 2, the equation between the payment for the service of a factor and the value of the marginal product of that factor plays no part in the discussion and derivation of equilibrium for the atemporal economy. The same is then necessarily true for equilibrium of the intertemporal economy, which is founded in the same analytical methods, and so *a fortiori* it is true for the semi-stationary state, which is after all a special case of intertemporal equilibrium. This observation is absolutely essential to an understanding of the place of marginal concepts in equilibrium analysis[1]. However, there is no implication that marginal ideas are in any way in conflict with the theory that has made no appeal to them, indeed in so far as marginal ideas are related to maximization a theory that is founded in the postulate of maximization by

[1] Some statements of the consequences for distribution of equilibrium are dependent for their validity on the correctness of the marginal principle. An example is the Austrian theory of 'imputation' according to which the price of a factor service is equal to the rate at which total utility would increase if more of that factor service were available. Among the many doubtful features of this construct is to be included the excessive identification which it involves between equilibrium and the marginal principle.

Dobb (1970) is correct to seize upon Walras' quoted statement: 'Though it is true that productive services are bought and sold in their own special markets, nevertheless the prices of these services are determined in the markets for products' as a good object for attack. However, Dobb should realize, as he seems not to have done, that Walras is wrong anyway, and even if definitional problems do not present themselves, if the words 'are determined in' are to carry anything like their seeming meaning.

various actors is necessarily in harmony with marginal concepts where these are applicable. The importance of remembering that marginal concepts are not primary, but follow upon the basic postulates of maximization, is that it guides us when the specification of marginal equations is unclear back to the postulated maximization for an answer. Also it should guard against a kind of confusion that may arise when certain specifications of marginal relations fail, whereupon the unwary too readily conclude that a crisis for economic analysis has arisen. Equilibrium analysis, being in no way dependent upon marginal concepts, can suffer no crisis on their account.

To say that marginal concepts are not fundamental to equilibrium analysis is not to say that they are unimportant. It so happens that the postulate that an actor maximizes can be expressed in more than one way. In some cases a necessary marginal condition for maximization may be a particularly felicitous vehicle for this postulate. The evidence for this claim is to be found in the history of economic analysis itself. The idea that economic actors maximize is an ancient one, but only in the second half of the nineteenth century were the implications of the idea fully realized. That realization coincided with, if it was not caused by, the widespread application of marginal ideas, with which came a great increase in the precision and clarity of economic theorizing. As Schumpeter (1954, p. 677) has written:

> But, as we have seen on other occasions, mere recognition of the element of productivity does not help us much unless it is streamlined by the notion of *marginal* productivity, exactly as the element of utility will not produce any serviceable theory of price unless streamlined by the notion of marginal utility.

One might summarize the status of marginal concepts in equilibrium analysis in the statement that these concepts, while finding no place in a catalogue of the postulates of equilibrium analysis, are, as derived relations, and as a means of straightening out ideas, important tools of that analysis.

The existence of capital poses two distinct but related problems for marginal analysis. Firstly, even considering the marginal product of another input, say labour time, one must confront the issue of what is to count as 'holding capital constant'. Secondly, there is of course the highly controversial issue of whether marginal principles have any application where capital itself is concerned. The existence of a connection between these two questions is immediate, for to ascertain what it is to hold capital constant is to ascertain at least in part what it is to change the quantity of capital employed and this is to take the first step towards an understanding of the relation between a change in the quantity of capital employed and the resultant change in production. We take the two questions in turn.

Reference must first be made to an important ambiguity concerning the notion of the marginal product of a factor input. The majority of textbooks define the marginal product of a factor in something more or less corresponding to the following definition (Samuelson, 1967, p. 514; the italics are mine):

> The marginal product of a productive factor is the extra product or output added by one extra unit of that factor, *while other factors are being held constant.* Labour's marginal product is the extra output you get when you add one unit of labour, holding *all other inputs constant.*

Now there is certainly nothing wrong with this definition but it is perhaps a little surprising that it does not bewilder students more than it seems to. Thinking of particular examples the reader might convince himself that it would very often be simply inefficient and foolish for a firm to adjust just the input of one factor without making any consequent alteration in any other input level. In that case, what is the relevance of the extra output that just an addition to the labour input would make possible to the task of characterizing the point at which the employment of labour will be set by a price-taking firm? An example will help to elucidate the answer.

Consider a firm which uses just three factors – horses, land and labour – to produce wheat. We suppose that each of these factors can be purchased at given prices and that wheat is likewise saleable at a given price. The production set of the firm is specified by a function f which designates the maximum output of wheat that may be obtained given a specified input combination. Let H be the input of horse time, J the input of the service of land, L the input of labour time and X the output of wheat. Then $(-H, -J, -L, X)$ is a feasible production plan for the firm if and only if

$$X \leqslant f(H, J, L). \tag{5.1}$$

The profit-maximization problem to which the firm is supposed to obtain a solution is

$$\max\ p^X X - p^H H - p^J J - p^L L \quad \text{subject to } X \leqslant f(H, J, L), \tag{5.2}$$

where $p^I (I = H, J, L, X)$ is the price of I. This problem may be split into two stages[2].

Stage I. Given an arbitrary non-negative value $\bar{L}$ choose H, J and X to solve

$$\max\ p^X X - p^H H - p^J J \quad \text{subject to } X \leqslant f(H, J, \bar{L}). \tag{5.3}$$

---

[2] The decomposition of the problem of choosing an overall profit-maximizing plan into two stages here discussed may be compared to a very common presentation in the textbooks. First, derive the minimum cost of producing each output level, then equate marginal cost to price. Of course, this is only an expository device. In principle, the problem of choosing input combinations to minimize cost and the problem of choosing the profit-maximizing output level are just different aspects of a single problem: choose all inputs and outputs to maximize profit subject to technical possibilities.

The solution to this problem, which depends upon the value of $\bar{L}$, may be denoted $\Pi(\bar{L})$. $\Pi(\bar{L})$ is simply the maximum profit, not including a charge for labour time, that may be realized by a firm which has its disposal $\bar{L}$ units of labour time.

Stage II. Choose L to solve

$$\max \Pi(L) - p^L L. \tag{5.4}$$

The quantity $\Pi(L)$ might be referred to as the *net value-product of labour* since it consists of the value of the product of labour less the value of the inputs co-operating with labour *when the levels of these inputs are chosen optimally so as to maximize profit*. If then it is always optimal in terms of profit to take on extra horses when labour employed is increased, the marginal net value product of labour will be the value of the extra output produced less the extra cost of horse time consequent upon the change in the employment of labour. Suppose now, for the sake of discussion, that Π is a differentiable function[3]. The reader may readily satisfy himself that a solution to (5.2) must embody solutions to both (5.3) and (5.4), i.e. if a solution to (5.2) is (H^*, J^*, L^*, X^*) then (H^*, J^*, X^*) must be a solution to (5.3) with $L = L^*$ and L^* must be a solution to (5.4). The rationale of this is obvious. A production plan which maximizes profit must necessarily maximize profit given that the labour input is fixed at the optimal level. Moreover, the labour input must be so adjusted to maximize the difference between the net value product of labour and the cost of labour.

Compare this analysis to the Marshallian analysis of equilibrium in the long and short periods. The problem (5.3) corresponds to the profit-maximizing decision of a firm for which one of the inputs is for the moment given, like the prices that it faces, while problem (5.4) corresponds to the choice of the level of that input in the 'long run', assuming that the other freely variable inputs will be optimally adjusted. To claim then that a solution to the problem of maximizing profit as in the problem (5.2) ('long-run profit maximization') must embody a solution to (5.3) ('short-run profit maximization') is to do no more than remind ourselves that every long-run problem is also a short-run problem (Samuelson, 1947, pp. 34–35; Viner, 1931), it is only that more in addition is involved in the long-run problem.

On the assumption that Π is a differentiable function, and assuming that the firm will employ a positive quantity of labour, a solution to (5.4) must satisfy

$$\mathrm{d}\Pi/\mathrm{d}L - p^L = 0. \tag{5.5}$$

[3] There is no reason why it need be differentiable but the conditions for it to be differenti able are weaker than the requirement that f be a differentiable function of its various arguments.

The wage rate of labour will equal the marginal net value product of labour. This is a concept of the marginal product of labour which goes beyond the standard definition according to which 'all other factors are held constant' (as opposed to being adjusted optimally) while including that standard concept as a special case, when it so happens that the optimal adjustment of all other inputs would in fact be zero. The notion that the optimal marginal adjustment of other inputs might typically not be zero seems particularly to have impressed Marshall (1920, pp. 426–430), whose definition of the marginal productivity of labour corresponds to net productivity as defined above[4]. The distinction between the marginal net value product of labour and the value of the marginal product of labour is obscured in traditional mathematical economics where all the functions that arise in the analysis are assumed to be differentiable. It may then be shown that the marginal net value product of labour is equal to the simple value of the marginal product of labour: the optimal marginal adjustment of other inputs is zero. At the margin (i.e. considering *rates of change* of profit instead of actual *changes* in profit) 'all factors are perfectly indifferent substitutes' (Samuelson, 1947, p. 35; Viner, 1937, pp. 515–516). Following the approach of traditional mathematical economics let the solution to (5.3) be specified by differentiable functions of $\bar{L}$.[5] Then

$$\frac{\mathrm{d}\Pi}{\mathrm{d}\bar{L}} = p^X \frac{\mathrm{d}X}{\mathrm{d}\bar{L}} - p^H \frac{\mathrm{d}H}{\mathrm{d}\bar{L}} - p^J \frac{\mathrm{d}J}{\mathrm{d}\bar{L}}. \tag{5.6}$$

However, by the theorem of Kuhn and Tucker[6], there exists a multiplier λ such that the form

$$p^X X - p^H H - p^J J - p^L L + \lambda[f(H,J,L) - X] \tag{5.7}$$

is maximized by (X, H, J, L). Hence, if X, J, H and L are all positive,

$$p^X = \lambda, \qquad -p^I = -\lambda \frac{\partial f}{\partial I} \qquad (I = H, J, L) \tag{5.8}$$

are satisfied by the solution to (5.2). Substituting into (5.6),

$$\frac{\mathrm{d}\Pi}{\mathrm{d}\bar{L}} = p^X \frac{\mathrm{d}X}{\mathrm{d}\bar{L}} - p^X \frac{\partial f}{\partial H}\frac{\mathrm{d}H}{\mathrm{d}\bar{L}} - p^X \frac{\partial f}{\partial J}\frac{\mathrm{d}J}{\mathrm{d}\bar{L}}. \tag{5.9}$$

---

[4] See also Hicks (1932, pp. 12–15) and Machlup (1963). I do not fully agree with Hicks' interpretation of Marshall.

[5] The reader may care to satisfy himself that this type of approach is not in every case valid by considering the example

$$p^X = p^H = p^J = p^L = 1, \qquad f(H,J,L) = (\min(H,J,L))^{1/2}.$$

[6] See the mathematical appendix, p. 358.

However, since $X = f(H, J, L)$ must be satisfied identically, we have

$$\frac{\mathrm{d}X}{\mathrm{d}\bar{L}} = \frac{\partial f}{\partial H}\frac{\mathrm{d}H}{\mathrm{d}\bar{L}} + \frac{\partial f}{\partial J}\frac{\mathrm{d}J}{\mathrm{d}\bar{L}} + \frac{\partial f}{\partial \bar{L}}. \tag{5.10}$$

Combining (5.9) and (5.10) one obtains

$$\mathrm{d}\Pi/\mathrm{d}\bar{L} = p^X \, \partial f/\partial \bar{L}. \tag{5.11}$$

The marginal net value product of labour in this case is simply the value of the marginal product of labour. This result is, of course, perfectly general as regards the number of factor inputs, but it is in another respect rather special and it is perhaps unfortunate that it has been given so much prominence by economic theorists. For the idea that every input might be smoothly substitutable for every other, which is what differentiability of f implies, is not at all convincing. Many people have felt that important aspects of reality are best represented by production possibilities generated by combining a finite set of fixed-coefficient activities, for each of which a specific scale of output demands a specific collection of factor inputs and no variation of this mix is possible. This may or may not be realistic. The point surely is that economic theory should be so formulated, unless this can be shown to be impossible, as to cover such a seemingly reasonable case. This the standard definition of a marginal product fails to do. There is no general guarantee that the marginal net value product of a factor will turn out to be well defined, but there is a much better chance that it will be, because it is a more general concept, including as it does, the value of the marginal product as a special case.

Figures 5.1 and 5.2 illustrate the traditional case and one of the possibilities of which the traditional analysis fails to take account. In each of the diagrams the curve of profit along which all inputs are varied so as to maximize profit naturally lies above, or certainly not below, the curve along which only the labour input may vary. Profit can never be increased by the addition of extra constraints on maximizing decisions. In the traditional case, however, this is of no consequence as far as the slope at (L^*, P^*) is concerned. The upper curve, being the envelope of all curves of the same type as the lower curve, has the same slope as the lower curve at the point at which the two curves meet. This common slope must be the wage rate p^L as was seen in ch. 2. In fig. 5.2 the lower curve is not differentiable – it has a corner at (L^*, P^*) – so that one cannot speak of the marginal product of labour according to the usual usage. The rate at which profit varies with labour input is steeper for reductions in labour than it is for increases.

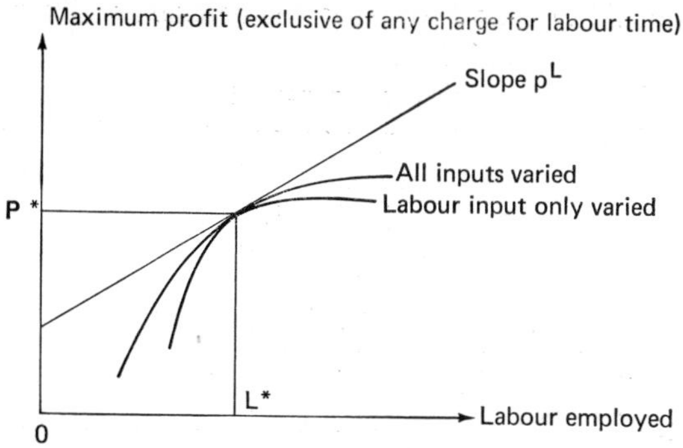

Fig. 5.1.

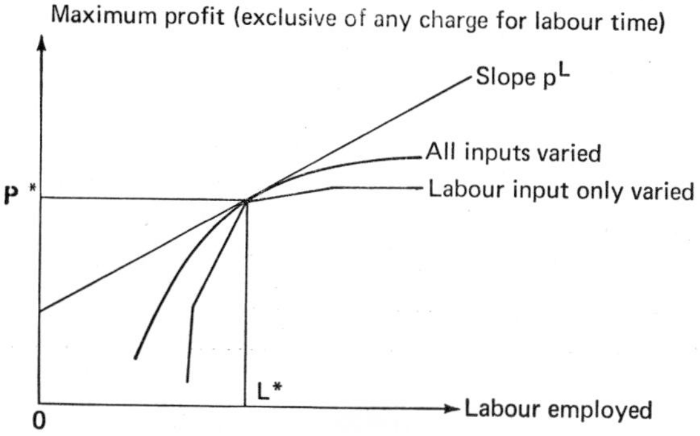

Fig. 5.2.

It is on account of the existence of examples such as the one illustrated in fig. 5.2 that care has been taken, in referring to marginal concepts and marginal-productivity equations, to always add some such rider as 'where these are applicable', for they may not apply and this, as has been remarked, has nothing to do with the viability of equilibrium theory. Figure 5.2 illustrates the basic point of our argument. If one wants an equation which will identify the wage rate of labour with a marginal-product construct then the slope of a curve which will do the job, if the slope of any curve will do the job, is the slope of the uppermost curve of figs. 5.1 and 5.2. We have called this slope the marginal net product of labour and if this cannot be defined, because even the uppermost curve is not differentiable (has a corner) at (L^*, P^*) then the wage rate of labour cannot be said to equal the marginal anything. Anyone who believes that our 'theory of income distribution' in equilibrium, such as it is, is destroyed when marginal concepts are taken from it is in the same confused state as a man would be who bemoaned the beheading of a friend who had done no more than remove his hat.

A major reason why the notion of marginal net product has not played a very central role in economic theory, particularly as it is taught to students, is the stress laid on the traditional mathematical formulation of equilibrium models under which every function in sight is assumed differentiable, there are no corners, all diagrams display only smooth curves and the marginal net product is none other than the marginal product by the envelope theorem shown above. But there is another point which merits a mention and which has perhaps a part to play in explaining why Marshall's construct has not been more influential. There is a view according to which a marginal product should be defined in purely physical terms. While the product price may be admitted to convert the marginal product to a marginal value product, on no account should factor prices appear in the definition of marginal products[7]. Since the purpose of marginal-productivity theory is to explain factor prices, how can marginal products be reasonably defined in terms of factor prices? The marginal net product of labour as we have defined it is not in accord with the requirement that it be defined independently of factor prices, for although p_L is not involved in the definition, it is necessary to know the prices of all other inputs to ascertain the optimal variation in these inputs. This is in contrast to the simple marginal product of labour, the calculation of which demands no more than a knowledge of the point of reference and the technical possibilities.

The belief that a principle of marginal productivity based upon the notion of the net productivity of factors is somehow inadequate for the purpose of explaining the prices of factor services in equilibrium, widespread though it is, is founded in a grotesque misconception. Someone who thinks that *net marginal products do not* do the job of explaining the prices of factor services presumably believes that *marginal products do* explain the prices of factor services – otherwise there would be nothing remarkable about the instance of marginal net productivity. Of course, as we have had reason to remark already, marginal products do not explain factor prices or isolate the causes

[7] This view has most commonly been advanced with respect to capital. The marginal product of capital it is argued should be defined independently of such values as prices and particularly interest rates. So many writers adhere to this view that it is hard to know which to mention but one associates it particularly with Cambridge economists. Cf. Keynes *General Theory* (1936, pp. 138 ff.), Kaldor (1955–1956, section III) and Robinson (1953–1954). Harcourt (1972), considering the marginal net product of labour and the wage rate, seems to think that one might be disconcerted that the equation between the two values does not 'explain the rate of profit'. What surprising things people think about the theory of distribution!

of these prices. Marginal products do determine factor prices, in the sole sense that knowing a marginal product in equilibrium one may infer, from the marginal productivity equation, the factor price. But it is equally true that the factor price determines, in this sense, the marginal net product. It is safest to state that marginal products, where these can be defined, are caused by the same primitive influences which cause factor prices, and when these causes operate through an equilibrium system then they must needs produce the same answer for a marginal product and for the corresponding factor price. There is no valid theory according to which factor prices are 'determined' in the sense of cause by effect by marginal products, and if the formulation of the marginal productivity concept in terms of net marginal productivity reminds us of this fact that is an extra argument in its favour.

It is very likely that this is all that Marshall meant when he wrote of the marginal productivity doctrine (1920, pp. 429–430):

> This doctrine has sometimes been put forward as a theory of wages. But there is no valid ground for any such pretension. The doctrine that the earnings of a worker tend to be equal to the net product of his work, has by itself no real meaning; since in order to estimate net product, we have to take for granted all the expenses of production of the commodity on which he works, other than his own wages.
>
> But though this objection is valid against a claim that it contains a theory of wages; it is not valid against a claim that the doctrine throws into clear light the action of one of the causes that govern wages.[8]

This passage has frequently been quoted but less frequently understood. Keynes, adhering to the 'marginal productivity theory of wages', thought that Marshall was wrong to maintain that there is no theory! Others (Kaldor for example) regard Marshall's admission as tantamount to a repudiation of the marginal productivity doctrine. All this reflects a lack of agreement about what a marginal theory is supposed to do, a question which Marshall intended to clarify.

Let us examine now the implications of the concept of marginal net productivity of labour for what is the crucial case; namely when labour co-operates with capital inputs in the production of output. It is particularly with capital inputs in mind that people have felt uncomfortable about the idea of a differentiable function relating labour inputs and all the various produced inputs to output. For let the labour input be increased, holding everything else (meaning each individual item) constant and perhaps output may be increased. Certainly a decrease in the level of the labour input, holding each other item constant, must bring about a loss of output unless labour is a

---

[8] The marginal notes read: 'This doctrine is not a theory of wages; but is a useful part of a theory.'

free good. But this is not the form that an increase in the labour input will normally take, for usually when more labour intensive production methods are adopted (the labour input is increased relative to the level of output) this is accompanied by *a change in the form of the capital inputs.*

Labour intensive production methods will normally call for different capital inputs and not merely less of the same capital inputs relative to labour. For example, if a ditch is to be dug by a very labour intensive method we may find men at work with shovels, one shovel in the hands of each man. If we take away some of the time of one man we will indeed lose some output, but we will at the same time render a shovel idle for that time which the man no longer works. If we increase the man-hours applied to digging the ditch, but hold constant the input of shovels, output may increase little relative to the increased labour input. As Taussig (1939, vol. II, p. 213) has remarked: 'There is no separate product of the tool on the one hand and of the labour using the tool on the other' (quoted by Robertson (1950)). What examples of this type indicate is not that the wage rate of labour may fail to equal the value of its marginal product in equilibrium. Rather they show that the common definition of the marginal product of labour as the partial derivative of output with respect to the input of labour may be otiose where, as might be expected to occur frequently where labour co-operates with capital inputs, there is no such partial derivative, output not being a differentiable function of labour, all other inputs constant.

The partial derivative of output with respect to the labour input is an academic concept. It is not what directly concerns the manager of a firm. There is nothing that constrains him when he conducts his mental experiments to see whether employing more or less labour would increase his profit, to vary only one input holding all the others constant. Indeed, it might very well not occur to him to do so. Let us assume that he has chanced upon a profit-maximizing plan. Suppose, for the sake of simplicity, that the firm produces only one output and that labour is the only non-produced input. As far as the particular discussion to follow is concerned it makes little difference whether or not we suppose the firm to be part of an economy in semi-stationary growth. So long as everything has a price the present value of a unit of output p^O and the present cost of a unit of labour input p^L are known, and the present cost of the use of capital inputs may be calculated. In ch. 4 the vector of unit costs of the capital services for all the firms taken together was $\rho \mathbf{p}$. However, that was a somewhat special case, taking into account as it did the fact that depreciation was all made good by all the firms taken together. Considering now a single firm, we must bear in mind that the cost of the service of the ith capital good is ρp_i, only if that good is perfectly durable and only if there is a single constant rate of interest. There is no need here to confine our attention to such a special case. More generally, the present-value cost of using the ith capital good for one production week t, supposing it to become one unit of capital good $i'(i)$ as a result of wear and tear in use[9], is $p_i^t - p_{i'(i)}^{t+1}$. This reduces to ρp_i^{t+1}, where $i'(i) = i$ and ρ is the one uniform rate of interest. Let $\boldsymbol{q}^t$ be the vector whose ith component is $p_i^t - p_{i'(i)}^{t+1}$. The superscript t will be dropped where (as here) it serves no purpose. A production plan for the firm during the week under consideration will comprise an output level O, a vector of capital inputs $\boldsymbol{k}$ and an employment level L. The subscript 1 will indicate the plan chosen and 2 an alternative plan included in the firm's production possibility set.

The present value of profit from the chosen plan must not be exceeded by that of any alternative feasible plan:

$$p_1^O O_1 - \boldsymbol{q}_1 \cdot \boldsymbol{k}_1 - p_1^L L_1 \geqslant p_1^O O_2 - \boldsymbol{q}_1 \cdot \boldsymbol{k}_2 - p_1^L L_2. \tag{5.12}$$

Hence,

$$p_1^O \Delta O - \boldsymbol{q}_1 \cdot \Delta \boldsymbol{k} - p_1^L \Delta L \leqslant 0.\text{[10]} \tag{5.13}$$

Now, upon dividing both sides of (5.13) by ΔL and bearing in mind that the sign of the inequality will be reversed where $\Delta L < 0$, we obtain

$$\left\{p_1^O \frac{\Delta O}{\Delta L} - \boldsymbol{q}_1 \cdot \Delta \boldsymbol{k}\left(\frac{1}{\Delta L}\right)\right\}_{\Delta L>0} \leqslant p_1^L \leqslant \left\{p_1^O \frac{\Delta O}{\Delta L} - \boldsymbol{q}_1 \cdot \Delta \boldsymbol{k}\left(\frac{1}{\Delta L}\right)\right\}_{\Delta L<0}. \tag{5.14}$$

If we consider only alternative plans with the same vector of capital inputs $\Delta \boldsymbol{k} \equiv \boldsymbol{0}$ (5.14) reduces to

$$p_1^O \left\{\frac{\Delta O}{\Delta L}\right\}_{\Delta L>0} \leqslant p_1^L \leqslant p_1^O \left\{\frac{\Delta O}{\Delta L}\right\}_{\Delta L<0}. \tag{5.15}$$

These two inequality relations are fundamental implications of the assumption of profit-maximizing choices by the managers of firms. The second reflects the approach most usually adopted by economic theorists whereby the marginal product of labour is taken to measure the rate at which output is added (subtracted) as labour is increased (decreased), all other inputs held constant. The relations of (5.15) indicate that the wage rate of labour p^L must lie between the rate of increase of product with respect to increased

[9] Here capital goods are indexed according to depreciation as well as type when new (see ch. 9). Good $i'(i)$ may be just the ith good measured in different units if depreciation is of the 'radioactive' type which decreases the quantity of a capital type without otherwise changing its form.

[10] As in ch. 4, Δx is defined as $x_2 - x_1$.

labour input and the rate of decrease of product with respect to decreased labour input. However, as has been remarked, the left- and the right-hand sides of (5.15) will very probably not be equal, or even tend to equality in the limit, as ΔL approaches zero. The relation (5.14) then reminds us that the wage rate of labour may nonetheless equal the rate at which output varies as the labour input is varied and it indicates precisely the necessary condition for this to be the case. We get to (5.15) from (5.14) if, for all alternative plans considered, $\boldsymbol{q}_1 \cdot \Delta \boldsymbol{k} = 0$. This condition is implied by $\Delta \boldsymbol{k} \equiv \boldsymbol{0}$ but it is, of course, much weaker than this last requirement. Thus, we arrive at marginal product inequalities, just like those derived under the assumption of everything else constant, if we assume that capital inputs are adjusted along with labour *but so as to keep their cost at the ruling prices the same.*

If we confine attention to the most profitable alternative plan in each case, then clearly the plans which are allowed to adjust the structure of the capital input cannot be less profitable than the most profitable plan which is constrained to leave capital inputs unchanged. Given then that equilibrium obtains and that the firm has chosen a production plan to maximize profit, what may one infer about the level of the wage rate from a knowledge of the production possibilities of firms? The answer may be summarized in the following marginal inequalities:

$$p_1^O \left\{\frac{\Delta O}{\Delta L}\right\}_{\substack{\Delta L>0 \\ \Delta \boldsymbol{k}=\boldsymbol{0}}} \leqslant p_1^O \left\{\frac{\Delta O}{\Delta L}\right\}_{\substack{\Delta L>0 \\ \boldsymbol{q}_1 \cdot \Delta \boldsymbol{k}=0}} \leqslant p_1^L \leqslant p_1^O \left\{\frac{\Delta O}{\Delta L}\right\}_{\substack{\Delta L<0 \\ \boldsymbol{q}_1 \cdot \Delta \boldsymbol{k}=0}} \leqslant p_1^O \left\{\frac{\Delta O}{\Delta L}\right\}_{\substack{\Delta L<0 \\ \Delta \boldsymbol{k}=\boldsymbol{0}}}. \tag{5.16}$$

These relations give mathematical expression to the implications of figs. 5.1 and 5.2 for the present case. The approach adopted here lies between the traditional approach and the thoroughgoing marginal-net-productivity approach. Adjustment of co-operating inputs is allowed but not all adjustments – only those that leave unchanged the total outlay on co-operating inputs at the prices ruling. Naturally, this makes the definition of the marginal product dependent upon prices of co-operating inputs but that is how it should be – the demand for labour is not independent of the prices of co-operating inputs! This approach is precisely the one that must be adopted if one wants, at the same time, the wage rate to equal the rate of change of product (not net of any deductions), and the greatest chance that the function relating product to labour input be differentiable.

In the type of example considered by traditional mathematical economics the limits of all these terms as $\Delta L \to O$ are equal so that it is possible to speak unambiguously of a value of the marginal product of labour without regard to whether ΔL is positive or negative and without regard to whether capital inputs are constant or whether they are adjusted optimally. Naturally, in this case the value of the marginal product of labour is equal to the wage rate. This, however, as we have seen, is a peculiarly special case. In general, while it can be shown that all the terms of (5.16) will possess well-defined limits as $\Delta L \to O$,[11] none of these limits need equal any other.

There is then no general theoretical justification for the view that the wage rate of labour will be equal in equilibrium to the value of the marginal product of labour. The view is not ill-founded because it asserts that the two quantities will be equal whereas in fact they might differ, for if the value of the marginal product of labour is well defined, as a single number, then that number must be the wage rate. The point is that the marginal product of labour, and hence the value of the marginal product of labour, may not be well defined. If one wants to work with marginal concepts – and remember that they are strictly 'optional extras' of equilibrium analysis – then presumably it makes sense to adopt the definition of a marginal product which is most likely to be well defined; and this, of course, is the slope of the upper curve of fig. 5.2, or, in the present instance, the limit of

$$\left\{\frac{\Delta O}{\Delta L}\right\}_{\mathbf{q}_1 \cdot \Delta \mathbf{k}=0} \quad \text{as } \Delta L \to O.$$

In conclusion, *holding capital constant for the purpose of determining the marginal product of labour should mean holding an index of the value of capital services based upon prices* $\mathbf{q}_1$ *constant.* If the value of the marginal product of labour can be defined unambiguously on this definition it will be equal to the wage rate in equilibrium. If it cannot be defined unambiguously it will nonetheless prove possible to define left- and right-hand marginal products and the wage rate will lie between the value of these. We get this from the assumption of profit maximization and it is all that we could hope to get from it. We have assumed that the firms of the economy are interested in making profit – they are not interested as such in marginal relations.

Finally, let it be noted that our failure to find a general justification for traditional statements of marginal productivity relations *has nothing to do with capital.* Marginal ideas as traditionally formulated depend inescapably upon differentiability of the functional relations between inputs and outputs. Since we may, if we wish, suppose these relations not to be differentiable no

---

[11] It may be shown because ΔO is in each case a concave function of ΔL. See the mathematical appendix, p. 355.

matter what inputs are involved, and we may do this without making any difference to equilibrium theory which has no need of differentiability, marginal theory as traditionally formulated lacks the generality of the concepts from which, when valid, it springs; namely, maximization and equilibrium. It is up to the individual theorist to decide how he will proceed from this point. What he decides to do will depend in part upon how he plans to use his theoretical construct. As has been remarked, the utility of marginal concepts lies in their being on some occasions excellent vehicles for the fundamental assumptions of equilibrium theory. For the most part, it is doubtful whether their utility in this regard extends beyond the cases for which the traditional formulation is valid, so that doubts about the validity of the traditional formulation give cause to doubt the utility of marginal principles. Whether working with the traditional type of model is very misleading is a matter of opinion: if it is very misleading where the theory of distribution is concerned, then it follows that if the world were to be modified just very slightly, so that all inputs could be smoothly substituted one for the other at the margin, even if only to an arbitrarily small extent, quite new principles would come to govern the distribution of income. Some people believe this to be the case.

It emerges, then, that from the formal point of view there is nothing exceptional as far as marginal principles are concerned about the services of capital goods as co-operating inputs alongside labour. But perhaps that case is particularly efficacious when it comes to reminding us that the assumptions of traditional mathematical economics are very likely not realistic. On the other hand, Robinson (1970, p. 234) is not correct in her belief that this lack of realism 'destroys the doctrine that wages are regulated by the marginal product of labour'[12]. Firstly, the doctrine is not a valid one even in the traditional case if it purports to be a theory or an explanation of the level of wages in equilibrium and cannot then be said to be destroyed by any consideration of a particular case. We have seen already that whatever it is that 'regulates' the level of wages in an equilibrium model it is not the marginal product of labour. Secondly, if the doctrine is to be the claim that the wage rate will 'measure' the marginal product of labour (Robertson, 1950, p. 221), for which at least there is support from the traditional analysis, then, as we have seen already, there may be a well-defined 'marginal product' of labour, the value of which will be measured by the wage rate of labour, even if the traditional

[12] It is far from clear what the phrase 'wages are regulated by' (which phrase goes back to von Thünen) means. However, it presumably means something different from 'wages are equal to'. We do not usually say that the area of the square on the hypotenuse of a right-angled triangle is regulated by the sum of the areas of the squares on the other two sides.

assumption that everything is differentiable is not satisfied. Let the firm produce one output at rate O, use a vector of capital services $\boldsymbol{k}$ priced $\boldsymbol{q}$ and employ labour L. Let the production set $\mathscr{T}$ be the set of all feasible plans $(O, -\boldsymbol{k}, -L)$. Formally this marginal product will be the derivative of $O(\bar{L})$, where $O(\bar{L})$ is the solution to the following problem:

$$\max O \quad \text{subject to } (O, -\boldsymbol{k}, -L) \in \mathscr{T}, \qquad L \leqslant \bar{L}, \qquad \boldsymbol{q}\cdot\boldsymbol{k} \leqslant \boldsymbol{q}\cdot\bar{\boldsymbol{k}}, \qquad (5.17)$$

with $\bar{\boldsymbol{k}}$ the profit-maximizing choice of capital inputs and $\bar{L}$ the profit-maximizing employment level.

Now notice two important implications of our departure from the familiar definition of the marginal product of labour in assuming that it is the value of capital at constant prices that is held constant as labour is varied and not each particular capital input. One consequence is that the value of the marginal product of labour may differ between two economies just because the prices of capital services differ and for no other reason. There is nothing paradoxical about this. What the wage rate measures in a competitive economy is the rate at which the application of labour can increase net value and that is something that by its nature cannot always be independent of the prices of inputs any more than it is independent of the prices of outputs. It is thus not strictly accurate to say that the marginal product of labour in terms of the output that it produces is a purely technological concept, although again in the case of the traditional analysis it turns out to be such.

Another consequence of the general approach to marginal productivity emerges when we turn our eyes from the individual firm to look at the economy as a whole. Does the marginal product of labour as defined above measure the rate at which the economy could increase the output concerned if more labour were to be made available? In general, it does not and a consideration of the reason why it does not can provide some indispensable insight into the implications of assuming an economy in which each actor is a 'price-taker'. A single firm faced with parametric prices for all goods, including capital goods, can adjust the structure of its capital stock from one week to the next, but the same is not true of the economy as a whole. The capital stock that exists in one week may be transformed slowly by normal productive activities and, given enough time, the economy might end up with a capital stock of any structure whatsoever. Within a single week, however, and for some time to an extent, the stock is given and the economy must make of it what it can. It follows that the wage rate of labour, when the function $O(L)$ is differentiable at $\bar{L}$, measures *the outcome of a hypothetical experiment which as a matter of fact the economy would not be capable of putting into effect even if extra labour were available*. Perhaps this is not always understood, but of course there is nothing puzzling about it. The very notion of marginal productivity is based on the idea of the outcomes of hypothetical experiments. 'Assume that the economy experiences a small increase in its available land area. But an economy cannot increase its land area – it is simply not possible! Yes, but just suppose that it could and calculate the extra production that this would permit[13].'

Let us now turn to the marginal product of capital. Fortunately, a great deal of the groundwork for a discussion of this concept has been done already in our investigation of the marginal product of labour. A good starting point for the present discussion is the inequality (4.10) of ch. 4 which reads

$$\boldsymbol{p}_c^1 \cdot \Delta \boldsymbol{c}(1+\gamma) + (\gamma - \rho^1)\boldsymbol{p}_k^1 \cdot \Delta \boldsymbol{k} \leqslant 0. \tag{5.18}$$

Let

$$[Y]_{\text{cp}(1)} = \boldsymbol{p}_c^1(1+\gamma)\cdot \boldsymbol{c} + \boldsymbol{p}_k^1 \gamma \cdot \boldsymbol{k}. \tag{5.19}$$

$[Y]_{\text{cp}(1)}$ is net product measured in terms of the price system of growth path 1, hence the subscript cp(1) meaning constant prices of growth path 1. Now,

$$\Delta[Y]_{\text{cp}(1)} = \boldsymbol{p}_c^1(1+\gamma)\cdot \Delta\boldsymbol{c} + \boldsymbol{p}_k^1 \gamma \cdot \Delta\boldsymbol{k} \tag{5.20}$$

measures the difference in net product between growth path 2 (another path) and growth path 1 from the point of view of growth path 1, i.e. in terms of the prices of growth path 1. Next, let

$$[K]_{\text{cp}(1)} = \boldsymbol{p}_k^1 \cdot \boldsymbol{k} \tag{5.21}$$

be capital measured in terms of the prices of growth path 1, so that

$$\Delta[K]_{\text{cp}(1)} = \boldsymbol{p}_k^1 \cdot \Delta\boldsymbol{k}. \tag{5.22}$$

Of course, all these measures are based on a parochial viewpoint in which everything is evaluated according to the prices of growth path 1, and there are different measures of product and capital implied by the alternative price systems of other growth paths. However, parochial though they are, these measures of product and capital are of central theoretical importance because they spring naturally from the assumption that the price system of growth

---

[13] In the instance considered by traditional mathematical economics the experiments are hypothetical only with regard to the availability of the input whose marginal product is measured since only this need vary. Evidently we have here a special case.

path 1 (the reference path) is parametric. In one sense these aggregations of product and capital are 'local' in that they are based on a particular reference path as starting point, and upon the price system of that path for the provision of the 'weights' that are used to form the weighted sums of disparate physical quantities. But from another point of view they are 'global' in that the product and capital of any growth path may be measured according to (5.19) and (5.21). Notice that all this is fully in accord with the treatment of capital adopted in the discussion of the marginal product of labour.

Now (5.18) may be rewritten as

$$\Delta[Y]_{\mathrm{cp}(1)} - \rho^1 \Delta[K]_{\mathrm{cp}(1)} \leqslant 0. \tag{5.23}$$

Upon dividing through by $\Delta[K]_{\mathrm{cp}(1)}$ and noting that the sense of the inequality is reversed when $\Delta[K]_{\mathrm{cp}(1)} < 0$, we obtain

$$\left\{\frac{\Delta[Y]_{\mathrm{cp}(1)}}{\Delta[K]_{\mathrm{cp}(1)}}\right\}_{[K]_{\mathrm{cp}(1)}>0} \leqslant \rho^1 \leqslant \left\{\frac{\Delta[Y]_{\mathrm{cp}(1)}}{\Delta[K]_{\mathrm{cp}(1)}}\right\}_{\Delta[K]_{\mathrm{cp}(1)}<0}. \tag{5.24}$$

It is not inappropriate to call a term of the form

$$\left\{\frac{\Delta[Y]_{\mathrm{cp}(1)}}{\Delta[K]_{\mathrm{cp}(1)}}\right\}, \tag{5.25}$$

and more particularly the limits of such terms as $\Delta[K]_{\mathrm{cp}(1)}$ is chosen very close to zero, a 'marginal product of capital', since it is nothing more nor less than a ratio of a change in product and a change in 'capital'. Here we need to distinguish between the left-hand marginal product of capital (the rate of change of product associated with a fall in the input of capital) and the right-hand marginal product of capital (the rate of change of product associated with a rise in the input of capital). The inequalities (5.24) now allow of the following interpretation: *the rate of interest lies between the left- and right-hand marginal products of capital.*

The limits of the left- and right-hand sides of (5.24) as $\Delta[K]_{\mathrm{cp}(1)}$ is chosen very close to zero may or may not be equal because the function relating the maximum 'product' to be obtained to the input of 'capital' may not be differentiable at the point $[K]_{\mathrm{cp}(1)} = \boldsymbol{p}_k^1 \cdot \boldsymbol{k}_1$. But we are now very well aware that this has nothing to do with capital; it is a general feature of marginal theory where differentiability is not imposed by the fiat of the analyst. If, on the other hand, the limits of right- and left-hand terms are equal then they can only together equal ρ^1 and the rate of interest will be equal to the marginal product of capital.

Our investigations have given us a precise indication of how capital must be measured if its marginal product is to be related to the rate of interest according to the usual formula. There is no need to rehearse again all the points that have been made above about what a marginal theory does and does not say, for they apply just as forcefully to the present instance. To consider just one point, there is of course no implication, even when the rate of interest is equal to the marginal product of capital, that the cause of the rate of interest is the marginal product of capital, any more than in a world where all men wore collars to fit their neck sizes collar sizes would be the causes, or the explanations of, the circumferences of necks. Marshall clearly perceived, as indicated by the passage quoted at the head of this chapter, that an equation between the marginal product of capital and the rate of interest cannot be taken to be a theory of interest. The above is elementary; but the reader may feel some different perplexities to which, if they have been correctly anticipated, we may now turn.

A first worry concerns the method proposed for the measurement of capital. It is clear now that if capital is measured according to (5.21) then its marginal product may be defined unambiguously, at least given the direction of the change in the amount of capital employed, and that it will be related to the rate of interest as any marginal product is related to a price. However, the measure of capital proposed is a parochial one, it is not independent of the point of reference. For some tasks, such as the construction of an aggregate production function, which is the subject matter of ch. 8, we necessarily require a measure of capital which is 'universal' so that no growth path plays a special role in the definition as a point of reference. This raises the problem of the existence of a global aggregation of the capital stocks of different growth paths, but that problem is not at issue in the present argument. *The marginal product of capital is a marginal concept: it does not depend for its justification upon the existence of global capital aggregates*[14]. Surely this is discomforting only to someone who is hoping that the marginal product of capital will be the cause of the rate of interest.

There is another likely cause of bewilderment. In ch. 4 a great deal of trouble

[14] Cf. Swan (1956, appendix). Theorists of the 'Cambridge school' have tended to identify the problem of making clear the meaning of the marginal product of capital with the problem of providing a measure of capital that will serve as an argument in an aggregate production function, so that showing the second task to be impossible in certain circumstances is taken as evidence that the first is impossible. Formally, however, the two problems are distinct. Examples of arguments that entangle one issue with the other are legion: cf. (but only by way of example) Robinson (1971, p. 37) and Kaldor (1966b). An exposition of the Cambridge view is to be found in Harcourt (1972). Lest an overly simple view be taken of the Cambridge argument it is as well that pp. 21 and 45 of that work be compared.

was taken to make it abundantly clear that if anything could be expected to be lower on a capital-rich growth path (although as a matter of fact there is no such expectation in general for any value) it would be the rental of the capital vector and not the rate of interest, because the former is the price of the use of capital (and the analogue of the wage rate of labour). There it was pointed out that the rate of interest is not the cost of using capital which is why, even in a stationary state, there is no implication that a capital-rich economy will not have a higher rate of interest. Now only one chapter later we are relating the marginal product of capital to the rate of interest. What is going on? The answer to this query is not difficult to comprehend. Where there was one capital vector we arbitrarily took one unit of capital to be a vector, chosen at random, the components of which were in the common proportions of all capital vectors, whereupon the price of the use of one unit of capital was $\rho\pi$. We could, however, *for one particular growth path*, so choose units in which to measure capital that π would be equal to 1. In other words, we are free if we wish to choose the unit of capital so that the price of that unit (not its rental) will be one unit of the *numeraire*. Naturally, this can only be done once, we cannot make it true for each growth path. The reason why the rental of capital turns out to be just the rate of interest in the present instance is that one unit of capital has been chosen to be one unit of the *numeraire* so that π in this case is 1 by definition; the unit of capital is £1 worth. Reasoning along these lines many theorists have convinced themselves that this is a necessary feature of the unit in which capital should be measured, not just locally by choice of units at a particular point, but globally. To take this path, however, is necessarily to depart from the idea that capital is a 'real' magnitude on a par with 'real product'. Perhaps this is the correct path to take, but taking it we should not be surprised to arrive at some rather unfamiliar results. To make anything that is not the *numeraire* have unit price by definition is not a step to be taken lightly.

Wicksell, as one might expect, puts the argument very clearly and directly:

> Whereas labour and land are measured each in terms of its own *technical* unit (e.g. working days or months, acre per annum) capital, on the other hand, as we have already shown, is reckoned, in common parlance, as a sum of *exchange value* – whether in money or as an average of products. In other words, each particular capital-good is measured by a unit extraneous to itself. However good the practical reasons for this may be, it is a theoretical anomaly which disturbs the correspondence that would otherwise exist between all the factors of production. The productive contribution of a piece of technical capital, such as a steam engine, is determined not by its cost but by the horse power which it develops, and by the excess or scarcity of similar machines. If capital were also to be measured in technical units, the defect would be remedied and the correspondence would be complete. But, in that case, productive capital would have to be distributed into as many categories as there are kinds of tools, machinery, and materials, etc., and a unified treatment of the rôle of capital in production would be impossible. Even then we should only know the *yield* of the

various objects at a particular moment, but nothing at all about the value of the goods themselves, which it is necessary to know in order to calculate the rate of interest, which in equilibrium is the same on all capital[15].

This, or a similar argument, has been repeated a thousand times, though never as eloquently as in the original statement.

Let us examine the argument of the quoted passage. Wicksell puts very lucidly the point that to measure a productive input in terms of its exchange value is to introduce a theoretical anomaly. He might have gone on to remark that this anomaly is not peculiar to capital. It would be just as anomalous, for example, to measure labour input (whether labour be homogeneous or heterogeneous) in terms of the annual wage bill and there would follow immediately the conclusion that the marginal product of labour time measured in terms of exchange value would not be equal to the wage rate except by purest chance[16]. However, what worried Wicksell about taking an alternative course was that it was not apparent to him how we may be sure that the ratios of the rentals of different perfectly durable capital goods will be equal to the relative prices of those goods, as must be the case in stationary conditions with a single constant rate of interest. To follow Walras in 'deriving the prices of capital goods from their own cost of production' would, according to Wicksell, 'be arguing in a circle' because interest is part of the cost of capital goods.

We have here an outstanding example of a severe difficulty which a number of writers have had in the past. It is one which still afflicts many writers today. It is hard to come to grips with the idea of an equilibrium system as a single entity in which the various magnitudes are so resolved (if indeed there is a unique solution, for which there is no guarantee) so that, except in the most exceptional circumstances, it makes no sense to seek first for the resolution of certain values and hence for the further resolution of another set of values[17]. If taking

---

[15] Wicksell (1934, p. 149).

[16] Consider a very simple example. There is one type of labour, the input of which is L, and one type of land, the input of which is N, and output is a traditional differentiable function $F(L,N)$. The product wage rate will be $\partial F/\partial L$. The exchange value of the labour time used is $V = L\,\partial F/\partial L$. Now

$$\frac{\mathrm{d}V}{\mathrm{d}L}=\frac{\partial F}{\partial L}+L\frac{\partial^2 F}{\partial L^2}. \tag{5.26}$$

Hence,

$$\frac{\partial V}{\partial F}=\frac{\partial F}{\partial L}\frac{\mathrm{d}L}{\mathrm{d}V}=(\partial F/\partial L)\Big/\left(\frac{\partial F}{\partial L}+L\frac{\partial^2 F}{\partial L^2}\right)=\frac{1}{1-\varepsilon}, \tag{5.27}$$

where ε is the elasticity of the schedule of the marginal product of labour.

[17] '. . . the neo-Keynesian critics really cannot be sloughed off as neo-Böhm-Bawerkians, spurning, as Stigler puts it, "mutual determination . . . for the older concept of cause and effect"' (Harcourt, 1972, p. 21). This claim would be more convincing if the immediately following works cited gave some support to it. However, they include the paper by Garegnani, from which the quotation below has been taken.

the view that the mathematical relations of an equilibrium system will usually resolve everything at once is 'arguing in a circle' then so be it, but let there be no doubt that it is not 'assuming what has to be proved'.

We know from the investigation of ch. 4, based on the more general theory of ch. 3, that there will always exist a semi-stationary equilibrium for an economy, given appropriate specifications. From the appendix to ch. 4 we know that a 'stationary' price system is always a possibility for such a state. In this way Wicksell's problem is automatically resolved: we obtain both an intertemporal price system in which producers are in equilibrium; so that the values of marginal products of particular capital goods, if these are defined, as Wicksell supposes them to be, will equal the rentals of these goods; so that the prices of capital goods in each week will be equal to their marginal costs of production, if those are well defined; and, finally, so that all present prices will be falling, as we look to future weeks, at the same proportional rate. This last feature of the equilibrium, as we saw in ch. 4, will guarantee that the rental of a perfectly durable capital good will be $\rho\pi_i$ for the ith such good, where π_i is the price of the good and ρ the common rate of interest.

It seems then that Wicksell's apprehensions were not well founded. He was, however, given these apprehensions, admirably consistent in following them through to their logical conclusions. Thus he rejected the idea that the marginal product of 'capital' could be related to the rate of interest, which he explained by claiming that part of the increased product arising from the increased use of capital would be 'absorbed' by price changes and changes in rents, so that not all the extra product would accrue to 'capital'. Let

$$[K]^i_{\text{vp}} = \boldsymbol{p}^i_k \cdot \boldsymbol{k}^i \qquad (i = 1, 2, \text{etc.}). \tag{5.28}$$

Here, in contrast to $[K]_{\text{cp(1)}}$, as defined by (5.21) the measure of 'capital' is the exchange value of the capital stock, not at the prices of a particular reference path, growth path 1, but at the prices of the particular path with which the capital vector $\boldsymbol{k}$ is associated. The subscript vp reminds us that capital is here measured in variable prices. Evidently,

$$\begin{aligned}\Delta[K]_{\text{vp}} &= \boldsymbol{p}^2_k \cdot \boldsymbol{k}^2 - \boldsymbol{p}^1_k \cdot \boldsymbol{k}^1 = (\boldsymbol{p}^2_k \cdot \boldsymbol{k}^2 - \boldsymbol{p}^1_k \cdot \boldsymbol{k}^2) + (\boldsymbol{p}^1_k \cdot \boldsymbol{k}^2 - \boldsymbol{p}^1_k \cdot \boldsymbol{k}^1)\\ &= \boldsymbol{k}^2 \cdot \Delta \boldsymbol{p}_k + \boldsymbol{p}^1_k \cdot \Delta \boldsymbol{k} = \boldsymbol{k}^2 \cdot \Delta \boldsymbol{p}_k + \Delta[K]_{\text{cp(1)}}.\end{aligned} \tag{5.29}$$

Substituting for $\Delta[K]_{\text{cp(1)}}$ into (5.23) one obtains

$$\Delta[Y]_{\text{cp(1)}} - \rho^1[\Delta[K]_{\text{vp}} - \boldsymbol{k}^2 \cdot \Delta \boldsymbol{p}_k] \leqslant 0, \tag{5.30}$$

so that

$$\left\{\frac{\Delta[Y]_{\text{cp}(1)}}{\Delta[K]_{\text{vp}}}\right\}_{\Delta[K]_{\text{vp}}>0} \leqslant \rho^1 - \frac{k^2 \cdot \Delta p_k}{\Delta[K]_{\text{vp}}} \leqslant \left\{\frac{\Delta[Y]_{\text{cp}(1)}}{\Delta[K]_{\text{vp}}}\right\}_{\Delta[K]_{\text{vp}}<0}. \tag{5.31}$$

Compare these inequalities to (5.24).

One might appropriately refer to

$$\left\{\frac{\Delta[Y]_{\text{cp}(1)}}{\Delta[K]_{\text{vp}}}\right\} \tag{5.32}$$

as the marginal 'real product' of 'exchange-value capital'[18], and so arrive at the conclusion of Wicksell's investigation. *The marginal product of exchange-value capital is neither, except by chance, equal to the rate of interest, nor is it even related to the rate of interest by the inequalities of general marginal theory.*

There is, of course, nothing surprising about this observation. We have seen how the marginal product is to be defined if there is to exist any presumption that it might be equal to the rate of interest, and the definition is not that embodied in (5.31). This is to be expected because the latter definition does not spring from, and is not in accord with, the magnitudes that revolve in the minds of price-taking managers of firms. The presence of an extra term in the middle of the inequalities (5.31) has been called 'the price-Wicksell effect' by Robinson. In general, we know nothing about the sign of the term

$$(k^2 \cdot \Delta p_k)/\Delta[K]_{\text{vp}}, \tag{5.33}$$

which measures the revaluation of the capital stock of growth path 2 that would follow upon changing from the price system of growth path 1 to 2 as a ratio of the change in capital measured in variable prices. In the model originally considered by Wicksell, in which capital consisted exclusively of maturing wine, growing trees, or the like (the point-input point-output model), it so happens that the price-Wicksell effect is always positive but this is a very

---

[18] The above derivations raise an issue which was not confronted by Wicksell because he confined his attention to stationary states: namely, if capital is to be measured in exchange value why is product not measured in exchange value, especially as, in a growing economy, net product includes accretions to the capital stock? We leave it as an exercise to derive the analogue of (5.31) where the numerator is to be $\Delta[Y]_{\text{vp}}$. It makes no difference to the present discussion which depends only on the presumption that the middle term of the inequalities is not necessarily ρ^1.

special case[19]. In general, as Wicksell discovered when he came to study late in life the model proposed by his pupil Dr. Akerman, the price-Wicksell effect may be of either sign. Special cases apart, economic theory cannot be expected to pronounce on the signs of terms like (5.33).

Thus Wicksell's analysis is directed towards a question about which we may now confidently declare that it will allow of no general unambiguous answer. Imagine two economies, each in semi-stationary growth, which *ab initio* differ only in one regard. In each economy the citizens are determined to hold capital goods of a specified value in terms of the *numeraire* and they will not be deflected from this aim no matter what equilibrium comes about. However, in economy 2 the citizens desire to hold a higher *numeraire* value of capital than the citizens of economy 1. How specifically will the economies differ with regard to total product produced? We have here an extremely contrived theoretical exercise, for it is evident that no convincing specification of the demand for capital would lead to a totally inelastic demand for a particular *numeraire value.* However, let that be. If the two economies were to end up, extraordinarily, with the same price systems and the same interest rate (the price-Wicksell effect would then be zero) then, evidently, the greater desire of the citizens of economy 2 could only be accommodated by their holding more 'capital' measured in the common price system of the two states. Hence, $\Delta[K]_{cp(1/2)}$ would be positive and the greater desire to hold 'capital' would, in Wicksell's terminology, be 'productively absorbed' by real capital accumulation[20]. However, price changes which have the effect of increasing

---

[19] Here is Wicksell's model. Let the amount of 'wood' in the trees that the labour force can plant be $f(t)$ when the trees are t years old. A 'forest owner' chooses T, the age at which a tree is felled, so as to maximize $e^{-\rho T}f(T)$, where ρ is the rate of interest; so that T will satisfy

$$\frac{1}{f(T)}\frac{df(T)}{dT} = \rho. \tag{5.34}$$

Then

$$K = \int_0^T f(t)e^{-\rho t}\,dt \tag{5.35}$$

is the present value of all the trees in a stationary state in terms of wood; this is our $[K]_{vp}$. Let Y be net output, here $f(T)$. Now

$$\frac{dY}{dK} = \frac{dY}{dT}\frac{dT}{dK} = \frac{df(T)}{dT}\frac{1}{f(T)}e^{\rho T} = \rho\, e^{\rho T} > \rho. \tag{5.36}$$

Hence, the rate of interest is less than the 'marginal product of "capital"' on account of 'unproductive absorption' $\rho(e^{\rho T}-1)$.

[20] The term 'real capital' is used here to correspond to 'real national income', so that an increase in 'real capital' means an increase in the quantity of capital measured in constant prices. There is no connection with Robinson's (1956) (surely most unfortunate) usage according to which 'real capital' means the exchange value of the capital stock in terms of labour time.

the exchange value of the capital stock in terms of *numeraire* can also help to accommodate the desire of the citizens to hold a capital stock of a specified exchange value and very often the two economies will have different price systems such that the price-Wicksell effect will not be zero. If the price-Wicksell effect is positive then part of the difference between the exchange values of the capital stocks of the two economies will be accounted for simply by 'capital appreciation' which favours the economy with more 'capital' – 'unproductive absorption' in Wicksell's terminology. However, and it is here that the point-input point-output model is deceptive, 'absorption' can equally well be 'productive'! If the price system of economy 2 assigns a lower exchange value to $\boldsymbol{k}^2$ than the price system of economy 1, then part of the larger holdings, in terms of exchange value, of economy 2 will have made good the negative price-Wicksell effect and the rate of interest will be larger than the 'marginal product of "capital"' on that account.

The foregoing argument is an absorbing one and worth recounting, both because of its historical interest, and also because it indicates the manner in which the influence of different holdings of capital are reflected in the exchange value of the capital stock; through 'real effects' and 'valuation effects'. It should be clear now what kind of question Wicksell's analysis serves to answer. Wicksell was wrong in his belief that his argument gave cause to doubt the validity of the marginal principle, properly understood; although it seems that, given his exaggerated idea of what a marginal principle might be expected to do, he was right to conclude that the marginal product of capital could not do it. And on one thing Wicksell was very clear: that to measure capital in terms of its exchange value for the *numeraire* is an anomaly. One might go further; it is something from which an economist should instinctively recoil. For to say that the 'quantity of capital' embodied in a collection of capital goods is to be measured by the exchange value of that collection of goods is to countenance the notion that a given collection of capital goods, precisely specified, item by item, is to count as a different 'quantity of capital' if it happens that prices so differ as to make the exchange value of that stock different. To proceed in this manner is to wilfully entangle quantity effects inextricably with price effects[21]. We have seen that where marginal analysis is concerned there is no necessity for this. There exists a 'local' measure of capital, which is all that marginal analysis demands, such that the marginal product of this capital, where well defined, is equal to the rate of interest on a

[21] Strangely no one seems to want to measure capital in terms of exchange value when there is only one kind of capital good, although if it is a good idea to measure capital in exchange value, why forgo the opportunity when all capital consists of one type of machine?

semi-stationary growth path, with the standard inequality relations holding where marginal product cannot be defined unambiguously. That is all that can be derived for any factor and so it is with capital.

If we insist on measuring quantities in terms of exchange value then marginal products in terms of those quantities will not correspond to prices, even when marginal products are well defined. This has nothing to do with capital or the heterogeneity of capital; there just is no presumption that the ratio of the change in product to the change in the exchange value of an input will bear a meaningful relation to any price.

The reader should understand that there is not agreement among economists on any of the foregoing points. Thus, for example, Garegnani can write (1970, p. 422):

> To give a marginal product equal to the *rate of interest*, 'capital' must be conceived as a magnitude homogeneous with the product and must therefore be measured as the *value* of the means of production and not in physical units as is the case with labour or land. This value, however, like that of other products, changes as the rate of interest and the wage rate change. Consequently, the 'quantities' of capital per worker corresponding to each system – and with it the 'production function' where those quantities appear – cannot be known independently of distribution. Every conclusion reached by postulating the contrary cannot be defended on *that* ground. And we have just seen that *one* of those conclusions is invalid: no definition of 'capital' allows us to say that its marginal product is equal to the rate of interest[22].

A full reconciliation of the argument of this chapter with the above passage would seem to be hard to achieve. It is, of course, absolutely correct that to give a marginal product of capital equal to the rate of interest capital must be so measured that a collection of capital goods, whose exchange value at the point at which the marginal product is desired is one, should count as one unit of capital. But this is not to say that the marginal unit of capital should be conceived as an increment of exchange value, as it was conceived by Wicksell. That is not the same thing at all and it is not demanded of us. Indeed, fluke cases apart, it is positively prohibited to us if we do want the marginal product of capital to relate to the rate of interest according to the usual equality or inequalities of marginal theory. The opening of the quoted passage seems to assert the exact opposite of the true state of affairs. All this has been known since Wicksell.

---

[22] The paper goes on to claim that '. . . traditional theory – reduced to its core as the explanation of distribution in terms of demand and supply – rests in fact on a single premise. This premise is that any change of system brought about by a fall of the rate of interest must increase the ratio of "capital" to labour in the production of the commodity . . .'. If by 'explanation of distribution in terms of demand and supply' the author means equilibrium theory (say of the intertemporal economy) then he has dreamed up this condition. That theory does not need aggregate notions like 'capital'. The premise to which he refers is not needed and is not used in deriving equilibrium of demand and supply. See above, ch. 3.

The closing sentence of the passage might also seem to be at variance with our earlier conclusions but here a reconciliation is not far to seek. It is evident that the author is concerned with global measures of capital and not just the local measure that a marginal theory requires, for he refers explicitly to capital as an argument of a production function. As our investigations have made abundantly clear, one cannot repeatedly, for one state and then another, keep choosing units of capital so as to make the exchange value of one unit of capital be one unit of the *numeraire*. Hence, even if a meaningful global capital aggregate could be constructed (and when we come to investigate that possibility in chs. 7 and 8 our conclusions will not be encouraging for the success of the enterprise) we could not expect the marginal product of aggregate capital to be *everywhere* equal to the rate of interest. If nothing else made this clear, a consideration of the simple case in which there is only one kind of capital basket would do so. There capital aggregation is trivial – the weight of the capital stock would provide a meaningful capital aggregate – but the exchange value of one unit of capital will typically vary. Thus, the rental of a unit of capital, which under appropriate conditions would equal the marginal product of capital, will not, except perhaps at one or two points, be equal to the rate of interest.

Wittgenstein once asserted that one of the tasks of philosophy is to heal the philosophical illnesses that afflict people when they try to philosophize. A similar claim might be advanced for economic theory and particularly for marginal analysis. As has been remarked, marginal analysis is not necessary to the description of an economy in equilibrium. It is not generally valid – depending as it does in the usual statements on the differentiability of functions that cannot always be shown to possess that property. It is of no use by itself in isolating the causes of factor earnings. And to top all this, it gives rise to misapprehensions and controversy. However, marginal ideas are a fact and they cannot be wished away. Moreover, it would be wrong to want to wish them away because properly understood, they can be useful and where there are 'philosophical illnesses' concerning marginal concepts their influence cannot easily be confined just to that particular field. So, while from one point of view, this whole chapter has been an unnecessary detour, it may yet be justified.

6

The Cambridge model

The comprehensive vision of the universal interdependence of all the elements of the economic system that haunted Thünen probably never cost Ricardo as much as an hour's sleep. His interest was in the clear-cut result of direct, practical significance. In order to get this he cut that general system to pieces, bundled up as large parts of it as possible, and put them into cold storage – so that as many things as possible should be frozen and 'given'. He then piled one simplifying assumption upon another until, having really settled everything by these assumptions, he was left with only a few aggregative variables between which, given these assumptions, he set up simple one-way relations so that, in the end, the desired results emerged almost as tautologies.

J. SCHUMPETER, *History of Economic Analysis* (1954)

There are two features of an economy growing through time that make the study of its development a taxing enterprise. One is that, usually, each week will be significantly different from the one that went before, so that a complete account of what occurs must detail separately the events of each week and, furthermore, the analysis must take into account the implications for individual behaviour and expectations of the fact that each week will bring with it new events, to which past experience cannot be a perfect guide. We have encountered already the most usual means of 'getting round' these difficulties: the analysis is confined to a semi-stationary state, so that each week is, in its essentials, exactly like every other, when it becomes less unreasonable to suppose that expectations might be both confident and correct.

Another feature which makes analysis difficult is that, typically, everything in the economy depends upon everything else and it is not possible to determine any quantity without doing most of the work needed to determine every quantity. In other words, a model of the economic system does not normally *decompose*. It is not usually allowed to the analyst to divide the primitive postulates into two classes, A and B; such that certain variables can be determined from postulates included in class A alone without regard to, or without even a knowledge of, the postulates of class B. Economists, however, are understandably tempted by the idea of an abbreviated list of the determinants of a particular quantity. It is not very interesting or very enlightening to be told on enquiring into the causes of the real wage of unskilled labour, or of the price of soap, to be presented with a list of all the primitive postulates of a model. However, there is no escape from this response (if we rightly insist upon including in lists of causes only primitive postulates) unless the model proposed decomposes.

The classic example of a decomposable model of the distribution of income is the one associated with the statistical investigations of Cobb and Douglas (1928) and the subsequent theoretical work that has made use of the Cobb–Douglas production function. If output depends upon 'capital' and labour through a differentiable constant-returns-to-scale function $F(K,L)$, and if factor earnings correspond to marginal products, the share of each factor in the product will be equal to the elasticity of output with respect to that factor, evaluated at the point concerned[1]. Now assume that the elasticity of output with respect to each factor is *constant*, which values are primitive postulates of the model, and then *these values alone are the causes of relative shares*. Here the analyst can say: so long as the economy has a Cobb–Douglas production function, then tell me only the parameters of that function and I will tell you relative shares in equilibrium. I do not need to know the rate of growth of the economy, saving behaviour, or whatever; just those parameters. Now this instance is a trivial one and we shall not examine it further. As it stands it is essentially a one-good model, for no interpretation of 'capital' is offered if there is more than one kind of output. Furthermore, the decomposition is manifestly the most special case, the function must take just that particular form. Immediately it does not do so everything must be solved to arrive at even a relative share. The decomposition here is, moreover, of a very unsubtle kind: either a relative share is a constant governed by a single primitive postulate, or else it is a variable governed by the complete solution of the model. Uninteresting though it is, the instance of the Cobb–Douglas production function serves well to illustrate a point: it is not impossible that some variables may be solved for from just part of the complete system. It is only 'typically' or 'generally' that everything depends upon everything else.

We turn now to another instance where the equilibrium of the semi-stationary state decomposes, and this is a far more interesting example. The construct is usually associated with economists of the 'Cambridge school', but the case has become a standard reference point for all theorists, and it should not be

---

[1] Considering labour, for example, the wage rate W will be equal to $\partial F/\partial L$. The share of wages in output will be

$$\frac{L}{F(K,L)}\frac{\partial F}{\partial L}. \tag{6.1}$$

thought that all members of that school adhere firmly to the simple model to be considered in this chapter. In the Cambridge model the irritations arising from the interdependent network of influences are circumvented by some special assumptions that have the effect of allowing the state of the economy to be solved out and discussed in three distinct stages:

(1) The rate of interest (here equal to the rate of profit) is determined by a relation, pertaining to the whole economy, between the need for investment funds[2] implied by the growth of the economy and the supply of these funds which is related to the level of profits. From this first step is derived the rate of interest.

(2) Given the rate of interest it is possible to determine, independently of demand conditions and the growth rate, the costs of production of all goods in terms of labour (i.e. in wage units) and the techniques of production that the economy will use. From this step come relative prices.

(3) Finally, demand conditions may be brought in to determine the rates of output, given the techniques of production; and hence the capital–output ratio in value terms for the whole economy; and hence, given the rate of interest, the share of profit in total output. In this chapter we will be concerned mainly with the first step of the above solution procedure. The conditions for the second and third steps will be the subject matter of ch. 11.

Here is an undeniably attractive scheme and it is not surprising that economists have found it absorbing. As a decomposable structure it has the advantage of simplicity; given a change in specification one ascertains which steps in the solution procedure are affected and it is then not difficult to work out the consequences and, particularly where an early step is involved, to obtain definite conclusions. It must be said that the assumptions that are needed to support this edifice are so restrictive that it is difficult to attach a great weight to it. But in the study of these assumptions, and the roles that they play, there are useful lessons to be learnt.

One needs in the first place assumptions that will allow of the possibility of semi-stationary growth. We have seen already, in ch. 4, what these assumptions are. Included among them is the assumption that the availability of every input that is not a produced input grows at rate γ, the rate of economic growth. As was then observed, this gives rise to difficulties where there is more than one non-produced input and, for this reason, it was not easy to give a convincing account of semi-stationary growth. In the case of the Cambridge model this point need not detain us; it is absolutely essential for the *second*

[2] The term is used loosely; it suggests the intervention of a monetary medium and, while there is nothing against this, the analysis does not make explicit any such institution.

step that there should be only one homogeneous non-produced input, which we will identify with labour. Is the growth rate γ then the growth rate of the labour supply? In the case of the semi-stationary growth equilibrium of ch. 4 this was the case; the growth rate of the economy was the growth rate of the supply of the services of (in that case all) non-produced factors. However, that feature of an equilibrium was definitional, the conditions for equilibrium entailing as they did that there should be neither involuntary unemployment of factor services, nor any excess demand for them. Writers of the Cambridge school have toyed with the idea of a 'disequilibrium' semi-stationary state with employment not equal to the forthcoming supply of labour. For the first stage of the three-step solution what is necessary, and all that is necessary, is that the growth rate of the system should be a datum, or that it should depend only on the rate of profit. For the time being let us assume that labour is fully employed in the semi-stationary state, for it is not entirely clear that any other assumption is viable for that circumstance, but let us keep track of some alternative specifications as we proceed.

If full employment of the labour supply is to be assumed then it is strictly necessary, if the delicate three-step solution structure is to be preserved, that the forces governing the growth of the labour supply should not include real wage levels. For if, as the classical economists assumed, the growth of the labour supply were to be responsive to the level of wages, there would be no amelioration of the complexities arising from interdependence. One cannot solve at the first step for the rate of interest, from a relation involving the growth rate γ, if that growth rate is itself dependent upon every feature of the complete solution. However, it is possible and imperative to make some concession to the old classical view in the recognition that there are standards of life so impoverished that, were they to be attained, a continued growth of population could no longer be forthcoming. In terms of the equilibrium models of the previous chapters this corresponds to a reformulation of the assumption that every household must be able to attain a point in its consumption set. Here we suppose that only if a subsistence level of consumption is attained will growth at rate γ be possible. What conditions must be satisfied for a solution that places each working household within its subsistence set? Happily the required condition, which will be established below, is a simple one: the rate of interest must not be too high.

Given a known growth rate of the economy the next requirement is a relation between the rates of investment and interest. There is more than one possibility here, and in later chapters some of these will come under examination. For the present, the assumption that gives to us the first step in the three-step solution is: *all investment is financed out of profits and an invariable fraction of profits is used to finance investment*. This is the basic assumption in its most direct form; there are various more or less equivalent formulations, usually in terms of savings. The above formulation, however, is a direct statement of what is demanded of this assumption; namely, that the value of investment be proportional to the total value of profits. Obviously one wants to give some intelligible economic content to the idea that investment and profits might be so related, at the very least a sketch of the mechanism that brings about this result. This has been done most commonly by means of the so-called '*classical*' *savings assumption*[3]. Under this assumption all income accruing to labour is spent immediately on consumption goods – the only source of saving is profits. And the relation between saving and profits is of the very simplest kind; the amount of profit saved is a constant fraction of the total, denoted π where $0 < \pi \leqslant 1$. We exclude $\pi \leqslant 0$ (i.e. no saving, or dissaving related to profits) but for plausibility, not because the analysis demands it.

Compare the accounting conventions given in (4.12) above. Profit in the present context is net product less the cost of non-produced factors (here only labour). Thus saving in week t is

$$\pi\{\boldsymbol{p}_c \cdot \boldsymbol{c}_t(1+\gamma) + \gamma \boldsymbol{p}_k \cdot \boldsymbol{k}_t - w(1+\rho)\lambda_t\} = \pi P_t = S_t, \qquad (6.2)$$

where λ_t is the labour employed in week t and P_t is profits in week t.

Without for the moment examining this assumption let us look at once at how it is used. If semi-stationary growth at rate γ, with labour fully employed, is to be possible, then saving and investment plans must be consistent at full employment. From the 'classical' savings postulate it is known that savings will be proportional to profits. Denote by I_t the rate of investment in week t. Then

$$I_t = \gamma \boldsymbol{p}_k \cdot \boldsymbol{k}_t = \pi\{\boldsymbol{p}_c \cdot \boldsymbol{c}_t(1+\gamma) + \gamma \boldsymbol{p}_k \cdot \boldsymbol{k}_t - w(1+\rho)\lambda_t\} = S_t, \qquad (6.3)$$

---

[3] This term is used by Hahn and Matthews (1964, pp. 793–794). The reference is to the 'Ricardian antecedents' of the assumption. Compare this passage from the famous ch. XXXI, 'On Machinery' (Ricardo, 1953, p. 396):

'I have before observed, too, that the increase of net incomes, estimated in commodities, which is always the consequence of improved machinery, will lead to new savings and accumulations. These savings, it must be remembered are annual, and must soon create a fund, much greater than the gross revenue, originally lost by the discovery of the machine, when the demand for labour will be as great as before, and the situation of the people will be further improved by the increased savings which the increased net revenue will still enable them to make.'

The idea did not become of major importance in 'classical' economic writings; Mill made nothing of it but it later turns up in the writings of Marx. Notice that Ricardo, along with Say, completely identifies saving with capital accumulation.

whence

$$\frac{\gamma}{\pi} = \frac{\mathbf{p}_c \cdot \mathbf{c}_t(1+\gamma) + \gamma \mathbf{p}_k \cdot \mathbf{k}_t - w(1+\rho)\lambda_t}{\mathbf{p}_k \cdot \mathbf{k}_t} = \frac{P_t}{\mathbf{p}_k \cdot \mathbf{k}_t}. \tag{6.4}$$

Now, if we further assume that there is constant returns to scale in all productive activities, so that profit is just an interest return at rate ρ, then we obtain

$$\mathbf{p}_c \cdot \mathbf{c}_t(1+\gamma) + \gamma \mathbf{p}_k \cdot \mathbf{k}_t - w(1+\rho)\lambda_t = \rho \mathbf{p}_k \cdot \mathbf{k}_t, \tag{6.5}$$

using reasoning parallel to that employed to derive (4.14). Since we must have the linearity assumption (4.13) satisfied for the second step of the three-step solution, we may as well assume it now. However, notice that, even without this assumption, (6.4) gives the ratio of all profits to the value of capital as equal to γ/π in any case. But only when constant returns are a feature of the economy is this ratio, as a rate of profit, of any particular significance. Assuming constant returns, so that (6.5) follows, and combining that equation with (6.4), we obtain

$$\gamma/\pi = \rho \mathbf{p}_k \cdot \mathbf{k}_t / \mathbf{p}_k \cdot \mathbf{k}_t = \rho \tag{6.6}$$

or

$$\gamma = \pi\rho. \tag{6.7}$$

Under the particular conditions of semi-stationary equilibrium growth, at rate γ with the linearity assumption valid, with 'classical' saving, (6.7) is a condition which must be satisfied. But two of the terms that appear in (6.7), γ and π, are known constants under the foregoing assumptions. From this it follows that the value of ρ must be γ/π which is 'given' in the circumstances postulated: this is the first step in the three-step solution procedure. There is only one rate of interest that is consistent with equality between full-employment investment and full-employment saving, so if we assume full-employment growth at rate γ that is what the interest rate must be.

So much for the consequences of assuming 'classical' saving and semi-stationary growth. From just a few assumptions there emerges a theory of the rate of interest. There has been no need to consider production possibilities, except to assume that they satisfy the linearity assumption, although it will later be seen that they must be brought in to pronounce whether γ/π is an admissible rate of interest. There has been no need to consider the structure of final demands, household preferences, or the distribution of income as measured by relative shares. Furthermore, the argument seems not to require any particular institutional or behavioural framework with regard to such matters as price setting or the choice of techniques of production. The interest rate of the smoothly expanding economy with 'classical' saving depends only upon the 'natural' rate of growth γ and the propensity to save out of profits π. Also, so simple is the formula for ρ that one may deduce immediately propositions such as the following: comparing two semi-stationary states, with the same growth rate γ, the state for which the value of π is the larger will have the lower rate of interest ρ.

Note well that there is no theory of the rate of interest embodied in (6.7) which, on one interpretation, is simply an identity. Consider an identity which is an immediate consequence of the saving–investment identity, namely,

$$I_t/K_t = (S_t/P_t)(P_t/K_t), \tag{6.8}$$

where P_t is the value of profits, I_t the value of investment and K_t the exchange value of the capital stock, all in week t. One may now define various 'actual' quantities, subscripting the variable concerned a, so that γ_a, for example, is the actual growth rate of the capital stock in value for week t, and π_a is the ratio of saving to profits, however determined. The identity (6.8) now translates to

$$\gamma_a \equiv \pi_a \rho_a, \tag{6.9}$$

which must be true of any economy in semi-stationary growth, no matter what is assumed of it. Here the actual 'rate of profit' in week t appears in a formula which is true by definition. Now assume that, or adopt assumptions which carry the implication that, *all other terms in the formula are constants.* The rate of profit then follows.

We have here an example of a general analytical method which proceeds by embedding the variable whose magnitude is desired in an equation in which all other terms are deemed by assumption to be constants[4]. The method has been called 'Ricardian' by Schumpeter (1954, pp. 472–473) and 'implicit theorizing' by Leontief (1936). The trouble with this method of treating problems is not merely that things are assumed to be constant which are certainly not constant, though that is indeed a tendency; but also that factors which ought to be analysed and made the subject of economic theories remain unanalysed, or are analysed only crudely.

By way of illustration, consider the specification of π, the ratio of aggregate savings to aggregate profits. For there to be any point in even attempting to

---

[4] Another, famous, example of the method is embodied in the 'crude quantity theory of money' which derives the price level from the identity $M \cdot V = P \cdot T$ by imposing enough assumptions to ensure that M, V and T are constants. Of course, no economist of any standing has gone quite so far as to adopt this theory.

construct an account of the determination of this ratio which is less than a description of the operation of the whole economy, one requires that it be natural to relate savings to profit income and to profit income only. After that has been justified, if it can be justified, one then needs to give an account of what regulates the proportion of profits that is actually saved. Here, however, a danger arises which threatens the whole method; a theory of the determination of π may reach the conclusion that it depends upon many variables from among the whole set of values that the model must determine. Perhaps, for example, π depends, among other things, upon ρ – then already the simple formula for ρ becomes more intricate. If π were to depend, say, upon the share of profit in total income, then there can no longer be any question of calculating ρ as a first step towards the solution of the whole system. The temptation in this situation is to assume that there is a certain 'propensity to save out of profits' and to denote this value by a constant π. The consequence of falling in with this approach is that the sources of saving are treated in a mechanical and superficial manner[5]. The habit of assuming 'propensities to save', here meaning given fractions of income or profit, has badly infected the theory of economic growth, so that the assumption that ratios of saving to other quantities are given constants is quite usual. Of course, there must be a propensity, *ex post*, in that a certain proportion of income or profit will be saved in the solution to the model. But to assume such a ratio constant in advance is to take as given something that ought to be the subject of economic analysis[6].

Robinson has proposed a model (1962, pp. 34–59) (cf. Kahn (1959)) which gives a broader interpretation to eq. (6.7), while still allowing this equation, on its own, to determine the rate of profit. As we have seen, what is basic to the first step of the three-step solution of the Cambridge model is that the rate of profit (or the rate of interest if this is the same value) should appear as the only unknown in an equation of the type (6.7). Just how it appears, so long as it allows of at least one solution, is a matter of secondary importance. As a consequence of this observation we may note that either the growth rate, or the proportion of profits saved, may be dependent upon the rate of profit without destroying anything but the simplicity of the foregoing argument. In Robinson's construct the rate of growth of the economy depends not upon

---

[5] Naturally these comments apply just as much if the propensity to save is related to income and not to profits.

[6] The author's own work is as much subject to this stricture as anyone else's; and if assuming a constant propensity to save out of *gross income* is much worse even than assuming a constant propensity to save out of *net income*, as arguably it is, then his paper 'On putty clay' (Bliss, 1968) is a particularly bad example.

an exogenously given rate of growth of labour, but rather upon the willingness of producers to accumulate capital in the light of the rate of profit that they realize. Apart from giving us an interesting model in its own right, a consideration of this example is valuable in throwing light on the relation between the rate of profit and the rate of interest.

Let the rate of interest be interpreted as the supply price of riskless capital, so that someone who wants to borrow at this rate must offer first-class security for the loan. If the investments undertaken by firms are felt by lenders to be riskless[7] then the firms will be able to borrow at the rate of interest and will not look for a higher return at the margin. Then, under the linearity assumption, the rate of profit on capital which will accrue to firms in semi-stationary conditions will be the rate of interest, no more and no less. In a world in which the outcome of investment is felt by the firm, or by those who lend to the firm, to be uncertain – which is to say in reality – the investment itself will not be an adequate security for the loan that suffices to purchase it. If the firm provides some alternative security, and thus takes the risk upon its own shoulders, it will not do so except in the expectation of a higher return on the investment. Or, if the lender bears the risk, he in turn will look to a return over and above the rate of interest on perfectly secured loans. We will look more closely at these ideas in ch. 13, but for the present they can be accepted on the basis of common sense. Imagine now that the rate of interest is simply given to us: there it is, the forces that act upon it have nothing to do with the variables that we are now considering. In this case, variations in the rate of profit are associated with exactly equivalent variations in the differential between the rate of profit and the rate of interest.

Robinson's idea is that changes in this differential affect changes in the willingness of firms to face up to the uncertainty which the act of investment involves and to accumulate capital. Specifically, the rate of growth of a semi-stationary state is related functionally to the rate of profit through this type of influence. The firm, or its creditors, feel investment to be more risky the faster the growth of the firm, perhaps because an increase in the growth rate of an individual firm is perceived as an increase in its growth rate relatively to other firms and so regarded as particularly risky[8]. We may denote the growth which firms would willingly undertake at a rate of profit ρ as $\gamma(\rho)$, where

$$d\gamma/d\rho > 0. \tag{6.10}$$

---

[7] The term 'risk' is here used in its ordinary popular sense, which sense is not the same as the one proposed by Knight (1921).

[8] It might be objected that this assumption is inconsistent with competition and the perfect capital market. Indeed it is, but it is not at all clear that competition in capital markets in the sense that we are assuming it for goods markets is a viable concept. See pp. 325–326.

Now (6.7) becomes

$$\gamma(\rho) = \pi\rho, \tag{6.11}$$

where, as before, π is to be regarded as a constant. So long as we suppose that the solution for γ which will emerge is consistent, at least for some time, with the supply conditions for labour, we can conceive of a semi-stationary growth of the economy in which the growth rate comes not from the growth rate of the labour supply, but rather from the equation (6.11) as an implication of the value of ρ.

Before, where γ was a constant, only one value of ρ could satisfy the condition, but now the matter is more complicated. Let the rate of interest be 0.05 and suppose that $\gamma(\rho)$ is given by

$$\gamma(\rho) = 0.20 - \frac{0.21}{\rho - 0.05}. \tag{6.12}$$

Here capital would be decumulated very rapidly as ρ fell towards the rate of interest, whereas no rate of profit, however high, would induce growth at rate 20% or higher. Let $\pi = 0.6$. Denote the difference between the rate of profit and rate of interest, $\rho - 0.05$, by μ; then only positive values of μ are admissible. In this special case (6.11) becomes

$$0.20 - (0.01/\mu) = 0.6\ (\mu + 0.05) \tag{6.13}$$

or

$$0.6\mu^2 - 0.17\mu + 0.01 = 0, \tag{6.14}$$

which is satisfied by

$$\mu = \frac{0.17 \pm 0.07}{1.2} = \frac{1}{12} \quad \text{or} \quad \frac{1}{5}. \tag{6.15}$$

Thus we have two perfectly admissible solutions, one involving a higher growth rate than the other. In this case the first step of the solution process, as specified by Robinson, gives us a multiplicity of possible rates of profit at which firms would be content with their rate of growth, in the light of the profit earned and the risks involved. At the same time, the saving from profit would just serve to finance investment.

Let us look more closely at this model. Notice first that it is based upon the introduction of risk and the consequences of risk for investment, and this is something that played no role in the semi-stationary state as it was set out in ch. 4. Can one have semi-stationary growth in an economy in which the productive activities take on the character of roulette wheels? If semi-stationary growth is interpreted according to the definition of ch. 4 then the answer would probably have to be a negative one. One could no doubt formally construct an economy in which the sum of firms' productive transformations would be non-random, although each firm would be subject to a random influence on its production, but this is hardly interesting. However, to say this is only to suggest that semi-stationary growth is conceived rather differently by the economists of the Cambridge school. For them the smooth progress of the 'golden age' is reflected in the experience of firms in general, it is not necessarily an attribute of any particular firm or sector. Kahn (1959) has written:

> The fact that in a golden age capitalists' expectations are realised *in the broad* does not exclude the risks involved in the vagaries of technical processes and of consumers' behaviour. For these reasons the risk-free rate of interest would even in a golden age lie below the rate of profit, with which yields on ordinary shares are more comparable since they involve the same kind of risks as physical investment. Imperfections of the financial and capital markets are also likely to be important factors limiting investment. To meet the requirements of a golden age it is only necessary to assume either that the number of capitalists grows at the golden age rate of growth or that the limits on the finance available to each expand on the average at the same rate of growth[9].

This is genuinely aggregative economics of the kind that tries to say something particular and definite about aggregates (or about the representative firm, which is a kind of aggregate) without being in a position to say anything definite about developments for any individual firm. While recognizing that here is a very different method from the one so far adopted let us examine it further.

Consider two golden age paths, on one of which the value of π is larger than on the other. If γ did not depend upon ρ, the golden age growth path with a high value of π would have a proportionately lower value of ρ. Now, allowing ρ to influence the growth rate, let the golden age with a low value of π have a lower value of ρ and a lower growth rate[10]. The central problem for the theory may now be posed in terms of the following question. Why on the golden age path with a low rate of profit (ρ smaller) is the lack of profit manifest in lower risk premiums, with a consequent discouragement of growth, as opposed to a lower riskless rate of interest? The critical issue is of the time-span of the model. At least since Keynes introduced the concept of liquidity preference economists have been well aware of the possibility that the rate of interest might fail to respond to the needs of the current condition of the economy on account of speculative positions being adopted which would have the effect of holding up the rate of interest. But it is hardly worth talking of golden age

[9] The approach is reminiscent of the treatment of firm and industry by Marshall (1920, pp. 377–382). The famous analogy of the forest and the trees that constitute that forest could be adapted easily to the present instance.

[10] There is no necessity for this, but the particular case meets our needs.

growth unless it continues for some considerable time. Is it then reasonable to postulate that the riskless rate of interest will stand at the same level no matter what developments come about and no matter for how long? Even if one were to neglect the effects that might be expected to follow from the involuntary unemployment of labour, with possibly falling wage rates, it would be difficult to accept the conclusions of this model without being satisfied that a less mechanical treatment of the rate of interest would allow the conclusions to remain. That these considerations make a continuing regular growth of the economy but, with the labour market in disequilibrium, a somewhat problematical construct, is recognized by Kahn (1959) who, however, does not mention changing expectations about interest rates:

> The possibility of a bastard golden age turns on the absence of any progressive tendency towards the easing of the state of finance, and, more particularly, towards a lowering of rates of interest and of yields on ordinary shares. If, for example, money-wage rates tend to fall progressively under the pressures of unemployment or the quantity of money tends to rise faster than money wages or the monetary authority in the face of unemployment deliberately makes credit progressively cheaper, there will be such a progressive tendency and this will undermine the equilibrium of the bastard golden age.

In seeking to get away from the full-employment semi-stationary state the Cambridge theorists have no doubt been repelled by the evidently 'classical' aspect of that edifice. However, this aspect is not a fortuitous feature of the construct. On the contrary, it must seriously be questioned whether the sources from which involuntary unemployment of labour, or other factors, spring are not foreign to the economy in which 'expectations are realized in the broad'. Keynes (1936, p. 293) drew a distinction between 'the theory of stationary equilibrium and the theory of shifting equilibrium – meaning by the latter the theory of a system in which changing views about the future are capable of influencing the present situation'. The theory of shifting equilibrium derives its importance precisely from the fact that the conditions of complex market economies subject to continuous change in knowledge, tastes and population are not conducive to the attainment of semi-stationary growth. And even if the underlying structure allowed semi-stationary growth we have as yet no theory that predicts the realization of that state. Because it seems doubtful whether the idea of involuntary unemployment in stationary conditions is a viable theoretical notion we will return now to the consideration of an economy in semi-stationary growth with its labour force fully employed. In that case a question which arises is whether the model for which the rate of interest emerges from (6.7) is a particular instance of the model of semi-stationary growth that was presented in ch. 4, or whether this specification demands a different type of model. The answer to that question turns on the determinants of saving in semi-stationary growth, and that is an issue to which we have neglected so far to give explicit consideration. However, that consideration is now becoming urgent, for which reason we turn to it at once.

First consider the intertemporal equilibrium of ch. 3. The hth household chooses a consumption plan in the form of a vector $\bar{x}_h - x_h(p, I)$ which satisfies the budget condition

$$p \cdot x_h(p, I_h) + I_h \geqslant 0, \tag{6.16}$$

where the plan and the prices are to be interpreted as covering dated quantities, so that the condition appears exactly as (2.2) but with a broader interpretation. Denoting the net sales vector of week t by x_h^t, and the present value in terms of the *numeraire* of transfers to the household in week t by I_h^t, we may write the budget condition in the 'long-hand' form as

$$\sum_{t=1}^{T} \{p_t \cdot x_h^t + I_h^t\} \geqslant 0. \tag{6.17}$$

As was indicated in ch. 3, there is only one budget condition and that condition carries no implication that an individual term of the series whose sum is given in (6.17) will not be negative. Thus if

$$p_t \cdot x_h^t + I_h^t > 0 \tag{6.18}$$

for week t, the household is consuming less for that week in terms of present value than the present value of all credits in its favour for that week – the household is dissaving. If, on the other hand,

$$p_t \cdot x_h^t + I_h^t < 0, \tag{6.19}$$

the household is a net saver in week t.

It follows that the saving behaviour of households is governed, as is the distribution of their expenditures between various goods inside one week, by the preference orderings. To take the investigation of this idea further we need to resolve an ambiguity which arises from the attempt to interpret a semi-stationary state as a special case of the intertemporal equilibrium of ch. 3: namely, if the semi-stationary state is an intertemporal equilibrium is there a finite horizon in that case, or does the semi-stationary state continue indefinitely and, what matters, are there individual households or firms whose horizons are unbounded? It is possible to resolve this issue in more than one way without affecting the main conclusions that will follow. For the sake of simplicity, however, we will resolve it in the most straightforward manner by assuming that the household is a mortal entity, and conceives itself as mortal when it comes to planning its future actions, so that the planned consumption vector of any household for the remaining weeks of its life will take the form of a vector with a finite number of components. The growth of the economy will now be associated with a parallel growth in the number of households, but so as to preserve a constant balanced age structure. A theory of saving cast in this type of mould is usually called a *life-cycle theory* (see Modigliani and Brumberg (1970) and Friedman (1957)).

In its most simple formulation the life-cycle model comes up against the problem that 'households' sometimes leave bequests and that in some cases these bequests are very considerable, so that it does not seem at first sight to be accurate to treat the household as planning only with a view to its own life-span. However, bequests are not troublesome for the theory as long as they can be treated as a particular type of 'consumption' that a household has at its disposal, and not as a proxy for the continued planned consumption of an immortal family line. In fact, it is surely for the most part more realistic to think of bequests as coming under the preference ordering of a household as a transfer that it may prefer to its own consumption than to imagine them the wherewithal for a continuation of an infinite plan for the family[11]. In this case bequests are simple to introduce. We suppose that the bequest is given in kind[12], that household h transfers a vector $\boldsymbol{b}_h$, at death, and we modify the budget condition (6.17) to make it read

$$\sum_{t=1}^{T} \{\boldsymbol{p}_t \cdot \boldsymbol{x}_h^t + I_h^t\} \geqslant \boldsymbol{p}_{t_h^\dagger} \cdot \boldsymbol{b}_h, \tag{6.20}$$

where $t_h^\dagger$ is the week at the end of which household h will end its existence Bequests received are part of the I_h^t totals.

Let every household persist for just L weeks, which assumption could be dispensed with, but it is evident that nothing important turns on it. The preference ordering of household h is defined over its lifetime consumption sequence and the real bequest that it leaves behind; that is over arrays of the form

$$\{\boldsymbol{c}_h^1, \boldsymbol{c}_h^2, \ldots, \boldsymbol{c}_h^\theta, \ldots, \boldsymbol{c}_h^L; \boldsymbol{b}_h\}, \tag{6.21}$$

[11] Reference should be made to the interesting and perceptive discussion of these issues by Meade (1968, chs. XII, XIII). In terms of his non-exhaustive taxonomy we are here treating the desire to leave a bequest as a desire *sui generis* – a departure from 'perfect selfishness' which yet does not have the character of 'perfect altruism'.

[12] This may appear to be odd, but something like it seems unavoidable. It does not make sense to assume that the preference relation is over bequests in terms of *numeraire* value without regard to what that value will purchase. If we put the 'money value' of the bequest into the preference ordering then we would have to put in prices as well and that would raise new considerations.

where c_h^θ is the consumption of household h in the θth week of its existence ($\theta = 1, \ldots, L$); that is in week $t_h^\dagger - L + \theta$. Similarly, θ attached to any variable ($\boldsymbol{p}$, $\bar{\boldsymbol{x}}$, etc.) indicates the value of the variable in the θth week of this household's existence. Now following more or less exactly the approach of ch. 2, we may assume that the household, when presented with the sequence of those present value prices which will be current at some time during its own lifetime, chooses from its intertemporal consumption set a lifetime plan,

$$\{c_h^{*1}, c_h^{*2}, \ldots, c_h^{*\theta}, \ldots, c_h^{*L}; b_h^*\}, \tag{6.22}$$

such that there exists no sequence

$$\{c_h^1, c_h^2, \ldots, c_h^\theta, \ldots, c_h^L; b_h\} \tag{6.23}$$

preferred by it to the starred sequence, and satisfying

$$\begin{aligned} &\text{(i)}\ \{c_h^1, c_h^2, \ldots, c_h^L; b_h\} \in \mathscr{C}_h, \\ &\text{(ii)}\ \sum_{\theta=1}^{L} \{p_\theta \cdot (\bar{x}_h^\theta - c_h^\theta) + I_h^\theta\} \geqslant p_L \cdot b_h. \end{aligned} \tag{6.24}$$

If we assume, in line with the approach of ch. 2, that there will always be a unique sequence satisfying the choice condition then it may be seen how household saving and dissaving emerge from a treatment of intertemporal consumption planning that is formally closely analogous to the static consumption theory of ch. 2.

There are three points that deserve mention concerning the theory of saving constructed from the extension of a preference ordering on consumption plans to include consumptions of many weeks, to include also bequests, but otherwise sticking very close to the atemporal theory of consumption choice subject to a budget condition and to a consumption set. Firstly, it should be noted that the theory, by construction, can take no account of the uncertainty of the future and the effect that that uncertainty has on the willingness of households to save. In fact, saving 'for a rainy day' is an important part of saving but a life-cycle theory can throw light only on life-cycle saving. Secondly, it will be noticed that this development of the theory in the direction of intertemporal choice does work the notion of choice subject to a single budget condition very hard, which notion, as we saw in ch. 3, carries with it the implication that every household is perfectly 'creditworthy'. Can we say that all the reasons that make the majority of households very far from perfectly creditworthy will not be present in a semi-stationary state? It seems that there could be no grounds for this claim, although, of course, those reasons which spring from uncertainty about the future would clearly be less important in semi-stationary conditions. Perhaps it would be better to build into a theory of intertemporal household behaviour, even for use in the theory of semi-stationary growth, some limitations on households which would have 'the effect' of prohibiting a household from holding negative net assets when the present value of future labour income is excluded from its assets[13]. This can be done and naturally a slightly different theory is the result. But the point is probably too obvious to need rehearsing here and the theory retains many of the same features; all that happens is that, aside from the overall budget condition, one has in addition a sequence of week-by-week 'solvency' conditions with which the household must comply. Finally, let us examine the role of saving by firms in intertemporal equilibrium. In the atemporal equilibrium the profits of firms were made available to their owners and these profits figured in the budget conditions of households. The same is true in the intertemporal equilibrium and one might suppose, if one wanted to, that a firm would distribute its profit in each week immediately to its owners. However, there is no necessity for this assumption, it is not at all a natural assumption to adopt, and a unique and unambiguous definition of profit on a week-by-week basis would be hard to provide.

The last point is clear: all that matters in the theory of intertemporal equilibrium is the present value of the profits of a firm. Thus, although in (6.17) we have detailed the individual transfers for each week in the form of the I_h^t values, what matters for the budget condition is the sum

$$\sum_{t=1}^{T} I_h^t. \tag{6.25}$$

Thus, if a firm is investing, it makes no difference in the intertemporal equilibrium whether it 'borrows', or whether it uses retained earnings, to finance the investment. The kind of considerations which make these important questions of company finance pertinent are simply not present in the intertemporal equilibrium, in which conditions a firm could announce dividend payments well in advance and have its announcements credited. So in the

---

[13] This is roughly the kind of constraint that faces households in reality. It is not quite accurate to say that households cannot borrow in excess of income but may only sell any assets that they happen to hold; for they usually can borrow, particularly for house purchase, if they can offer a negotiable security for the loan. The assumption that only the present value of lifetime receipts and outlays constrains a household's choice is frequently equated in the literature with something called a 'perfect capital market', on which it seems, by analogy with a perfect commodity market, any actor may transact as he wishes without influencing the terms available to him. A necessary condition for a perfect commodity market is that the commodity be homogeneous so that the name of the seller is of no interest to the buyer and, conversely, it is of the nature of personal loans that there cannot be a perfect market for them in this sense.

intertemporal equilibrium, and so in particular in the semi-stationary state, it is households that 'call the tune' when it comes to saving, not because only households can save, but because when firms save (retain earnings for investment) the ownership rights in those firms appreciate in value along with the new investment and so increase the net worth of the households that share in the ownership of firms, and hence increase their ability to consume if they so wish[14]. Thus there is no reason to expect that an increase in the retention of earnings by firms will lower consumption on the part of households. Now all this is wildly unrealistic and as a matter of fact company saving is without doubt an important independent cause of aggregate saving. But the conditions of semi-stationary growth are wildly unrealistic and, if we are to treat of them as a theoretical exercise, it were better if they were not sweetened by grafting onto them 'realistic' embellishments that are in fact quite foreign to stationary conditions.

It was important that mention was made of the issue of saving by firms because at least one writer has emphasized it in connection with the view that the propensity to save out of profit is larger than the propensity to save out of other types of income. Kaldor has written (1966b, p. 310):

> I cannot of course speak for Dr. Pasinetti, but as far as my own ideas are concerned, I have always regarded the high saving propensity out of profits as something which attaches to the nature of business income, and not to the wealth (or other peculiarities) of the individuals who own property[15].

Everyone would recognize the importance of business income as a peculiar category in working out, for example, the short-run effects of fiscal policy changes. What is less obvious is that the peculiarity of business income allows us to attach to it a high saving propensity (*qua* business income and not *qua* the personal income of wealth owners) for an indefinitely prolonged period.

---

[14] The statement should not be misunderstood. There is no question here of saving causing investment – both are simultaneously determined in the solution of the intertemporal equilibrium. All that is claimed is that company retention policy is not, in this kind of world, one of the influences that act upon saving.

[15] In the model proposed in this paper saving and investment decisions are made quite independently of each other by firms who also issue securities independently of these decisions. The mechanism which then brings aggregate saving into equality with the investment rate of the firms is changes in the market valuation of the securities, which is not associated in any way with the discounted value of the dividends, but settles at that level which will call forth the appropriate level of personal saving. This model is the exact converse of the 'classical' intertemporal equilibrium model. The difficulty with interpreting it as a long-run theory is to understand why the firms persist with an arbitrary and mechanical financial policy, and to see why the institution of fixed-interest borrowing and lending does not arise, which institution would ensure that the value of a security could not be wildly out of line with a reasonable actuarial valuation.

According to another most ingenious line of argument, which we owe to Pasinetti, it is wrong in the context of long-run equilibrium to consider an arbitrary distribution of initial wealth because continued saving at different rates by different groups will lead to redistribution of wealth. Long-run equilibrium will then require that the distribution of wealth itself be stationary and for this it is now known to be necessary *either* that the ratio of aggregate saving to profit be the same as the saving propensity of a group which derives income only from profit *or* that any such group owns a negligible proportion of total wealth. Fortunately, it is not necessary for us to enter here into the shameful controversy, that followed upon the announcement of the above results, concerning the logical standing of the two cases mentioned, because the model is wholly unconvincing on account of its assumptions. It is bad enough to assume propensities to save as if they were personal and group characteristics on the determination of which economic theory could throw no light, but to further assume that these saving propensities then go on forever and independently of income sources or income levels or whatever, and to work these assumptions so hard, is to compound a dubious assumption with a dubious application[16].

If one allows that the rate of saving in a semi-stationary state must be one with which the households are content after taking into account the profits of the firms that they 'own' (which is not to disclaim causes operating on saving that come from the side of the firms but is merely to suppose that these causes will operate via prices and interest rates) then one may learn something about the aggregate saving rate from a consideration of those intertemporal plans that will satisfy the households' preferences, subject to their budget conditions and consumption sets. An exhaustive discussion of all the possibilities here would not be a worthwhile enterprise in view of our present particular concerns. Furthermore, it would be a new enterprise to a very considerable extent because the literature has only considered a few cases which would appear to be very special ones when viewed against the background of our present fairly general construct. We are especially concerned here with that question which the Cambridge model must bring particularly to our notice: namely, under what conditions will the ratio of aggregate saving to profit be a value that is independent of any other solution values, except perhaps the rate of interest or the growth rate?

At this point we encounter at once a serious difficulty. It is very easy, on the one hand, to assume that saving comes from profit and interest income only and that the proportion of this income saved is a constant; the number of

---

[16] The original reference is to Pasinetti (1962).

journal papers and books that have adopted this assumption must by now run into hundreds. To give viable theoretical support to this assumption, however, is a very different matter. One possibility of which advantage has been taken by some writers is to put saving into the preference ordering for each week, along with the competing uses of income, just like any other 'consumption'[17]. Then, for example, if the preference ordering is represented by a utility function linear in the logarithms of the various 'consumptions' expenditure shares will be constants given by the parameters of the utility function so that saving will be a constant proportion of income. If profit and interest income accrues to a completely separate class of individuals from those who earn income from labour or rents, one may assign a different utility function to this group. However, this observation is not very enlightening. To put saving into the utility function, along with bread and cheese, is to wrongly entangle utility with indirect utility. Saving presumably is not desired for the most part as an end in itself, but rather as a means to future consumption or bequest. The basis of the life-cycle approach is just such a treatment of the decision to save. It is almost a necessary consequence of that approach that the rate of saving of any particular household will vary over the course of its life-span. Of course, the saving rate of a group of households of the same type may be constant, just as the reproduction rate of a group may be constant notwithstanding the fact that the reproduction rate of an individual family varies over its lifetime.

The conclusion seems inescapable that the classical saving model is not an appropriate one to a modern capitalist economy. One can imagine an economy divided into two quite distinct social classes – the capitalists on the one hand and the labourers on the other. The labourers may be imagined to live in a traditional extended family system, sharing family income collectively among the young, those of working age and the old. They would then have no need to save for the reason of making provision for old age[18] although they might be encouraged to do so if they could get a positive interest rate. The capitalist class consists of those who are wealthy, interested in the accumulation of property and in passing it on to their offspring. As owners of estates and the entrepreneurs of industrial enterprises they have access to good outlets for their saving so that their saving will respond directly and simply to changes in

---

[17] As is done by Hahn (1965) and Morishima (1969).

[18] Provision for old age does not generate net saving from one household over its whole lifetime because saving during early life is later offset by dissaving in late life (and indeed more than offset if the savings have accumulated at a rate of interest). However, where population growth takes place there are more young households saving than old households dissaving on account of the age structure which characterizes a growing population.

their income. Of course, that income would include a considerable proportion of rent for the use of land and property so that it is not strictly accurate, even in this context, to speak of saving as related solely to profit and interest income. This model, as stylized economic models go, may not be too bad as a representation of the state of England in the eighteenth or early nineteenth centuries, but as an even stylized representation of a modern economy it is simply not adequate.

While it remains true even today that the ownership of wealth is extremely concentrated, so that a great deal of profit and interest income accrues to a small proportion of the population, there have been other changes which have had the effect of altering the roles and forms of wealth, saving and social class. The entrepreneurial function is now very considerably separated from the ownership of wealth, so that profit and interest income, present and projected, is to a great extent the personal income of a propertied class which does not engage in the management of the enterprise capital that it owns. For a number of reasons the propertied classes may save a high proportion of income. Most notably, the desire to bequeath considerable estates is common in this class (and not only where the form of property ownership is the traditional family business or farm). Also it may be that the wealthy are more willing to save – it is sometimes argued that taking a long view is easier with a full stomach.

From considerations such as the above it can be seen that there might be reasons why, even in conditions of semi-stationary growth, a large share of profit would be associated with more saving than would be associated with a low share of profit. The explanation would not reside in a 'high propensity to save out of profit', but rather in a high propensity to save out of the high incomes that would accrue to certain large-scale receivers of profit – the converse of Kaldor's view quoted above. Even here one could hardly be justified in neglecting any consideration of saving arising from non-profit income – for in a modern economy some such is undoubtedly to be found – but most writers have recognized that the classical saving hypothesis is not strictly valid. Of course, if the hypothesis is not valid the simple first step in the solution procedure is denied to us.

Even where the classical saving hypothesis is valid there remains the question of why π, the ratio of saving to profit income, is a constant *ab initio*. Why is it not influenced by the growth rate or the rate of interest or the price of champagne? Assuming saving decisions to come from preference orderings, budget conditions and consumptions sets, the conditions that would have to be satisfied for us to be able to declare the value of π in advance of any knowledge of other magnitudes are clearly very special, although they have not been closely investigated. Most people would not be impressed by a theory that derived the rate of interest from a propensity on the part of households to discount the future assumed a known constant in advance. But the treatment of π adopted by a multitude of writers of different schools is no better.

Despite its manifest elegance the Cambridge model (that is the first stage of its solution that has concerned us in this chapter) is seen to depend so critically upon certain dubious assumptions that no great weight can be attached to it. But as a very special case it remains a useful reference point. No doubt the majority of writers who have made use of the classical savings assumption in conjunction with semi-stationary growth have thought of it as nothing more than a convenient analytical short-cut. However, where the Cambridge school itself is concerned it seems perhaps that a greater significance is attached to the special case, which has sometimes even seemed to be seen as a distinctive theory of interest, an alternative to marginal productivity theory. By now there is no need to explain that this view, were it to be advanced, would be founded in a serious misunderstanding.

As a theory of the interest rate the Cambridge example is not an alternative to a marginal theory. There is no valid 'marginal productivity theory of interest', if by a 'theory of interest' is intended an economic argument which isolates the primitive causes of the rate of interest. In that sense a model like the Cambridge model is doing something that the marginal productivity principle (which is less than a theory of a factor price) could not aspire to do. However, there is no conflict with the idea that the rate of interest *might be* (or *will be* if we are willing to forget that sometimes our functions are not differentiable) equal to the marginal product of capital. The conflict arises in quite another direction and with an approach the aim of which, properly understood, is the same as that of the Cambridge model. The Cambridge approach is in irreconcilable conflict with 'the comprehensive vision of the universal interdependence of all the elements of the economic system . . .' as contained in the semi-stationary growth model regarded as a particular case of the general intertemporal equilibrium. That second approach can assign a value to the rate of interest, but not necessarily a unique value, just as well as the first stage of the Cambridge model. The solution, however, cannot be obtained from a few lines of calculation. So if the assumptions that underlie the Cambridge model could be credited we would all have good reason to be pleased, for it would then be far easier to solve for equilibrium values than it would be if the equilibrium system were not to obligingly decompose and so facilitate our calculations. It only remains to decide whether the assumptions are credible.

Part III

AGGREGATION

7

The aggregation of miscellaneous objects

To say that net output today is greater, but the price level lower, than ten years ago or one year ago, is a proposition of a similar character to the statement that Queen Victoria was a better queen but not a happier woman than Queen Elizabeth – a proposition not without meaning and not without interest, but unsuitable as material for the differential calculus.

J. M. KEYNES, *The General Theory of Employment, Interest and Money* (1936)

This chapter will be devoted to an examination of some of the problems that must be confronted whenever we attempt to compress the description of a collection of inputs or outputs into a simple scalar measure. Such a summary of a heterogeneous collection in a single number will be called an *aggregate*. The enquiry as to the conditions that would allow of the legitimate construction of aggregates will be called *the theory of aggregation*. In ch. 8 we will consider some problems in the theory of aggregation that are peculiar to the theory of capital, but for the present it is not only the aggregation of capital that is our concern. We will also consider explicitly the aggregation of labour and the argument that will unwind turns out to find an application also to the aggregation of outputs.

Let it be understood that the theory of aggregation is a large subject with a considerable literature of its own. It is an area to which some of the most refined minds in economic analysis have given their attention and it would be foolhardy to attempt to lay out the nice and intricate theorems that have resulted in one short chapter. For a full and balanced coverage the reader is referred to one of the specialized treatments of the subject[1].

Our concerns here are more particular than a general discussion of the theory of aggregation. We want to discover what conditions would have to be

[1] As for example the survey volume by Green (1964). Although the theory of aggregation is for the most part a post-war development, its literature is already an extensive one. The interested reader might begin by consulting some of the following references: Fisher (1965); Gorman (1959, 1968); Klein (1946); Leontief (1947); Morishima (1961); Nataf (1948); and Theil (1954).

satisfied to make it legitimate to treat of a certain group of capital goods, or perhaps all the capital goods, as if there were only one quantity, the quantity of capital, instead of the many different quantities that together specify the capital vector. In declaring that to be our concern we set aside quite large tracts of the theory of aggregation as being outside our universe of discourse. Hence, for example, a lot of the literature on aggregation is concerned with the aggregation of functional relations. One asks whether it is possible to combine together the demand functions of a group of households so as to obtain an aggregate demand function for that group which contains as arguments only aggregates of household incomes and other relevant variables. Clearly there is some relation between this type of problem and the problem of aggregating a group of quantities in a single relation, say the production set for the whole economy. But they remain different problems for which somewhat different approaches are demanded.

Given that our concern is with the aggregation of capital it might be wondered why time is to be wasted on the problem of the aggregation of labour, or other inputs. There are two reasons why it is important that the aggregation of labour be examined. Firstly, it is essential to have a point of reference from which to consider the aggregation of capital in a proper perspective. Naturally, it is interesting to know whether the aggregation of capital is in some absolute sense difficult or easy, but that knowledge alone would not serve to evaluate the very widespread idea that the aggregation of capital is not merely difficult, but that it is *peculiarly difficult*. In other words, there are two questions that demand an answer of our investigation: how stringent are the conditions that would allow of capital aggregation, and are these more or less stringent than the parallel conditions that apply to labour or another type of input? A second reason for taking time to examine the case of labour is that it will turn out eventually to have cost very little in terms of time and space. The reason is simple: as far as the problems of this chapter are concerned there are not distinct and separate sets of aggregation conditions for capital on the one hand, and for labour on the other. There is only one condition. If it is satisfied by any group of inputs, then they may be aggregated and treated as if they were one input; if it is not satisfied then aggregation is impossible. This is as true for capital as it is for labour or any other input and that is the most important lesson to be learnt from what follows.

In case the claim that there is nothing distinctive in the problem of aggregating capital seems mysterious or incredible, let it be made clear at once that the reference here is to the aggregation of a capital stock conceived as an arbitrary collection. In other words, we are assuming that the aggregation procedure is to be good for a miscellaneous collection of capital quantities, no matter how implausible, and no matter whether any economy would ever be likely to accumulate the particular collection concerned. A wholly different type of problem presents itself if we want to consider aggregation over a limited set of capital vectors, as for example those that could figure in semi-stationary equilibrium with a constant-rate-of-interest price system. We will refer to the latter type of problem as *stationary-equilibrium aggregation* and to an approach not restricted by the conditions of the semi-stationary state as *general aggregation*. In this chapter we are concerned with general aggregation, while stationary-equilibrium aggregation will be the subject matter of ch. 8.

The distinction between general and stationary-equilibrium aggregation is one that is peculiar to capital as produced means of production. With any other type of input we must assume that the composition of the input vector is something that cannot be restricted, not even if we are considering conditions of long-run equilibrium. This is obvious in the case of 'natural resources', the composition of which depend upon the whim of nature. It would be equally obvious in the case of labour if it were possible to draw a clear boundary between labour and capital. As is well known, this boundary is by no means easy to draw because of the widespread tendency to augment the economic worth of labour by training and other 'investments in human capital'. Similarly, in the case of land, actual land is a mixture of natural resources and capital investments in the improvement and maintenance of the land, so that it is not easy to disentangle a pure element of natural resources. However, while these are real problems, they do not affect the argument that capital goods, wherever they may appear, are different in that their composition, at least in a semi-stationary equilibrium, is not a matter of chance, and because it is not a matter of chance we are presented with a different kind of problem when we come to try to aggregate equilibrium capital stocks.

It is because the components of an equilibrium capital stock are not independent of each other that we argued in ch. 1 that capital in some sense 'invites aggregation' in a way that other groups of inputs do not. It is perhaps in the context of this observation that we should view the supposed difficulty of aggregating capital; so that, even if it could be shown that it is no harder to aggregate capital than it is to aggregate other inputs, the problem of aggregating capital would retain a peculiar significance. To attempt to aggregate capital across semi-stationary equilibria, and to fail, is to have failed in an enterprise for which one might reasonably hope for success. But all this concerns the argument of ch. 8. This is not the moment to embark upon that argument. For the time being we are to be concerned with any collection of capital goods, no matter how made up. So long as capital is so conceived its status as produced means of production is not particularly pertinent to the problem of aggregation. It is for this reason that we will arrive at similar conclusions for capital and other kinds of inputs.

Let us now examine the problem of aggregation formally, bearing in mind that it is general aggregation that is to be considered. Consider the productive transformations of one week of the intertemporal economy. The inputs to production will be represented by two vectors, because we want to distinguish between produced and non-produced inputs. We hold to the convention that a positive number represents the net production of a good, so that inputs are represented by negative numbers. Hence, $\boldsymbol{k}$ is a non-positive vector representing the capital inputs to production. Similarly, $\boldsymbol{z}$ is a non-positive vector representing the use of non-produced inputs. At the start of the following week a vector of goods will be made available and this will be non-negative since these are outputs. We denote the vector of outputs by $\boldsymbol{q}$. In this way we can represent the productive activity of the whole economy for one week by a triple $(\boldsymbol{z}, \boldsymbol{k}, \boldsymbol{q})$. Both types of input and the output are represented by vectors, so that we can imagine that the number of goods distinguished is as large as appropriate.

The set of all transformations of the type $(\boldsymbol{z}, \boldsymbol{k}, \boldsymbol{q})$ that are feasible for the economy as a whole will comprise a set $\mathscr{T}$. We are interested in the possibility of finding a more compressed form of $\mathscr{T}$ in which the vector $\boldsymbol{z}$ will have been replaced by a scalar magnitude, being the aggregate of non-produced inputs. We will assume that all the non-produced inputs are to be aggregated together. It may be, of course, that only some of these inputs will be aggregated together, say all types of labour, but the conditions for this are the same as the conditions for all the inputs that go to make up $\boldsymbol{z}$.

Notice that there is another kind of aggregation from the one which we are about to investigate involved in our starting out from the production set of the whole economy, instead of starting from the production sets of individual productive units or firms. This is an aggregation of functional relations and it represents a type of problem with which we are not now concerned. However, some consideration was given to this type of problem in ch. 4, where it was seen that a group of producers may be treated as if they were a single producer subject to the sum of the individual production sets, provided only that all producers face the same prices and maximize net profit at those prices.

The conditions that will have to be satisfied if we are to form an aggregate depend not unnaturally, but critically, upon the properties demanded of the aggregate. In truth there is no such thing as *the* aggregation problem, or *the* index-number problem; rather there are as many problems as there are conditions that one might require of the aggregate. It is this that gives to the theory of aggregation its richness and interest. The first and most basic property is almost definitional of what we are going to mean by an aggregate.

The aggregate value of z will be a scalar Z which depends only upon z. In other words, the values of $\boldsymbol{k}$ and $\boldsymbol{q}$ should not be relevant to the formation of the aggregate of z. Hence, we postulate a function which relates the aggregate of non-produced inputs Z to z:

$$Z = \phi(z). \tag{7.1}$$

We will now consider some properties of the aggregate of z that might seem interesting or desirable. Having first explained each property we will elucidate the conditions that give rise to it.

Property 1 (perfect representation of production possibilities). There exists a set $\mathscr{T}_0$ *with elements of the form* $(Z, \boldsymbol{k}, \boldsymbol{q})$, *where* Z *is a scalar, such that* $(Z, \boldsymbol{k}, \boldsymbol{q}) \in \mathscr{T}_0$ *and* $Z = \phi(z)$, *if and only if* $(z, \boldsymbol{k}, \boldsymbol{q}) \in \mathscr{T}$.

If property 1 is satisfied there is no loss of information concerning production possibilities from dealing only with the aggregate of z. To determine whether a vector z forms a feasible production plan along with $\boldsymbol{k}$ and $\boldsymbol{q}$ *one does not need to know* z *but only the aggregate of* z. Given $\phi(z)$ one can confirm whether $(\phi(z), \boldsymbol{k}, \boldsymbol{q})$ is in $\mathscr{T}_0$ and if it is then $(z, \boldsymbol{k}, \boldsymbol{q}) \in \mathscr{T}$.

Now it might be remarked that this is rather an odd idea, that absolutely nothing would be lost by aggregation. One normally thinks of aggregation as a necessary evil to reduce reality to manageable proportions, and perfect aggregation might seem not particularly relevant. However, the theory of aggregation has largely, and perhaps inevitably, concerned itself with those cases where aggregation can do everything that a fully disaggregated approach can achieve. The theory of aggregation and the practice are still some way apart.

Theorem 7.1 below throws some light on the conditions that would have to be satisfied for property 1. It is in fact little more than a translation of the property into a closely related statement, but as such it is useful in elucidating what is involved in replacing a heterogeneous collection of inputs by an aggregate. The following definition is needed for theorem 7.1.

Definition 7.1. A collection of subsets of the n-dimensional vector space R^n will be said to be *nested* if, for any two subsets $\mathscr{S}_1$ and $\mathscr{S}_2$ included in the collection, we have

$$\textit{either} \quad `\mathscr{S}_1 \subseteq \mathscr{S}_2' \quad \textit{or} \quad `\mathscr{S}_2 \subseteq \mathscr{S}_1'. \tag{7.2}$$

The implication of definition 7.1 may be illustrated in a Venn diagram as fig. 7.1. Definition 7.1 implies that we may have fig. 7.1. However, we may not have fig. 7.2.

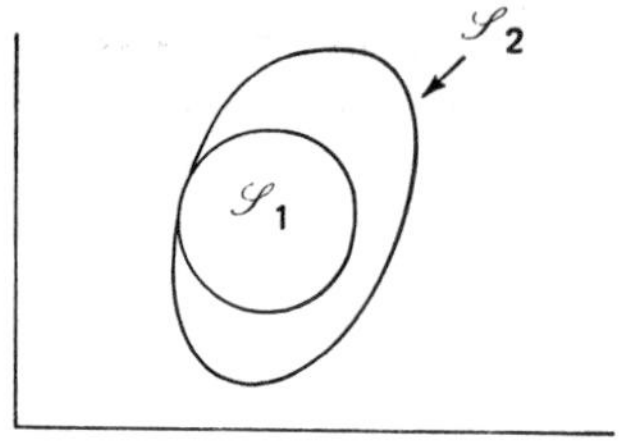

Fig. 7.1.

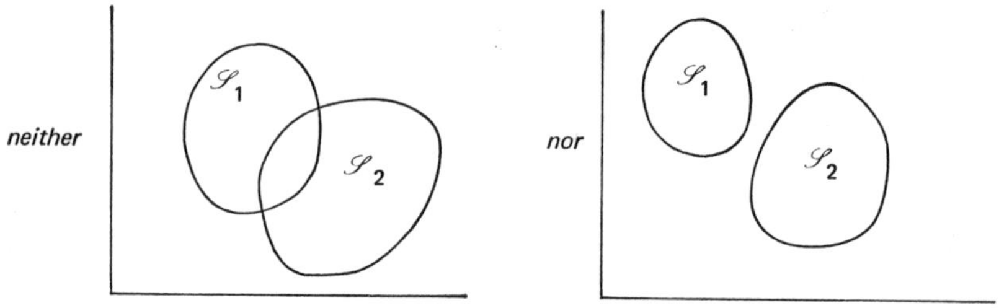

Fig. 7.2.

The proof of theorem 7.1 is unavoidably lengthy. However, the argument consists of several independent steps. The reader who cares to may skip the proof or read on and return to it later.

Theorem 7.1. Property 1 will hold if and only if the sets

$$\mathscr{C}(\boldsymbol{k},\boldsymbol{q})=\{z|(z,\boldsymbol{k},\boldsymbol{q})\in\mathscr{T}\} \tag{7.3}$$

are nested.

Proof.

(i) Necessity. Suppose that there exists a function $\phi(z)$ and a set $\mathscr{T}_0$ such that property 1 holds. We may suppose that $\phi(z)$ is a non-decreasing function of its arguments. We thereby rule out cases where the aggregate has been chosen to decrease with an increase in the components of z, but where an increase in the aggregate is assumed to make a negative contribution to production. Consider two pairs $(\bar{\boldsymbol{k}}_1, \bar{\boldsymbol{q}}_1)$ and $(\bar{\boldsymbol{k}}_2, \bar{\boldsymbol{q}}_2)$. Suppose, contrary to the theorem, that the sets $\mathscr{C}(\bar{\boldsymbol{k}}_1, \bar{\boldsymbol{q}}_1)$ and $\mathscr{C}(\bar{\boldsymbol{k}}_2, \bar{\boldsymbol{q}}_2)$ are not nested. Then there exist

$$\begin{aligned} &z_1\in\mathscr{C}(\bar{\boldsymbol{k}}_1,\bar{\boldsymbol{q}}_1) \quad \text{and} \quad z_1\notin\mathscr{C}(\bar{\boldsymbol{k}}_2,\bar{\boldsymbol{q}}_2)\\ \text{and}&\\ &z_2\in\mathscr{C}(\bar{\boldsymbol{k}}_2,\bar{\boldsymbol{q}}_2) \quad \text{and} \quad z_2\notin\mathscr{C}(\bar{\boldsymbol{k}}_1,\bar{\boldsymbol{q}}_1). \end{aligned} \tag{7.4}$$

That is,

$$(z_1, \bar{k}_1, \bar{q}_1) \in \mathcal{T}, \qquad (z_1, \bar{k}_2, \bar{q}_2) \notin \mathcal{T}$$
and
$$(z_2, \bar{k}_2, \bar{q}_2) \in \mathcal{T}, \qquad (z_2, \bar{k}_1, \bar{q}_1) \notin \mathcal{T}. \tag{7.5}$$

But, on account of property 1, (7.5) implies

$$[\phi(z_1), \bar{k}_1, \bar{q}_1] \in \mathcal{T}_0 \quad \text{and} \quad [\phi(z_2), \bar{k}_1, \bar{q}_1] \notin \mathcal{T}_0 \tag{7.6}$$

so that

$$\phi(z_1) < \phi(z_2). \tag{7.7}$$

However, again on account of property 1, (7.5) also implies

$$[\phi(z_2), \bar{k}_2, \bar{q}_2] \in \mathcal{T}_0 \quad \text{and} \quad [\phi(z_1), \bar{k}_2, \bar{q}_2] \notin \mathcal{T}_0, \tag{7.8}$$

so that

$$\phi(z_2) < \phi(z_1), \tag{7.9}$$

which contradicts (7.7).

(ii) Sufficiency. Suppose that the sets $\mathscr{C}(\boldsymbol{k}, \boldsymbol{q})$ are nested. It is first shown that this implies the existence of a *complete pre-ordering* of the non-positive vectors z. The ordering will be denoted '$\gtrsim$' and it is derived as follows:

$$z_1 \gtrsim z_2 \quad \text{if for all } \boldsymbol{k} \text{ and } \boldsymbol{q}, \text{ `}(z_1, \boldsymbol{k}, \boldsymbol{q}) \in \mathcal{T}\text{'} \Rightarrow \text{`}(z_2, \boldsymbol{k}, \boldsymbol{q}) \in \mathcal{T}\text{'}. \tag{7.10}$$

To establish that (7.10) defines a complete pre-ordering we have to show that the two definitional properties of a complete pre-ordering are satisfied.

(a) *Connectivity*. For all z_1 and z_2, *either* '$z_1 \gtrsim z_2$' *or* '$z_2 \gtrsim z_1$'. Suppose that we do not have connectivity. Then there must exist z_1 and z_2, both non-positive, and two couples $(\boldsymbol{k}_1, \boldsymbol{q}_1)$ and $(\boldsymbol{k}_2, \boldsymbol{q}_2)$ such that

$$(z_1, \boldsymbol{k}_1, \boldsymbol{q}_1) \in \mathcal{T} \quad \text{and} \quad (z_2, \boldsymbol{k}_1, \boldsymbol{q}_1) \notin \mathcal{T}$$
and
$$(z_2, \boldsymbol{k}_2, \boldsymbol{q}_2) \in \mathcal{T} \quad \text{and} \quad (z_1, \boldsymbol{k}_2, \boldsymbol{q}_2) \notin \mathcal{T}. \tag{7.11}$$

But this is to say that

$$z_1 \in \mathscr{C}(\boldsymbol{k}_1, \boldsymbol{q}_1) \quad \text{and} \quad z_2 \notin \mathscr{C}(\boldsymbol{k}_1, \boldsymbol{q}_1)$$
and
$$z_2 \in \mathscr{C}(\boldsymbol{k}_2, \boldsymbol{q}_2) \quad \text{and} \quad z_1 \notin \mathscr{C}(\boldsymbol{k}_2, \boldsymbol{q}_2), \tag{7.12}$$

so that the sets $\mathscr{C}(\boldsymbol{k}, \boldsymbol{q})$ are not nested, contrary to assumption.

(b) *Transitivity*. '$z_1 \succsim z_2$' and '$z_2 \succsim z_3$', $\Rightarrow$ '$z_1 \succsim z_3$'. Transitivity is more or less immediate. For, evidently, if

$$(z_1, \boldsymbol{k}, \boldsymbol{q}) \in \mathscr{T} \Rightarrow (z_2, \boldsymbol{k}, \boldsymbol{q}) \in \mathscr{T} \quad \text{for all } (\boldsymbol{k}, \boldsymbol{q})$$

and

$$(z_2, \boldsymbol{k}, \boldsymbol{q}) \in \mathscr{T} \Rightarrow (z_3, \boldsymbol{k}, \boldsymbol{q}) \in \mathscr{T} \quad \text{for all } (\boldsymbol{k}, \boldsymbol{q}), \tag{7.13}$$

then

$$(z_1, \boldsymbol{k}, \boldsymbol{q}) \in \mathscr{T} \Rightarrow (z_3, \boldsymbol{k}, \boldsymbol{q}) \in \mathscr{T} \quad \text{for all } (\boldsymbol{k}, \boldsymbol{q}),$$

which is what transitivity entails here.

It is now known that (7.10) defines a complete pre-ordering of the vectors of non-produced inputs z. We can give an economic interpretation to the relation '$\succsim$'; '$z_1 \succsim z_2$' can be read as 'z_1 is a smaller input (a larger output) than z_2'. The nested-set property makes it possible to say that one vector of inputs is not less productive than another, regardless of the co-operating inputs and output mix.

Next, note that, provided that $\mathscr{T}$ is a closed set, the pre-ordering $\succsim$ is *continuous*; meaning that, for any given z_0, the sets

$$\{z \mid z \succsim z_0\} \quad \text{and} \quad \{z \mid z_0 \succsim z\} \tag{7.14}$$

are closed[2]. It is known that a continuous pre-ordering may be represented by a 'utility function' ϕ such that

$$z_1 \succsim z_2 \quad \text{if and only if } \phi(z_1) \geqslant \phi(z_2).^3 \tag{7.15}$$

It is further known that ϕ may be chosen a continuous function. The aggregate of z, $\phi(z)$, will be a functional representation of the pre-ordering $\succsim$. The set $\mathscr{T}_0$ may now be specified as

$$(Z, \boldsymbol{k}, \boldsymbol{q}) \in \mathscr{T}_0 \quad \text{if} \quad \exists\, (z, \boldsymbol{k}, \boldsymbol{q}) \in \mathscr{T} \quad \text{such that } \phi(z) \geqslant Z. \tag{7.16}$$

Suppose that $(z_1, \boldsymbol{k}, \boldsymbol{q}) \in \mathscr{T}$. We show that $[\phi(z_1), \boldsymbol{k}, \boldsymbol{q}] \in \mathscr{T}_0$. Suppose not. Then $(z, \boldsymbol{k}, \boldsymbol{q}) \in \mathscr{T} \Rightarrow \phi(z) < \phi(z_1)$. But this contradicts $(z_1, \boldsymbol{k}, \boldsymbol{q}) \in \mathscr{T}$ and (7.16).

---

[2] The details of the proof of this proposition are left as an exercise. Here is a sketch proof of the closedness of $\{z \mid z \succsim z_0\}$.

Suppose that $\{z \mid z \succsim z_0\}$ is not closed. Then there exists a limit point of $\{z \mid z \succsim z_0\}$, z^*, such that z^* is not $\succsim z_0$. Hence $(z^*, \boldsymbol{k}, \boldsymbol{q}) \in \mathscr{T}$ does not imply $(z_0, \boldsymbol{k}, \boldsymbol{q}) \in \mathscr{T}$, although there exist points arbitrarily close to z^* such that $(z, \boldsymbol{k}, \boldsymbol{q}) \in \mathscr{T}$ does imply $(z_0, \boldsymbol{k}, \boldsymbol{q}) \in \mathscr{T}$. This is inconsistent with the assumption that $\mathscr{T}$ is a closed set.

[3] Cf. Debreu (1959, pp. 56–59) and Arrow and Hahn (1971, ch. 4).

Suppose that $(Z, \boldsymbol{k}, \boldsymbol{q}) \in \mathscr{T}_0$, as defined by (7.16), and $\phi(z_1) \leqslant Z$. We show that $(z_1, \boldsymbol{k}, \boldsymbol{q}) \in \mathscr{T}$. Since $(Z, \boldsymbol{k}, \boldsymbol{q}) \in \mathscr{T}_0$, $\exists$ some z_2 such that $(z_2, \boldsymbol{k}, \boldsymbol{q}) \in \mathscr{T}$ and $\phi(z_2) \geqslant Z$. Hence, we have

$$\phi(z_2) \geqslant Z \geqslant \phi(z_1). \tag{7.17}$$

Hence,

$$z_2 \gtrsim z_1. \tag{7.18}$$

Hence,

$$(z_2, \boldsymbol{k}, \boldsymbol{q}) \in \mathscr{T} \Rightarrow (z_1, \boldsymbol{k}, \boldsymbol{q}) \in \mathscr{T}, \tag{7.19}$$

as required. The proof of theorem 7.1 is now complete.

As was remarked, theorem 7.1 is only a translation of the condition for aggregation. It is, however, a rather enlightening translation. We now know that aggregation will prove possible if and only if the sets $\mathscr{C}(\boldsymbol{k}, \boldsymbol{q})$ are nested. Hence, it is possible to examine a production set to see whether this condition is satisfied or not, and if it is satisfied we have a constructive method of arriving at ϕ and $\mathscr{T}_0$. But what is the economic meaning of the nested set condition? Without knowing this we cannot assess whether it is reasonable to assume it satisfied.

Consider a simple case where there are only two non-produced inputs, measured by $z = (z_1, z_2)$, and only one type of output measured by y. The production set $\mathscr{T}$ can be represented by a *differentiable* function T such that

$$(z, \boldsymbol{k}, y) \in \mathscr{T} \quad \text{if and only if } T(z, \boldsymbol{k}, y) \leqslant 0. \tag{7.20}$$

The sets $\mathscr{C}(\boldsymbol{k}, \boldsymbol{q})$ take the form

$$\{z | T(z, \boldsymbol{k}, y)\} \leqslant 0. \tag{7.21}$$

For given $\boldsymbol{k}$ these sets depend upon y and the upper limit of z values consistent with a particular value of y is

$$\{z | T(z, \boldsymbol{k}, y) = 0\}. \tag{7.22}$$

Fig. 7.3 illustrates a few of the loci defined by (7.22) for a particular k. These loci are the familiar 'isoquants' of traditional mathematical economics. Because T is assumed to be differentiable they are smooth without corners. The numbering of the isoquants shows the output level obtainable from various combinations of z_1 and z_2, *for a given* $\boldsymbol{k}$ *vector*, $\boldsymbol{k}_1$. Obviously there are infinitely many loci satisfying (7.22), even when $\boldsymbol{k}$ takes a particular value, so only a few have been drawn on the figure. The shading in the figure reminds us that each isoquant is the upper boundary of a set $\mathscr{C}(\boldsymbol{k}, y)$; here the shaded

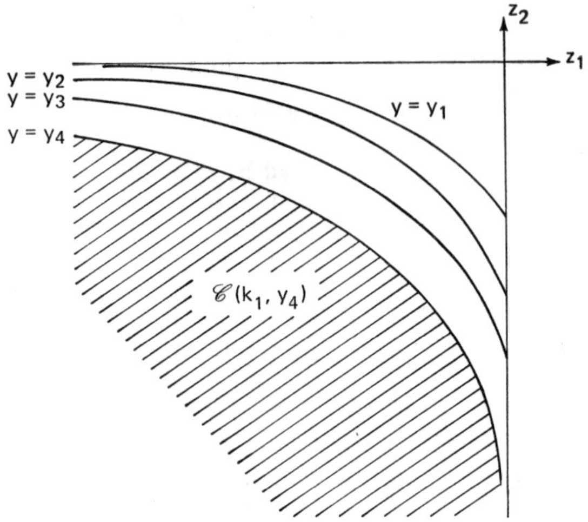

Fig. 7.3. Loci of $\{z|T(z, k, y) = 0\}$ for $k = k_1$.

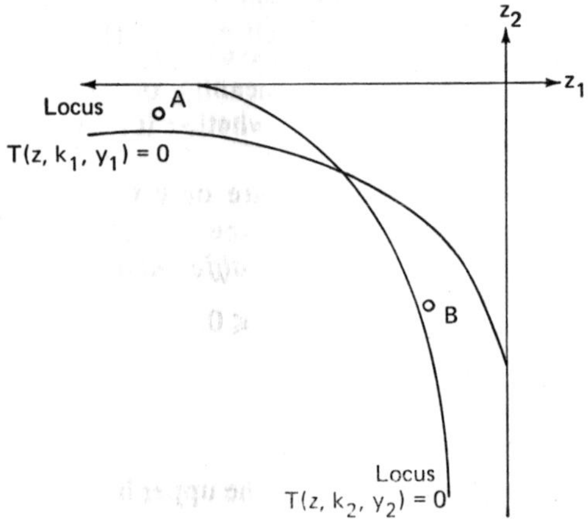

Fig. 7.4.

area is $\mathscr{C}(k_1, y_4)$. Suppose now that we redraw fig. 7.3, but for $k = k_2$ $(k_1 \neq k_2)$. Clearly, we get a new collection of sets $\mathscr{C}(k_2, y)$ so that the figure must be altered. But notice that *none of the new loci shall intersect the old loci*, i.e .we must not have the situation of fig. 7.4. For if the situation depicted in fig. 7.4 were to arise we would have

$$A \in \mathscr{C}(k_2, y_2) \quad \text{and} \quad A \notin \mathscr{C}(k_1, y_1)$$

and (7.23)

$$B \in \mathscr{C}(k_1, y_1) \quad \text{and} \quad B \notin \mathscr{C}(k_2, y_2).$$

The sets $\mathscr{C}(\boldsymbol{k}, y)$ would not be nested. So what must happen if the new isoquants can never intersect the old? All that can be altered are *the output levels corresponding to the various isoquants*. In other words, there is really only one figure of the type of 7.3. An alteration is $\boldsymbol{k}$ does not render the figure redundant, but only the output numbering. It is this feature which allows us to pre-order the z vectors in the proof of theorem 7.1, for it is as if we had indifference curves that never cross.

Now something that does not depend upon the output numbering, but only upon the shape of the isoquant, is the *marginal rate of substitution between* z_1 *and* z_2. Hence, we can aggregate *only if the marginal rate of substitution between two inputs is independent of the output level and capital vector* $\boldsymbol{k}$. This condition is familiar from the work of Leontief and is usually known as the *Leontief condition*[4].

The Leontief condition is useful in helping us to assess the plausibility of the case where aggregation is possible. The conclusion at which it helps us to arrive is that the condition for aggregation is so implausible that it is hardly to be taken seriously. The following are some, evidently very special, cases in which we will have the conditions for aggregation:

(1) The non-produced inputs are perfect substitutes for each other. Suppose that we distinguish seven kinds of unskilled labour: labour of men born on a Monday; labour of men born on a Tuesday; labour of men born on a Wednesday; etc. According to the nursery rhyme, labour born on a Saturday 'works hard for its living', but we will here assume that there are no efficiency differences depending upon the day of birth. In that case there is a trivial aggregation:

$$\phi(L_{\mathrm{M}}, L_{\mathrm{TU}}, L_{\mathrm{W}}, L_{\mathrm{TH}}, L_{\mathrm{F}}, L_{\mathrm{SAT}}, L_{\mathrm{SUN}}) = L_{\mathrm{M}} + L_{\mathrm{TU}} + L_{\mathrm{W}} + L_{\mathrm{TH}} + L_{\mathrm{F}} + L_{\mathrm{SAT}} + L_{\mathrm{SUN}}. \quad (7.24)$$

The aggregation is possible because all interior boundaries of the sets $\mathscr{C}(\boldsymbol{k}, \boldsymbol{q})$ are parallel hyperplanes; hence these sets are necessarily nested. Whenever the boundaries of the sets $\mathscr{C}(\boldsymbol{k}, \boldsymbol{q})$ are parallel hyperplanes, the components of z can be measured in units such that only their sum matters. In this case, all the non-produced inputs *are really the same input* so that naturally aggregation is possible.

(2) The non-produced inputs are used in fixed proportions. Suppose that plumbers and plumbers' mates always work in pairs, one man of each kind. Then what matters for production is not the number of plumbers, or the

---

[4] Cf. Leontief (1947) and Solow (1955–1956).

number of plumbers' mates, but the number of teams consisting of one plumber and one mate. Hence,

$$\phi \text{ (plumbers, mates)} = \min \text{ (plumbers, mates)} \tag{7.25}$$

is an aggregation. Here the sets $\mathscr{C}(\boldsymbol{k}, \boldsymbol{q})$ are regions for which plumbers $\geqslant a$ and mates $\geqslant a$, and so are necessarily nested. In general, if the $\mathscr{C}(\boldsymbol{k}, \boldsymbol{q})$ are hypercubes with collinear corners, then they must be nested, and the aggregate will take the form

$$\phi(z) = \min[\alpha_1 z_1, \alpha_2 z_2, \ldots, \alpha_i z_i, \ldots, \alpha_n z_n]. \tag{7.26}$$

Notice that aggregation is straightforward when the elasticity of substitution is infinity, and again when it is zero; it is the values in between that give rise to doubt!

(3) Provision of an intermediate service. The above example suggests a more general case. One might say that the true input is the work of a two-man team (plumber and mate) and that the role of plumbers and mates is as inputs to the provision of the work of these teams. Aggregation will be possible whenever a group of inputs is used independently of other inputs to provide a service. Suppose that there is one type of furnace which can take many fuels. The heat generated depends upon the fuel input vector $\boldsymbol{x}$ as

$$\text{heat} = F(\boldsymbol{x}). \tag{7.27}$$

Heat in turn is an input, regardless of how it is generated. In this case there is a natural aggregation, which reflects a structural feature of the technology. The aggregate of fuel input can be taken to be heat generated. Here the nested-set property is present because the marginal rate of substitution between two fuels depends only upon the rate at which they can be substituted in the generation of heat, and in no way depends upon how heat is being combined with other productive inputs.

It is evident that each of the foregoing examples is special and atypical. If one were to consider, say, the aggregation of different types of labour time, it is simply incredible that any of these features would hold for more than a few labour types. Yet it is very hard to think of further plausible cases that would give rise to the nested-set condition. Viewed either as a formal mathematical condition, or in the light of economic rationalizations of it, the nested-set condition is so strong that it cannot be credited. And if the condition cannot be credited then there can be no aggregation in the sense of property 1: we must know the detailed composition of the input vector z, and not simply its aggregate measure, before we can pronounce on the feasibility of a production plan.

Of course, these are not unexpected conclusions. To ask for perfect aggregation in the sense of property 1 is to ask for a great deal and we cannot reasonably expect to get it 'on the cheap'. In fact, as theorem 7.1 has demonstrated, the 'price', in terms of restrictions on production possibilities, is very high.

Now so far our discussion has concerned itself, at least overtly, with aggregation of non-produced inputs. The conclusion has been that, from the theoretical point of view, and excepting only some very special cases, aggregation cannot be rigorously justified. It must then be regarded as a procedure to which recourse is had by virtue of necessity; because we cannot avoid some aggregation; because some heterogeneous objects at least must be treated as if they were a single good. What would the conclusion be if, instead of considering the aggregation of $\boldsymbol{z}$, we were to consider the aggregation of the vector $\boldsymbol{k}$ into a scalar index? The reader will readily see that there is no necessity to embark now upon a new investigation to see what conditions must be satisfied if there is to exist an aggregate of $\boldsymbol{k}$ in the sense of property 1. It is purely fortuitous that the discussion until now has concerned itself with non-produced inputs. In fact, the interpretation of $\boldsymbol{z}$ as a vector of non-produced inputs is arbitrary: it could as well be the vector of capital inputs and $\boldsymbol{k}$ the vector of non-produced inputs. In the argument of theorem 7.1 what we have in fact been considering are the conditions for any group of inputs to be formed into an aggregate. Indeed, our argument applies equally to outputs, say to the aggregation of $\boldsymbol{q}$, for we have treated inputs as negative outputs. Hence, $\boldsymbol{z}$ is a non-positive vector, so that inputs and outputs are treated in a manner that allows one to switch from the consideration of one to the consideration of the other very easily. All that is involved is a change of signs. And now notice that the proof of theorem 7.1 has at no point depended upon the signs of components of $\boldsymbol{z}$, so that $\boldsymbol{z}$ could as well have been a non-negative vector – it could as well have been $\boldsymbol{q}$.

The investigation of the conditions for aggregation could be wound up at this point. The conclusion implied by theorem 7.1 is so negative for the whole enterprise that it might be deemed a waste of time to detail the further niceties of the theory. However, for the sake of completeness, to give a clear overview, and because it does not need very much extra space to complete the job, we will present some further results.

Property 2 (convexity). $\mathcal{T}_0$ is convex provided that $\mathcal{T}$ is convex.

This is a very reasonable property to look for. If $\mathcal{T}_0$ is to represent production possibilities, then not only should it do so, but it should represent them in a form which is in harmony with the underlying technology as embodied in $\mathcal{T}$. The next theorem shows what condition will give us property 2.

Theorem 7.2. Property 2 can be satisfied if ϕ can be chosen concave.

Proof. Suppose that $\mathscr{T}$ is convex and ϕ is a concave function. Suppose that $\mathscr{T}_0$ is not convex. Then there exists $(Z_1, \boldsymbol{k}_1, \boldsymbol{q}_1) \in \mathscr{T}_0$ and $(Z_2, \boldsymbol{k}_2, \boldsymbol{q}_2) \in \mathscr{T}_0$ such that

$$[\lambda Z_1 + (1-\lambda) Z_2, \lambda \boldsymbol{k}_1 + (1-\lambda)\boldsymbol{k}_2, \lambda \boldsymbol{q}_1 + (1-\lambda)\boldsymbol{q}_2] \notin \mathscr{T}_0 \quad \text{for } 0 < \lambda < 1. \tag{7.28}$$

Choose z_1 so that $\phi(z_1) = Z_1$. This must be possible, for otherwise, by construction $(Z_1, \boldsymbol{k}_1, \boldsymbol{q}_1)$ could not be in $\mathscr{T}_0$. Similarly, choose z_2 so that $\phi(z_2) = Z_2$. By property 1, $(z_1, \boldsymbol{k}_1, \boldsymbol{q}_1) \in \mathscr{T}$ because $[\phi(z_1), \boldsymbol{k}_1, \boldsymbol{q}_1] \in \mathscr{T}_0$. Similarly, $(z_2, \boldsymbol{k}_2, \boldsymbol{q}_2) \in \mathscr{T}$. Hence, $\mathscr{T}$ being convex,

$$[\lambda z_1 + (1-\lambda) z_2, \lambda \boldsymbol{k}_1 + (1-\lambda)\boldsymbol{k}_2, \lambda \boldsymbol{q}_1 + (1-\lambda)\boldsymbol{q}_2] \in \mathscr{T}. \tag{7.29}$$

Hence, again by property 1,

$$[\phi\{\lambda z_1 + (1-\lambda) z_2\}, \lambda \boldsymbol{k}_1 + (1-\lambda)\boldsymbol{k}_2, \lambda \boldsymbol{q}_1 + (1-\lambda)\boldsymbol{q}_2] \in \mathscr{T}_0. \tag{7.30}$$

Next note that

$$\phi\{\lambda z_1 + (1-\lambda) z_2\} \geqslant \lambda \phi(z_1) + (1-\lambda)\phi(z_2) = \lambda Z_1 + (1-\lambda) Z_2, \tag{7.31}$$

ϕ being a concave function. Hence, given (7.30),

$$[\lambda Z_1 + (1-\lambda) Z_2, \lambda \boldsymbol{k}_1 + (1-\lambda)\boldsymbol{k}_2, \lambda \boldsymbol{q}_1 + (1-\lambda)\boldsymbol{q}_2] \in \mathscr{T}_0. \tag{7.32}$$

This contradicts (7.28). Thus $\mathscr{T}_0$ is convex, as required.

The theorem is useful in indicating the extra condition that must be imposed on the function ϕ to give us convexity of $\mathscr{T}_0$. How strong is this condition? Notice that ϕ, being a representation of a pre-ordering relation '$\gtrsim$' is arbitrary up to an order-preserving transformation. So the question is not 'is ϕ concave?', but rather, 'can ϕ be chosen concave?' A necessary condition for it to be possible to represent the relation '$\gtrsim$' by a concave function is that the relation itself should own a property of *convexity*, namely the following.

Definition 7.2. The relation '$\gtrsim$' will be said to be *quasi-concave* if all sets of the form

$$\{z | z \gtrsim z_0\} \tag{7.33}$$

are convex sets.

The reader may confirm that the relation $\gtrsim$ as defined in (7.10) is quasi-concave provided only that $\mathscr{T}$ is a convex set. For, suppose that '$[z_1, \boldsymbol{k}, \boldsymbol{q}] \in \mathscr{T} \Rightarrow [z_0, \boldsymbol{k}, \boldsymbol{q}] \in \mathscr{T}$' and '$[z_2, \boldsymbol{k}, \boldsymbol{q}] \in \mathscr{T} \Rightarrow [z_0, \boldsymbol{k}, \boldsymbol{q}] \in \mathscr{T}$', but for some $(\bar{\boldsymbol{k}}, \bar{\boldsymbol{q}})$,

$$[\lambda z_1 + (1-\lambda) z_2, \bar{\boldsymbol{k}}, \bar{\boldsymbol{q}}] \in \mathscr{T} \quad \text{and} \quad [z_0, \bar{\boldsymbol{k}}, \bar{\boldsymbol{q}}] \notin \mathscr{T}. \tag{7.34}$$

Then $[z_1, \bar{k}, \bar{q}] \notin \mathscr{T}$, for otherwise '$[z_0, \bar{k}, \bar{q}] \in \mathscr{T}$' would be implied; and similarly $[z_2, \bar{k}, \bar{q}] \notin \mathscr{T}$. Hence, $\mathscr{T}$ is not a convex set, contrary to our assumption.

It is known that, under some not too strong conditions, a continuous pre-ordering that is convex may be represented by a function that is concave (see Fenchel, 1953, pp. 115–126). Hence, we may reasonably assume that ϕ, the representation of a convex pre-ordering, has been chosen concave. It follows that theorem 7.2 can be interpreted to state that there are no considerable difficulties regarding the convexity of $\mathscr{T}_0$.

The last property that we will consider is one for which the formal statement is best preceded by some explanation. We have derived conditions under which the production possibility set $\mathscr{T}$ may be represented by another set $\mathscr{T}_0$, in which some of the variables (here the components of z) have been aggregated. Under the conditions of theorem 7.1 there is no loss of precision following on the adoption of the aggregate representation, although information concerning the composition of z is naturally lost.

But what is the interest of the construct? What can one do with the synthetic set $\mathscr{T}_0$? All that is so far possible is a game which might proceed as follows. There are three players, A, B and C, connected by a telephone system so that any player can talk to any other without the third player overhearing. The idea of the game is that A will think up arrays $(z, \boldsymbol{k}, \boldsymbol{q})$ and he will be told whether his arrays are in $\mathscr{T}$ or not. However, no player, not A and not even B or C, knows the form of $\mathscr{T}$. B knows the function ϕ. C knows the set $\mathscr{T}_0$. The set $\mathscr{T}$ is not known and cannot be inferred by any player. A thinks up an array $(z, \boldsymbol{k}, \boldsymbol{q})$. He communicates z to B and $(\boldsymbol{k}, \boldsymbol{q})$ to C. Then B calculates $\phi(z)$ and communicates this number to C. Now C has $[\phi(z), \boldsymbol{k}, \boldsymbol{q}]$ and he can check whether this is included in $\mathscr{T}_0$. If it is, he tells A that his proposal is a feasible one – his array is included in $\mathscr{T}$. He does not know the array and does not know $\mathscr{T}$, but he can supply this piece of information. If not, he tells A that his array is not included in $\mathscr{T}$. It is to be hoped that the players will derive some amusement from this game. However, whether the game is amusing or not, it has nothing much to do with economic analysis. For aggregation to be of interest to the economic analyst we must be able to do something with the synthetic set $\mathscr{T}_0$ beyond merely admiring it.

Something that we might hope to do is summarized in the term *two-stage maximization*. Property 2 gives a hint that we may be able to forge a link between a value-maximizing point of $\mathscr{T}$ and a value-maximizing point of $\mathscr{T}_0$, since to do this we would surely need convexity of both these sets. Under two-stage maximization we are first presented with a price array $[\Pi, \boldsymbol{p}_k, \boldsymbol{p}_q]$, for which we choose a point of $\mathscr{T}_0$ so that $\Pi Z + \boldsymbol{p}_k \cdot \boldsymbol{k} + \boldsymbol{p}_q \cdot \boldsymbol{q}$ is maximized for

$[Z,\boldsymbol{k},\boldsymbol{q}] \in \mathscr{T}_0$. In other words, we maximize the net value of output, but treating of only Z, the aggregate of the components of z, for which the price is Π. That is the first stage. At the second stage we are given the relative prices of the components of z and using these we choose z so as to make up the aggregate at minimum cost. If two-stage maximization is to make sense, then the vector z obtained in the two stages must be one of the very vectors that we might obtain by solving the underlying one-stage problem of maximizing the net value of $(z,\boldsymbol{k},\boldsymbol{q})$ subject to $(z,\boldsymbol{k},\boldsymbol{q}) \in \mathscr{T}$. Where we have this feature we say that two-stage maximization is *consistent*. Where two-stage maximization is consistent we really can boast that the set $\mathscr{T}_0$ is more than a toy. We can use $\mathscr{T}_0$, for example, to obtain a value-maximizing array $[Z,\boldsymbol{k},\boldsymbol{q}]$ which is explicit with regard to $\boldsymbol{k}$ and $\boldsymbol{q}$. We do not know z, but we do know that there is some z such that $[z,\boldsymbol{k},\boldsymbol{q}]$ is value maximizing.

Property 3 (consistent two-stage maximization). There exists a function $\Pi(\boldsymbol{p}_z)$ such that $(z^*,\boldsymbol{k}^*,\boldsymbol{q}^*)$ is a solution to

$$\max \boldsymbol{p}_z \cdot z + \boldsymbol{p}_k \cdot \boldsymbol{k} + \boldsymbol{p}_q \cdot \boldsymbol{q} \quad \text{subject to } (z,\boldsymbol{k},\boldsymbol{q}) \in \mathscr{T}, \tag{7.35}$$

if and only if the following conditions are satisfied:

(*i*) $[\phi(z^*),\boldsymbol{k}^*,\boldsymbol{q}^*]$ *is a solution to*

$$\max \Pi(\boldsymbol{p}_z) Z + \boldsymbol{p}_k \cdot \boldsymbol{k} + \boldsymbol{p}_q \cdot \boldsymbol{q} \quad \text{subject to } (Z,\boldsymbol{k},\boldsymbol{q}) \in \mathscr{T}_0; \tag{7.36}$$

(*ii*) z^* *is a solution to*

$$\max \boldsymbol{p}_z \cdot z \quad \text{subject to } \phi(z) = \phi(z^*). \tag{7.37}$$

For the discussion of property 3 it is necessary to assume something definite about vector z, either that it is non-negative, or that it is non-positive. Since we are thinking of inputs we will assume $z \leqq \mathbf{0}$. Hence, ϕ is defined only on the non-negative z vectors. Since the numerical representation of a pre-ordering relation is arbitrary up to an order preserving transformation we may choose ϕ so that $\phi(\mathbf{0}) = 0$. Then ϕ will not be positive for admissible z values. The argument goes through on the very same track if z is non-negative and $\phi(z) \geqslant 0$.

Recall that our confining interest to the non-produced input is not of consequence for the mathematical argument, so that this property, like the previous ones, may be predicted of the vector $\boldsymbol{k}$ and its aggregate just as for z and Z. The next theorem gives a sufficient condition for property 3.

Theorem 7.3. A sufficient condition for property 3 is that ϕ be homogeneous of degree one[5].

Proof. Consider the three following mathematical programmes; it will be readily seen that they are equivalent one to the other:

$$\max \boldsymbol{p}_z \cdot \boldsymbol{z} + \boldsymbol{p}_k \cdot \boldsymbol{k} + \boldsymbol{p}_q \cdot \boldsymbol{q} \quad \text{subject to } (\boldsymbol{z}, \boldsymbol{k}, \boldsymbol{q}) \in \mathscr{T}. \tag{7.38}$$

$$\max \boldsymbol{p}_z \cdot \boldsymbol{z} + \boldsymbol{p}_k \cdot \boldsymbol{k} + \boldsymbol{p}_q \cdot \boldsymbol{q} \quad \text{subject to } [Z, \boldsymbol{k}, \boldsymbol{q}] \in \mathscr{T}_0, \qquad Z = \phi(\boldsymbol{z}). \tag{7.39}$$

$$\max \Pi Z + \boldsymbol{p}_k \cdot \boldsymbol{k} + \boldsymbol{p}_q \cdot \boldsymbol{q} \quad \text{subject to } [Z, \boldsymbol{k}, \boldsymbol{q}] \in \mathscr{T}_0, \qquad Z = \phi(\boldsymbol{z}), \quad \Pi Z \leqslant \boldsymbol{p}_z \cdot \boldsymbol{z}, \tag{7.40}$$

where in (7.40) Π is a choice-variable along with $[Z, \boldsymbol{k}, \boldsymbol{q}]$. Evidently these programmes, being (7.38) or rearrangements of the same making use of property 1, have the same value. If $(\boldsymbol{z}^*, \boldsymbol{k}^*, \boldsymbol{q}^*)$ solves (7.38), then it will also solve (7.39), and $[\phi(\boldsymbol{z}^*), \boldsymbol{k}^*, \boldsymbol{q}^*]$ will solve (7.40), and conversely. What we have to show is that (7.40), and hence (7.38) and (7.39) are equivalent to

$$\max \Pi(\boldsymbol{p}_z) Z + \boldsymbol{p}_k \cdot \boldsymbol{k} + \boldsymbol{p}_q \cdot \boldsymbol{q} \quad \text{subject to } [Z, \boldsymbol{k}, \boldsymbol{q}] \in \mathscr{T}_0. \tag{7.41}$$

In other words, we have to show that only the first condition in the constraints of (7.40) carries any force.

To this end define $V(\boldsymbol{p}_z, \boldsymbol{z}^0)$ to be the value of the programme

$$\max \boldsymbol{p}_z \cdot \boldsymbol{z} \quad \text{subject to } \phi(\boldsymbol{z}) = \phi(\boldsymbol{z}_0). \tag{7.42}$$

Let

$$\Pi(\boldsymbol{p}_z) = V(\boldsymbol{p}_z, \boldsymbol{z}^0)/\phi(\boldsymbol{z}_0). \tag{7.43}$$

We show that (7.43) gives a well-defined function of $\boldsymbol{p}_z$, i.e. the right-hand side does not depend upon $\boldsymbol{z}^0$.[6]

Suppose that $V(\boldsymbol{p}_z, \boldsymbol{z}^0)/\phi(\boldsymbol{z}^0)$ is not independent of $\boldsymbol{z}^0$. Then there exists a $\boldsymbol{p}_z$ and vectors $\boldsymbol{z}_1^0$ and $\boldsymbol{z}_2^0$ such that

$$V(\boldsymbol{p}_z, \boldsymbol{z}_1^0)/\phi(\boldsymbol{z}_1^0) > V(\boldsymbol{p}_z, \boldsymbol{z}_2^0)/\phi(\boldsymbol{z}_2^0). \tag{7.44}$$

Let $\boldsymbol{z}_1^*$ be a solution to (7.42) with $\phi(\boldsymbol{z})$ constrained to equal $\phi(\boldsymbol{z}_1^0)$ and let $\boldsymbol{z}_2^*$ be a solution to (7.42) with $\phi(\boldsymbol{z})$ constrained to equal $\phi(\boldsymbol{z}_2^0)$. Then,

$$\boldsymbol{p}_z \cdot \boldsymbol{z}_1^*/\phi(\boldsymbol{z}_1^0) > \boldsymbol{p}_z \cdot \boldsymbol{z}_2^*/\phi(\boldsymbol{z}_2^0). \tag{7.45}$$

---

[5] The function ϕ will be said to be homogeneous of degree one if, for any scalar $\lambda > 0$, $\phi(\lambda \boldsymbol{z}) = \lambda \phi(\boldsymbol{z})$. Actually this is a strong requirement and rather more than we need, which is that ϕ be homogeneous of degree one over the range of $\boldsymbol{z}$ vectors under consideration. Of course, ϕ, being a numerical representation of a pre-ordering is arbitrary, so what is being postulated is that ϕ can be (and has been) chosen to satisfy homogeneity of degree one. If $\lambda = 0$ is admissible note that $\phi(\boldsymbol{0})$ must equal 0.

[6] Except that it were better that $\phi(\boldsymbol{z}^0) \neq 0$, for if it were we would have to make appeal to limiting arguments.

Choose $\lambda = \phi(z_1^0)/\phi(z_2^0)$ and consider λz_2^* as a possible solution to (7.42) with $\phi(z)$ constrained to equal $\phi(z_1)$. Since

$$\phi(\lambda z_2^*) = \lambda\phi(z_2^*) = \lambda\phi(z_2^0) = \frac{\phi(z_1^0)}{\phi(z_2^0)}\phi(z_2^0) = \phi(z_1^0), \tag{7.46}$$

λz_2^* is feasible for this programme. Hence,

$$\boldsymbol{p}_z \cdot z_1^* \geq \frac{\phi(z_1^0)}{\phi(z_2^0)} \boldsymbol{p}_z \cdot z_2^*. \tag{7.47}$$

Thus, bearing in mind that $\phi(z_1^0) < 0$,

$$\boldsymbol{p}_z \cdot z_1^*/\phi(z_1^0) \leq \boldsymbol{p}_z \cdot z_2^*/\phi(z_2^0), \tag{7.48}$$

in contradiction to (7.45).

It remains to show that, given $[Z, \boldsymbol{k}, \boldsymbol{q}] \in \mathscr{T}_0$, no extra constraint is imposed by

$$Z = \phi(z) \quad \text{and} \quad \Pi(\boldsymbol{p}_z) \leq \boldsymbol{p}_z \cdot z. \tag{7.48a}$$

In other words, given $[Z, \boldsymbol{k}, \boldsymbol{q}]$ in $\mathscr{T}_0$, (7.48a) may be automatically satisfied. Given Z from $[Z, \boldsymbol{k}, \boldsymbol{q}]$ we may obviously choose $\boldsymbol{z}$ so that $Z = \phi(z)$, for otherwise $[Z, \boldsymbol{k}, \boldsymbol{q}]$ would not be a point of $\mathscr{T}_0$, by construction. Now choose $\boldsymbol{z}$ to solve

$$\max \boldsymbol{p}_z \cdot \boldsymbol{z} \quad \text{subject to } \phi(z) = Z, \tag{7.49}$$

hence ensuring that (7.37) will be satisfied. We will then have

$$\boldsymbol{p}_z \cdot \boldsymbol{z} = V(\boldsymbol{p}_z, z) = \Pi(\boldsymbol{p}_z)\phi(z) = \Pi(\boldsymbol{p}_z)Z, \tag{7.50}$$

so that (7.36) will be satisfied. Hence, $[\phi(z^*), \boldsymbol{k}^*, \boldsymbol{q}^*]$ solves not merely (7.40) but (7.41) as required.

Suppose now that $[Z^*, \boldsymbol{k}^*, \boldsymbol{q}^*]$ solves (7.41) and $\boldsymbol{z}^*$ solves

$$\max \boldsymbol{p}_z \cdot \boldsymbol{z} \quad \text{subject to } \phi(z) = Z^*.$$

Clearly, $[z^*, \boldsymbol{k}^*, \boldsymbol{q}^*]$ solves (7.40) and then $[z^*, \boldsymbol{k}^*, \boldsymbol{q}^*]$ must solve (7.38). The proof of theorem 7.3 is complete[7].

---

[7] It may help the reader to get a feel for theorem 7.3 if he considers the type of case in which $\mathscr{T}_0$ is specified by a differentiable function which must be non-negative and ϕ is differentiable. The Lagrangian of the problem

$$\max \boldsymbol{p}_z \cdot \boldsymbol{z} + \boldsymbol{p}_k \cdot \boldsymbol{k} + \boldsymbol{p}_q \cdot \boldsymbol{q} \quad \text{subject to } Z = \phi(z), \qquad F_0(Z, \boldsymbol{k}, \boldsymbol{q}) \geq 0,$$

is

$$\boldsymbol{p}_z \cdot \boldsymbol{z} + \boldsymbol{p}_k \cdot \boldsymbol{k} + \boldsymbol{p}_q \cdot \boldsymbol{q} + \mu[Z - \phi(z)] + \zeta F_0(Z, \boldsymbol{k}, \boldsymbol{q}),$$

and it will be maximized by a solution $(z^*, \boldsymbol{k}^*, \boldsymbol{q}^*)$. Hence, z^* must maximize $\boldsymbol{p}_z \cdot \boldsymbol{z} - \mu[Z - \phi(z)]$, which is the Lagrangian of

$$\max \boldsymbol{p}_z \cdot \boldsymbol{z} \quad \text{subject to } \boldsymbol{z} = \phi(z).$$

It remains to append some remarks concerning the stringency of the condition the ϕ be homogeneous of degree one. From one point of view the condition is not so strong as one might at first think, for we are not demanding that *any* aggregation of z have the property of homogeneity but just that some aggregation will own this property. However, that said, it must be conceded that the requirement is a very strong one and not very likely to be satisfied. That this is so can be seen by considering the type of case for which all functional relations are differentiable, so that the Leontief conditions apply. In that case the marginal rate of substitution between two components of z must be independent, not merely of $\boldsymbol{k}$ and $\boldsymbol{q}$, but also of the scale of z. If one thinks of the earlier example of different types of fuel helping to generate heat, it will at once be clear that homogeneity is a strong assumption on top of the strong assumption already necessary for property 1.

Theorem 7.3. states that ϕ homogeneous of degree one is a sufficient condition for property 3. Note also that as $\Pi(\boldsymbol{p}_z)$ was constructed we have

$$\phi(z^*)\,\Pi(\boldsymbol{p}_z) = \boldsymbol{p}_z \cdot z^*. \tag{7.51}$$

Hence,

$$\frac{\phi(z^*)\,\Pi(\boldsymbol{p}_z)}{\phi(z^*)\,\Pi(\boldsymbol{p}_z) + \boldsymbol{p}_k \cdot \boldsymbol{k}^* + \boldsymbol{p}_q \cdot \boldsymbol{q}^*} = \frac{\boldsymbol{p}_z \cdot z^*}{\boldsymbol{p}_z \cdot z^* + \boldsymbol{p}_k \cdot \boldsymbol{k}^* + \boldsymbol{p}_q \cdot \boldsymbol{q}^*}. \tag{7.52}$$

It follows that, maximizing on the synthetic production set, we will obtain an exact measure of the share of net value which non-produced inputs will command. If we demand this feature of the two-stage maximization procedure then it is rather clear that homogeneity is a necessary condition. For in that case we must have

$$\Pi(\boldsymbol{p}_z) = V(\boldsymbol{p}_z, z^0)/\phi(z^0), \tag{7.53}$$

as in (7.43), and this will not be independent of z^0 unless ϕ is homogeneous of degree one, as the proof of theorem 7.3 has made clear.

We have looked long enough now at the theory of general aggregation to learn the lessons that impinge directly upon the aggregation of capital as we will here be concerned with it. Our discussion has not done justice to the theory in all its breadth and finesse. We could, were our concerns different, go on to consider simultaneous aggregation of several vectors; consistent two-stage maximization without the requirement (7.53); and many other problems. Yet enough has been done here to allow some clear conclusions to emerge. These are:

(1) If capital inputs can be aggregated in the sense of properties 1, 2 and 3 then we are fully justified in treating 'capital' as an aggregate which behaves

just like a single good. We will follow an image of the real underlying production set, we can maximize, and so obtain production equilibria, treating only of the aggregate, and doing this we will obtain exactly the true figure for the total payment to capital.

(2) The conditions that must be imposed to admit of the above desirable features are so strong that we may safely dismiss them from serious consideration as actualities. We must conclude then that general aggregation of capital is a theoretical possibility but that the theory gives no support to widespread use of the approach. In particular, a theory which is genuinely dependent upon the possibility of general capital aggregation is confined to instances so special that it would be hard to find parallels elsewhere in economic theory for such a constrained theory.

(3) While our conclusions concerning general capital aggregation are very damaging for the whole idea, *the investigation has provided no support whatsoever for the idea that the aggregation of capital is relatively difficult.* The conditions for general capital aggregation are identical to the conditions for the aggregation of labour, or of output. We may thus conclude that the widespread belief that there is a notable, particular and distinct problem posed by capital aggregation is at best an ill-formulated idea, and at worst is based simply on ignorance.

These are the major conclusions of the present chapter. Before we go on to examine stationary equilibrium aggregation in ch. 8 there are two outstanding matters which are relevant to the present, and also to later, investigations. Because they are closely connected we will consider them together.

Two questions might occur to the reader. Suppose that we are told that an aggregate of capital exists, conforming to all the desirable properties (1–3): how can we discover the function ϕ? Evidently this might be done in more than one way, but one way of tackling the problem connects up nicely with the second question. What is the relation of $\Pi(\boldsymbol{p}_z)$, as defined in (7.43), to the ordinary familiar price index of general usage, which is after all formed as a *linear sum* of prices weighted by quantities?

Both these questions can be elucidated, and the ground laid out for the discussion of ch. 8 as well, if we now introduce the idea of *chain-index aggregation* (Divisia, 1925, 1928; Jorgenson and Griliches, 1967). However, to do this fully, and on the basis only of the assumptions concerning production possibilities to which we have so far had recourse, would involve us in a discussion more lengthy than that for which the reader is likely to have an appetite at this stage. Also the most general treatment is not particularly useful to us since we will make no demands on it in what follows. We will therefore examine firstly the theory of chain-index aggregation as it applies to the type of case considered by traditional mathematical economics, in which production possibilities are represented by differentiable functions. This allows of brevity and will serve to give some plausibility to the chain-index method, which would otherwise appear to be more than a little arbitrary. The theory having been developed in the traditional framework, we will append some remarks concerning departures from the traditional case, without, however, laying out a full and rigorous treatment of these cases.

Since we have remarked more than once that there is no difference from the formal point of view between the general aggregation of $\boldsymbol{k}$ and the general aggregation of z, we may as well, in what follows, treat of $\boldsymbol{k}$ as the vector for which properties 1–3 are satisfied. Then let $\phi(\boldsymbol{k})$ be the aggregate of $\boldsymbol{k}$. Suppose that the synthetic production set $\mathscr{T}_0$ can be represented by a differentiable function F, which is non-negative for a point of $\mathscr{T}_0$. The problem of maximizing the net value of output will take the form:

$$\begin{aligned} &\max \boldsymbol{p}_z \cdot z + \boldsymbol{p}_k \cdot \boldsymbol{k} + \boldsymbol{p}_q \cdot \boldsymbol{q} \quad \text{subject to } F[z, \phi(\boldsymbol{k}), \boldsymbol{q}] \geqslant 0, \\ &z \leqq \mathbf{0}, \qquad \boldsymbol{k} \leqq \mathbf{0}, \qquad \boldsymbol{q} \geqq \mathbf{0}. \end{aligned} \tag{7.54}$$

The Kuhn–Tucker conditions[8] for this problem are

$$\begin{aligned} &\boldsymbol{p}_z + \mu \boldsymbol{f}_z \quad\;\; \geqq \mathbf{0} \text{ comp. } z \leqq \mathbf{0}, \\ &\boldsymbol{p}_k + \mu F_\phi \boldsymbol{\phi}_k \geqq \mathbf{0} \text{ comp. } \boldsymbol{k} \leqq \mathbf{0}, \\ &\boldsymbol{p}_q + \mu \boldsymbol{f}_q \quad\;\; \leqq \mathbf{0} \text{ comp. } \boldsymbol{q} \geqq \mathbf{0}, \end{aligned} \tag{7.55}$$

where μ is the Lagrange multiplier of the production constraint; $\boldsymbol{f}_z$, $\boldsymbol{f}_q$ and $\boldsymbol{\phi}_k$ are vectors of first-order partials of respectively F with respect to z, F with respect to $\boldsymbol{q}$, and ϕ with respect to $\boldsymbol{k}$; and F_ϕ is the partial derivative of F with respect to ϕ. From the second line of (7.55) we obtain

$$\boldsymbol{p}_k \cdot \boldsymbol{k} + \mu F_\phi \boldsymbol{\phi}_k \cdot \boldsymbol{k} = 0. \tag{7.56}$$

However, note that ϕ is homogeneous of degree one by property 3, so that Euler's theorem implies that $\boldsymbol{\phi}_k \cdot \boldsymbol{k} = \phi(k)$. Hence, (7.56) reduces to

$$\boldsymbol{p}_k \cdot \boldsymbol{k} + \mu F_\phi \phi(\boldsymbol{k}) = 0. \tag{7.57}$$

Next note that, at least for the purposes of integration, we may assume that whenever a component of the $\boldsymbol{k}$ vector is zero the time rate of change of that component is zero. Hence, denoting the vector of time rates of change of $\boldsymbol{k}$ by $\dot{\boldsymbol{k}}$ we will have

$$\boldsymbol{p}_k \cdot \dot{\boldsymbol{k}} + \mu F_\phi \boldsymbol{\phi}_k \cdot \dot{\boldsymbol{k}} = 0. \tag{7.58}$$

---

[8] See the mathematical appendix, pp. 360–362.

However, $\phi_k \cdot \dot{k}$ is simply $\dot{\phi}$, the time rate of change of ϕ. Now combining (7.57) and (7.58) we have

$$\frac{\mathrm{d}}{\mathrm{d}t}\{\log\phi\} = \frac{\dot{\phi}}{\phi} = \frac{p_k \cdot \dot{k}}{p_k \cdot k}, \tag{7.59}$$

which is a differential equation in the logarithm of ϕ. If the prices (p_z, p_k, p_q) are a continuous function of time and if we suppose the solution to (7.50) to be a unique and continuous function of the prices, as is appropriate in the context of a traditional analysis, then we may obtain a solution to (7.59) which will allow us to assign a value of ϕ to any particular k. The method is as follows:

(1) Choose a $k^0 \neq 0$ such that k^0 is part of the solution to (7.54) for prices (p_z^0, p_k^0, p_q^0), the full solution being (z^0, k^0, q^0).[9]

(2) Assign an arbitrary value, say – 100, to $\phi(k^0)$.

(3) Given another k^T, which can be included in a solution to (7.54) for prices $[p_z^T, p_k^T, p_q^T]$, choose a scalar $t \geqslant 0$ and let the price system at t $(0 \leqslant t \leqslant T)$ be

$$\left[\frac{t}{T}p_z^0 + \frac{(T-t)}{T}p_z^T ; \frac{t}{T}p_k^0 + \frac{(T-t)}{T}p_k^T ; \frac{t}{T}p_q^0 + \frac{(T-t)}{T}p_q^T\right]. \tag{7.60}$$

Now as t goes from 0 to T the prices vary continuously and the solution for k, $k(t)$, will vary continuously. We suppose $k(t)$ differentiable with respect to t.

Now,

$$\phi(k^T) + 100 = \int_0^T \frac{p_k \cdot \dot{k}}{p_k \cdot k}\phi(t)\,\mathrm{d}t. \tag{7.61}$$

In this way we can discover the value of ϕ corresponding to any k.

Now it is evident that the procedure described above for arriving at a value of ϕ in no way depends upon the conditions for the existence of a capital aggregate. However, the function ϕ defined by (7.61) does depend upon the point of departure k^0, so that we might write the solution to (7.61) as $\phi(k^T, k^0)$. If we are to have a meaningful capital aggregate, as we will if properties 1–3 are satisfied, then the values $\phi(k^T, k^0)$ must differ only by a factor of proportionality which will depend only upon k^0. In other words, we must get the same measure of capital, except perhaps for an arbitrary change in the base unit, wherever we start from. The condition that must be imposed is that

$$\phi(k^T, k^0)/\phi(k^S, k^0) = \phi(k^T, k^{00})/\phi(k^S, k^{00}). \tag{7.62}$$

---

[9] In assuming unique solutions for each price array we are seemingly ruling out constant returns to scale. However, if we have constant returns so that $F[\lambda z, \lambda\phi, \lambda q] = \lambda F[z, \phi, q]$, we can consider just cross-sections of solutions for which some normalization is satisfied, say $z^2 + q^2 = 1$, and use the chain-index approach over just this set.

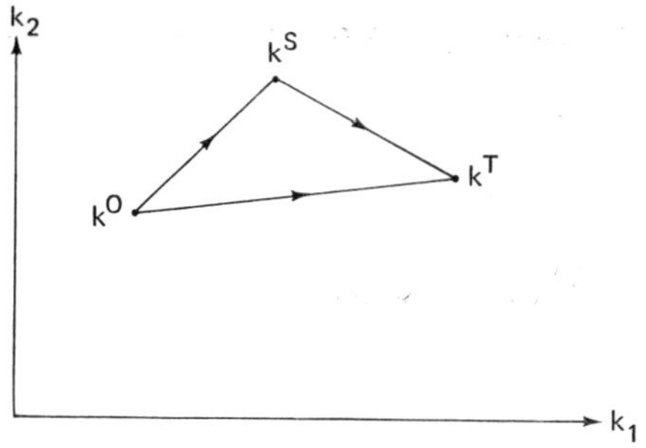

Fig. 7.5.

Or, while $\phi(\boldsymbol{k}^T, \boldsymbol{k}^0)$ may depend upon $\boldsymbol{k}^0$, it must do so only as regards a factor of proportionality. Now setting $\boldsymbol{k}^{00}$ in (7.62) equal to $\boldsymbol{k}^S$ we obtain

$$\phi(\boldsymbol{k}^T, \boldsymbol{k}^0) = \phi(\boldsymbol{k}^S, \boldsymbol{k}^0) \frac{\phi(\boldsymbol{k}^T, \boldsymbol{k}^S)}{\phi(\boldsymbol{k}^S, \boldsymbol{k}^S)}, \tag{7.63}$$

which has an important interpretation. The left-hand side of (7.63) is the capital measure, based upon $\phi(\boldsymbol{k}^0) = -100$, at $\boldsymbol{k}^T$. The right-hand side is the product of the measure at $\boldsymbol{k}^S$ and the proportionate increase in the measure that is recorded upon going from $\boldsymbol{k}^S$ to $\boldsymbol{k}^T$. The force of (7.63) is that these two values should be equal. Fig. 7.5 illustrates.

Imagine that we are journeying in mountainous country. We start at $\boldsymbol{k}^0$ and move directly, by the shortest route to $\boldsymbol{k}^T$. We could instead have gone firstly to a camp at $\boldsymbol{k}^S$ and only then on to $\boldsymbol{k}^T$. If we record on each route the net gain (or loss) in elevation above sea level then the final answer should be independent of the route chosen. It is the same with a measure of capital. It is not enough that we should measure $\phi(\boldsymbol{k})$ unambiguously, as we do through (7.61), but we must also find that our measure is invariant with regard to the route which we choose to follow. Note that if the condition (7.63) is not satisfied we may go from $\boldsymbol{k}^0$ to $\boldsymbol{k}^T$ and on to $\boldsymbol{k}^S$ and back to $\boldsymbol{k}^0$, and we may not arrive at -100, the starting point.

To sum up, if there exists a capital aggregate, we can discover it by the chain-index method of aggregation. If we apply the chain-index method where no capital aggregate exists we will run into nonsense. Our measure at one point will change as the economy follows one path rather than another. Hence, the conditions, properties 1–3, are required for the chain-index method, as here applied, to produce a meaningful measure of capital.

To turn now to the price function $\Pi(\boldsymbol{p}_k)$, consider the relation

$$\boldsymbol{p}_k \cdot \boldsymbol{k} + \mu F_\phi \phi(\boldsymbol{k}) = 0, \tag{7.64}$$

as given in (7.57). We know also, from (7.53), that $\Pi(\boldsymbol{p}_k)$ will satisfy

$$\Pi(\boldsymbol{p}_k) = \boldsymbol{p}_k \cdot \boldsymbol{k}/\phi(\boldsymbol{k}). \tag{7.65}$$

Hence,

$$\Pi(\boldsymbol{p}_k) = -\mu F_\phi \tag{7.66}$$

and (7.64) can be written as

$$\boldsymbol{p}_k \cdot \boldsymbol{k} - \Pi(\boldsymbol{p}_k)\phi(\boldsymbol{k}) = 0. \tag{7.67}$$

Since (7.67) holds at all t the time derivative of the left-hand side must be zero, so that

$$\dot{\boldsymbol{p}}_k \cdot \boldsymbol{k} + \boldsymbol{p}_k \cdot \dot{\boldsymbol{k}} - \dot{\Pi}\phi - \Pi\dot{\phi} = 0. \tag{7.68}$$

Hence,

$$\frac{\dot{\boldsymbol{p}}_k \cdot \boldsymbol{k}}{\boldsymbol{p}_k \cdot \boldsymbol{k}} + \frac{\boldsymbol{p}_k \cdot \dot{\boldsymbol{k}}}{\boldsymbol{p}_k \cdot \boldsymbol{k}} - \frac{\dot{\Pi}}{\Pi} - \frac{\dot{\phi}}{\phi} = 0, \tag{7.69}$$

which, taking into account (7.59), reduces to

$$\dot{\Pi}/\Pi = \dot{\boldsymbol{p}}_k \cdot \boldsymbol{k}/\boldsymbol{p}_k \cdot \boldsymbol{k}. \tag{7.70}$$

Compare this to (7.59). It will be seen that the price function Π satisfies the equation for a chain-index derivation just as does the quantity function ϕ. In the derivation of the price function the rate of change of the price measure at any moment of time involves a linear function of price changes $\dot{\boldsymbol{p}}_k \cdot \boldsymbol{k}$. However, the weights are changing constantly, as one expects with a price index, to reflect the changing role played by various capital items in making up the total cost of capital.

It only remains to remind the reader that our treatment of the theory of chain-index aggregation has not been a general one. We have not previously assumed uniqueness and differentiability of the value-maximizing production plans and we would surely be unhappy with any approach confined solely to that case. However, we need have no fear of this. Other cases can be covered by the chain-index method, and while we will not provide here a full account of how this is done, we can indicate the amendments that must be made.

Since we are assuming convex sets, what the assumption of 'smoothness' does is to rule out 'corners' and 'flats' in the production surfaces. A corner will mean that the rate of change of the value-maximizing solution will be discontinuous and a flat will give us non-unique maximizing points and discontinuities. However, with some modifications, these features can be put to good advantage. One of the difficulties of the type of case considered by

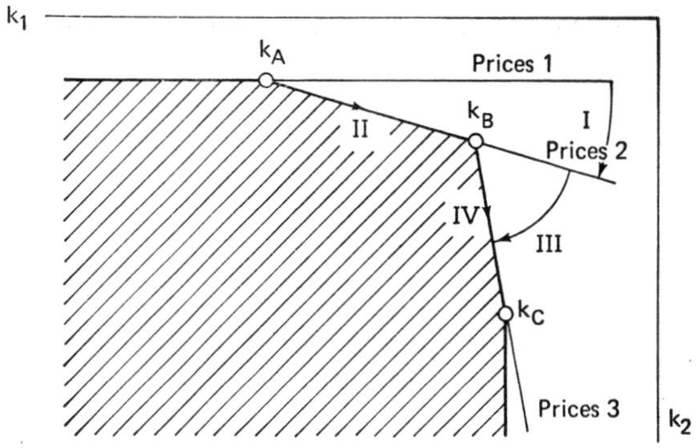

Fig. 7.6.

traditional mathematical economics is that there is simultaneous variation in prices and quantities. This is awkward for the chain-index method because a function such as $\boldsymbol{p}_k \cdot \dot{\boldsymbol{k}}$, which appears to be linear is in fact not so, because $\boldsymbol{p}_k$ is implicitly a function of $\boldsymbol{k}$. However, if we had a production set with a frontier consisting only of corners and flats then we could vary prices only at corners, with the value-maximizing point remaining unchanged, and vary quantities only along planed 'faces' of the production set at constant prices. In this case it is possible, and indeed quite easy, to obtain ϕ or Π by the chain-index method *exactly*, i.e. without recourse to the approximations normally employed for the solution of differential equations.

Figure 7.6 illustrates the decomposition of movements along the production frontier into periods of pure quantity change and periods of pure price change. Of course, we should think of this as occurring in n dimensions and not just two, but that will not give rise to difficulties.

We start at A with prices 1. The first period I is occupied by a continuous movement of prices from prices 1 to prices 2. During this period the value-maximizing point continues to be A. The change in the quantity chain index is zero, there being no change in any quantity and the change in the chain index of price is

$$\boldsymbol{k}_A[\boldsymbol{p}_k^2 - \boldsymbol{p}_k^1], \tag{7.71}$$

because the weights on price changes are invariant. The next period, II, is occupied by a movement along the line $\boldsymbol{k}_A\boldsymbol{k}_B$, prices being throughout $\boldsymbol{p}_k^2$. Only the quantity index registers any change and, the weights being constant, the total change is

$$\boldsymbol{p}_k^2[\boldsymbol{k}_B - \boldsymbol{k}_A]. \tag{7.72}$$

Period III is again one of price changes, the total change being

$$\boldsymbol{k}_{\mathrm{B}}[\boldsymbol{p}_k^3 - \boldsymbol{p}_k^2]. \tag{7.73}$$

Lastly, period IV involves a quantity change from $\boldsymbol{k}_{\mathrm{B}}$ to $\boldsymbol{k}_{\mathrm{C}}$ and the change in the quantity index is

$$\boldsymbol{p}_k^3[\boldsymbol{k}_{\mathrm{C}} - \boldsymbol{k}_{\mathrm{B}}]. \tag{7.74}$$

It will be observed that this type of angular case is really much easier than the traditional case. For we can write out the chain indices exactly without any integration. We will encounter this type of approach again in ch. 8. There we will apply the basic aggregation ideas that have been set forth in this chapter to the new situation of aggregation across semi-stationary states.

8

The production function

Moreover, the production function has been a powerful instrument of miseducation. The student of economic theory is taught to write $O = f(L, C)$ where L is a quantity of labour, C a quantity of capital and O a rate of output of commodities. He is instructed to assume all workers alike, and to measure L in man-hours of labour; he is told something about the index-number problem involved in choosing a unit of output; and then is hurried on to the next question, in the hope that he will forget to ask in what units C is measured. Before ever he does ask, he has become a professor, and so sloppy habits of thought are handed on from one generation to the next.

JOAN ROBINSON, *The Production Function and The Theory of Capital* (1953–1954)

According to one interpretation the production function is a representation of the production possibilities that are open to an economic system. As such it is a concept which is neither particularly revolutionary nor controversial. All are agreed that some transformations are possible for a particular economy, while others are not possible. This is what we are saying when we state that $(z_1, \boldsymbol{k}_1, \boldsymbol{q}_1)$ is a feasible transformation for the economy with production set $\mathscr{T}$, while $(z_2, \boldsymbol{k}_2, \boldsymbol{q}_2)$ is infeasible for the same economy. That such statements make sense, and that they are sometimes important, is not to be doubted.

However, to many students of economics the term *production function* will evoke something which differs in certain critical respects from the general disaggregated representation of production possibilities to which reference has been made. Let us examine some of these differences. According to a quite usual usage the production function:

(i) pertains to the activity of the whole economy – as does the transformation set $\mathscr{T}$;

(ii) represents the rate of production of a single final output depending upon the input of capital (being here just one input), labour and possibly some other non-produced inputs;

(iii) exhibits constant returns to scale (homogeneity of degree one); and

(iv) satisfies the condition that the product of an input, labour or capital, and the marginal product of that input in terms of output, gives the total payment to the owners of that input in terms of output.

Let us put aside the last item for the time being, for unless we can construct a production function in the sense of (i)–(iii) there is little point in worrying about whether this extra restriction can be complied with as well. Furthermore, (iii) need not detain us. We have not until now imposed constant returns, although condition 4.1 came close to it; but it is a small thing as regards our present concerns, so let us assume that $\mathscr{T}$ satisfies

$$(\boldsymbol{z}, \boldsymbol{k}, \boldsymbol{q}) \in \mathscr{T} \Rightarrow (\lambda \boldsymbol{z}, \lambda \boldsymbol{k}, \lambda \boldsymbol{q}) \in \mathscr{T}, \quad \text{for any } \lambda > 0, \tag{8.1}$$

and then look for a constant-returns-to-scale production function.

With (ii) we get to the heart of the problem. Our production function is to take the form

$$Y = f[K, \boldsymbol{z}], \tag{8.2}$$

where Y is the rate of production of output, represented by a scalar; K is the stock of capital, again represented by a scalar; and $\boldsymbol{z}$ is the vector of non-produced inputs, such as labour. If there were only one non-produced input, homogeneous labour, then we could represent it by a scalar L, when (8.2) would reduce to

$$Y = f[K, L]. \tag{8.3}$$

It seems more than a little unsatisfactory to treat of only one non-produced input, as labour, to the neglect of land and variegated human labour. However, this has been done so frequently that today economists very often do not even note the force of the assumption. Here we will adopt the same assumption, but the reader should note that some of our results could not be derived without it. The problem of justifying a production function of the form (8.3) has typically been seen as a problem of vindicating the practice of representing capital by an aggregate. This is the problem which Robinson has advertised[1] and the existence of which excites some economists, while depressing others and filling them with feelings of insecurity and doubt.

However, before we tackle K, what about Y? If the production function is to describe the productive activities of the entire economy, and if that economy

---

[1] Notably in her classic paper 'The production function and the theory of capital' (1953–1954). Many later papers are addressed in one way or another to answering Robinson's challenge. Immediately following the above was published an over-modestly-titled paper, 'The production function and the theory of capital: a comment', by Champernowne (1953–1954). Strangely, this last paper seems to have attracted scarcely any readers, so that its results are still neglected, or have had to be rediscovered in later years. The approach to the production function adopted in this chapter is based on the marvellously ingenious creation of Champernowne.

can, and typically does, produce more than one kind of final output, then is there not a parallel problem of justifying the representation of Y by a single number? It would be a serious mistake to dismiss this last probelm as just 'an index-number problem' (whatever that means) while supposing that the problem of aggregating capital is in some sense more profound and intractable. However, it may be useful to cut through the problem of output by supposing that only one final output is produced. As our argument proceeds this will turn out to amount to assuming that there is only one kind of consumption good, and that the economy is in a stationary state, a semi-stationary state with $\gamma = 0$. But more of that later.

Have we not already settled the question of a justification of the production function in ch. 7? After all, it is transparently clear that (8.3) is only a special case of a synthetic production set in disguise. We express the conditions of production by saying that a production plan $(z, \boldsymbol{k}, \boldsymbol{q})$ is feasible only if $(z, \boldsymbol{k}, \boldsymbol{q})$ belongs to $\mathscr{T}$. We can just as well measure output net rather than gross as $\boldsymbol{y} = \boldsymbol{q} - \boldsymbol{k}$ and represent production by a triple $(z, \boldsymbol{k}, \boldsymbol{y})$, which triple will be feasible only if it belongs to $\mathscr{T}_1$, the set of feasible triples expressed in terms of net output. Furthermore, if only one net output is ever positive, we may replace $\boldsymbol{y}$ by the scalar Y measuring the rate of production of that output. Our triple now takes the form $(z, \boldsymbol{k}, Y)$. Next suppose that z, similarly, has only one element, here denoted by L to evoke the idea of labour. Then the triple has the form $(L, \boldsymbol{k}, Y)$. Note that $\boldsymbol{k}$ and L are non-positive so that the capital *input* is $-\boldsymbol{k}$ and the labour *input* is $-L$. Now define a function as follows:

$$f(-\boldsymbol{k}, -L) = \max Y, \qquad (L, \boldsymbol{k}, Y) \in \mathscr{T}_1. \tag{8.4}$$

Less formally, Y is the largest output producible with inputs $-\boldsymbol{k}$ and $-L$. Hence, a production function may be derived from a production set. If we have a case in which a synthetic production set may be derived, in which $\boldsymbol{k}$ is replaced by a scalar K, then in such a case we may derive a production function in which $-\boldsymbol{k}$ is replaced by a scalar. In no other case may we do so.

Is there then no more to be said? The answer to this question turns on an important issue of interpretation. Historically the production function was introduced at a time when the central focus of macroeconomic analysis was on the stationary state. The primary employment of the production function was to assist with the analysis of comparisons of stationary states which were assumed to differ with regard to capital intensity of production methods. On one interpretation, therefore, the production function is not concerned with states of the economy that do not correspond to some or other stationary state. One thing at least is clear: unless we give some such specialized interpretation to the production function (8.3) we have already disposed of the problem of justifying the aggregate representation of capital or output in ch. 7. The conclusion there it will be remembered was not favourable to the idea.

So let us examine the implications of confining our attention to stationary states. If we do so then the net output of the economies that we will consider will consist only of consumption goods and this, or rather this and more, is vitally important to the construction of a production function because that enterprise can succeed only if the relation between capital per head and output per head is *independent of the composition of final output*. Why so? Suppose that final output comprises more than one type of output. Suppose further that of the components that make up final output some are more capital intensive than others, meaning that more capital[2] and less labour is used to produce a unit of some components of final output than others in all states of price equilibrium. Then we have only to alter the composition of final output, so as to leave the total unaffected, and we will require more (or less) capital in combination with a given input of labour, to produce the same level of output. There is an important message herein contained: the construction of an aggregate production function comes up against two quite distinct difficulties. On the one hand, there is the problem of giving a meaning to K, aggregate capital – but even if that were no problem we would still be hard pressed to relate the level of output uniquely to a given pair of inputs if the composition of the output might change haphazardly.

It is here that the assumption that the economy is in stationary equilibrium, allied to the assumption that there is only one kind of consumption, is peculiarly efficacious in dissolving the problem of composition of output and allowing the analysis to focus clearly on the problem of capital aggregation. For if there is only one kind of consumption and if there is no capital accumulation, then the composition of final output is determined and we need be concerned only with the level of final output relative to labour. By proceeding with the assumptions that have been detailed we are best equipped to throw light on the debate concerning the meaning of 'capital' in a production function. However, let it not be forgotten that in focusing our attention so exclusively on the aggregation of capital we are carried away by the fetishistic preoccupation of the authors of that debate. Naturally, the problem of aggregating

---

[2] The meaning of the term 'capital' in this sentence with its overtones of aggregation need not cause us concern. For the sake of the argument just at this point we can well assume that all capital is alike, or consists of proportional vectors. Even the two-sector models, in which problems of aggregating capital are assumed not to exist, are rich enough to demonstrate that the capital–output ratio is not independent of the division of output between consumption and capital accumulation. See, for example, Hahn and Matthews (1964).

capital appears to be peculiarly awesome if the problems of aggregating everything else, and notably output, have simply been assumed away.

The analysis that will follow admits of an alternative interpretation of which mention should be made. We have so far supposed that our production function will describe the whole economy. Hence, if it is important that final output be homogeneous, we must impose assumptions to give us a homogeneous final output for the whole economy. Instead, we might simply require that our production function describe just one sector of an economy so designated that its final output will be all of one kind. This alternative interpretation is available and it indicates that the restriction to the stationary state is not as crippling as it might at first seem. If we cannot construct an aggregate production function we may yet be able to construct sectoral production functions in each of which the inputs are labour and aggregate capital, but the aggregate capitals of different sectors may be incomparable. However, notice that this notion of a 'sector' of an economy does not correspond to the usual one, the one familiar from industry studies and input–output analysis. An economy in stationary equilibrium is a fully vertically integrated production process for producing the consumption good. If capital equipment wears out and has to be replaced then part of the activity of the stationary state consists in producing capital goods. It follows that an analysis derived for stationary states applies directly only to fully integrated production sectors, self-sufficient with respect to their replacement demands for capital equipment, but not self-sufficient with respect to additions to capital equipment[3].

Aside from dissolving the problem of the composition of output, the assumption of stationary equilibrium is important in another aspect. What it does is to largely remove the analysis from the jurisdiction of the theorems of ch. 7. This it achieves by considerably weakening the requirements on the capital-aggregation function. In ch. 7 we postulated a function ϕ the value of which was the aggregate of its arguments z. If we think of aggregation of the capital inputs, then an aggregation is a rule for associating an aggregate measure K with a vector of capitals $\boldsymbol{k}$. Let that rule be embodied in the function ϕ:

$$K = \phi(\boldsymbol{k}), \qquad \boldsymbol{k} \in \mathscr{D}, \tag{8.5}$$

---

[3] The example of the two-sector model may help to clarify the point. If capital equipment is perfectly durable then the consumption sector of the two-sector model is a 'sector' in our sense. If capital equipment wears out, however, then we would have to combine the consumption activity with just enough capital-producing activity to maintain capital intact. We would then get the fully integrated consumption sector, i.e. the production activity of the two-sector economy in stationary equilibrium.

where $\mathscr{D}$ is the domain of the function ϕ, the set of all $\boldsymbol{k}$s to which the aggregation procedure is applicable. The domain of ϕ did not play much of a role in ch. 7, because there more or less any $\boldsymbol{k}$, of the right sign at least, was admissible. However, the reader may confirm for himself that the derivations of ch. 7 are good for $\boldsymbol{k}$ restricted to an arbitrary closed domain, except that if $\mathscr{D}$ is not identical to all the $\boldsymbol{k}$ values that occur in the production set we will not be able to rehearse arguments that depend upon convexity or the maximization of net value at equilibrium prices. Thus, if we are to successfully aggregate over equilibrium stationary states we must have the nested-set condition satisfied over the subset of the production set which corresponds to the transformations of equilibrium stationary states. However, with the set of transformations so severely restricted, the nested-set condition (7.3) is rather a faint condition, at once not difficult to satisfy but at the same time when satisfied not a condition from which one gets very much. The problem of aggregating over equilibrium stationary states is best approached rather differently from the approach that proved fruitful in ch. 7.

Nevertheless, we can retain some continuity between the argument of ch. 7 and that of the present argument as follows. Towards the end of ch. 7 we addressed ourselves to the question: suppose that there exists an aggregate of capital, how could one go about computing the function ϕ? There we discovered that the chain-index method would discover ϕ whenever that function existed. Recall that in that context the chain index method could always be applied and would always generate a function $\phi(\boldsymbol{k})$. However, unless the conditions for perfect representation of production possibilities were satisfied, the form of the function ϕ would depend upon the choice of initial capital vector.

One reason for considering the chain-index method as a likely tool for constructing the production function is that this method is an appropriate and fruitful one in the context of general aggregation. By adopting it again we are thus able to forge a link between the general aggregation problem of ch. 7 and the more particular concerns of this chapter. But another reason is yet more compelling. We have already had a 'first run' at the problem of aggregating capital in ch. 5, where we examined the notion of the marginal product of capital. There we were able to make some progress in delineating the principles for measuring capital as an aggregate. In particular, we noted that a change in aggregate capital should be measured in *constant prices*. Thus we were enabled to define the marginal product of capital and relate it to the rate of interest. However, as was there remarked, the measure of capital that emerged from that investigation was a 'parochial' one, meaning that it depended upon the point of reference of a particular growth path (called in chs. 4 and 5 growth path 1). All changes in capital were evaluated as changes away from this reference path.

To arrive at a global measure of capital, for the purpose of constructing a production function, we must put behind us the parochial approach that was adequate for ch. 5. The natural way of doing this is to construct a capital aggregate by the use of the chain-index method. For the purpose of production-function construction the chain-index method has two notable advantages:

(1) it incorporates the principle that a change in capital is a change in the value of capital measured at constant prices[4];

(2) it is non-parochial: the prices associated with any particular state are used to evaluate movements away from that state, but the same is true of every other state and its own price system. Thus, no price system is given a special or privileged status in the construction of the index.

The chain index then commends itself in the context of stationary-state aggregation: unfortunately there are certain difficulties in the way of applying it to that context. The source of these difficulties is not hard to comprehend. When we applied the chain-index method in ch. 7 what we did was to take prices along a straight line (the distance being represented by the scalar t) and compute the variation continuously along this line. Of course, to get the whole function ϕ one would have to repeat this process an indefinitely large number of times, but the point is that in any single and particular application of the method *prices varied continuously.* As the prices varied continuously we passed sequentially through various states of the economy hence arranging these states in a sequence, or imposing upon them a particular *linear structure.* This was not an accidental feature, in fact it is basic to the chain-index method. The method can only be applied if the states for which an aggregate is to be constructed *can be arranged along a line, along which line prices at which the states are equilibria vary continuously*[5].

How are we going to arrange all the equilibrium stationary states of an economy along a line, along which line prices will vary continuously? If we cannot do this we are certainly in difficulties even in applying the chain-index method. We want a parameter which will rank stationary states but this must be a parameter with respect to which the variation in relative prices of capital goods is continuous.

---

[4] Hence, in particular, the chain index will record a change only when at least one real capital quantity has changed.

[5] Of course, in the general aggregation of ch. 7 the states were arranged along many lines converging on (p_z^0, p_k^0, p_q^0). But then, as we saw, one needs strong conditions to ensure that an unambiguous and meaningful aggregate will emerge.

The chain-index method has frequently been associated with a time-series context. There the linear structure springs from the temporal sequencing of states and there we might be willing to assume for theoretical purposes that prices vary continuously through time.

As regards this parameter, there is only one possible candidate and that is the rate of interest[6]. As we have seen in ch. 4, a semi-stationary state, and hence in particular a stationary state, might be an equilibrium at intertemporal prices that do not correspond to a constant rate of interest and to relative prices that are invariant over time. It is, however, the peculiar feature of a semi-stationary state that it can be supported by a constant-rate-of-interest price system (appendix to ch. 4). Hence, with any stationary state we may associate a set of interest rates at which that state could be an equilibrium, meaning that for each value in the set there exists an intertemporal price system, with a constant rate of interest of that value, at which prices the stationary state concerned is an equilibrium.

To be able to use the rate of interest as a parameter by means of which stationary states may be arranged in a linear sequence we need to make some special assumptions. None of these is inconsequential, but some are more forceful than others, and we will in due course examine each of them in turn[7]. Henceforth, whenever we refer to the prices or wage rates of stationary states, these are in terms of the current consumption good which will be supposed not to be a free good in any stationary state under consideration. From now on we will always consider stationary states with the same labour forces so that questions of the size of the economy do not obscure comparisons of the other features.

The stationary states that are equilibrium at some prices can be divided into two mutually exclusive groups, labelled *pure* and *blended.* Every equilibrium stationary state is either of the pure or blended type. A blended stationary state can be obtained by combining two or more distinct stationary states in

---

[6] There are various alternatives that might come into consideration but none of them will do. Consider, for example, ranking stationary states by consumption (per capita). This is unambiguous as regards arranging the states along a line, but there is no reason to believe (although it could happen) that the states so arranged will have equilibrium price systems varying continuously along the line.

[7] We are following Champernowne (1953–1954). However, our treatment differs from his in a number of details and in terminology. Also there is an ambiguity involved in his assumption 5 ('At any level of food-wages of labour, the rate of interest will settle at the highest level which any employer can pay without making losses.'). The highest level of interest which an employer can pay depends in general not merely upon the food wage rate but on other prices as well. What this assumption is designed to do is to ensure that relative prices, including the consumption wage rate, will be uniquely determined given the wage rate or the rate of interest. Also, it is implicitly assumed that relative prices vary continuously with the wage rate. However, to guarantee these features we need to make more assumptions than are laid out by the author. A discussion of the matter may well be deferred until ch. 11, when we will go into it rather fully. However, let it be noted at once that more is involved than the manifestly innocuous assumption that employers will pay the highest possible rate of interest given *all* the prices that rule.

suitable proportions. Consider three distinct stationary states, numbered arbitrarily 1, 2 and 3. Recall that all these states have the same total labour supply. Suppose that stationary state 3 is equivalent to 40% of the labour force working in a state exactly similar to stationary state 1 (except for the reduction in scale) together with 60% of the labour force working in a state exactly similar (except for scale) to stationary state 2. Then we say that stationary state 3 is a *blended stationary state*. If there exists no pair of distinct stationary states such that stationary state 3 is a blend of these two states then we say that stationary state 3 is a *pure stationary state*. Notice that we are always concerned only with equilibrium stationary states.

The assumptions that we are going to impose now follow. They are first listed and then elucidated:

(1) The number of pure stationary states is finite.

(2) *Either*, for each rate of interest in a non-empty closed interval of admissible rates of interest, having zero at its lower end and a maximum rate of interest (ρ_{max}) at its upper end; *or* for each non-negative rate of interest, there exists a price system embodying that rate of interest at which at least one stationary state is an equilibrium. Where the alternative *either* applies, for no rate of interest higher than ρ_{max} does there exist a price system at which a stationary state is an equilibrium.

(3) The price system associated with an admissible interest rate is unique and each price is a continuous function of the interest rate on the range of admissible values.

(4) At the price system associated with any interest rate not more than two distinct pure stationary states are equilibria.

(5) For any pair of distinct stationary states there exists at most one rate of interest for which both these states are equilibria at the price system of that interest rate.

(6) The set of rate of interest values which give rise to price systems at which any particular stationary state is an equilibrium is a closed connected set.

Assumption (1) is not necessary to what follows but it makes for simplicity and has been much favoured by writers on this subject. Also the currently fashionable *curiosa* of capital theory come forth most readily in the context of a model with a finite number of basic techniques of production. An added convenience of working with this assumption is that the chain-index method is easy to apply, for reasons which the closing pages of ch. 7 will have made apparent. Finally, let it be noted that a finite model is necessarily richer in possibilities for comparisons of equilibria than a non-finite one; this because any case that can arise in the non-finite model can arise also in a finite model where only the two equilibrium techniques of the non-finite model are admissible.

Assumption (2) is not at all unreasonable. We are supposing that there will be stationary-state equilibria for all non-negative values of the rate of interest, at least up to some maximum rate. However, the assumption is not quite vacuous and one can construct examples that fail to satisfy it[8].

With assumption (3) we come to a really strong and restrictive assumption. Notice that this assumption is the one that underlies the second stage of the Cambridge model. There is no general guarantee that the price system of a stationary state will be uniquely determined given the rate of interest. In fact, there is not even a guarantee that the wage rate will be uniquely determined by the rate of interest. Hence the *factor price frontier*, a functional relation between the rate of interest and the equilibrium wage rate, which has proved to be a popular tool in recent times, requires some special assumptions for its justification. In ch. 11 we will detail what these assumptions amount to. In the meantime, here is an example to vindicate our claim that there is real force behind assumption (3). Notice that the stationary states of the example are both ones in which the technique for producing the capital good covers its costs, although in a stationary state it will not be employed. Hence, we are not surreptitiously introducing another non-produced good apart from labour.

Example 8.1. There are only two productive activities and one kind of capital good. The activities are

1 labour ⊕ 1 capital good ⊖ 2 consumption good ⊕ 1 capital good,
1 labour ⊕ 2 capital good ⊖ 2 consumption good ⊕ 3 capital good.

The reader may confirm for himself that both these activities break even at each of the following price systems (the consumption good is the *numeraire*):

$$\begin{aligned} \rho &= 1, \quad w = 1, \quad \pi = 1, \\ \rho &= 1, \quad w = \tfrac{3}{4}, \quad \pi = \tfrac{5}{4}. \end{aligned} \tag{8.6}$$

Hence, neither relative goods prices nor the wage rate are necessarily uniquely determined by the rate of interest. The argument of ch. 11 will give some insight into what kind of assumptions one would have to impose to rule out example 8.1, or any similar example.

Assumption (4) once again carries a certain amount of force but is both convenient and basically harmless. If we take a complete price system at

[8] See below, ch. 11, p. 274.

random, we would normally expect that only one pure stationary state would be an equilibrium at those prices. But since as the prices change we will eventually find another stationary state to be an equilibrium it is clear that there will be *tie points*[9], meaning values of the rate of interest giving rise to price systems at which two pure stationary states, and hence all blends of these states, constitute equilibria. Once we have two pure states tying at a particular value of the rate of interest, and if we can construct our examples at will, we evidently may choose a distinct third state such that it will again be an equilibrium at the very same price system. However, such examples are always contrived, in the sense that small random variation in the coefficients of their activities will destroy the special feature of three pure states being simultaneously equilibria. Hence, we do well to put such improbable cases aside.

Assumption (5) carries two somewhat distinct implications which we may consider in turn. Without loss of anything of importance for the present discussion, consider a case in which there are just two pure stationary states that are equilibria at any rate of interest. Consider the values of the rate of interest, between zero and $\rho_{\max}$, at which the two pure stationary states, here denoted I and II, are equilibria. These are illustrated in figs. 8.1 and 8.2 which feature two particular types of case that assumption (5) is designed to exclude.

In fig. 8.1, assumption (5) is violated because the range of rates of interest at which I can be an equilibrium (0 to ρ_2) *overlaps* with the range of rates of interest at which II can be an equilibrium (ρ_1 to $\rho_{\max}$). While this might occur, it is inherently improbable, because it means that over the range ρ_1–ρ_2 the movement in prices that takes place affects the cost of production of the consumption good for two distinct techniques of production in an identical manner. This is hardly a possibility that need cause us concern. The type of case illustrated by fig. 8.2, however, is an altogether more likely possibility. Here the two stationary states only tie at particular and isolated values of the rate of interest – we have *tie points* rather than one or more ranges of rate-of-interest values over which the two stationary states are tied. But there is more than one tie point for these two particular stationary states. However, assumption (6) is one that rules out this type of case and more as well; so the special force of assumption (5), in the context of the complete list of assumptions, is to rule out the case of fig. 8.1. Viewed from this angle the assumption is not unreasonable and we need not allow it to detain us further, but may proceed at once to a discussion of the wider ranging and critical assumption (6).

[9] The usual terminology is *switch point*. In case that term may have too many overtones of a change from one equilibrium to another, which changes, of course, are not involved in the argument, we prefer the more exact connotation of a tie.

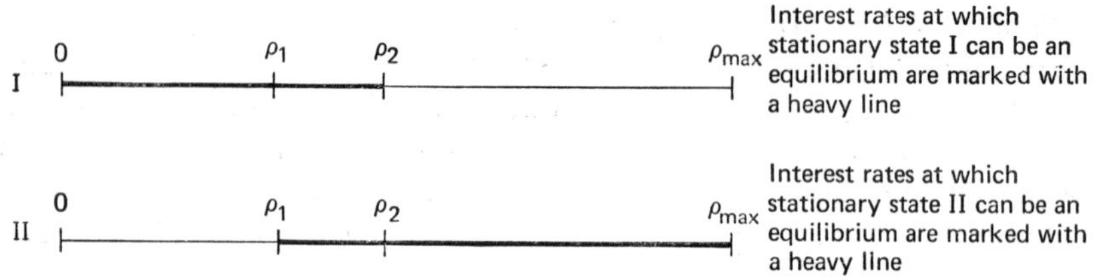

Fig. 8.1.

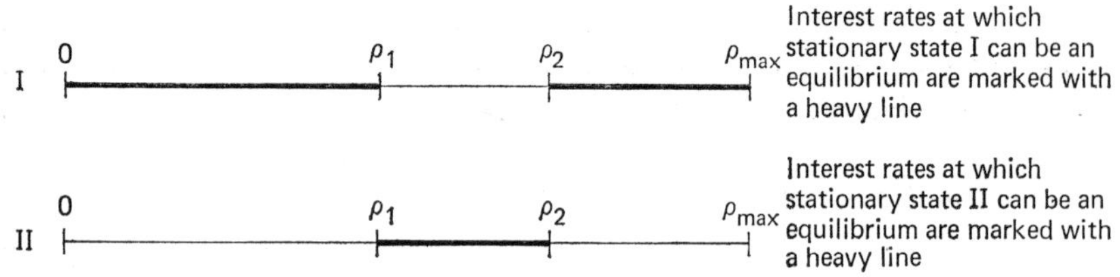

Fig. 8.2.

We are following up the idea that the rate of interest might serve to arrange stationary states in a linear sequence. For this we require that the rate of interest will place each state at some point in the sequence – that is essential. But it would also be helpful if no stationary state appeared more than once in the sequence. We want the chain-index measure of capital to be constructed by moving along the sequence and applying the chain-index rule. If, however, some stationary state appears more than once in the sequence, we will obtain more than one measure of the quantity of capital in that state. In that case, we would have to impose extra conditions, and strong ones as well, to ensure that the different measure of capital would be consistent. Assumption (6) has the implication that any particular stationary state will appear only over one range of values of the rate of interest. However, there is no guarantee whatsoever that the assumption will be satisfied, as the following example indicates.

Example 8.2. There are three productive activities which allow of two distinct stationary states, called I and II. Stationary state I is characterized by the following activities breaking even:

I: 1 labour $\oplus$ 1 durable good $\ominus$ 5 consumption good $\oplus$ 1 durable good
4 labour $\ominus$ 1 durable good.

In the case of stationary state II only one activity comes into consideration. This is

II: 1 labour $\oplus$ 2 consumption good $\ominus$ 5 consumption good.

In the case of the present example, the stationary state will be an equilibrium at any particular value of ρ which can pay the highest wage rate at that value of ρ.[10] We can calculate what the maximum wage will be for each stationary state as follows. Let ρ denote the rate of interest, ω the wage rate in terms of the consumption good in the input week and π the price of the durable good in terms of the consumption good. Then, when I is an equilibrium we have

$$\begin{aligned} &\omega + (1+\rho)\pi = 5 + \pi, \\ &4\omega = \pi, \end{aligned} \tag{8.7}$$

by the condition that the present value of output be equal to the present value of inputs. Eliminating π from (8.7) one obtains

$$\frac{5-\omega}{\rho} - 4\omega = 0 \tag{8.8}$$

or

$$\boxed{\omega_{\mathrm{I}} = \frac{5}{4\rho + 1},} \tag{8.9}$$

where the subscript I reminds us that this is the wage rate of stationary state I when the rate of interest is ρ.

When II is an equilibrium we have

$$\omega + 2(1+\rho) = 5, \tag{8.10}$$

again by the condition that the present value of inputs shall be equal to the present value of outputs. Hence,

$$\boxed{\omega_{\mathrm{II}} = 3 - 2\rho.} \tag{8.11}$$

It is immediately evident that this example will give rise to a violation of assumption (6). Clearly ω_{I} exceeds ω_{II} for high values of ρ and the same is true when $\rho = 0$. However, for $\rho = 0.5$ $\omega_{\mathrm{II}} > \omega_{\mathrm{I}}$. Hence, the range of values of ρ for which I is the equilibrium is not connected. Fig. 8.3 illustrates. The tie points are at ($\rho = 0.25$, $\omega = 2.5$) and at ($\rho = 1.0$, $\omega = 1.0$). The set of values of ρ at which I can be an equilibrium comprises the pair of disconnected intervals [0, 0.25] and [1.0, $+\infty$]. Assumption (6) is violated[11].

Some remarks may prove useful. The example is not contrived. Since it depends upon the manner in which the ω_{I} function intersects the linear ω_{II}

---

[10] This is not generally true, see the discussion in footnote 7, p. 176.

[11] On the meaning of all this we will have more to say later. See below, pp. 238–240 and 242–243.

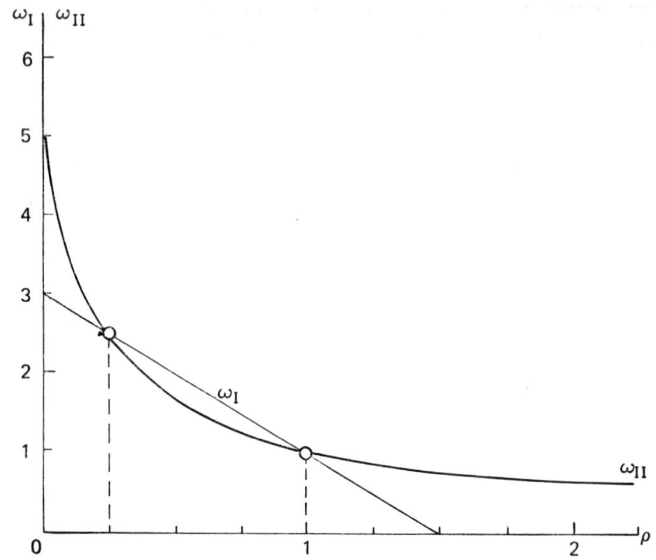

Fig. 8.3.

function twice, small changes in the parameters of the example, which will only bring about small shifts in the curves of the figure will not destroy the pertinent features of the example. Next, note that this example, as it happens, also violates assumption (5) because there are two tie points for I and II. However, this is incidental. The reader may confirm for himself that adding another pure stationary state (III), which employs only the activity

$$1 \text{ labour} \oplus 1 \text{ consumption good} \ominus 3.5 \text{ consumption good}, \tag{8.12}$$

with a wage equation

$$\boxed{\omega_{III} = 2.5 - \rho,} \tag{8.13}$$

'takes out' the tie point ($\rho = 1.0$, $\omega = 1.0$). However, the set of values of ρ for which I is an equilibrium will still be disconnected. In this case [0, 0.25] and $[9/8 + \sqrt{41}/8, +\infty]$.

It is clear then that assumption (6) is a strong one and according to one view the production function founders on this rock. However, the failure of assumption (6) does not mean that the chain-index method cannot be applied – it means rather that the method when applied leads to some unsatisfactory results. To see exactly what does happen we need to become better acquainted with the chain-index method.

To apply the method proceed as follows. Denote the prices of capital goods, in terms of the consumption good, of the price system corresponding to ρ by $\boldsymbol{p}_k(\rho)$. Set ρ equal to zero. By assumption (4) there are at most two pure stationary states which are equilibria at the price system corresponding to $\rho = 0$. Let us suppose, which is to assume rather little, that there is a pure stationary state, equilibrium at $\rho = 0$, in which some capital is used, and such that this stationary state is an equilibrium for some positive value of ρ. Let the capital vector of this state (at the scale where the labour used is 1) be $\boldsymbol{k}_0$. Let $\boldsymbol{k}_0$ count as 1.0 units of aggregate capital. There is no loss of generality here: we must arbitrarily choose units for our aggregate capital and this can be done once. Now the price index of one unit of capital at $\rho = 0$, in terms of the consumption good, will be $\boldsymbol{p}_k(0) \cdot \boldsymbol{k}_0$.

There may be one other pure stationary state also equilibrium at $\rho = 0$. If so, denote its capital vector by $\boldsymbol{k}_0'$. The aggregate of $\boldsymbol{k}_0'$ is given by the formula

$$\phi(\boldsymbol{k}_0') = \phi(\boldsymbol{k}_0')/\phi(\boldsymbol{k}_0) = \boldsymbol{p}_k(0) \cdot \boldsymbol{k}_0'/\boldsymbol{p}_k(0) \cdot \boldsymbol{k}_0. \tag{8.14}$$

This is a particular example of the general principle of the chain index. *The quantities of 'capital' in two stationary states which tie at rate of interest ρ are in the ratios of the values of capital in these two states evaluated at prices $\boldsymbol{p}_k(\rho)$.* This principle assigns capital quantities also to blended stationary states.

We have now assigned quantities of capital to all stationary states which are equilibria at rate of interest 0. Now consider a small positive rate of interest. For rates small enough we will be in the range of values between zero and the lowest tie point above zero. In this range a pure stationary state which is an equilibrium at $\rho = 0$ will be the unique equilibrium. This we know because our assumptions suffice to guarantee that the range $[0, \rho_{max}]$, or $[0, \infty]$ as the case may be, will be divided up into closed intervals, overlapping only at isolated tie points, on which intervals a particular pure stationary state will be an equilibrium. At a tie point two pure states are equilibria; it then follows that all blends of these pure states are equilibria as well. Except at isolated tie points the equilibrium stationary state is unique.

As ρ increases from zero to the value corresponding to the next tie point, ρ_1, we have no work to do with regard to compiling the index of the quantity of capital. The reason is plain. It is fundamental to the method that two states of the economy shall be deemed to contain different quantities of capital *only if their capital vectors are unequal.* However, we need not be idle. We have a price index to compile as well as a quantity index and while the capital vector is not varying the price vector is. The rule for measuring the price of aggregate capital in terms of the consumption good is again the chain-index method.

Denote the price index for ρ by $\pi(\rho)$. For ρ not greater than the value corresponding to the first tie point above $\rho = 0$, ρ_1, we have

$$\pi(\rho)/\pi(0) = \boldsymbol{p}_k(\rho)\cdot\boldsymbol{k}_0/\boldsymbol{p}_k(0)\cdot\boldsymbol{k}_0, \qquad \rho \leqslant \rho_1. \tag{8.15}$$

Proceeding thus we arrive at the first tie point above $\rho = 0$. At ρ_1 a pure stationary state is tied with the state with capital vector $\boldsymbol{k}_0$. Let that state have a capital vector $\boldsymbol{k}_1$. Again applying the chain-index rule we obtain

$$\phi(\boldsymbol{k}_1) = \{\phi(\boldsymbol{k}_1)/\phi(\boldsymbol{k}_0)\} = \{\boldsymbol{p}_k(\rho_1)\cdot\boldsymbol{k}_1/\boldsymbol{p}_k(\rho_1)\cdot\boldsymbol{k}_0\}. \tag{8.16}$$

Now for $\rho > \rho_1$ we enter a range of values on which the unique equilibrium has capital vector $\boldsymbol{k}_1$. Again, because there is no change in the capital vector along this range, there will be no alteration in the index of capital. However, the price index will be subject to alteration. The cumulative effect of these alterations is to give an index satisfying

$$\frac{\pi(\rho)}{\pi(0)} = \frac{\pi(\rho_1)}{\pi(0)}\frac{\pi(\rho)}{\pi(\rho_1)} = \frac{\boldsymbol{p}_k(\rho_1)\cdot\boldsymbol{k}_0}{\boldsymbol{p}_k(0)\cdot\boldsymbol{k}_0}\frac{\boldsymbol{p}_k(\rho)\cdot\boldsymbol{k}_1}{\boldsymbol{p}_k(\rho_1)\cdot\boldsymbol{k}_1}, \qquad \rho_1 \leqslant \rho \leqslant \rho_2. \tag{8.17}$$

And so to ρ_2, the next point, if there is one. Here we again amend the capital index. The capital vector of the pure stationary state that ties with $\boldsymbol{k}_1$ at ρ_2 is $\boldsymbol{k}_2$. The index measure of $\boldsymbol{k}_2$ satisfies

$$\phi(\boldsymbol{k}_2) = \frac{\phi(\boldsymbol{k}_2)}{\phi(\boldsymbol{k}_0)} = \frac{\phi(\boldsymbol{k}_1)\phi(\boldsymbol{k}_2)}{\phi(\boldsymbol{k}_0)\phi(\boldsymbol{k}_1)} = \frac{\boldsymbol{p}_k(\rho_1)\cdot\boldsymbol{k}_1\,\boldsymbol{p}_k(\rho_2)\cdot\boldsymbol{k}_2}{\boldsymbol{p}_k(\rho_1)\cdot\boldsymbol{k}_0\,\boldsymbol{p}_k(\rho_2)\cdot\boldsymbol{k}_1}. \tag{8.18}$$

We may now continue in a similar manner up to the largest tie point. To each pure-stationary-state capital vector we will have assigned a unique aggregate measure. The measure will be unique because, by assumption, and particularly assumption (6), a pure stationary state will appear once only on a closed range of values of ρ. On that range the chain-index measure is everywhere the same, so that it follows that the measure will be unique. The capital measure of a blended stationary state is an average of the capital measures of the pure stationary states from which it is composed (this is in accord with the chain-index measure) the weights being the proportions of the labour force in each of the stationary states. Consider, for example, the states tied at ρ_1. Construct a blended state as follows. Place λ labour in the stationary state of the type of the pure state that is an equilibrium at $\rho < \rho_1$ and $(1-\lambda)$ labour in the stationary state of the type of the other tied state $(0 < \lambda < 1)$. The capital vector of this blended state is

$$\lambda\boldsymbol{k}_0 + (1-\lambda)\,\boldsymbol{k}_1 \tag{8.19}$$

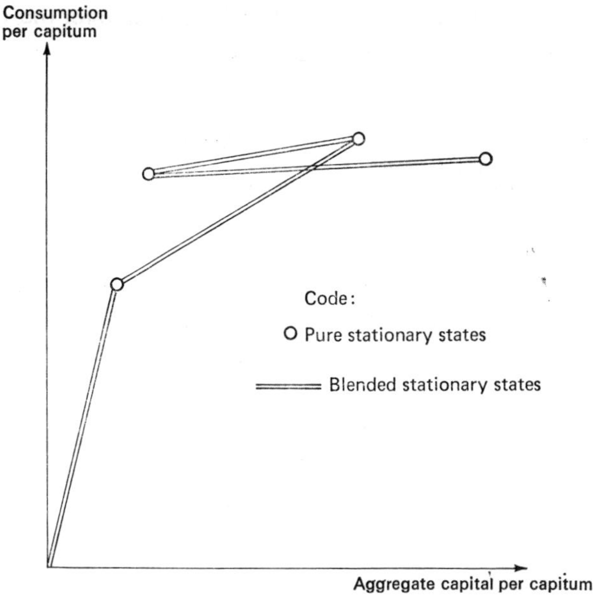

Fig. 8.4.

and the aggregate of that capital is

$$\lambda\phi(\boldsymbol{k}_0) + (1 - \lambda)\phi(\boldsymbol{k}_1). \tag{8.20}$$

With each pure or blended equilibrium stationary state we have now associated a capital measure. Each stationary state also has an output rate, which is no more than its level of consumption, there being no other final output. Can we now enter points on the graph of fig. 8.4 and so map out a function? Notice that whenever two points correspond to a pair of stationary states tied at some value of ρ we may connect them by a straight line indicating the various blends of those two pure tied states.

It now emerges that we have not yet necessarily arrived at a production function – not even with our lengthy list of assumptions. The reason is implicit in fig. 8.4. There points are entered corresponding to pure stationary states and tied states are connected by straight lines.

The graph twists around and ties a knot – it does not form a nicely shaped cross-section of a production function. We will shortly examine an example which gives rise to the type of case illustrated in fig. 8.4. But first it may be useful to examine an example which does give rise to a production function. The reader may use the example as an exercise to test his understanding of the chain-index method.

Example 8.3. There are six activities from which emerge four pure stationary states. The equation for the factor price frontier is given with each stationary state.

Stationary states	Activities
I	1. 1 labour ⊖ 2 consumption good
	$\omega = 2.$
II	2. 4 labour ⊕ 1 consumption good ⊖ 17 consumption good
	$\omega = 4 - \frac{\rho}{4}.$
III	3. 1 labour ⊕ 1 capital good (1) ⊖ 6 consumption good ⊕ 1 capital good (1)
	4. 1 labour ⊖ 2 capital good (1)
	$\omega = \frac{12}{2+\rho}.$
IV	5. 1 labour ⊕ 1 capital good (2) ⊖ 8 consumption good ⊕ 1 capital good (2)
	6. 1 labour ⊕ 2 capital good (2) ⊖ 3 capital good (2).
	$\omega = 8\frac{1-2\rho}{1-\rho}.$

Fig. 8.5 illustrates the form of the factor price frontiers.

Let us now apply the chain-index method. The stationary states are equilibria in inverse order as the rate of interest rises. At $\rho = 0$ the unique equilibrium stationary state is IV. Thence, one unit of capital good 2 must contain one unit of aggregate capital. At $\rho = 0$ the wage rate for IV is 8.0 and the cost of producing one extra unit of capital good (2) is also 8.0. Hence, the price index of 'capital' at $\rho = 0$ is 8.0. On the range [0, 0.25] it is again IV that is the equilibrium so that the quantity of capital is unchanged at 1.0. However, the price index is altered. The price of one unit of capital good (2) is $8/(1-\rho)$ $(\rho = 0, 0.25)$.[12]

[12] This is one of many statements in this example, the validity of which the reader should satisfy himself as an exercise.

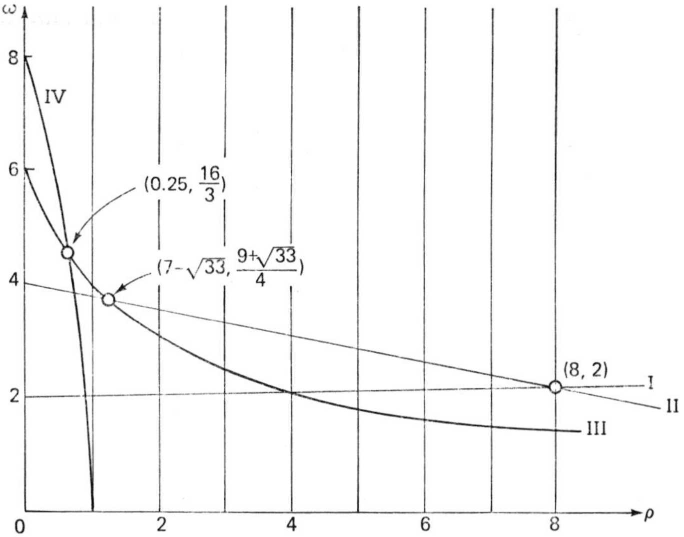

Fig. 8.5.

At $\rho = 0.25$ we reach our first tie point. Here we may rest the price index and turn our attention to the quantity index. Pure stationary state III ties with IV at $\rho = 0.25$, $\omega = \frac{16}{3}$. At that point the cost of one unit of capital good (1) is half the wage rate, $\frac{8}{3}$. The cost of one unit of capital good (2) is 8/0.75. Hence,

$$\frac{\phi\ [\text{one unit of capital good (1)}]}{\phi\ [\text{one unit of capital good (2)}]} = \frac{8/3}{8/0.75} = 0.25. \tag{8.21}$$

Since ϕ [one unit of capital good (2)] = 1.0, by construction, the quantity of capital in pure stationary state III is 0.25.

Next we enter the range of $(0.25, 7 - \sqrt{33})$ on which stationary state III is the unique equilibrium. The price index on this range is four times the cost of one unit of capital good (1) because capital good (1) contains 0.25 units of capital, i.e. $24/(2 + \rho)$. This brings us to the next tie point at $\rho = 7 - \sqrt{33}$. Here stationary state III is tied with stationary state II, and we have

$$\frac{\phi\ [0.25 \text{ units of the consumption good}]}{\phi\ [\text{one unit of capital good (1)}]} = \frac{0.25}{6/(2 + 7 - \sqrt{33})}, \tag{8.22}$$

$$\phi\ [0.25 \text{ units of the consumption good}] = (9 - \sqrt{33})/96. \tag{8.23}$$

The rest of our calculations are simple. Since in pure stationary state II the capital stock is a quantity of the consumption good there will be no more changes in the price index. Now ρ may go as high as 8.0 and the equilibrium

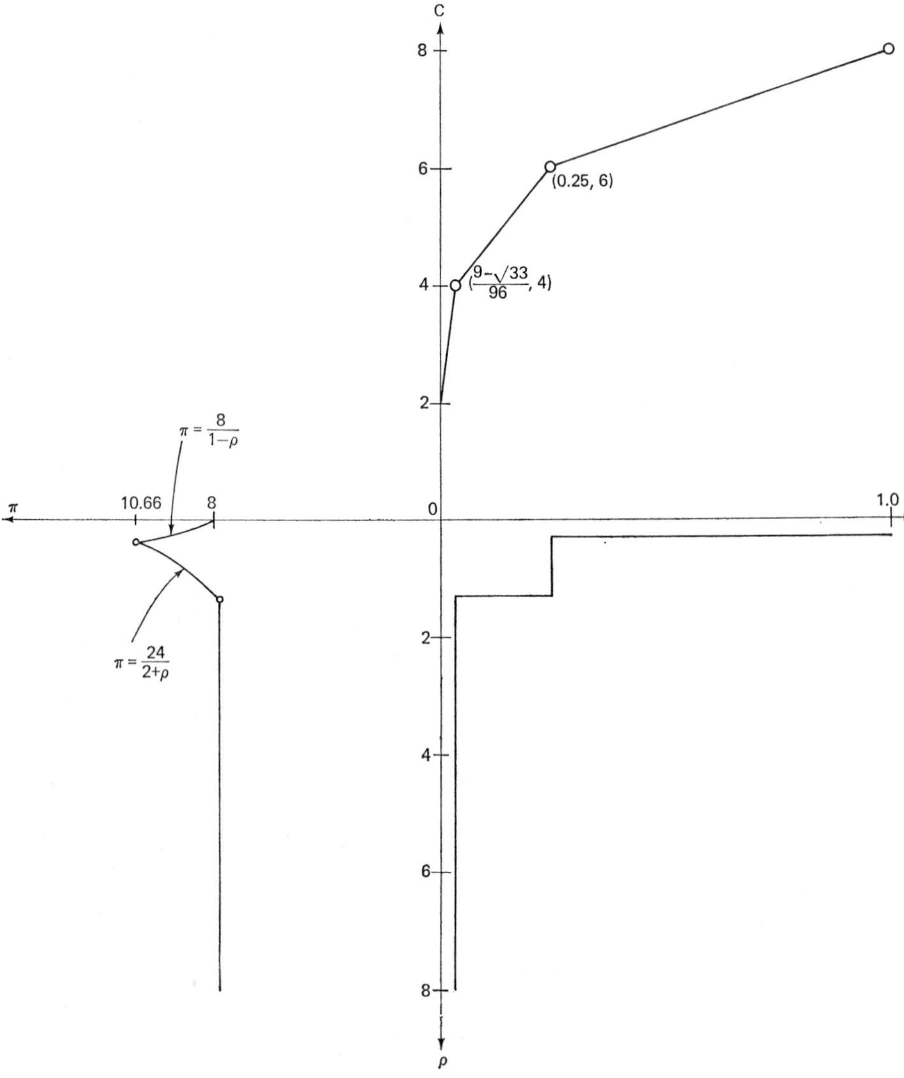
C
8
6
4
2
0
(0.25, 6)
$(\frac{9-\sqrt{33}}{96}, 4)$
$\pi = \frac{8}{1-\rho}$
π
10.66
8
1.0
$\pi = \frac{24}{2+\rho}$
2
4
6
8
ρ

Fig. 8.6.

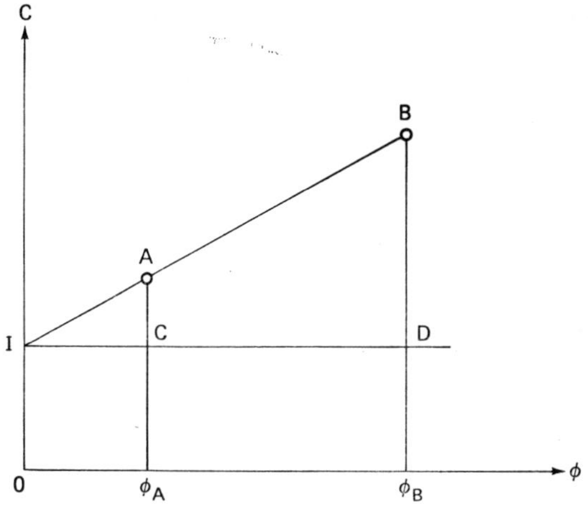

Fig. 8.7.

stationary state is still II. Finally, for ρ still higher we switch to stationary state I, which contains no capital. Fig. 8.6 illustrates. The production function is graphed in the upper right-hand quadrant, the relation between ρ and the chain index of capital in the lower right-hand quadrant, and the relationship between ρ and the price index of capital in the lower left-hand quadrant. At the tie points there is more than one possible value of ϕ because there are blended equilibrium states. These blended states serve to connect up with straight lines the points that we have calculated for the production function.

We can now note a very important property of a production function constructed by the chain-index method. Fig. 8.7 illustrates a pair of points on such a function, being tied stationary states, denoted A and B, and the line segment AB joining them which is one of the 'flats' of the function. Let the stationary states have consumption levels of C_A and C_B respectively. Let the stationary states corresponding to points A and B be tied at a rate of interest $\rho(A, B)$. Let the price index of capital at $\rho = \rho(A, B)$ be $\pi\{\rho(A, B)\}$. We will show that the intercept of the tangent to the production function (AB extended) on the vertical axis OI is the wage rate corresponding to $\rho = \rho(A, B)$. The importance of this observation will not elude the reader's notice. It means that when our production function is differentiable, so that marginal theory may be applied, the payment to one unit of the factor labour is equal to the marginal product of that factor in terms of output. It follows then, because we are treating of a cross-section of a constant-returns production function, that the payment to one unit of capital is the marginal product of capital in terms of output[13].

To demonstrate the result note that the price index of capital satisfies, by construction, the condition that the payment to capital is the product of the rate of interest, the index of 'capital' and the price index. Hence, we have

$$C_A = \rho(A, B)\pi\{\rho(A, B)\}\phi_A + \omega \tag{8.24}$$

and

$$C_B = \rho(A, B)\pi\{(\rho(A, B)\}\phi_B + \omega, \tag{8.25}$$

because whatever part of consumption does not accrue to capital is paid in wages. Then,

$$(C_A - \omega)/(C_B - \omega) = \phi_A/\phi_B. \tag{8.26}$$

However, inspection of fig. 8.7 reveals that

$$\frac{C_A - OI}{\phi_A} = \frac{AC}{IC} = \frac{BD}{ID} = \frac{C_B - OI}{\phi_B}. \tag{8.27}$$

Hence,

$$(C_A - OI)/(C_B - OI) = \phi_A/\phi_B, \tag{8.28}$$

so that, taking (8.26) and (8.28) together, $OI = \omega$. Thus our production function, when we can construct it, is more than a relation between capital per head and output per head. It is also a function the derivatives of which give unit payments to labour and capital in competitive equilibrium.

We have now examined an example of the construction of a production function by means of chain-index aggregation of capital. However, it is no more than an example and it exhibits certain features that are not general. The critical property which example 8.3 embodies, and on account of which the

---

[13] Of course, the marginal product of capital is not necessarily the rate of interest because capital is not necessarily homogeneous with consumption. Suppose we have $C = F[\phi, L]$, the production function. We have graphed

$$C/L = F[\phi/L, 1],$$

the cross-section of the production function. The intercept when the function is differentiable, with first partial derivative F_1, is

$$(C/L) - (F_1\phi/L).$$

If the intercept is equal to ω we have

$$C - \omega L = F_1\phi,$$

i.e. the payment to capital is the product of the quantity of capital and the marginal product of capital.

resulting function nowhere resembles that of fig. 8.4 is that *when two pure stationary states are tied at rate of interest $\bar{\rho}$ the state which is an equilibrium for $\rho > \bar{\rho}$ has a smaller chain-index measure of capital per head.* Examples in which this property is violated will be said to exhibit *capital reversal.* That capital reversals are a real possibility is already apparent from our having considered already the popular type of *double switching*[14] example (example 8.2). We will now briefly examine two more simple examples, each of which exhibits capital reversal, and see how the chain-index method is affected.

Example 8.4. There are three activities and two stationary states.

Stationary states	Activities
I	1. 1 labour ⊕ 2 consumption good ⊖ 5 consumption good
II	2. 1 labour ⊕ 1 capital good ⊖ 5 consumption good ⊕ 1 capital good
	3. 4 labour ⊖ 1 capital good

Factor price frontiers: I $\boxed{\omega = 3 - 2\rho,}$ II $\boxed{\omega = \dfrac{5}{1 + 4\rho}\cdot}$

Fig. 8.8 illustrates.

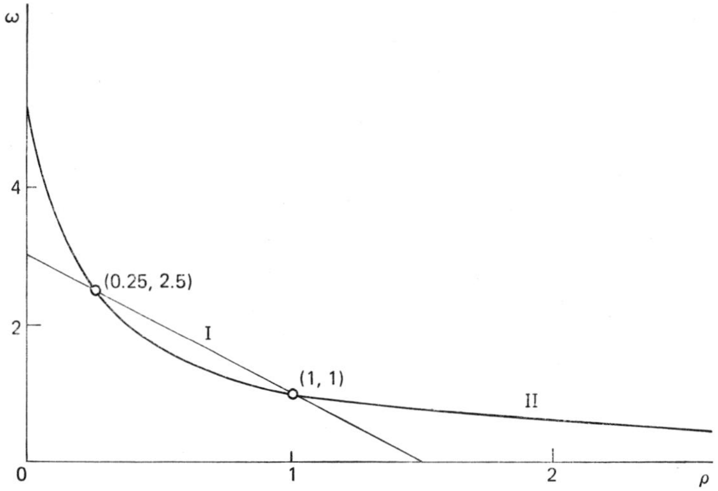

Fig. 8.8.

[14] This terminology is unfortunate for the same reason as 'switch point' is unfortunate. However, it is so generally known and used that it has to be accepted.

Clearly II is the equilibrium state at very high or very low ρ. We have multiple tie points and double switching. At $\rho = 0$ the equilibrium state is II. The chain-index measure of capital is 1.0 and output is 5.0. The price index of capital is four times the wage rate so long as II is the equilibrium, i.e. $\pi = 20/(1+4\rho)$, $0 \leqslant \rho \leqslant 0.25$. There is a tie point at $\rho = 0.25$, $\omega = 2.5$. At that point the value of the chain index of capital in I, ϕ_{I}, is given by the formula

$$\phi_{\text{I}} = \frac{\phi_{\text{I}}}{\phi_{\text{II}}} = \frac{2}{20}\{1 + 4\,(0.25)\} = \frac{1}{5}. \tag{8.29}$$

Hence, the 'quantity of capital' in state I is 0.2 and the output is 3. On the range $\rho = (0.25,\ 1.0)$ there is no change in the price index because here the capital good is the consumption good. The next tie point is at $\rho = 1.0$, $\omega = 1.0$. Again applying the chain-index formula we get *another* measure of the quantity of capital in stationary state II, viz.

$$\phi_{\text{II}}/\phi_{\text{I}} = 4/2 = 2.0. \tag{8.30}$$

Hence, on the new measure $\phi_{\text{II}} = 2.0 \times \frac{1}{5} = 0.4$. Fig. 8.9 illustrates.

Now this example has violated assumption (6), but notice that there is nothing to stop us mechanically applying the chain-index method in this case. However, the 'production function' that arises (it hardly merits that title) is of a rather strange appearance. In particular it is no longer enough to know the index value of ϕ to know output per head. One has to know as well on which branch of the graph the economy finds itself; so strictly there is no function. Note also that there is a violation of a basic principle which the chain index embodies in other contexts. The two points on the graph of (C, ϕ) values labelled II in fig. 8.9 *correspond to identical real states of the production sectors of the economy*[15]. Naturally the price systems are different so that it is perfectly appropriate that we should find ourselves at different points on the (ρ, π) graph. But we argued earlier (ch. 5) that counting two different states of the economy to contain different quantities of capital *only because their price systems were different and for no other reason* is something to be avoided. And here, because we have double switching, and the chain-index method has been applied twice over to the same stationary state, we have failed to avoid this objectionable feature. The 'capital reversal' in the example occurs at $\rho = 1.0$, as fig. 8.9 shows, where capital per head 'goes up' from 0.2 to 0.4 for a larger rate of interest.

Now the fact that the above example embodies double switching and hence violates assumption (6), which assumption is clearly rather important to the

[15] Of course, 'who consumes what' will not be the same in each case.

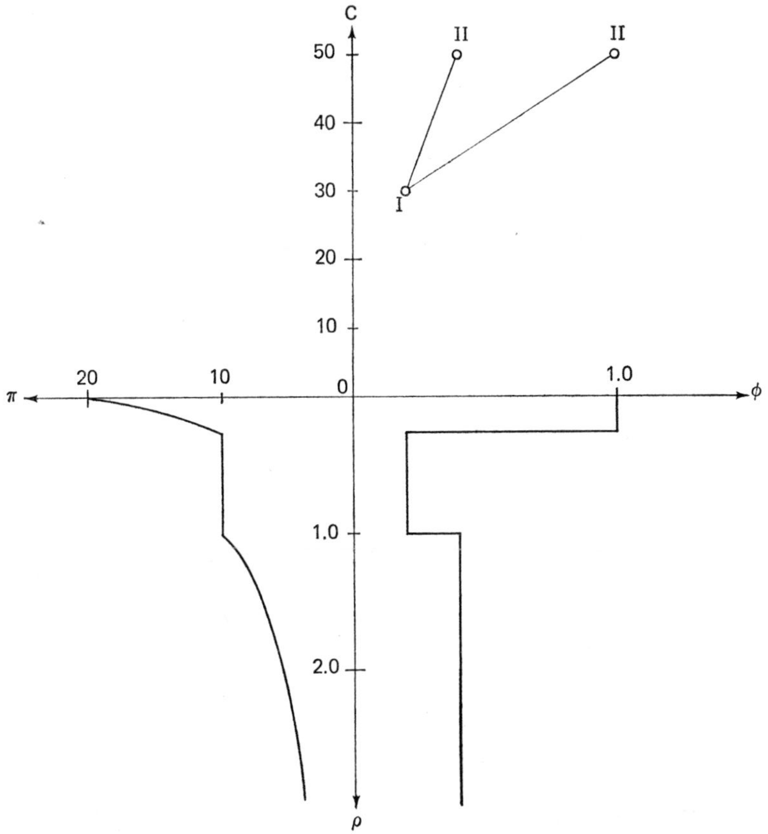

Fig. 8.9.

rationale of the chain-index method as here applied, is incidental to the feature of capital reversal. To see that this is so, slightly modify example 8.4.

Example 8.5. Modify example 8.4 as follows. Add another stationary state III.

Stationary state		Activity
III	4.	1 labour ⊕ 14 consumption good ⊖ 21 consumption good

Factor price frontier: III $\boxed{\omega = 7 - 14\rho.}$

Fig. 8.10 illustrates. Stationary state III dominates stationary states I and II at low values of ρ and so 'cuts out' the double-switching feature. But we still have a capital reversal at the tie point (1, 1).

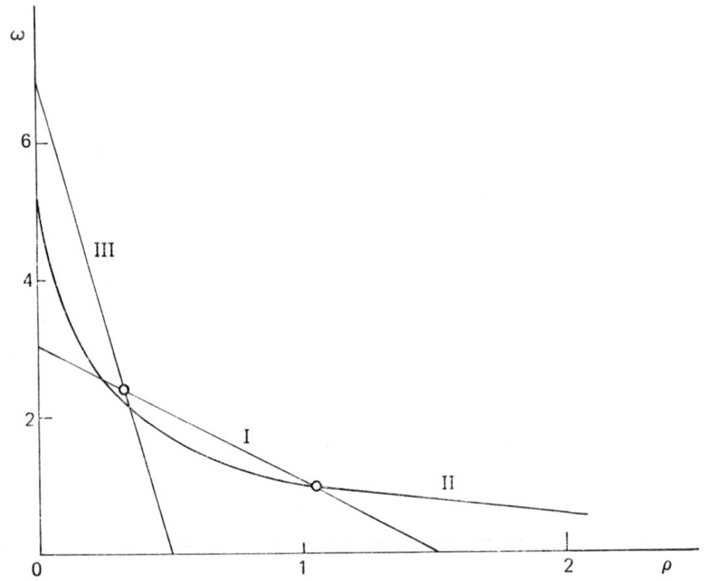

Fig. 8.10.

Let us now attempt a summary. In ch. 7 we saw that the chain-index method of aggregation is a natural and theoretically reasonable method when aggregation is possible. Hence, the idea of applying it to the rather different problem of aggregation across equilibrium stationary states is an attractive one. It is evident that to succeed with this enterprise we will not need conditions anything like as strong as the nested-set condition of ch. 7. However, to apply the chain-index method we need to travel across all the stationary states that we want to take into consideration with prices varying continuously and so that we pass to and from any particular stationary state only once. It seems that the only way that we might do this is to hope that the rate of interest would arrange our stationary states in a linear structure, and give us the desired continuity of prices. We have seen by example, however, that there is no guarantee that it will serve us in this regard.

Moreover, even if the rate of interest will arrange equilibrium stationary states 'in line' for us, we do not necessarily obtain a very acceptable production function. This is because the chain-index measure of capital may be larger for states corresponding to higher rates of interest. It is interesting to see how different is our problem here in ch. 8 from the problems of general aggregation discussed in ch. 7. There, if we could aggregate at all (and one might say that usually we could not do so), there were no serious problems concerning the convexity of the resulting aggregate production set. Here we can usually aggregate (i.e. the chain-index method may be applied), but whether we get a convex relation when we have aggregated is another question. And because we are only concerned with equilibrium stationary states, the convexity of the underlying production set gives us little purchase on the problem.

Lastly, let it be noted that the argument concerning the intercept of a tangent to the production function and the equality of marginal products and factor payments *in no way depends upon the shape of the* (C, ϕ) *graph*. Hence we are able to confirm again, and contrary to the beliefs of some economists of the 'Cambridge school', that the existence of a satisfactory production function and the validity of marginal principles *are separate and independent issues*. Naturally, in a case such as the one considered in example 8.4 we may have two points on two 'flats' of the (C, ϕ) graph corresponding to the same blended stationary state. Then there are two intercepts and two marginal-product measures according to the price system that rules. But following upon the discussion of ch. 5 this is by now familiar ground. Contrary to the attempts of some economists (including members of the other 'Cambridge school') to make marginal productivity measures purely real and independent of prices, in general marginal products are in terms of net value at constant prices, and hence may well depend upon what those prices happen to be. All this then is as it should be.

Part IV

EFFICIENCY

9

The linear production model

Could commodities themselves speak, they would say: 'Our use-value may be a thing that interests men. It is no part of us as objects. What, however, does belong to us as objects, is our value. Our natural intercourse as commodities proves it. In the eyes of each other we are nothing but exchange-values.'

KARL MARX, *Capital*, vol. I

The linear production model is one in which all production is governed by constant returns to scale. Any productive activity may be magnified or diminished to any extent, provided only that there are no distortions, i.e. so that all ratios between inputs and outputs are conserved. In this we depart from our earlier treatment of production sets under which the linearity assumption (4.13) was frequently dispensed with. Here it will be basic to some of the developments that follow.

The assumption of *linearity* is very usual in economic theorizing of the abstract kind and economists have become quite accustomed to it. Nonetheless, it is an unrealistic assumption and it is necessary to keep in view at all times the fragility of results that are critically dependent upon it. In the following chapters the assumption will appear sometimes as a convenient simplification, which could be relaxed without undermining the results derived: but in ch. 11 we will examine a body of results for which the assumption is strictly indispensable. From time to time we will note in passing what happens when the assumption is relaxed. Aside from such detours, however, it will usually be assumed throughout this section that the economy under consideration satisfies the constant returns-to-scale property, so that we may seek to represent it by the linear production model of the title.

It is evident that the validity of the linearity assumption will depend upon which inputs are taken into account. Diminishing returns may arise because, while levels of inputs considered have risen, the level of another input, not considered, has remained constant. Alternatively, if an input is indivisible, there is a sense in which the quantity of it present when production takes place is a poor measure of the service that it provides. This might account for output increasing proportionately to some inputs while others have remained unchanged. Yet attempts to claim that linearity must be satisfied at some suitably refined level of classifying inputs are misconceived and fruitless (see Samuelson (1947, pp. 83ff.)) and it is here supposed that the list of inputs taken into account explicitly has been selected so as to include those items that will satisfy the assumptions made about inputs. Given this list of inputs, linearity is an assumption, and a strong one. It is also a useful assumption and one which underlies many of the established results of the theory of capital, and it is for this reason that it is given so much prominence in what follows.

Apart from constant returns to scale as it is usually understood the linear production model satisfies another condition, the mathematical term for which is *additivity*. The economic interpretation of this property is the absence of external effects and interrelationships between productive activities. In this case the economic consequence of two productive activities carried on at the same time is the arithmetic sum of the consequences of the two activities taken one at a time. If trawlers adversely affect the catches of other trawlers, or if beekeeping enhances the productivity of apple orchards, as in Meade's (1952) classic example, additivity is violated. As with the constant returns-to-scale assumption, so with the present assumption, there is endless scope for hair-splitting discussions about whether or not there has to be additivity as a matter of logical necessity. The claim that additivity must be satisfied would be supported in the case of an example such as Meade's beekeeping and apple-growing case by maintaining that the example requires the recognition of extra, and joint, 'products'; e.g. a pollination service provided by bees. As with the earlier discussion, this line of argument could at best lead to an entirely circular and useless classification of inputs and outputs, in terms of which, however, there would necessarily be additivity. It also ignores the consideration that the inputs and outputs considered must be economically relevant ones in terms of the standard economic assumptions. Additivity then is a genuine assumption, and indeed not always a realistic one, but we adopt it nonetheless for reasons of convenience and because many issues and problems of capital theory are not related in any significant way to the problem of external effects.

Production is based on a finite set of activities, which are combined together in a simple additive manner, and each of which can be scaled at will so long as the appropriate ratios are conserved. Our method of giving expression to production possibilities is the one famously adopted by von Neumann (1945–1946) in his paper on economic growth[1]. However, the present production

[1] We depart from von Neumann's model most importantly in allowing non-produced inputs in production.

model is not identical to von Neumann's construct, and von Neumann's major concern, economic growth at the maximal rate, is only an incidental concern of the present discussion. Thus, although in conception and notation we follow von Neumann, the term *linear production model* is to be preferred to the possibly confusing term, von Neumann model.

There are *M linear activities* (indexed by $i = 1, \ldots, M$) where the ith activity, run at unit level, requires a vector of inputs $\boldsymbol{a}^i$ and produces a vector of outputs $\boldsymbol{b}^i$, which outputs will be available one week later. There are *N goods* distinguished in the model (indexed by $j = 1, \ldots, N$). The concept of a good is a very general one; including, for example, non-produced inputs, such as labour services, and producer goods not desired for consumption. Hence, $\boldsymbol{a}^i$ and $\boldsymbol{b}^i$ are N-dimensional real vectors whose elements are non-negative by definition. The matrix whose ith column is $\boldsymbol{a}^i$ is denoted $\boldsymbol{A}$, the *input matrix*, and the matrix whose ith column is $\boldsymbol{b}^i$ is denoted $\boldsymbol{B}$, the *output matrix*. Thus, given a list of goods, a pair of non-negative $N \times M$ matrices[2] define a body of technological knowledge.

Some examples will illustrate the great power of this simple notational device. First notice that joint production is not excluded. If carpentry shops use wood and man-hours to produce chairs and sawdust, the matrix $\boldsymbol{B}$ will have a column, the output vector for this activity, which has positive elements both in the chair row and in the sawdust row. This is, of course, joint production in the ordinary familiar sense, but the possibility that a column of $\boldsymbol{B}$ will have more than one positive element allows the treatment of various features of production processes which may not be seen immediately as joint production. Indeed, it is through the introduction of more than one positive element in a column of $\boldsymbol{B}$ that the participation in production of capital equipment of the fixed or durable variety can be represented. If production demands the presence of goods that are not themselves completely used up in production, the carpenter's saw for example, then these goods can be treated both as inputs and as outputs of the activity. One may think of the activity as 'swallowing' the durable goods of which it makes use, but then 'regurgitating' them one week later. From there it is a short step to allowing the good 'regurgitated' to be different in some respect from the good that originally went into production, and in this way depreciation of capital inputs can be included. Suppose, for example, that a certain durable good, which may as well for the sake of illustration be the carpenter's saw again, has a useful life of 100 weeks. There will than have to 100 different chair-making activities, all of the same broad type,

---

[2] By assumption, $\boldsymbol{a}^i \geqq \boldsymbol{0}$, $i = 1, \ldots, M$; and $\boldsymbol{b}^i \geqq \boldsymbol{0}$, $i = 1, \ldots, M$. A matrix is said to be non-negative if none of its components is negative, i.e. each column is a non-negative vector.

each one using a saw of a different age, and each one producing along with other outputs a saw one week older than the one that was used as input. This illustration makes clear how it is that it is possible to represent many, and also very complicated, productive processes in such a simple format as a matrix pair. The von Neumann representation deals with complexity by multiplying the number of goods considered and reducing every productive activity to a set of elementary transformations of inputs into outputs. Like many a brilliant innovation it is essentially a very simple idea[3].

Another matter to be considered is the treatment of intermediate goods. If only one productive process were possible, and if that process occupied σ hours from start to finish, then one might, if σ were small enough, take σ hours as the production period and ignore any intermediate products of unfinished goods involved in the working out of the stages of this process. This would only be acceptable if σ were fairly small, because otherwise the possibility of various cycles of the process running out of phase would become one of considerable economic importance. However, when there are many productive processes available it will typically be necessary to recognize explicitly the existence of intermediate products and it may even be necessary to invent particular goods just for the requirements of the analysis, for example, a part-finished house with a certain number of hours needed to complete it. With two processes demanding σ_1 and σ_2 hours to complete the production period must be at least as short as the highest common factor of these two numbers, considered as whole numbers, which is not preceded by an uncommon factor. Or perhaps one should not take period analysis so seriously and regard the assumption that all the activities in the von Neumann construct take one common production period to complete as a simplifying assumption of no great import. In that case the foregoing discussion of the choice of production period shows that any gross unrealism in the assumption of discrete production periods could be removed by the admission of a shorter period, with a consequent increase in the number of activities and a more refined classification of goods. Notice that the concept of an activity is not the same as the concept of a productive process. The latter, which comprises complex endeavours, such as the building of a ship or the manufacture of an industrial product, may include large numbers of activities; indeed it must do if the process takes several periods to complete.

[3] In his paper (1945–1946) von Neumann not only allowed the matrices ***A*** and ***B*** to have many positive elements in any column, he went so far as to require that all the elements of these matrices be positive. It has since been shown that this assumption is not necessary for von Neumann's results. See, for example, Gale (1960, ch. 9).

Suppose, for example, that a crop is produced by planting seed in land prepared for the purpose, doing nothing for 20 weeks and then harvesting. Let the production period be one week. Then one cannot represent directly in an input matrix and an output matrix such a 20-week production lag. The manner of treating this case is to invent a sequence of intermediate inputs and break the whole process down into a sequence of activities which use and produce these intermediate inputs. The process is then conceived as follows: various inputs, including seed and unsown land, produce one week later one-week-sown land; one-week-sown land produces one week later two-week-sown land; and so on. In this manner the whole process is reduced to a combination of activities, the outputs of which are made available one week later. Of course, some of these inputs and outputs are purely notional. We do not think, in the everyday sense of the word 'produce', of 10-week-sown land 'producing' 11-week-sown land without the intervention of any other input. Nonetheless, by an extension of the concept of a good to include various contrived goods introduced for the purpose of the analysis, it is possible to encompass a very wide class of technological possibilities within the formally elementary format of a pair of non-negative matrices.

It is possible, with sufficient ingenuity, to fit into the format of the linear production model many examples of technological structure which may seem at first sight outside its scope. An impressive example of what imagination can achieve in this respect is provided by Morishima's (1969, p. 90) observation that the von Neumann framework can accommodate 'immobile' capital goods. Consider the case where a machine of a particular type can be installed costlessly, or at low cost, in any sector of the economy when it is newly manufactured, but later on it is transferred to another sector only at high cost, or not at all. One could then distinguish, for each sector characterized by this immobility of the capital good concerned, two different 'species' of the machine – the newly produced mobile version and the second-hand immobile version. Certain activities would then be seen as transforming among other things the newly produced version into, one week later, the installed and immobile version.

The von Neumann framework, which is the basis of the present linear production model, is an extremely flexible and powerful one, so much so in fact that it includes as special cases nearly all the capital models that have been proposed by theorists in the past. This generality is to be greatly welcomed, for there is nothing more boring than a catalogue of examples. Yet one must retain a sense of proportion; von Neumann did not solve, by means of one brilliant insight, all the problems of capital theory. Since his construct is such a simple one, as we see clearly after the event, it follows that he cannot have solved by means of it problems that were not fundamentally fairly simple ones[4].

The point can be illustrated by a consideration of Morishima's proposal that immobile capital goods can be incorporated, effortlessly it seems, into the framework of the linear production model. Assumptions that capital goods move freely and easily between different sectors of the economy have worried economists for more than one reason. One is a feeling that where an aggregate measure of capital is employed, even if the aggregation involved is very partial, say only for one group of capital goods, one loses sight of the fact that the particular goods within the group are likely to be somewhat specific to particular uses. This would make aggregate capital for that group 'immobile' even if the very specific items within the group were highly mobile. Now this is a consequence of aggregation, a procedure which is out of place in the von Neumann framework since his model proposes no aggregation at all[5].

But there is another reason for feeling doubtful about the assumption that capital is highly mobile between sectors. This is based upon considerations more of a behavioural than a technological nature. It may be that the managers of firms are sluggish and unresponsive to economic incentives when it comes to the reconsideration of the uses to which capital goods installed in the past should be put. If this were to be a feature of the economy it would be of some importance with respect to certain investigations into how the economy behaves. When one considers that markets for second-hand capital goods are very imperfect, if they exist at all, and that decisions concerning drastic redeployment of existing investment goods might well be taken in a fog of uncertainty, some degree of immobility of a behavioural or institutional nature is seen to be a not implausible assumption. There are no doubt investigations in which this issue would not be involved very crucially. Equally, there are problems, of a dynamic nature, where it would be very important to take into account any immobility of capital goods. What Morishima's observation shows is that some types of capital immobility, including all cases where the immobility is of a technological type, do not really introduce into economic analysis fundamental new principles or the need for entirely novel and radical tools. In contrast, however, other types of capital immobility will raise

[4] Morishima (1969, preface) writes of a 'von Neumann revolution' in dynamic economics brought about by grafting von Neumann on Walras, which might be compared in importance with the Keynesian revolution in static economics. If he is right it will necessarily be on account of the analytical methods employed, and the ideas that emerged, and not just because of the formulation of production relations.

[5] On the epistemology of capital aggregation, see ch. 7.

problems of a more fundamental character and these will not be buried in an avalance of notional goods and activities.

The reader will notice that our discussion of immobile capital goods has raised in passing the question of what one does when one displays a set of activities as comprising, at some moment, the technological knowledge of an economy. This is a large question and it is unlikely that economists alone could provide an answer to it. We confine ourselves to a few observations. The transformations of inputs into outputs which lie within the capacity of the economy depend in part upon the level of scientific understanding which the learned inhabitants of that economy have attained, and in part upon more general social and socio-economic factors that will determine how effectively the economy realizes the potential of its scientific understanding[6]. The precise form which the input matrix $\boldsymbol{A}$ and the output matrix $\boldsymbol{B}$ take will normally reflect more than just engineering knowledge.

The line between assumptions about technology and assumptions about how individuals behave in the light of that technology is not a sharp one. Examples can readily be constructed such that one might as well classify an aspect of the economy under one heading as another. Consider, by way of illustration, a known method of production which is rejected by producers on ethical grounds. It might, for example, be generally maintained in the society concerned that women should not undertake certain kinds of work of which they are physically capable. Do we exclude this technique and all its constituent activities from the statement of the technological possibilities, or do we include it and add a proviso, in the form of a behavioural specification, that this method is never employed? In the present instance it makes no difference which we do. On the other hand, there are plausible types of behavioural assumption that cannot be written into the statement of the technology. Suppose that capital goods will shift from one sector to another if and only if there is an earnings differential of at least 2%. This is a case where capital is somewhat immobile between sectors but not completely immobile. It is clear that only this specific assumption will incorporate the requirement of the case. There can be no question of inventing new goods and activities to cover this case as if it were a feature of the technology, for prices enter essentially into the condition for the transfer of capital goods and prices have no place in a statement of technological relations.

---

[6] There is by no means general agreement among economists on the validity of this point, witness the claim that international differences in production efficiency *must* reflect inputs of different quality or some other factor than basically different production relations. For such a view, see Pearce (1970, pp. 323ff). For a parallel type of argument, see Kaldor (1966a, p. 13).

If the list of goods includes non-produced inputs, the matrix ***B*** will have one or more rows of zeros. Economic theory traditionally divides factors of production[7] into three groups: capital, labour and natural resources – the triad. Does the linear production model require a triad? The logic of the model demands only two classes of inputs, divided according to one distinction, that between produced and non-produced inputs, the latter being defined as inputs available in quantities independent of productive decisions but not necessarily constant over time. Capital inputs clearly belong to the produced category and natural resources such as land to the non-produced category and where does labour belong? It was the distinctive features of labour that led the classical economists to set it apart from other factor inputs and within their vision this was appropriate, indeed necessary. For labour was seen as supplied elastically in the long run given a sufficiently high wage level. It was thus distinguished from land, the factor in inelastic supply *par excellence*, on the one hand, and from capital, on the other hand, whose long-run supply conditions were unclear, but not the same as those pertaining to labour. In the present context, however, the case for putting labour in with natural resources is clear. Even if labour supply responds to economic variables, as it can hardly fail to do to some extent, the supply will be independent of individual activity levels and, in particular, it will not vary because the rate of production of activities which produce labour as an output have been altered for economic profit-maximizing motives. To treat labour supply as given from the point of view of technical feasibility and profit-guided economic decisions is not to exclude consideration of induced population growth[8].

The treatment of labour as a non-produced input applies, naturally, only to labour 'in the raw'. The training of labour is like investment in a capital good and trained labour can be regarded as a produced good whose production requires the input of a non-produced good. Furthermore, there is no reason why a good should not be included both in the produced and in the non-produced category. There exist, for example, natural lakes, but it is also possible

[7] A factor of production is defined as something whose presence may augment production, on which definition the place of capital inputs in the triad cannot be disputed. Economists in the past have hotly disputed whether capital has a place among the factors of production; hence the definition, usually not explicit, cannot have been the foregoing one. See Schumpeter (1954, pp. 557ff.).

[8] In the model of von Neumann (1945–1946) only produced inputs are considered explicitly. It was assumed of natural factors of production, including labour, that these could be 'expanded in unlimited quantities'. This assumption, together with the assumption that the necessities of life consumed by workers are to be included in inputs, amounts to the same thing as assuming that labour is available in infinitely elastic supply, and *instantaneously*, at a minimum subsistence level defined by a specific consumption basket.

to construct artificial lakes. It may be useful in such a case to treat the produced and the non-producible version as different goods which as inputs are perfect substitutes in the case of many or all activities. Finally, the reader is reminded that the supply of a non-produced input may vary over time. This is what happens, for example, when the labour force expands on account of purely demographic forces.

In reality the matrices $\boldsymbol{A}$ and $\boldsymbol{B}$ are changing all the time as the forces of technical progress and social change make themselves felt in terms of new coefficients, new activities and even new goods. However, really substantial issues arising from technical change are ones that will be put aside for the time being: so, for the moment, we settle for an extremely superficial observation. One can if one wants simply admit a different matrix pair for each week and label the input and output matrices accordingly. Thus $\boldsymbol{A}_t$ is the input matrix for activities initiated in week t and $\boldsymbol{B}_t$ is the corresponding output matrix. There are some investigations in which it makes little difference to the analysis whether the matrices vary over time or not. This is the case with the formal efficiency theorems of ch. 10. Where such investigations are involved we may as well avail ourselves freely of the greater generality obtainable by varying the matrices from week to week. But no one will fail to understand that this disposes only of the most trivial aspect of technical change – that it involves a change in technical knowledge. The importance of such changes for economic theory resides, of course, in the fact that the consideration of technical change forces upon us the recognition of uncertainty. It is simply incredible to assume that technical knowledge and attainment will change in a manner that can be precisely forecast. So the subscripted matrices take on, as it were, a different character; it is harder for us to assume them known data. Obviously there is nothing to stop us from assuming them known from the formal point of view and it is slightly useful to do so in certain contexts[9], but there should be no question of claiming that technical progress and all the problems that it raises have thereby been overcome.

Enough has been said now to make it clear that the linear production model includes as a special case the great majority of models of capitalistic[10] production. This should not blind us to the fact that there are production models whose shape does not permit them to be squeezed into the simple linear

[9] Subscripting the input and output matrices has some importance independently of the problem of technical progress as such. One might, for example, want to include cycles in productive possibilities such as might arise from seasons.

[10] For the meaning of the term 'capitalistic' see above, p. 5, footnote 2.

framework. And the importance of these models is in no way diminished by the fact that they have not figured very largely in the literature.

Obviously all models which embody increasing returns to scale are excluded, but this is more true by construction than because there is any great barrier in the way of extending the linear production model to embrace non-linear processes. As the model stands the *i*th activity, run at unit level, transforms the vector $\boldsymbol{a}^i$ to the vector $\boldsymbol{b}^i$ one week later. Because of the linearity property this information alone completely specifies the possibilities inherent in the *i*th activity. We may infer at once that the *i*th activity can transform $\lambda \boldsymbol{a}^i$ to $\lambda \boldsymbol{b}_i$ one week later, for any $\lambda > 0$. More generally, assume that the *i*th activity run at level $\lambda_i \geqslant 0$ transforms

$$\boldsymbol{a}^i(\lambda_i) \ominus \boldsymbol{b}^i(\lambda_i), \tag{9.1}$$

one week later; where the input and output vector are functions of the activity level (cf. Arrow and Hurwicz (1960)). In this manner we may represent an arbitrary non-linear production transformation. We could at will adopt this more general framework, and some of the results of ch. 10, but not all of them could still be established. However, the gain in generality seems not worth the price in complicating the exposition and having to change models according to the subject under investigation. For the results of ch. 11 linearity is indispensable.

There are further models that cannot be fitted into the framework of our linear production model. As an interesting example, consider the one-good model proposed by Kaldor (1957; 1961, pp. 177–222) which includes what he calls 'the technical progress function'. This is a relation between the rate of growth of the capital stock and the rate of growth of the output flow, these two being assumed measured, in homogeneous units, per capita. The output relevant to the technical progress function is net of the input rate, while in the von Neumann formulation output is measured gross, i.e. it includes all goods available after production has taken place. However, ignoring this distinction, which is not critical for the present discussion, one can formulate a relation between inputs and outputs, in the spirit of the technical progress function, as

$$\frac{\mathrm{y}_t - \mathrm{y}_{t-1}}{\mathrm{y}_{t-1}} = f\left[\frac{\mathrm{x}_{t-1} - \mathrm{x}_{t-2}}{\mathrm{x}_{t-2}}\right], \tag{9.2}$$

where x_t is the input level in week *t* and y_t the output available at the beginning of week *t*, each for activities employing one unit of labour. Relation (9.2) defines an infinite number of activities, each of which is consistent with the form of *f*, and scaled by the requirement that the labour input be unity. Note, however, that (9.2) takes the form of a difference equation, so that one requires more than a knowledge of x_{t-1} to know whether y_t is a possible value. One would have to know also the values y_{t-1} and x_{t-2}. The fact that 'current' input (i.e. the input of the previous week) does not uniquely determine output in Kaldor's formulation reflects the dependence of output on the history of capital accumulation in previous weeks. This immediately implies that the linear production model cannot accommodate this specification. Indeed, Kaldor proposes his function as an alternative to the neoclassical production function, as more than simply a relationship between inputs and outputs[11]. The implication of this example is clear; there exist production models which can neither be included within the linear production model, nor can they be dismissed as absurd.

It may be useful to present an explicit example of the translation of a set of statements of technological possibilities into the format demanded by the linear production model – a pair of matrices. The example, which is fanciful, as any simple example must be, concerns an economy in which the only output for final consumption is fish. Fish can be caught in two ways: one man fishing for one week with the aid of a net can catch 50 fish; while three men fishing for a week with two nets and a boat can catch 200 fish. One man takes a week to make one net with a useful life of four weeks. Two men take three weeks to make a perfectly durable boat. There are only four types of input and output; man-days, nets, boats and fish. But the list of goods must be expanded to take account of intermediate outputs and wear and tear. The production period is a week. Let us call the result of a week's work from two men towards the construction of a boat a boat (1); the result of two week's work from two men a boat (2); and a completed boat a boat (3). Let a net which has been used for fishing for s days be a net (s), ($s = 0, 1, 2, 3$). A net (0) is a new unused net. We can ignore net (4)s, and so on, because they have no economic use.

Table 9.1 gives the form of the input and output matrices for the example. The reader unfamiliar with the technique of translating from a natural statement can test his understanding by checking the correctness of the translation. As would usually be the case, so in this example, the matrices are large with many zero entries. Notice that we are here concerned with the basic set of activities from which the rest can be generated. There is no reason why two

[11] As has been noted by a number of writers, Kaldor's technical progress function is equivalent to a production function when f is a linear relation. This is the special case where the history of capital accumulation matters only through its implication for the final capital level. See, for example, Black (1962) and Kaldor (1961, p. 215 footnote). The argument of this footnote is obscure; one should recognize that the arbitrary constant B appears in the integrated form only because units for measuring the capital input relatively to output have to be specified arbitrarily; it has no deeper economic significance.

Table 9.1.

***A* matrix**

Goods/		Fishing from land 1	2	3	4	Fishing from boats 5	6	7	8	Making nets 9	Boat-building 10	11	12
Man-days	1	1	1 1	1	1	3	3	3	3	1	2	2	2
Net (0)	2	1	–	–	–	2	–	–	–	–	–	–	–
Net (1)	3	–	1	–	–	–	2	–	–	–	–	–	–
Net (2)	4	–	–	1	–	–	–	2	–	–	–	–	–
Net (3)	5	–	–	–	1	–	–	–	2	–	–	–	–
Boat (1)	6	–	–	–	–	–	–	–	–	–	–	1	–
Boat (2)	7	–	–	–	–	–	–	–	–	–	–	–	1
Boat (3)	8	–	–	–	–	1	1	1	1	–	–	–	–
Fish	9	–	–	–	–	–	–	–	–	–	–	–	–

***B* matrix**

Goods/		Fishing from land 1	2	3	4	Fishing from boats 5	6	7	8	Making nets 9	Boat-building 10	11	12
Man-days	1	–	–	–	–	–	–	–	–	–	–	–	–
Net (0)	2	–	–	–	–	–	–	–	–	1	–	–	–
Net (1)	3	1	–	–	–	2	–	–	–	–	–	–	–
Net (2)	4	–	1	–	–	–	2	–	–	–	–	–	–
Net (3)	5	–	–	1	–	–	–	2	–	–	–	–	–
Boat (1)	6	–	–	–	–	–	–	–	–	–	1	–	–
Boat (2)	7	–	–	–	–	–	–	–	–	–	–	1	–
Boat (3)	8	–	–	–	–	1	1	1	1	–	–	–	1
Fish	9	50	50	50	50	200	200	200	200	–	–	–	–

men should not go out fishing with one new net and one three-day-old net, but this is to be regarded as a combination of activities 5 and 8, each at a level 0.5.

We will make use of a system of notation, which is much the same as the one embodied in fig. 4.2, to express the constraints on production and consumption imposed by a linear technology, as follows. Let $\boldsymbol{q}_t$ be the vector of produced goods available to the economy at the start of week t, including the durable capital goods still extant. $\boldsymbol{q}_t$ has something of the nature of a capital stock, but it includes also the produced goods to be consumed during week t. Notice that $\boldsymbol{q}_t$ is necessarily non-negative. Consumption in week t is $\boldsymbol{c}_t$, and since the supply of certain factor services may be included as negative consumption, $\boldsymbol{c}_t$ is not required to be non-negative. The capital stock of week t, $\boldsymbol{k}_t$ is defined by

$$\boldsymbol{k}_t = \boldsymbol{q}_t - \boldsymbol{c}_t \tag{9.3}$$

and this vector, which defines the upper limits on inputs to production must be non-negative. The vector $\boldsymbol{z}_t$ is a non-negative vector of non-produced inputs available for use in week t. Included in this vector, for example, will be the services of land. There is some arbitrariness about whether a non-produced input should be included as a negative component of $\boldsymbol{c}_t$ or a positive component of $\boldsymbol{z}_t$ and indeed the distinction between these vectors is not strictly necessary to the analysis that follows. All the same, there is no harm in making the distinction, and it is sometimes useful to distinguish non-produced inputs which have the character of negative consumptions from the point of view of welfare (e.g. labour supplies) from those which do not.

The vector $\boldsymbol{x}_t$ is the non-negative *activity levels* for week t. The inputs that the productive activities of the week t will require are

$$\sum_{i=1}^{M} \boldsymbol{a}^i x_{it} = \boldsymbol{A}\cdot\boldsymbol{x}_t, \tag{9.4}$$

where x_{it} is the ith component of the vector $\boldsymbol{x}_t$. For the time being the matrix $\boldsymbol{A}$ is assumed the same for each week. The resources available at the start of the week must be sufficient to provide both for the consumption and the input requirements of that week. Thus, for week t,

$$\boldsymbol{c}_t + \boldsymbol{A}\cdot\boldsymbol{x}_t \leqq \boldsymbol{q}_t + \boldsymbol{z}_t. \tag{9.5}$$

Or, we may express this condition in terms of the capital stock, using (9.3), as

$$\boldsymbol{A}\cdot\boldsymbol{x}_t \leqq \boldsymbol{k}_t + \boldsymbol{z}_t. \tag{9.6}$$

Now, $\boldsymbol{q}_t$ is by definition simply the result of the productive activities of the previous week, so that

$$\boldsymbol{q}_{t+1} = \boldsymbol{c}_{t+1} + \boldsymbol{k}_{t+1} = \boldsymbol{B}\cdot\boldsymbol{x}_t. \tag{9.7}$$

Consider now four hypothetical sequences of vectors:

$$\begin{array}{ll} (\boldsymbol{x}_1, \boldsymbol{x}_2, \ldots, \boldsymbol{x}_t, \ldots), & (\boldsymbol{c}_1, \boldsymbol{c}_2, \ldots, \boldsymbol{c}_t, \ldots), \\ (\boldsymbol{k}_1, \boldsymbol{k}_2, \ldots, \boldsymbol{k}_t, \ldots), & (\boldsymbol{z}_1, \boldsymbol{z}_2, \ldots, \boldsymbol{z}_t, \ldots). \end{array} \tag{9.8}$$

These vector sequences define a *development of the economy* over time. For week t $(t=1, 2, \ldots)$ the tth terms of the sequences give, respectively, the activity levels, the consumption vector, the capital stock vector and the inflow of non-produced goods, all for week t. Naturally some developments would be mere fantasy – these would not be consistent with technical possibilities, even supposing that inflows of non-produced goods as specified by the sequence of z vectors could be made available, and even supposing the sequence of c vectors possible. In contrast to these daydreams, a development of the economy will be said to be a *feasible development* if the sequences satisfy (9.6) and (9.7) for each t. The feasibility conditions are no more than balancing relations which add up quantities of various goods required and compare the totals to the quantities available.

Feasibility as defined above might be called, more exactly, technical feasibility. Whether the economy could actually put into effect what the development proposes would depend upon whether or not the sequence $(z_1, z_2, \ldots, z_t, \ldots)$ is one which is possible for the economy concerned. To consider an explicit example, the supply of land is not included among the feasibility conditions. So an economy might be unable to attain one of its feasible development paths for want of land. Naturally if one takes care to only consider developments for which the z sequence is a possible one, and for which the c sequence lies in the aggregate consumption set, then feasibility entails a possible development.

We turn next to prices. Given a feasible development of the economy, a sequence of non-negative vectors, $(p_1, p_2, \ldots, p_t, \ldots)$, will be said to be *production prices* for that development if

$$p_{t+1} \cdot B \leqq p_t \cdot A \qquad t=1,2,\ldots, \tag{9.9}$$

and these inequalities are *complementary* to the inequalities

$$x_t \geqq 0, \tag{9.10}$$

and the inequalities

$$c_t + A \cdot x_t - q_t - z_t \leqq 0 \qquad t=1,2,\ldots, \tag{9.11}$$

are *complementary* to the inequalities.

$$p_t \geqq 0. \tag{9.12}$$

Recall from ch. 3 that the price vectors p_t have the interpretation of present value prices. So (9.9) is to be interpreted as requiring that no activity shall show an excess of present value of output over present value of input cost. Where there is strict inequality, say for the ith activity, we have

$$p_{t+1} \cdot b^i < p_t \cdot a^i, \tag{9.13}$$

so that the condition that there be a complementary relation between the inequalities (9.9) and (9.10) now requires that

$$x_{it} = 0. \tag{9.14}$$

The condition that the inequalities (9.11) be complementary to the inequalities (9.12) has the interpretation that a good which is produced in surplus by the development must be priced at zero. Thus the requirements on production price sequences are twofold: the prices must assign no pure present gain to any activity at any time, and if they assign a pure present loss, then it must only be to an activity which is not used; and goods in excess supply must be free goods.

The definition of equilibrium prices is purely a formal one and as such is independent of any particular institutional interpretation in terms of price-guided behaviour. But no doubt a great part of the interest of the concept lies in the possibility of interpretations in terms of such behaviour; even if, perhaps, in the pure theory of production, the concept of production prices has an interest in its own right. The reason for offering a formal definition is that there is more than one possible institutional interpretation.

The linear production model is now before our eyes. But we have yet to do anything with it. It is still no more than a framework within which, and from which, many problems and theories of capital accumulation can be discussed. In ch. 10 we will make use of the model to indicate the relationship between *efficient* developments of the economy and the existence of production prices. Aside from the inherent interest of this exercise it serves to throw some light on recent debates concerning the meaning of the rate of interest which is embedded in the price system of a semi-stationary development, and in particular the question of whether that interest rate can be interpreted as a rate of return. We will be able also to view in an entirely new light the phenomenon of 'double switching' that we encountered in ch. 8.

10

Efficiency, production prices and rates of return

In optimum conditions, that is to say, production should be so organised as to produce in the most efficient manner compatible with delivery at the dates at which consumers' demand is expected to become effective. It is no use to produce for delivery at a different date from this, even though the physical output could be increased by changing the date of delivery; – except in so far as the prospect of a larger meal, so to speak, induces the consumer to anticipate or postpone the hour of dinner. If, after hearing full particulars of the meals he can get by fixing dinner at different hours, the consumer is expected to decide in favour of 8 o'clock, it is the business of the cook to provide the best dinner he can for service at that hour, irrespective of whether 7.30, 8 o'clock or 8.30 is the hour which would suit him best if time counted for nothing, one way or the other, and his only task was to produce the absolutely best dinner.

J. M. KEYNES, *General Theory of Employment Interest and Money* (1936, ch. 16)

In ch. 9 we took note that of the many developments of the economy as specified by sequences

$$(x_1, x_2, \ldots, x_t, \ldots), \qquad (c_1, c_2, \ldots, c_t, \ldots), \qquad (z_1, z_2, \ldots, z_t, \ldots), \tag{10.1}$$

only some are *feasible*. However, even the class of feasible developments is far wider than the developments in which we are likely to be interested. It may be feasible to dig holes in the ground and fill them up again but that is not a fruitful way to apply scarce resources. We want to concentrate attention on those developments which cannot be improved upon. And to get to the notion of 'improving upon' which relates most closely to the existence of production prices we need to focus attention upon improvements of the Pareto variety – those which provide more of some particular type of final consumption for some week without providing less of any final consumption in that same week or in any other week. Of course, some final consumptions may be negative in which case 'more consumption' means less of that item supplied to the production sector (e.g. less labour services used in production counts as more consumption).

Now evidently it is not difficult to improve upon a development of the economy unless we in some way restrict the alternative developments to be considered. To count as an improvement the alternative must constitute a rearrangement of the existing or future resources and not merely a contemplation of what might be achieved if only the $\boldsymbol{Z}$ sequence were more bountiful, or $\boldsymbol{q}_1$ were more lavish. We call a development *efficient* if no alternative development with the same $\boldsymbol{Z}$ sequence and the same value of $\boldsymbol{q}_1$ (and, of course, with the same technical possibilities) can dominate its final consumption offering. In terms of a formal definition we have the following.

Definition 10.1. The development $(\boldsymbol{X}, \boldsymbol{C}, \boldsymbol{Z})$ will be said to be *efficient* if there exist no vector sequences $\boldsymbol{X}'$ and $\boldsymbol{C}'$ such that:

(i) $\boldsymbol{c}_1 + \boldsymbol{A}_1 \cdot \boldsymbol{x}_1 \geqq \boldsymbol{c}_1' + \boldsymbol{A}_1 \cdot \boldsymbol{x}_1'$;
(ii) $(\boldsymbol{X}'\ \boldsymbol{C}'\ \boldsymbol{Z}')$ is a feasible development; and
(iii) $\boldsymbol{c}_t' \geqq \boldsymbol{c}_t$ $(t = 1, 2, \ldots)$ with $\boldsymbol{C}$ and $\boldsymbol{C}'$ not identical sequences.

Condition (i) of the definition implies that

$$\boldsymbol{c}_1 - \boldsymbol{z}_1 + \boldsymbol{A}_1 \cdot \boldsymbol{x}_1 \geqq \boldsymbol{c}_1' - \boldsymbol{z}_1 + \boldsymbol{A}_1 \cdot \boldsymbol{x}_1', \tag{10.2}$$

so that the development $(\boldsymbol{X}', \boldsymbol{C}', \boldsymbol{Z})$ does not start from a larger initial vector of produced goods than does the development $(\boldsymbol{X}, \boldsymbol{C}, \boldsymbol{Z})$. Condition (iii) of the definition implies that no component of the consumption sequence $\boldsymbol{C}'$ is ever less than the corresponding component of the sequence $\boldsymbol{C}$; but, because these two sequences are not identical, there must be at least one consumption in at least one week for which $c_{it}' > c_{it}$. Thus the import of definition 10.1 is that an efficient sequence cannot be dominated, with regard to its consumption sequence, by another feasible development with the same initial state and subject to the same availability of the services of non-produced factors.

Efficiency is a term that seems to carry with it commendatory overtones, so that it is as well that we pause to note that the definition as it stands is too broad to carry any such implication. A development is inefficient if any final output can be augmented without cost to another output level. However, some outputs may not be desired for final consumption, and who cares if the economic system could produce more sulphuric acid but not more of anything else? As we proceed we shall see that the definition could be modified, in the obvious manner, so as to define efficiency relative to a particular set of goods desired for final consumption.

Definition 10.1 defines efficiency in terms of the lack of any feasible rearrangement of the development so as to improve upon its final consumption. Suppose that a development is not efficient, so that a rearrangement improving upon it is possible: what form will that rearrangement take? One may distinguish, arguing fairly loosely for the moment, between two types of case. In one case the organization of economic activity within a span of a few weeks can be improved upon. During certain weeks coke is being delivered to cider factories and apples to steel works – swop these deliveries around and output can be increased at both plants. This is a kind of inefficiency that is familiar from atemporal production theory. However, this type of case does not exhaust the possibilities. An example will help to illustrate another type of situation.

Example 10.1. There is only one produced good in the economy, called 'stuff'. There are four activities available, indexed by n, each of the following type:

$$1 \text{ unit of stuff} \oplus n \text{ man-hours of labour time} \ominus \frac{2n+1}{n+1} \text{ units of stuff} \qquad (n = 0, 1, 2, 3). \quad (10.3)$$

We consider an economy of this type in which the number of man-hours of labour available grows at a rate of 50% per week. The economy starts in week 1 with one man-hour of labour time available and one unit of stuff. In each week all the labour time and all the stuff are used in activity 1, so that at the beginning of week 2 there are 1.5 units of stuff available and these are combined with the labour time of week 2, 1.5 man-hours, to fuel activity 1, and to provide 2.25 units of stuff for the beginning of week 3; and so on. The economy continues according to this semi-stationary pattern indefinitely.

Now it is immediately clear that this development is not efficient. It provides no consumption at all, while a straightforward modification of the development (say reinvesting only 80% of the stuff at the start of each week and consuming the rest) would both provide some consumption and save on the labour time used. But it cannot be said that the inefficiency arises from a misallocation of resources as that term is usually understood: it is not that the resources go to the wrong activity. This is evident from the observation that the demonstration that the development is inefficient did not in any way depend upon the form, or even the existence, of the other activities. No, the fault is of a different kind: in the case of the example the whole direction of the development is wrong. It is too much concerned with accumulation and not enough concerned with consumption. As we shall see below, the development of example 10.1 is rational according to its own peculiar direction, for it is not possible to gain more consumption in any week without 'suffering' a permanent diminution of the stock of stuff that will be available at the start of the subsequent weeks. Because the value of output is credited to producers regardless of whether it goes to consumption or to the augmentation of capital it is perhaps not astounding that the development is a production price equilibrium,

Table 10.1.

	Week 1		Week 2		
	Stuff	Labour time	Stuff	Labour time	
$\gamma = 0.5$	1	1	1.5	–	Goods
$p = 0.3$	1.3	0.2	1	$\frac{2}{13}$	Prices

notwithstanding its inefficiency. Since the example exhibits a semi-stationary state we may present it in table 10.1, with the prices, in the format of table 4.1. The reader may confirm that at these prices none of the other activities are profitable.

So a production price equilibrium is not necessarily efficient. What can one say then of a production price equilibrium? We are here confronting a problem that is peculiarly a problem of capital theory, for in atemporal production theory it is known that a state of the economy is a production price equilibrium if and only if it is efficient[1]. To answer the question we need to introduce some new concepts.

Take the first T weeks of the development (10.1) and consider it as an entity in its own right. We have

$$(\boldsymbol{x}_1, \boldsymbol{x}_2, \ldots, \boldsymbol{x}_T), \qquad (\boldsymbol{c}_1, \boldsymbol{c}_2, \ldots, \boldsymbol{c}_T), \qquad (\boldsymbol{z}_1, \boldsymbol{z}_2, \ldots, \boldsymbol{z}_T). \tag{10.4}$$

Notice that productive activity continues in week T, so that produced outputs will be available at the start of week $T+1$, and the vector $\boldsymbol{B}_T \cdot \boldsymbol{x}_T$ records what the weeks that follow after week T will inherit. A finite development of the form of (10.4) will be called a *T overture*. From a development of the economy we may pick out an infinity of overtures of various durations each of which may be regarded as the beginning of an unending development that follows upon the completion of the overture. An alternative approach, closer to the spirit of ch. 3, is to look upon the overture as a completed account of the development of an economy which will have no history after week $T+1$. Just as we have defined *feasibility* and *efficiency* for developments, so we may define them, in an obvious manner, for overtures; but in the case of efficiency there is a small new consideration. Efficiency for a development was defined as relative to an initial vector $(\boldsymbol{k}_1 + \boldsymbol{c}_1 - \boldsymbol{z}_1)$ because obviously it would usually prove possible to improve upon a development given a more generous starting point. Similarly with an overture efficiency must be relative to an initial vector, but now

[1] Refer, for example, to Koopmans (1957). Formally, the difference between the two cases is that the number of goods is finite in the case of the atemporal example.

also to a terminal vector $B_T \cdot x_T$, for again it will usually prove possible to improve upon any development if we are willing to settle for a smaller final endowment.

Definition 10.2. The T overture

$$(x_1, x_2, \ldots, x_T), \qquad (c_1, c_2, \ldots, c_T), \qquad (z_1, z_2, \ldots, z_T), \tag{10.5}$$

will be said to be *efficient* if there exist no vectors

$$(x_1', x_2', \ldots, x_T'), \qquad (c_1', c_2', \ldots, c_T'), \tag{10.6}$$

which together with $(z_1, z_2, \ldots, z_T)$ constitute a feasible overture, and such that

$$\begin{aligned} &\text{(i) } c_1 + A_1 \cdot x_1 \geqq c_1' + A_1 \cdot x_1'; \\ &\text{(ii) } B_T \cdot x_T \leqq B_T \cdot x_T'; \\ &\text{(iii) } c_t' \geqq c_t, \ (t = 1, \ldots, T) \quad \text{with } (c_1, c_2, \ldots, c_T) \quad \text{and} \\ &\qquad\qquad (c_1', c_2', \ldots, c_T') \text{ not identical sequences.} \end{aligned} \tag{10.7}$$

The relation between efficiency of a development and efficiency of overtures is clear in the light of example 10.1, and the discussion that accompanied it. It is immediately evident that a development is efficient only if all its overtures are efficient, for if a development commences with an inefficient overture a re-arrangement just of its first T weeks can produce extra consumption without prejudice to later possibilities. However, in the case of a development such as that of example 10.1 we shall see soon, if it is not already obvious, that the inefficiency does not arise because any overture is inefficient, but rather on account of the misdirection of the whole development. To increase consumption in this type of example the course of the development must be diverted, *never to return to the original course.* We call this type of path, one which follows efficiently development in a certain direction, *pseudo-efficient.*

Definition 10.3. A development of the economy is *pseudo-efficient* if all its overtures are efficient.

Evidently an efficient development must be pseudo-efficient so that efficiency is the stronger requirement. It so happens that the property of being a production price equilibrium is more associated with pseudo-efficiency than with efficiency. For this reason we shall investigate the existence, and later the interpretation, of production prices for a development assumed to be pseudo-efficient, but which may or may not be efficient. We show first that production prices may be associated with an efficient overture. This is done by establishing that a price sequence will satisfy the requirements of (9.9) and (9.10) if and only if they are a solution to the dual of a linear programme – the question of the existence of production prices is thus reduced to the well-known theory concerning duality of linear programmes[2].

Suppose that the feasible T overture

$$(\bar{\boldsymbol{x}}_1, \bar{\boldsymbol{x}}_2, \ldots, \bar{\boldsymbol{x}}_T), \qquad (\bar{\boldsymbol{c}}_1, \bar{\boldsymbol{c}}_2, \ldots, \bar{\boldsymbol{c}}_T), \qquad (\bar{\boldsymbol{z}}_1, \bar{\boldsymbol{z}}_2, \ldots, \bar{\boldsymbol{z}}_T), \tag{10.8}$$

is efficient. Then it must maximize the level of consumption in week 1 subject to initial endowment, technology, the other consumption levels and the final stock. In other words, $\theta = 0$, $\boldsymbol{x}_t = \bar{\boldsymbol{x}}_t$ $(t = 1, \ldots, T)$, is a solution to the linear programme:

$$\left.\begin{array}{l} \text{maximize } \theta \text{ subject to} \\ \boldsymbol{A}_1 \cdot \boldsymbol{x}_1 + \bar{\boldsymbol{c}}_1 + \theta \bar{\boldsymbol{u}} \leqq \boldsymbol{A}_1 \cdot \bar{\boldsymbol{x}}_1 + \bar{\boldsymbol{c}}_1, \\ \boldsymbol{A}_t \cdot \boldsymbol{x}_t + \bar{\boldsymbol{c}}_t \leqq \boldsymbol{B}_{t-1} \cdot \boldsymbol{x}_{t-1} + \bar{\boldsymbol{z}}_t \qquad (t = 2, \ldots, T), \\ \boldsymbol{B}_T \cdot \bar{\boldsymbol{x}}_T \leqq \boldsymbol{B}_T \cdot \boldsymbol{x}_T, \\ \boldsymbol{x}_t \geqq \boldsymbol{0} \qquad (t = 1, \ldots, T), \end{array}\right\} \tag{10.9}$$

where $\bar{\boldsymbol{u}} \geqslant \boldsymbol{0}$ is an arbitrary vector.

The idea of the linear programme is to add to the consumption of week 1 the largest possible vector in the proportions of $\bar{\boldsymbol{u}}$ without lowering any other consumption vector in a later week. The parameter θ, which may be of any sign, measures the extent to which extra consumption is provided. The constraints impose feasibility. The first line requires that the solution to the linear programme in week 1 uses no more resources net of non-produced factor services than does the original overture. The next set of constraints require for weeks 2 to T that, in each of these weeks, the total use of resources (inputs to production plus consumption) shall not exceed the total availability of resources (outputs from the previous week plus non-produced factor services). Finally, the last conditions ensure that the overture yields a final resource vector at least as large as $\boldsymbol{B}_T \cdot \bar{\boldsymbol{x}}_T$, and that no activity levels are negative.

---

[2] The method is familiar to economists from, for example, the work of Dorfman *et al.* (1958). Proofs of the results of linear programming theory in harmony with the arguments of this section will be found in the mathematical appendix.

Arranging (10.9) in the standard form it reads:

maximize θ subject to

$$\begin{bmatrix} \bar{\boldsymbol{u}} & \boldsymbol{A}_1 & & & & & \\ & -\boldsymbol{B}_1 & \boldsymbol{A}_2 & & & & \\ & & -\boldsymbol{B}_2 & \boldsymbol{A}_3 & & & \\ & & & \ddots & \ddots & & \\ & & & & \ddots & \ddots & \\ & & & & & -\boldsymbol{B}_{t-1} & \boldsymbol{A}_T \\ & & & & & & -\boldsymbol{B}_T \end{bmatrix} \begin{bmatrix} \theta \\ \boldsymbol{x}_1 \\ \cdot \\ \cdot \\ \cdot \\ \cdot \\ \cdot \\ \boldsymbol{x}_T \end{bmatrix} \leqq \begin{bmatrix} \boldsymbol{A}_1 \cdot \bar{\boldsymbol{x}}_1 \\ \bar{\boldsymbol{z}}_2 - \bar{\boldsymbol{c}}_2 \\ \cdot \\ \cdot \\ \cdot \\ \cdot \\ \bar{\boldsymbol{z}}_T - \bar{\boldsymbol{c}}_T \\ -\boldsymbol{B}_T \cdot \bar{\boldsymbol{x}}_T \end{bmatrix} \tag{10.10}$$

and

$$\begin{bmatrix} \boldsymbol{x}_1 \\ \cdot \\ \cdot \\ \cdot \\ \boldsymbol{x}_T \end{bmatrix} \geqq \boldsymbol{0}.$$

If an overture is efficient its activity vectors and $\theta = 0$ must evidently solve (10.10). The dual of (10.10) is:

$$\text{minimize } \boldsymbol{p}_1 \cdot \boldsymbol{A}_1 \cdot \bar{\boldsymbol{x}}_1 + \sum_{t=2}^{T} \boldsymbol{p}_t \cdot (\bar{\boldsymbol{z}}_t - \bar{\boldsymbol{c}}_t) - \boldsymbol{p}_{T+1} \cdot \boldsymbol{B}_T \cdot \bar{\boldsymbol{x}}_T$$

subject to

$$[\boldsymbol{p}_1, \boldsymbol{p}_2, \ldots, \boldsymbol{p}_{T+1}] \begin{bmatrix} \bar{\boldsymbol{u}} & \boldsymbol{A}_1 & & & & & \\ & -\boldsymbol{B}_1 & \boldsymbol{A}_2 & & & & \\ & & -\boldsymbol{B}_2 & \boldsymbol{A}_3 & & & \\ & & & \ddots & \ddots & & \\ & & & & \ddots & \ddots & \\ & & & & & -\boldsymbol{B}_{T-1} & \boldsymbol{A}_T \\ & & & & & & -\boldsymbol{B}_T \end{bmatrix} \geqq \begin{bmatrix} 1 \\ 0 \\ \cdot \\ \cdot \\ \cdot \\ \cdot \\ 0 \end{bmatrix} \tag{10.11}$$

and

$$\boldsymbol{p}_t \geqq \boldsymbol{0} \qquad (t = 1, \ldots, T+1).$$

We see then that there is a correspondence, and an exact one, between a feasible efficient overture and a pair of dual linear programmes of the form (10.10) and (10.11). This fact is the basis of the following result.

Theorem 10.1. An efficient overture is a production price equilibrium.

Proof. The activity vectors of an efficient overture (together with $\theta = 0$) must be the solution to a linear programme of the form (10.10) for otherwise there could be an increase in first week consumption in the direction $\bar{\boldsymbol{u}}$, without loss of consumption in any later week. Hence, since (10.10) has this solution, (10.11) must have at least one solution which will have inequality relations complementary to the sign constraints of (10.10). The first constraint complementary to the unsigned θ gives us

$$\boldsymbol{p}_1 \cdot \bar{\boldsymbol{u}} = 1, \tag{10.12}$$

so that $\bar{\boldsymbol{u}}$, chosen arbitrarily, is now seen to be the *numeraire*. A vector of goods $\bar{\boldsymbol{u}}$ delivered in week 1 has the value one. The remaining constraints are all of the type

$$\boldsymbol{p}_t \cdot \boldsymbol{A}_t - \boldsymbol{p}_{t+1} \cdot \boldsymbol{B}_t \geqq \boldsymbol{0} \qquad (t = 1, \ldots, T) \tag{10.13}$$

and these are complementary to the inequalities

$$\boldsymbol{x}_t \geqq \boldsymbol{0} \qquad (t = 1, \ldots, T). \tag{10.14}$$

Comparing (10.13) and (10.14) to (9.10) and (9.11) it will be seen that the first conditions for a production price equilibrium are satisfied. Note next that the dual variables $(\boldsymbol{p}_1, \boldsymbol{p}_2, \ldots, \boldsymbol{p}_{T+1})$ are themselves constrained by sign conditions complementary to the constraints of (10.10). Hence, the inequalities

$$\boldsymbol{p}_t \geqq \boldsymbol{0} \qquad (t = 1, \ldots, T + 1), \tag{10.15}$$

will be complementary to the inequalities

$$\begin{aligned} &\bar{\boldsymbol{c}}_t + \boldsymbol{A}_t \cdot \boldsymbol{x}_t \leqq \boldsymbol{B}_{t-1} \cdot \boldsymbol{x}_{t-1} + \bar{\boldsymbol{z}}_t \qquad (t = 1, \ldots, T) \\ \text{and} \\ &\boldsymbol{B}_T \cdot \bar{\boldsymbol{x}}_T \leqq \boldsymbol{B}_T \cdot \boldsymbol{x}_T, \end{aligned} \tag{10.16}$$

as required. The proof of the theorem is now complete.

The converse of theorem 10.1 cannot be established: a production price equilibrium is not necessarily efficient; however, if it can be dominated it will be only with respect to consumptions of free goods. In other words, a production price equilibrium is efficient except that, perhaps, the consumption of one or more of its free goods might be increased without cost to another consumption. The next theorem provides a formal statement and proof of this result. The argument could well make use, as did the proof of theorem 10.1, of linear programming theory, but a more elementary argument suffices.

Theorem 10.2. Consider two feasible T overtures

$$\begin{array}{ll} (x_1, x_2, \ldots, x_T), & (x_1', x_2', \ldots, x_T'), \\ (c_1, c_2, \ldots, c_T), \quad \textit{and} & (c_1', c_2', \ldots, c_T'), \\ (z_1, z_2, \ldots, z_T), & (z_1, z_2, \ldots, z_T), \end{array} \tag{10.17}$$

each starting from initial produced resources $\bar{q}_1$ *and finishing with produced resources* $\bar{q}_{T+1}$ *at the start of week* $T+1$. *Let the unprimed sequences define a T overture which is a production price equilibrium at prices*

$$(p_1, p_2, \ldots, p_{T+1}). \tag{10.18}$$

Let the primed sequences define a T overture for which

$$c_{js}' \geqslant c_{js} \qquad (j=1,\ldots,n; s=1,\ldots,T) \quad \textit{and} \quad c_{kt}' > c_{kt}. \tag{10.19}$$

Then

$$p_{kt} = 0. \tag{10.20}$$

Proof. Because both sequences define feasible *T* overtures we have

$$\left\{\begin{array}{r} \bar{q}_1 + z_1 - A_1 \cdot x_1 - c_1 \geqq 0 \\ B_1 \cdot x_1 + z_2 - A_2 \cdot x_2 - c_2 \geqq 0 \\ \cdot \quad \cdot \\ \cdot \quad \cdot \\ B_{t-1} \cdot x_{t-1} + z_t - A_t \cdot x_t - c_t \geqq 0 \\ \cdot \quad \cdot \\ B_{T-1} \cdot x_{T-1} + z_T - A_T \cdot x_T - c_T \geqq 0 \\ B_T \cdot x_T - \bar{q}_{T+1} \geqq 0 \end{array}\right\}$$

and (10.21)

$$\left\{\begin{array}{r} \bar{q}_1 + z_1 - A_1 \cdot x_1' - c_1' \geqq 0 \\ B_1 \cdot x_1' + z_2 - A_2 \cdot x_2' - c_2' \geqq 0 \\ \cdot \quad \cdot \\ \cdot \quad \cdot \\ B_{t-1} \cdot x_{t-1}' + z_t - A_t \cdot x_t' - c_t' \geqq 0 \\ \cdot \quad \cdot \\ B_{T-1} \cdot x_{T-1}' + z_T - A_T \cdot x_T' - c_T' \geqq 0 \\ B_T \cdot x_T' - \bar{q}_{T+1} \geqq 0 \end{array}\right\}.$$

Now consider the first part of (10.21). On multiplying the tth line by p_t the inequalities are eliminated, since whenever a line has strict inequality the relevant price must be zero, by the definition of production prices. The same operation on the second part of (10.21) may leave inequalities, because the primed overture is not necessarily a production price equilibrium at prices $(p_1, \ldots, p_{T+1})$. Hence, we obtain

$$\left\{\begin{aligned} p_1\cdot\bar{q}_1+p_1\cdot z_1-p_1\cdot A_1\cdot x_1-p_1\cdot c_1&=0\\ p_2\cdot B_1\cdot x_1+p_2\cdot z_2-p_2\cdot A_2\cdot x_2-p_2\cdot c_2&=0\\ &\;\vdots\\ p_t\cdot B_{t-1}\cdot x_{t-1}+p_t\cdot z_t-p_t\cdot A_t\cdot x_t-p_t\cdot c_t&=0\\ &\;\vdots\\ p_{T+1}\cdot B_T\cdot x_T-p_{T+1}\cdot\bar{q}_{T+1}&=0 \end{aligned}\right\}$$

and (10.22)

$$\left\{\begin{aligned} p_1\cdot\bar{q}_1+p_1\cdot z_1-p_1\cdot A_1\cdot x_1'-p_1\cdot c_1'&\geqslant 0\\ p_2\cdot B_1\cdot x_1'+p_2\cdot z_2-p_2\cdot A_2\cdot x_2'-p_2\cdot c_2'&\geqslant 0\\ &\;\vdots\\ p_t\cdot B_{t-1}\cdot x_{t-1}'+p_t\cdot z_t-p_t\cdot A_t\cdot x_t'-p_t\cdot c_t'&\geqslant 0\\ &\;\vdots\\ p_{T+1}\cdot B_T\cdot x_T'-p_{T+1}\cdot\bar{q}_{T+1}&\geqslant 0 \end{aligned}\right\}.$$

Now, on adding together all the lines of each part of (10.22) and noting that terms of the form

$$p_{t+1}\cdot B_t\cdot x_t-p_t\cdot A_t\cdot x_t \tag{10.23}$$

vanish, by the complementary conditions on a production price equilibrium, while terms of the form

$$p_{t+1}\cdot B_t\cdot x_t'-p_t\cdot A_t\cdot x_t' \tag{10.24}$$

are non-positive, one obtains the following equations:

$$p_1\cdot\bar{q}_1+\sum_{t=1}^{T}p_t\cdot(z_t-c_t)-p_{T+1}\cdot\bar{q}_{T+1}=0, \tag{10.25}$$

$$p_1\cdot\bar{q}_1+\sum_{t=1}^{T}p_t\cdot(z_t-c_t')-p_{T+1}\cdot\bar{q}_{T+1}\geqslant 0. \tag{10.26}$$

On subtracting (10.25) from (10.26) there remains

$$\sum_{t=1}^{T}p_t\cdot(c_t-c_t')\geqslant 0. \tag{10.27}$$

From (10.19) it follows that no term in the summation of (10.27) can be positive. If therefore one of the consumption differences were to be negative, as the argument postulates, the corresponding price must be zero. Thus the theorem follows as an implication of (10.27).

Notice that in obtaining production prices for a T overture we obtain them *en passant* for all the overtures shorter than T weeks, because the complementary inequality relations hold as much for the early weeks of an overture as they do for the complete overture. But we have not yet obtained production prices for a development. We do know already that a development will be a production price equilibrium *only if* it is pseudo-efficient[3]: for if a development is a production price equilibrium we can cut from it a T-week overture for any T, and the first $T+1$ price vectors will then constitute production prices for the overture (this because the complementary inequality conditions of the definition of production prices will be satisfied). However, what can be said of the converse type of result: is every pseudo-efficient development a production price equilibrium? This question demands for its answer some rather tricky analysis the difficulty of which is out of all proportion to the importance of the question. For this reason we relegate detailed discussion of the issue to the appendix to this chapter, while noting here that a negative answer to the question will be returned in that appendix. There are developments that are pseudo-efficient but for which there exist no production prices. However, a slight and probably not unreasonable condition will ensure that a pseudo-efficient development is a production price equilibrium as the argument of the appendix serves to demonstrate.

For the present one observation will suffice: *there is a problem in establishing that a development will have production prices only because the production prices of an overture even when normalized need not be unique.* For just suppose that every efficient overture had unique production prices[4]. Take two overtures from the same development of duration T_1 and T_2 ($T_2 > T_1$) with production prices

$$(p_1^1, p_2^1, \ldots, p_{T_1}^1, p_{T_1+1}^1)$$

and (10.28)

$$(p_1^2, p_2^2, \ldots, p_{T_1}^2, p_{T_1+1}^2, \ldots, p_{T_2}^2, p_{T_2+1}^2).$$

Now it is evident that the prices

$$(p_1^2, p_2^2, \ldots, p_{T_1}^2, p_{T_1+1}^2) \tag{10.29}$$

must be production prices for the T_1 overture, for in satisfying the complementary inequality conditions for the duration of T_2 weeks they must necessarily do so for the first T_1 weeks. Then if production prices are always unique we must have

$$p_t^1 = p_t^2 \qquad (t = 1, \ldots, T_1 + 1). \tag{10.30}$$

---

[3] Or, to put it more accurately, the development must be pseudo-efficient with respect to consumptions of goods that are not free at its production prices.

[4] To talk of uniqueness or non-uniqueness of production prices we must first normalize all the price sequences by choice of a common *numeraire*. Otherwise doubling all prices produces another set of production prices.

In this case, we may write out a sequence of price vectors, as far as is desired, knowing that this specific sequence can be continued indefinitely while satisfying for each week the conditions for production prices. We then have production prices for the unending development (we can generate any term of the infinite series by taking any overture of sufficient length and writing out the production prices of that overture).

Where, however, an overture has more than one set of production prices we suffer on account of the embarrassment of riches. There may now be production prices for a T_1 overture which are not the first $T_1 + 1$ terms of any production price sequences for overtures of duration $T_2 (T_2 > T_1)$ or longer. As we lengthen the duration of the overtures that we consider we are imposing more and more stringent requirements on the price vectors of the initial weeks. At the outset the production prices for a 99 overture must simply satisfy the complementary inequality conditions for 100 weeks. But the first 100 terms of the production prices for a 100 overture must not only constitute a set of production prices for the 99 overture but also be one which may be continued to complete production prices for a 100 overture. And the first 100 terms of the production prices for a 150 overture must not only constitute a set of production prices for the 99 overture but of all such sets it must be one to which may be added a further 50 terms to give a production price sequence for a 150 overture, and so on. The question to be taken up in the appendix is this: can we find a price set for each particular overture that can be continued indefinitely to form production price sequences for longer overtures? Obviously this is not a trivial question.

Putting aside the question for the moment let us confine our attention to developments that are production-price equilibria. The reader may satisfy himself, by consulting the appendix, that this is nearly equivalent to examining pseudo-efficient developments. But take note that there are some odd cases where a pseudo-efficient development is not a production price equilibrium. From example 10.1 we know that a production price equilibrium is not necessarily efficient, even with regard to goods that are not free goods at its production prices. However, except perhaps for goods that are free at its production prices, a production-price equilibrium is necessarily pseudo-efficient – this is an immediate consequence of theorem 10.2.

To learn more about the relationship between production-price equilibrium and efficiency we take note of the fact that a development is necessarily efficient with respect to the consumption of goods that are not free if it *maximizes the present value of consumption* at its own prices. The demonstration of this result will follow. To give a clear and precise meaning to this idea we need to clarify the notion of maximization, and for present purposes we will work with a rather general notion of maximization.

Definition 10.4. A sequence $\boldsymbol{C}$ will be said to *maximize the present value of consumption* at prices $\boldsymbol{P}$ if for each alternative sequence $\boldsymbol{C}'$, feasible for the same initial resource vector and non-produced resources $\boldsymbol{Z}$, we have

$$\limsup_{T\to\infty} \sum_{t=1}^{T} \boldsymbol{p}_t \cdot (\boldsymbol{c}_t' - \boldsymbol{c}_t) \leqslant 0. \tag{10.31}$$

Relation (10.31) is to be read to include the case where the left-hand side is minus infinity.

Definition 10.4 includes as special cases examples in which the present value of consumption converges to a finite value but is more general than that. The 'golden rule' path in a one good neoclassical model, for example, maximizes the present value of consumption in the sense of definition 10.4 although not in the stronger sense which requires that the discounted value of consumption approach a finite limit[5].

Broadly speaking, a sequence will have the present value maximizing property provided that the present values go to zero sufficiently rapidly as one goes towards the distant future. In the constant-rate-of-interest case this is equivalent to saying that the rate of interest must be sufficiently large. The following theorem is an example of the kind of result that may be established.

Theorem 10.3. A sufficient condition for a development to maximize the present value of consumption is that the price sequence $\boldsymbol{P}$ *is one for which the development is a production-price equilibrium, and such that*

$$\lim_{T\to\infty} \boldsymbol{p}_T \cdot \boldsymbol{k}_T = \lim_{T\to\infty} \boldsymbol{p}_T \cdot \boldsymbol{A}_T \cdot \boldsymbol{x}_T = 0, \tag{10.33}$$

for any feasible development with the samc initial resource vector and non-produced factor service flow $\boldsymbol{Z}$.

Proof. The argument is closely parallel to the proof of theorem 10.2 to which reference will be made whenever possible. Let an overture of duration T be cut from the development which is a production-price equilibrium at prices

---

[5] As, for example, the growth model in which output Y_{t+1} (including only net additions to the capital stock and not gross capital as in the linear production model) is a function of capital K_t and labour time L_t as

$$\begin{aligned} Y_{t+1} &= K_t^{1/2} \cdot L_t^{1/2}, \qquad & L_t &= (1.02)^{t-1}, \\ K_t &= 625\,(1.02)^{t-1}, \qquad & C_{t+1} &= Y_{t+1} - (K_{t+1} - K_t) = 12.5\,(1.02)^{t-1}. \end{aligned} \tag{10.32}$$

The reader may satisfy himself that (10.32) is a golden rule path, that the present value of consumption is unbounded, but that (10.31) is satisfied.

$\boldsymbol{P}$, and let the activity vectors of this overture be represented, as in (10.22) by unprimed vectors. The primed vectors will again represent an alternative development feasible from the same initial resource vector $\bar{\boldsymbol{q}}_1$ and with the same z_t values. Again, multiplying feasibility conditions by prices and adding, and noting the complementary inequality conditions, we obtain terms summing to zero, as with (10.25). The sole difference here is that, since the development continues after week $T+1$, no term involving $\bar{\boldsymbol{q}}_{T+1}$ appears, but instead simply $-\boldsymbol{p}_T \cdot \boldsymbol{A}_T \cdot \boldsymbol{X}_T$ is the only term involving an activity vector that does not cancel out when the terms are summed. Thus, we obtain

$$\boldsymbol{p}_1 \cdot \bar{\boldsymbol{q}}_1 + \sum_{t=1}^{T} \boldsymbol{p}_t \cdot (\boldsymbol{z}_t - \boldsymbol{c}_t) - \boldsymbol{p}_T \cdot \boldsymbol{A}_T \cdot \boldsymbol{x}_T = 0, \tag{10.34}$$

which may be compared to (10.25). Again, in an exactly parallel fashion, we obtain for the primed development the condition

$$\boldsymbol{p}_1 \cdot \bar{\boldsymbol{q}}_1 + \sum_{t=1}^{T} \boldsymbol{p}_t \cdot (\boldsymbol{z}_t - \boldsymbol{c}'_t) - \boldsymbol{p}_T \cdot \boldsymbol{A}_T \cdot \boldsymbol{x}'_T \geqslant 0, \tag{10.35}$$

which may be compared to (10.26).

On subtracting (10.34) from (10.35) and rearranging there remains

$$\sum_{t=1}^{T} \boldsymbol{p}_t \cdot (\boldsymbol{c}'_t - \boldsymbol{c}_t) \leqslant \boldsymbol{p}_T \cdot \boldsymbol{A}_T \cdot (\boldsymbol{x}_T - \boldsymbol{x}'_T). \tag{10.36}$$

Taking limits as $T \to \infty$, and taking into account (10.33), the limit of the right-hand side of (10.36) is zero. The left-hand side of (10.36) may not converge, it could go to $-\infty$ or oscillate, but in any case must have

$$\limsup_{T \to \infty} \sum_{t=1}^{T} \boldsymbol{p}_t \cdot (\boldsymbol{c}'_t - \boldsymbol{c}_t) \leqslant 0, \tag{10.37}$$

so that the present value of consumption is maximized, as required.

An immediate corollary of (10.37) is the efficiency of the unprimed sequences. The limiting condition (10.33) is familiar from the work of Malinvaud (1953). It is clearly not a necessary condition. Furthermore, it is possible to obtain sufficient conditions for (10.33) to be satisfied. If, for example, there is labour in the model growing at rate γ and semi-stationary growth with an interest rate ρ, strictly greater than γ, then a sufficient condition for (10.33) to hold is that the value of output in any week in terms of the *numeraire* in that week has an upper bound subject to a limited labour supply. This will be the case if every activity requires a positive labour input, though even this is not necessary. If the rate of growth is equal to the rate of interest ($\rho = \gamma$) not even these conditions will do and, indeed, the discounted value of consumption will not in general be maximized, as the following example indicates.

Example 10.2. This example is similar to example 10.1, except that there are only two activities. These are

$$1 \text{ unit of stuff} \oplus n \text{ man-hours of labour time} \ominus \frac{2n+1}{n+1} \text{units of stuff} \quad (n=0, 1). \tag{10.38}$$

A semi-stationary state which is a production-price equilibrium is presented in the format of table 4.1 to which it is identical except that the prices are different (see table 10.2). Again activity 1 is the only one employed, but now activities 2 and 3 would be more profitable were they available, which here they are not. As before, the development is clearly inefficient, there being no consumption at all, and it evidently does not maximize the present value of consumption.

Table 10.2.

	Week 1		Week 2		
	Stuff	Labour time	Stuff	Labour time	
$\gamma=0.5$	1	1	1.5	–	Goods
$\rho=0.5$	1.5	0	1.0	0	Prices

Reviewing the conclusions at which we have so far arrived we may note that a sufficient condition for the efficiency of a development which constitutes a production-price equilibrium is that the 'present value of capital', defined as $\boldsymbol{p}_T \cdot \boldsymbol{k}_T = \boldsymbol{p}_T \cdot \boldsymbol{A}_T \cdot \boldsymbol{x}_T$, goes to zero as T goes to infinity. However, this is not a necessary condition: there are efficient paths for which the present value of capital is unbounded, but there are also inefficient paths with this property. In the appendix we will evolve a direct economic interpretation of the limit of the present value of capital and this will enable us to see just why there is some association between the behaviour of this limit and the efficiency of a production-price equilibrium, but also why this feature of a development cannot be made into an unambiguous and foolproof indicator of its efficiency.

Let us return now to the proof of theorem 10.3 to consider a special case which has attracted attention. In the argument of that proof the primed development was any alternative development. It did not have to be an equilibrium at the prices $\boldsymbol{P}$, for which reason some of the activities to which it assigned a positive activity level might not be profitable at prices $\boldsymbol{P}$, hence the possibility of strict inequality in (10.35). Suppose, however, focusing attention upon a special type of instance, that the alternative development $\boldsymbol{X}'$, as well as being feasible for the same initial-resource vector $\bar{\boldsymbol{q}}_1$ and non-produced factor-service sequence $\boldsymbol{Z}$, is also a production-price equilibrium at prices $\boldsymbol{P}$. This involves two separate considerations:

(i) the alternative development X' must not assign a positive activity level to any activity that returns a present-value loss at prices $\boldsymbol{P}$; and

(ii) the alternative development X' must not make any commodity a 'free good' (i.e. bring it about that the full supply is not all used) unless that commodity has price zero at prices $\boldsymbol{P}$.

That these are very strong requirements will be evident, so we have here a very special case. The implication of the special case is that (10.35) is replaced by

$$\boldsymbol{p}_1 \cdot \bar{\boldsymbol{q}}_1 + \sum_{t=1}^{T} \boldsymbol{p}_t \cdot (\boldsymbol{z}_t - \boldsymbol{c}_t') - \boldsymbol{p}_T \cdot \boldsymbol{A}_T \cdot \boldsymbol{x}_T' = 0. \tag{10.39}$$

From this equation, following the line of the previous argument and assuming the limiting condition (10.30), we arrive at

$$\lim_{T\to\infty} \sum_{t=1}^{T} \boldsymbol{p}_t \cdot (\boldsymbol{c}_t' - \boldsymbol{c}_t) = 0, \tag{10.40}$$

which may be compared to the general result (10.37)

An examination of the inequality (10.37), or the special case of it (10.40), suggests that the production price system may give to us some indication about alternative possibilities relative to a particular development which is a production-price equilibrium at those prices. This is indeed the case, but it is important to be clear about what interpretation the production prices (and the rates of interest implicit in an intertemporal price system) will and will not bear. In this context there is nothing to be said for confining the discussion to semi-stationary developments with constant rates of interest, but since the discussion has been so confined by some writers we will include a specific consideration of that case. In the semi-stationary case the prices may be expressed in the form

$$\left(\boldsymbol{p}, \frac{1}{1+\rho}\boldsymbol{p}, \frac{1}{(1+\rho)^2}\boldsymbol{p}, \dots\right), \tag{10.41}$$

where $\boldsymbol{p}$ is the prices of week 1 and also the relative prices of all subsequent weeks. ρ is the rate of interest. In this case (10.37) reduces to

$$\limsup_{T\to\infty} \sum_{t=1}^{T} \boldsymbol{p} \cdot (\boldsymbol{c}_t' - \boldsymbol{c}_t) \left(\frac{1}{1+\rho}\right)^{t-1} \leqslant 0 \tag{10.42}$$

and (10.40) to

$$\lim_{T\to\infty} \sum_{t=1}^{T} \boldsymbol{p} \cdot (\boldsymbol{c}_t' - \boldsymbol{c}_t) \left(\frac{1}{1+\rho}\right)^{t-1} = 0. \tag{10.43}$$

Solow has sought to establish the rate of return to saving as one of the fundamental, perhaps the fundamental, concept of the theory of capital[6]. In terms of our notation and definitions it is possible to present Solow's argument concisely. But first there is a conceptual problem to be faced. In certain production models it is possible to make changes in the sequence $\boldsymbol{C}$ involving the consumption of two weeks only and these will sometimes be adjacent weeks. In such cases there is no difficulty in deciding how to define the rate of return to a decision to give up Δc_t of a consumption in week t in order to gain Δc_{t+1} of the same consumption in week $t+1$. This is

$$(\Delta c_{t+1}/\Delta c_t) - 1. \tag{10.44}$$

Expression (10.44) measures the rate of return where only one good is involved and a similar expression in price weighted sums does so where the change involves more than one good. It turns out, however, that a linear model does not always offer us such simple possibilities. We may have to choose between making no changes at all and changes leading to variations in the consumption vectors of three or more weeks. An example of this kind of case is presented below. It is then necessary to decide what is the appropriate generalization of (10.44). Solow's answer to this problem is contained in the following definition.

Definition 10.5. Consider two developments, both feasible for the same $\bar{\boldsymbol{q}}_1$ and $\boldsymbol{Z}$ values, with consumption sequences $\boldsymbol{C}$ and $\boldsymbol{C}'$. The first (unprimed) development is a production-price equilibrium at a price system for which relative prices, denoted $\boldsymbol{p}$, are the same in each week. The *rate of return* on a change from the first to the second development is a number σ such that

$$\sum_{t=1}^{\infty} \boldsymbol{p}\cdot(\boldsymbol{c}_t' - \boldsymbol{c}_t)\left(\frac{1}{1+\sigma}\right)^{t-1} = 0. \tag{10.45}$$

Clearly there could in principle be more than one value of σ satisfying (10.45). In the special case where $\boldsymbol{c}_t$ differs from $\boldsymbol{c}_t'$ in only two weeks (10.45) has a unique root. Another special case is that in which $\boldsymbol{c}_t$ and $\boldsymbol{c}_t'$ have at most one component, always the same one, different from zero at each t. Then only one good is consumed, the prices cancel out of (10.45), in which case we may dispense with the requirement that relative prices be invariant, and we are looking for a discount rate that will discount changes in consumption to zero.

---

[6] See Solow (1963) and, in the context of the linear production model, Solow (1967). On whether it is *the* rate of return to saving, or a *complete structure* of rates of return, that should be regarded as fundamental, these contributions are less explicit than would seem desirable. True, attention is largely confined to semi-stationary growth, but that does not resolve the issue, as the argument of ch. 4 has shown.

One of the results that Solow (1967) obtains in his paper is the following.

*Theorem 10.4. Let **X** define a semi-stationary development which is a production-price equilibrium with rate of interest ρ and prices proportional to **p** and let the associated consumption vectors be proportional to **c**, which is strictly positive (except perhaps for one component 'labour') and ρ strictly greater than the rate of growth γ. Let **X**$'$ define another semi-stationary development, also an equilibrium, at the same production prices with consumption vectors proportional to **c**$'$ and rate of growth γ. Then a sufficiently small proportion of the labour force can be transferred to working activities proportional to those of the **X**$'$ path in one week ('labour' can be any input common to both developments) and the rate of return to this change is ρ.*

It is not necessary at this point to give a full demonstration of the result. It is enough to indicate that the switch is indeed feasible in one week and the theorem then follows as a special case of theorem 10.5 below. That a one-week switch is possible can be seen by noting that since the consumption vector is strictly positive it is possible to subtract from it a set of inputs required for the primed activities while leaving a non-negative vector remaining, provided that the scale of the primed activities is sufficiently small. Let a proportion λ of the labour force be switched to activities proportional to those of the primed path, then the new consumption has the form

$$\boldsymbol{B}\cdot\boldsymbol{x} - (1+\gamma)\boldsymbol{A}\cdot[(1-\lambda)\boldsymbol{x} + \lambda\boldsymbol{x}'] = \boldsymbol{c} - \lambda(1+\gamma)\boldsymbol{A}\cdot(\boldsymbol{x}'-\boldsymbol{x}), \tag{10.46}$$

which is a non-negative vector for λ sufficiently small.

Solow obtains also some further related results for cases in which it is not possible to make a one-week switch without changes in prices. In such cases (10.45) may have more than one root for a slower change to activities of the primed proportions and this is related to the double-switching phenomenon. Now these results are without doubt neat but, as Solow himself points out, the assumptions are very restrictive. A change in activities will usually involve a change in prices, a possibility excluded throughout Solow's investigation. The assumption required for theorem 10.4, that all goods used as inputs by the primed sequence are consumed at positive levels, is, when one thinks of goods like crude oil and coke ovens, hard to swallow. Furthermore, an interest in results of this kind springs from a belief that the rate of return *as defined in definition 10.5* is a useful and fundamental concept in this kind of economic theory, which is Solow's view. Our approach is a different one which is already clear from the discussion of ch. 3.

The really fundamental concepts in this area are present-value prices, what we shall call *generalized marginal rates of substitution* between consumption in one week and consumption in another week, and the relation between these two. Since the rate of return in the sense of definition 10.5 can be related to these concepts only tenuously, if at all, its introduction is at best not very useful and at worst misleading. To say this is not to say that there is no place for the concept of a rate of return. Indeed, it will emerge that there is a straightforward relation between present values of consumption in different weeks and the possibilities for trading consumption in one week for consumption in another, even when the trade-off takes place at different rates according to whether consumption in one of the weeks is increased or decreased. This is the basic relation between shadow rates of interest and rates of return. But notice that this statement involves changes in consumption levels in just two weeks. The notion of the rate of return is one that takes into consideration two weeks only and it does so *even if efficient changes in consumption involving just two weeks cannot take place*. If a decrease in consumption in one week and an increase in another can only take place efficiently if consumption also changes in other weeks then these further changes are simply ignored for the purpose of defining the rate of return. Such basic rates of return (or rather their limits as changes in consumption approach zero) are the ones that relate directly to equilibrium prices. The same cannot be said of the rate of return as defined in definition 10.5.

A belief that the rate of return of definition 10.5 is of fundamental importance necessitates confining attention to rather special cases, which is anyway an unfortunate general tendency in capital theory. Some special cases are unavoidable, but in many cases the results that matter are quite general.

Consider next a more general version of theorem 10.4.

Theorem 10.5. Let $\mathbf{X}$ *define a semi-stationary development which is a production-price equilibrium with rate of interest* ρ *and prices proportional to* $\mathbf{p}$, *and* ρ *strictly greater than the rate of growth* γ. *Let* $\mathbf{X}'$ *define another development, feasible from the same initial conditions and non-produced factor-service flow* $\mathbf{Z}$, *and also a production-price equilibrium at the same prices. Then* ρ *is a rate of return to a change from the development* $\mathbf{X}$ *to the development* $\mathbf{X}'$.

Proof. The assumptions of the theorem give us all that is necessary to deduce (10.43) which we may write as

$$\sum_{t=1}^{\infty} \mathbf{p}\cdot(\mathbf{c}'_t - \mathbf{c}_t)\left(\frac{1}{1+\rho}\right)^{t-1} = 0, \tag{10.47}$$

so that ρ is a root of (10.45) as required.

There might, of course, be other real roots to (10.45). It may now be seen that a rate of return result, as theorem 10.4 or 10.5, is but a special case of the analysis of theorem 10.3. Suppose we take the general case, admitting the possibility that a change in activities will involve a change in prices[7], but continue to suppose that the unprimed sequence is an equilibrium at a constant rate of interest ρ, and let us now add the assumption that

$$\sum_{t=1}^{\infty} \boldsymbol{p}\cdot(c_t' - c_t)\left(\frac{1}{1+\rho}\right)^{t-1} \tag{10.48}$$

converges to a limit. In this case all we know of ρ is that it satisfies the inequality

$$\sum_{t=1}^{\infty} \boldsymbol{p}\cdot(c_t' - c_t)\left(\frac{1}{1+\rho}\right)^{t-1} \leqslant 0, \tag{10.49}$$

while to qualify as 'the rate of return' to this change in activities σ must satisfy

$$\sum_{t=1}^{\infty} \boldsymbol{p}\cdot(c_t' - c_t)\left(\frac{1}{1+\sigma}\right)^{t-1} = 0. \tag{10.50}$$

Now (10.49) and (10.50) together do not give us even an inequality between ρ and σ. There is first of all the possibility that (10.50) may have multiple real roots. But, even if there were only one real root, there is nothing to tell one in general whether it will lie above or below ρ, because that depends upon whether the left-hand side of (10.49) is an increasing or a decreasing function of ρ, a question of no consequence from the point of view of economic theory. Yet it still remains true that the unprimed sequences are equilibrium sequences, and it still remains true in a wide class of cases that the present value of consumption is maximized. Any feeling of perplexity which comes over the reader as he confronts alternatively (10.49) and (10.50) does not arise because economic theory fails to provide general and interesting results. It arises from the mis-

---

[7] The assumption that semi-stationary equilibria share a common price system $\boldsymbol{p}$, the 'switching' price system, does not guarantee that one can move resources from one to the other without price changes. This observation alone suffices to dispose of Pasinetti's (1969) nonsensical claim that Solow has merely exhibited a tautology and proved nothing, because:

'After *calling* "social rate of return" the rate of profit at which two economic systems are equally profitable one should not be surprised to find that the social rate of return so defined is indeed, in all circumstances, equal to the rate of profit at which the two economic systems are equally profitable.'

Solow's definition corresponds to our definition 10.5 and as such is not a statement about the rate of profit. For this reason Solow's type of analysis and the kind of result he seeks will *fail* where a change in prices is necessary for the switch of resources. Tautologies do not fail us in this manner.

taken belief that the concept of the rate of return, defined according to definition 10.5, has a role to play in presenting the results.

We have seen above (in the proof of theorem 10.1) what many writers have already noted, that there is a complete equivalence between the study of production prices for overtures and the study of the solution to the linear programme (10.9) and its dual (10.10). We know also, as examples have illustrated, and as is perhaps to be expected in a linear production model, that there is frequently more than one possible sequence of production prices that will do for a particular development. This means that the solution to (10.10) will commonly be non-unique. On the face of things it might seem extremely unlikely that a linear programme (or the dual of a linear programme) would not have a unique solution. For we know that for the optimal value to be attainable with more than one set of values of the choice variables the coefficients have to take on special values such that a hyperplane corresponding to a constant value of the objective function meets the set of feasible values of the choice variables along a flat face. If the coefficients were to be chosen at random this would be 'almost certain' not to happen. However, this argument, while valid on its own terms, has no application to the present case. The coefficients of the linear programmes of the form of (10.10) are by no means chosen at random; the programmes have a special structure and only the coefficients of the matrices $\boldsymbol{A}$ and $\boldsymbol{B}$ could in any sense be said to be random.

Anyway, for whatever reason, it is very easy to construct examples of developments that are equilibrium for more than one production price system. Indeed, it will be seen below that a development has more than one production-price system whenever the rate of trade-off between consumption of one good in one week against another good consumed in another week is different according to the direction of the change; not an uncommon occurrence in a linear model. If one confines attention to a subset of possible price systems, such as constant-rate-of-interest price systems, this makes it less likely that there will be more than one production-price system, but it does not guarantee that there will be only one. This has been demonstrated incidentally by the double-switching examples, although it does not need a double-switching example to demonstrate the point, and the authors of the examples have usually thought of themselves as demonstrating something different. Because our analysis can throw some light on the phenomenon of double-switching we choose an example of that type.

Example 10.3. There are three goods: labour time, a good that is consumed and a durable good. There are two ways of making the consumption good:

from labour and itself by activity 1, and from labour and the capital good by means of activity 2. The durable capital good is made from labour time alone by activity 3. The three activities are

$$\begin{aligned}&1 \text{ unit of labour time} \oplus 1 \text{ unit of the consumption good}\\&\quad \ominus 3 \text{ units of the consumption good;}\\&1 \text{ unit of labour time} \oplus 2 \text{ units of the capital good} \ominus 3 \text{ units}\\&\quad \text{of the consumption good} \oplus 2 \text{ units of the capital good;}\\&1 \text{ unit of labour time} \ominus 1 \text{ unit of the capital good.}\end{aligned} \tag{10.51}$$

Let the consumption good have unit price as output (i.e. in week 2); labour time as input (i.e. in week 1) have price ω; and the capital good as output have price π. The economy has two possible types of semi-stationary state (or as below stationary states) according to whether activity 1 is used to produce the consumption good, or whether it is activities 2 and 3. There are also combinations of these two basic types of state in which all activities are used. In this last case all activities must break even. If we now decide arbitrarily to confine our attention to constant rate of interest price systems we obtain

$$\omega + (1+\rho) = 3, \qquad \omega + 2\rho\pi = 3, \qquad \omega = \pi. \tag{10.52}$$

These are the equations for each activity to break even at a constant rate of interest ρ. The equations (10.52) have two sets of solutions:

$$\rho = 0.5 \text{ or } 1.0, \qquad \omega = 1.5 \text{ or } 1.0, \qquad \pi = 1.5 \text{ or } 1.0. \tag{10.53}$$

This is the now familiar double-switching phenomenon. In such a case the linear programme (10.10) must have more than one solution. Here then the state in which both types of method are used to make the consumption good (the tie point) has more than one possible set of constant-rate-of-interest production prices.

Suppose that, starting from a state in which only activity 1 is used, one wishes to transfer some labour to making the consumption good by activity 2. For this to be possible some labour has first to be transferred to activity 3 so that some of the durable capital good will be available. Table 10.3 gives the history of the economy supposing that λ units of labour are transferred at the start of week 1 to activity 3.

It so happens in this instance that the switch can be made without a change in prices if, for example, prices were initially at one of the set of values given in (10.53). Notice how the switch of table 10.3 maintains the total labour time employed constant – a necessary feature of an example in which the switch

Table 10.3.

(i) Week	(ii) Labour in activity 1	(iii) Labour in activity 2	(iv) Labour in activity 3	(v) Consumption good available	(vi) Consumption good demanded by activity 1	(vii) Difference (v) – (vi) = consumption
–1	1	0	0	3	1	2
0	1	0	0	3	1	2
1	$1-\lambda$	0	λ	3	$1-\lambda$	$2+\lambda$
2	$1-\frac{1}{2}\lambda$	$\frac{1}{2}\lambda$	0	$3(1-\lambda)$	$1-\frac{1}{2}\lambda$	$2-2.5\lambda$
3	$1-\frac{1}{2}\lambda$	$\frac{1}{2}\lambda$	0	3	$1-\frac{1}{2}\lambda$	$2+\frac{1}{2}\lambda$
..	..	..	..	..	..	..

could occur without price changes, but not a general feature. Now the rate of return equation (10.45) becomes

$$1-2.5\frac{1}{1+\sigma}+0.5\left(\frac{1}{1+\sigma}\right)^2\left(1+\frac{1}{1+\sigma}+\left(\frac{1}{1+\sigma}\right)^2+\cdots\right)=0. \qquad (10.54)$$

That is

$$1-2.5\frac{1}{1+\sigma}+0.5\left(\frac{1}{1+\sigma}\right)^2\left(\frac{1+\sigma}{\sigma}\right)=0 \qquad (10.55)$$

or

$$(2\sigma-1)(\sigma-1)=0, \qquad (10.56)$$

which has two solutions, just as the equations (10.52) had the same two solutions in ρ. Of course, this is only a special case of theorem 10.5. Notice that the argument of theorem 10.4 fails in this case because there is no consumption of the durable capital good.

Example 10.3 and the following discussion illustrate several points pertinent to our present concerns. In the first place it shows that the set of possible consumption sequences available from a linear model, given the initial conditions, can be quite intricate and, in certain cases, may not include any efficient elements with a structure such that the difference between two sequences is anything as simple as an initial fall in consumption followed by a uniform rise. It is also interesting to look at this example in the light of theorem 10.3. Here is a state of the economy that maximizes the present value of consumption at a discount rate equal to one-half and also maximizes the present value of consumption at a discount rate equal to unity. However, it does not maximize the present value of consumption at discount rates between one-half and one.

This brings us to a point of central importance, one sadly neglected in the literature on double switching. Let the weights assigned to consumption in various weeks be W and an alternative set of weights W' (these are either complete price systems or parts of price systems according to the number of goods consumed). If a state of the economy maximizes the present value of consumption when the weights or discount factors are W, and it also maximizes the present value of consumption when the weights are W', then it maximizes the present value of consumption when the weights are any convex combination of W and W'.[8] The discount factors, or weights attached to consumption in different weeks, or the present-value prices, are the fundamental quantities. In the theory of planning, for example, it is these weights that must separate the set of feasible consumption streams from the set of consumption streams preferred by the planner to the optimal stream. It has been seen that the weights W can be identified with dual prices of a linear programme. These dual prices may not be unique, but if two vectors are a solution to the programme (10.10) then so is any convex combination of them. Again one has the property of *convexity* in the set of solutions. *Convexity* implies *connectedness* and one may thus conclude that the set of production price equilibria consistent with a development of the economy is a connected set; it is not possible to have two disjoint sets of prices (i.e. complete price systems) at each of which a development of the economy is a production-price equilibrium.

The connectedness of the set of equilibrium price systems consistent with a specified development of the economy is clear once one works in the natural space for analysis of these models: the space of sequences of non-negative shadow price vectors. Unfortunately, the habit has grown of working in a less rich space than this: the space of price sequences corresponding to constant rates of interest (or Ws corresponding to constant discount rates). On this we can only reiterate what has been said repeatedly above. No doubt it is

---

[8] Let $W = \{w_1, w_2, \ldots, w_t, \ldots\}$ and $W' = \{w'_1, w'_2, \ldots, w'_t \ldots\}$. Suppose that $\{c_1, c_2, \ldots, c_t, \ldots\}$ maximizes

$$\sum_{t=1}^{\infty} w_t \cdot c_t \quad \text{and} \quad \sum_{t=1}^{\infty} w'_t \cdot c_t, \tag{10.57}$$

but does not maximize

$$\sum_{t=1}^{\infty} [\theta w_t + (1-\theta) w'_t] \cdot c_t, \qquad 0 < \theta < 1. \tag{10.58}$$

Then there must exist a feasible sequence $\{c_1^0, c_2^0, \ldots, c_t^0, \ldots\}$ such that

$$\sum_{t=1}^{\infty} [\theta w_t + (1-\theta) w'_t] \cdot c_t^0 > \sum_{t=1}^{\infty} [\theta w_t + (1-\theta) w'_t] \cdot c_t. \tag{10.59}$$

This is clearly not possible unless either

$$\sum_{t=1}^{\infty} w_t \cdot c_t^0 > \sum_{t=1}^{\infty} w_t \cdot c_t \quad \text{or} \quad \sum_{t=1}^{\infty} w'_t \cdot c_t^0 > \sum_{t=1}^{\infty} w'_t \cdot c_t. \tag{10.60}$$

sometimes useful in the study of capital theory to confine attention to price sequences corresponding to constant rates of interest. But such sequences have no logical priority over other sequences. There are perfectly good efficient developments of the economy that are not equilibrium at any constant-rate-of-interest price system and there is no reason to suppose that the economy will not (or should not) follow such a path. Furthermore, a simplifying assumption should only be employed as long as it simplifies matters. For all but the most elementary exercises the space of constant-rate-of-interest price systems is a peculiarly *difficult* one to work with because it is not even closed under the elementary algebraic operation of addition; hence not closed under the formation of convex combinations. As has been demonstrated, if a sequence of activities is an equilibrium for two price sequences, then it is equilibrium for any convex combination of these price sequences. But if the two price sequences were constant-rate-of-interest price sequences for different values of the rate of interest a convex combination of them will not be a constant-rate-of-interest sequence and, as such, will be excluded from an analysis which confines its attention to constant-rate-of-interest price sequences. When dealing with geometric progressions let it never be forgotten that the sum (or the average) of two geometric progressions is not a geometric progression.

Surely part of the excitement caused by the demonstration that double switching was seemingly a fairly 'common' phenomenon, in the sense that the examples do not depend upon choosing very special values for the parameters, arose not from the fact that a technique could be chosen by firms at more than one value of the rate of interest, an obvious consequence of the sparseness of a finite linear production model, but because it seemed that the set of values at which a technique might be chosen was not connected. *But this is an optical illusion.* Firms do not choose plans in the light of rates of interest alone. They choose plans in the light of complete intertemporal price systems. The price systems consistent with the choice of a development using particular production techniques are, as has been seen, necessarily connected. The fact that the subset of price sequences consistent with such a path that are also constant-rate-of-interest price sequences may not be connected[9] is well established by the double-switching examples. It is not clear, however, that the phenomenon has been properly comprehended. Why should great interest

[9] The concept of a connected set is being used rather loosely here. To make it precise one has to specify a topology for the price sequences $\boldsymbol{P}$. If the price sequences are bounded, the distance between two sequences can be taken to be the supremum of the absolute values of difference between their components taken one at a time. In this case the sequences are first normalized by setting one common price equal to unity, so that the distance between two sequences that differ only by a multiplicative factor will be zero.

be thought to attach to disconnectedness of just those price sequences that correspond to a single rate of interest?

In the mathematical appendix it is shown that the dual variables of a linear programme can be interpreted as the partial derivatives of the maximized value of the programme with respect to constraining constants. When the maximized value of the programme is a differentiable function of one of the constraining constants at the point concerned this gives to us a notion of a marginal contribution of that constant. Even when one does not have differentiability it turns out that right- and left-hand derivatives always exist. This leads naturally to a generalization of the notion of a marginal contribution to a range of values, at or between the left- and right-hand derivatives, replacing the single value of the more familiar differentiable case. A well-known result, proved in the mathematical appendix, is the following. If there is a solution to the dual then the shadow price associated with any constraint in that solution lies in the closed range of values bounded by the left- and right-hand derivatives of the maximized programme value with respect to the constant of that constraint[10]. In fact, the converse of this proposition is also true. If one chooses a value anywhere at or between the left- and right-hand derivatives associated with the constant of a particular constraint then there exists a solution to the dual such that the shadow price for this constraint will take the chosen value provided that the other shadow prices take appropriate values. In other words, the range of values given by the left- and right-hand derivatives above is the smallest range to which the shadow price can be confined. This last result is less well known but again it is demonstrated in the mathematical appendix.

Since we have identified production prices as dual variables of linear programmes of the form (10.10) we may apply theorems on linear programming, such as those detailed above, to the interpretation of production prices. Let us examine the exact extent to which dual prices can take different values while remaining solutions to (10.10).

An alteration in one of the constants on the right-hand side of (10.9), excluding $-\boldsymbol{B}_T \cdot \bar{\boldsymbol{x}}_T$, corresponds to a variation in the level of consumption of some good to be attained in a particular week. Such a variation may lead to a change in the maximum value of θ. To be specific, let us suppose that the target, or minimum, level of consumption of the jth good in week t, denoted $\bar{c}_{jt}$, is varied. The generalized marginal contribution in this case measures limits of the form

$$\lim_{c_{jt} \to \bar{c}_{jt}} \left\{ \frac{V(\bar{c}_{jt}) - V(c_{jt})}{c_{jt} - \bar{c}_{jt}} \right\} = \lim_{c_{jt} \to \bar{c}_{jt}} \left\{ \frac{\theta(\bar{c}_{jt}) - \theta(c_{jt})}{c_{jt} - \bar{c}_{jt}} \right\}, \tag{10.61}$$

[10] See the mathematical appendix, theorems 16.8 and 16.9.

where the above limits are either for c_{jt} tending to $\bar{c}_{jt}$ from above, or for c_{jt} tending to $\bar{c}_{jt}$ from below. The argument of the mathematical appendix assures us that these limits will exist, though they may not be equal for upward and downward variations in the consumption target. Notice the change of sign in the denominator of (10.61) because the constant that actually appears in (10.10) is $-\bar{c}_{jt}$.

The economic interpretation of terms like (10.61) is clear. They measure rates at which consumption of the composite good in week 1 can be traded for consumption of good j in week t. It is arbitrary that the earlier week is numbered 1. These rates of trade-off, or marginal rates of substitution, between different components of the consumption sequence measure rates of return of the most simple kind. They are defined to involve only two components of the whole consumption sequence (one a composite good) although we know from earlier discussion, and from example 10.3, that an increase in consumption in one week may involve, of necessity, changes in consumption in several other weeks. In other words, such variations may lead to a number of the constraints in (10.10) becoming non-binding, because consumption targets are over-fulfilled. There is then a temptation to define rates of return, as in definition 10.5, in such a way as to take account of these extra changes. This temptation should be resisted. Instead, define the rate of return involved in a trade-off between the *numeraire* $\boldsymbol{u}$ in week 1 and good j in week t – $\sigma_{u,j}(1, t)$ – by

$$\frac{1}{\sigma_{u,j}(1,t)+1} = \lim_{c_{jt}\to\bar{c}_{jt}} \left\{\frac{\theta(\bar{c}_{jt}) - \theta(c_{jt})}{c_{jt} - \bar{c}_{jt}}\right\}. \tag{10.62}$$

If the limits in (10.62) differ according to whether we take a left- or right-hand limit, this gives us two values for the rate of return as defined in (10.62) according to the direction of the trade-off considered. Denote the rate of return for c_{jt} tending to $\bar{c}_{jt}$ from above (the rate of return to 'saving') by the symbol $\sigma^{+}_{u,j}(1, t)$, and the rate of return for c_{jt} tending to $\bar{c}_{jt}$ from below (the rate of return to 'dissaving') by the symbol $\sigma^{-}_{u,j}(1, t)$. Note that $c_{jt} > \bar{c}_{jt}$ implies $-c_{jt} < -\bar{c}_{jt}$ so that it is the left-hand limit that gives $\sigma^{+}_{u,j}(1, t)$.

Our linear programming theorems now have the following implications for the present case. Let p_{jt} be the production price of the jth good in week t. Recall that

$$\boldsymbol{p}_1 \cdot \boldsymbol{u} = 1, \tag{10.63}$$

so that p_{jt} is also $p_{jt}/\boldsymbol{p}_1 \cdot \boldsymbol{u}$. Now we may write

$$\frac{1}{\sigma^{-}_{u,j}(1,t)+1} \leqslant \frac{p_{jt}}{\boldsymbol{p}_1 \cdot \boldsymbol{u}} \leqslant \frac{1}{\sigma^{+}_{u,j}(1,t)+1}. \tag{10.64}$$

We may arrange this condition in another way as follows:

$$p_{jt} = \frac{p_{jt}}{p_1 \cdot u} = \frac{p_{jt}}{p_t \cdot u} \cdot \frac{p_t \cdot u}{p_1 \cdot u} = \frac{p_{jt}}{p_t \cdot u} \frac{1}{1 + R_u(1,t)}, \tag{10.65}$$

where $R_u(1, t)$ is the own-rate of interest for the *numeraire* good $\boldsymbol{u}$ for a loan starting at week 1 and closing at week t. In the constant-rate-of-interest case all own-rates of interest are equal (and this is true for composites) and we have

$$1 + R_u(1,t) = (1 + \rho)^{t-1}. \tag{10.66}$$

Now (10.64) becomes

$$\frac{1}{\sigma^-_{u,j}(1,t) + 1} \leqslant \frac{p_{jt}}{p_t \cdot u} \frac{1}{(1 + \rho)^{t-1}} \leqslant \frac{1}{\sigma^+_{u,j}(1,t) + 1}. \tag{10.67}$$

This relation tells us that the relevant rate of interest must lie between the two rates of return. Furthermore, our knowledge of the interpretation of dual prices as 'partial derivatives' indicates that we can choose p_{jt}, or choose that particular interest rate, so that it lies anywhere on the range at or between $\sigma^+_{u,j}(1, t)$ and $\sigma^-_{u,j}(1, t)$.

This last result has an interesting economic implication. It is one that justifies the use of the simple notion of the rate of return here employed and the rejection of the kind of concept incorporated in definition 10.5. In spite of the fact that a linear model may offer in any particular case no simple trade-off between consumption of two goods available at different weeks, still if one looks at the rate at which such a trade-off can take place, noting any difference between the rate appropriate for one direction and the rate appropriate for the other, but ignoring any bonus increases in consumption in other weeks, then one will have discovered the maximum possible range of variation for the dual price of the one good in a particular week relative to the dual price of the other (possibly the same) good in the other week. Conversely, the maximum possible range of variation of the ratio of the two dual prices is exactly the interval bounded by the appropriate rate of return factors, as in (10.64). Of course, the choice of a complete price system is affected by all the changes in consumption levels that follow on a change of activities. But the implication of this is that, having chosen one dual price, anywhere one likes on the range given by the left- and right-hand rates of return, one must then, perhaps, be willing to choose all other prices appropriately. The derivative interpretation of dual prices guarantees in general only one free choice of a dual price on the range bounded by the rate of return terms.

It may be useful to bring these last results to bear on the double-switching examples. Let us suppose, for example, that some particular semi-stationary state of the linear production model is a production-price equilibrium for price systems corresponding to constant rates of interest from 0 to 5% and from 10% to 15%. Now this does not tell us what range of choice we have for any particular dual price. It only gives a minimum estimate of the range. Let us set the shadow price of the *numeraire* in week 1 equal to 1. Then we know that there exist price systems such that p_{it} is as high as 1 ($\rho = 0$) and also price systems for which p_{it} is as low as

$$(1/1.15)^{t-1}. \tag{10.68}$$

But then there must exist price systems, also consistent with the same semi-stationary state, for which p_{it} takes on any value between the above limits. This follows from the convexity of the set of equilibrium price systems. However, it may well be that the maximum possible range of variation for p_{it} is still wider than the above limits, because there are price systems not corresponding to any constant value of the rate of interest which have p_{it} outside this range. Evidently, in such a case, if one computes the rates of return on, for example, transfers between consumption levels of one good in two adjacent weeks, there will be a difference of at least 15% between the rate for change in one direction and the rate for change in another. But there may well be a still larger difference. One can only discover just how large the difference is by stepping outside the world of constant-rate-of-interest price systems and asking, among all possible equilibrium price systems, what is the maximum possible range of variations of p_{it}.

A reader of much of the recent literature on price equilibrium in linear production models might well take away with him the conclusion that the subject is incredibly complex, almost devoid of general results, and that the existence of the double-switching phenomenon was perhaps the most important feature of these models. Through an approach to those problems founded in the theory of linear programming we have been able to show that this is not at all the true state of affairs. There are two very general results available. Under specifiable conditions, wide enough to make the result of great interest, an equilibrium is such as to maximize the present value of consumption using the equilibrium production prices as weights or discount factors. Also, the equilibrium or the dual prices are related to marginal rates of substitution between consumptions of different goods and different weeks by inequality relations of exactly the kind one would expect from a model in which functions relating one consumption level to another are not always differentiable. These are completely general and useful rate-of-return relationships. An attempt to define the rate of return as the root of a polynomial, as in definition 10.5, only obscures these facts and forces one to treat of very special cases.

To some extent these are boring and unexciting results. For they assert that an intertemporal capital model has very much the properties of an atemporal equilibrium model, once one has become used to interpreting goods available in different weeks as different goods. Yet how could it be otherwise? If, for example, the double-switching phenomenon really was of fundamental import and really did exhibit a non-connected set of equilibrium price systems, then there would have to be an atemporal model with a similar property. It would simply be a matter of taking the formal mathematical structure and giving to it an atemporal intepretation. Of course, one must take care not to assert too much. There are fundamental differences between atemporal and intertemporal theories, as was seen in ch. 3. They have to do with uncertainty, and the open-endedness of the intertemporal model. The data cannot be assumed known and the number of goods cannot reasonably be taken to be finite. It is a measure of how badly disorientated the literature has become that recent controversies have managed to centre themselves around disputes in which, as it happens, these genuinely different features are not essentially involved.

Appendix: Prices and efficiency for infinite developments

A.1. The existence of prices for infinite developments

We want to show the existence of shadow prices for a pseudo-efficient development. To do this we impose an extra assumption. The question of how far this assumption can be dispensed with and what exactly must replace it is a highly technical one and beyond the scope of the present volume. The interested reader should consult papers specifically devoted to this topic, or to closely related topics[11]. Our assumption is the following[12].

The axiom of substitutability. There exists a vector $\bar{\boldsymbol{u}} \geqq 0$ such that for each pair of values (i, t), and for all $T \geqslant t+1$, there are numbers $\varepsilon_{it} > 0$, and $\bar{\theta}_{it}$ such that the programme (10.9) with $\bar{c}_t$ replaced by $\bar{c}_t + \varepsilon_{it} u^i$ admits of a solution with $\theta \geqslant \bar{\theta}_{it}$.

The meaning of the assumption is the following. We may impose a (perhaps only slightly) stronger version of the constraint regarding any commodity in

---

[11] In particular, Kurz (1969) and references cited therein.

[12] It is closely related to the assumption of Malinvaud (1953) while not being the identical assumption. Specifically, our assumption is a little easier to work with, partly on account of the fact that it is less primitive.

any week (i.e. consume more of it or have less provided as non-produced input) and this will be feasible, no matter how long the overture, provided that we are willing to decrease consumption in week 1 (or increase the initial endowment) by as much as $\bar{\boldsymbol{u}}\bar{\theta}_{it}$. Notice that ε_{it} and $\bar{\theta}_{it}$ depend upon i, t (but not upon $T \geqslant t+1$) while the vector $\bar{\boldsymbol{u}}$ must be the same for all i and t.

The effect of the axiom of substitutability is to bound the prices that attach to the overtures above and hence to give us compactness of the set of equilibrium prices – an essential property given the way in which the argument will proceed. The axiom gives us a bound immediately, as may be seen from the following. Consider the price of the ith commodity in week t, p_{it}; specifically one that will do for a T-week overture ($T \geqslant t+1$). From (10.27) we know that the valuation of net consumption is maximized at the equilibrium prices. Hence, the feasible rearrangement postulated in the statement of the axiom cannot increase the present value of consumption. For week 1, 'consumption' is consumption less any initial endowment which is here considered to be variable. Hence, we must have

$$p_{it}\,\varepsilon_{it} \leqslant \bar{\theta}_{it}\boldsymbol{p}_1 \cdot \bar{\boldsymbol{u}} = \bar{\theta}_{it} \tag{A10.1}$$

or

$$p_{it} \leqslant \bar{\theta}_{it}/\varepsilon_{it}. \tag{A10.2}$$

Furthermore, this inequality is satisfied for all $T \geqslant t+1$.

Theorem A10.1. If the axiom of substitutability is satisfied a pseudo-efficient development has production prices.

Proof. Take an arbitrary T and consider overtures longer than T. Let $\mathscr{P}_{T+S}$ be the set of all vector sequences $\{\boldsymbol{p}_1, \ldots, \boldsymbol{p}_{T+1}, \ldots, \boldsymbol{p}_{T+S+1}\}$ which are production prices for the overture of duration $T+S$, normalized so that $\boldsymbol{p}_1 \cdot \bar{\boldsymbol{u}} = 1$, where $\bar{\boldsymbol{u}}$ conforms to the requirements of the axiom of substitutability. Let $\mathscr{Q}_{T,S}$ be the set of the first $T+1$ terms of such sequences. Formally, the sequence

$$\{\boldsymbol{p}_1, \boldsymbol{p}_2, \ldots, \boldsymbol{p}_t, \ldots, \boldsymbol{p}_{T+1}\} \in \mathscr{Q}_{T,S}$$

if there exists a sequence $\{\boldsymbol{p}_{T+2}, \ldots, \boldsymbol{p}_{T+S+1}\}$ such that

$$\{\boldsymbol{p}_1, \boldsymbol{p}_2, \ldots, \boldsymbol{p}_{T+1}; \boldsymbol{p}_{T+2}, \ldots, \boldsymbol{p}_{T+S+1}\} \in \mathscr{P}_{T+S}.$$

The sets $\mathscr{Q}_{T,S}$ are non-empty closed subsets of the set of vector sequences $\mathscr{T}$ defined by

$$\mathscr{T} = \{(\boldsymbol{p}_1, \ldots \boldsymbol{p}_{T+1}) | 0 \leqslant p_{it} \leqslant \bar{\theta}_{it}/\varepsilon_{it}\ (i=1, \ldots, n;\ t=1, \ldots, T+1)\}. \tag{A10.3}$$

Notice that $\mathscr{T}$ is compact. Furthermore, $\mathscr{Q}_{T,S+1} \subseteqq \mathscr{Q}_{T,S}$ (i.e. these sets are nested). Hence, for any finite collection of values of S the corresponding sets $\mathscr{Q}_{T,S}$ have a non-empty intersection. Therefore, since $\mathscr{T}$ is a compact space, the infinite collection of sets $\mathscr{Q}_{T,S}$ has a non-empty intersection[13]. Choose any element from this intersection, this sequence can be prices for weeks 1 to $T+1$. If it is now desired to extend the sequence, say to $T'+1$ ($T'>T$), the method can be applied again to find the non-empty intersection of the sets $\mathscr{Q}_{T',S}$ and by construction this intersection must contain a sequence whose first $T+1$ terms are those which were chosen from the intersection of the sets $\mathscr{Q}_{T,S}$. The proof is complete.

A.2. The present value of the final stock of capital

Theorem 10.3 asserted that a development would be efficient (at least with regard to positively valued goods) if the present value of final capital tended to zero for all feasible developments of sufficient duration. This result can be seen to be a very natural one if we take note of the fact that the present value of final capital has a simple economic interpretation as a kind of price; a price which is related, as prices usually are, to substitution possibilities. To make clear this interpretation we introduce a *possibility frontier*.

In the linear programme (10.9) write the terminal capital stock in the form $(1+\lambda)\bar{k}_{T+1}$, where $\lambda > -1$ is a scalar parameter. Given all other constants in the linear programme (10.9), the value of the programme is a function of λ, defined over those values of λ for which (10.9) remains feasible. Denote this functional relation as follows:

$$\theta = f_T(\lambda). \tag{A10.4}$$

It is easily verified that: (a) f_T is monotonically decreasing; and (b) f_T is concave. Fig. A10.1 illustrates.

It is worth remarking that, while the definition of the possibility frontier is perfectly general, and the analysis to follow requires no extra assumptions on the technology or the growth programme, some very trivial cases are included in the present approach. The point is that the interest in the possibility frontier lies in its illustrating for us the possibilities of 'trading' present (i.e. first week) consumption of goods for the scale of the capital stock at the end of the programme horizon, all other consumptions being maintained at least at minimum levels. For this approach to be of any use, such trades should be technically possible. If they are not possible, $f_T(\lambda)$ will be undefined for $\lambda > 0$ and will take the value 0 for $\lambda \leqq 0$. The frontier will then be simply two sides of a rectangle with the corner at (0, 0).

---

[13] See, for example, Simmons (1963, p. 112).

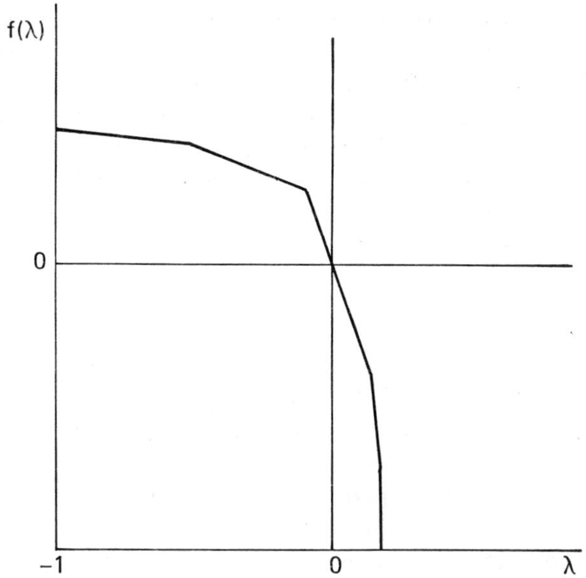

Fig. A10.1.

The existence of rather trivial cases in which the possibility frontier is rectangular has been noted. A question to which some attention must now be given therefore is whether non-trivial cases are at all common or plausible. No exhaustive discussion of this question is attempted, but the following remarks are relevant:

(a) The choice of $\bar{\boldsymbol{u}}$ in the linear programme (10.9) is arbitrary except that the choice must conform to the requirements of the axiom of substitutability. Thus the real question is whether one can choose any collection of goods for which there is a non-trival possibility frontier.

(b) The presence in the technology of substitution possibilities in the form of activities with the same outputs but different input combinations is favourable to a frontier of the non-trivial kind. Suppose, for example, that the *numeraire* good is labour. Then variations in $\boldsymbol{c}_1$ correspond to variations in the net inflow of labour in week 1. If some of the activities have more labour-intensive versions with higher output levels for some outputs then changes in the supply of labour need not render any other inputs redundant and this favours a smooth frontier.

(c) The productive system should be indecomposable. Otherwise, changes in some input levels may not make it possible to vary the whole $\bar{\boldsymbol{k}}_{T+1}$ vector proportionately.

(d) The existence of storage activities is favourable to a smoother frontier. Consider, for example, a decrease in the consumption of cigarettes in week 1. Suppose that all the cigarettes available initially would have been smoked in the first week, and productive activities would have been initiated in the first week to make available cigarettes to be smoked in the second week, and so on. Suppose further that cigarettes cannot be used as productive inputs. Under these conditions a decrease in the first-week consumption level for cigarettes allows no scalar increase in the capital stock in the future, however small that increase, and however far into the future. If, however, cigarettes can be stored, which means that there exist activities which use cigarettes as input and produce valuable output (including in this case cigarettes) then some inputs which would have been used to produce cigarettes for second-week consumption can be diverted to increasing some capital levels. This in turn will allow larger capital stocks in later weeks and so on.

Since f_T is concave it has left- and right-hand derivatives at $\lambda = 0$. Denote these derivatives $f_T'(0)^-$ and $f_T'(0)^+$ respectively. Of course, f_T may be undefined for $\lambda > 0$, but we can adopt the convention, just to avoid having to mention this case explicitly in statements of results, of allowing $f_T'(0)^+ =$ '$-\infty$'.

Theorem A10.2. For any solution of the linear programme (10.9) and its dual,

$$-f_T'(0)^- \leqq \boldsymbol{p}_{T+1} \cdot \bar{\boldsymbol{k}}_{T+1} \leqq -f_T'(0)^+. \tag{A10.5}$$

Proof. The method of proof is exactly the same as that used to demonstrate the marginal interpretation of dual prices in the mathematical appendix, p. 365. The only difference here is that the variation is in several parameters simultaneously instead of just one parameter. Since this makes little difference to the argument the proof is left to the interested reader as an exercise.

One can also establish that where there is a corner in the frontier at $\lambda = 0$ it is possible to choose prices such that the value $\boldsymbol{p}_{T+1} \cdot \bar{\boldsymbol{k}}_{T+1}$ will lie anywhere between the limits imposed by the theorem, including the endpoints. Once again the proof is closely parallel to the one given in the mathematical appendix for a single constraint and it is omitted.

The foregoing discussion has thrown some light on the relation between the present value of final capital and the shape of the possibility frontier. It follows that as $T \to \infty$ the same tangency type of relation must be maintained, since it holds for each T, and that one can therefore deduce that the limiting form of the possibility frontier constrains the limiting value of the present value of the capital stock. Some results can then be obtained immediately. Suppose, for example, that for some $\lambda_0 >$ one has

$$\lim_{T \to \infty} f_T(\lambda_0) = 0, \tag{A10.6}$$

then it is easily seen that this taken together with theorem A10.2 implies

$$\lim_{T\to\infty} p_{T+1}\cdot \bar{k}_{T+1} = 0, \qquad \text{(A10.7)}$$

which in turn implies an efficient development. The condition (A10.6) is closely related to a property which McFadden (1967) has called 'reachability' since it says in effect that the amount of consumption that one has to give up to attain a given scalar increase in final capital goes to zero as the time allowed to attain that increase goes to infinity.

To get more results one needs to know what efficiency implies for the limiting form of the possibility frontier. This is the subject of the next theorem. However, before embarking on this theorem we need a definition.

Definition A10.1. Consider all the developments which are feasible for a particular technology and a sequence $\{z_1, z_2 \ldots, z_t, \ldots\}$. These developments will be said to be *confined* if there exists an infinite sequence $\{\hat{x}_1, \hat{x}_2, \ldots, \hat{x}_t, \ldots\}$ such that the addition of the constraints on the activity vectors

$$x_t < \hat{x}_t \qquad \text{(A10.8)}$$

excludes no efficient development.

The assumption that the developments are confined is very reasonable if one is assuming that there are non-produced resources which play a critical role in production.

Theorem A10.3. Let developments be confined. If a development is efficient then the limit of the possibility frontier $f_T(\lambda)$ as $T \to \infty$, for any $\lambda > 0$, is the horizontal axis $y = 0$. That is

$$\lim_{T\to\infty} f_T(\lambda) = 0 \quad \textit{for each } \lambda < 0. \qquad \text{(A10.9)}$$

Remark. This result is very natural and satisfying from the economic point of view. It says that the amount of extra present consumption one can get from an efficient development by accepting a scalar decrease in final capital tends to zero as the date at which one accepts the given proportionate reduction in capital is pushed indefinitely far into the future. Note that the theorem does not state that the approach of $f_T(\lambda)$ to 0 is even eventually monotonic.

Proof. Suppose that there is an efficient development which does not satisfy the requirement of the theorem. Then for some $\lambda < 0$, $f_T(\lambda) > \mu_0$ for some arbitrarily large T, where μ_0 is a positive constant. Hence, there exists a sequence of T values $T_1, T_2, \ldots, T_S, \ldots$ strictly increasing such that

$$f_{T_S}(\lambda) > \mu_0 \tag{A10.10}$$

for each value of T_S. Now we have overtures of duration $T_1, T_2, \ldots, T_S, \ldots$; and final capital vectors $\bar{\boldsymbol{k}}_{T_1+1}, \bar{\boldsymbol{k}}_{T_2+1}, \ldots, \bar{\boldsymbol{k}}_{T_S+1}, \ldots$, which can be chosen with θ at least as large as μ_0, for each value of T_S. Consider any value of T, say T^*. To each of the above overtures longer than T^* there corresponds a set of activity vector sequences $(\boldsymbol{x}_1, \boldsymbol{x}_2, \ldots, \boldsymbol{x}_{T^*})$ which achieve an initial consumption at least as large as $\bar{\boldsymbol{c}}_1 + \mu_0\bar{\boldsymbol{u}}$ and all other consumption levels of the growth programme up to T^*. Because developments are confined these sets may be chosen compact and they are nested. The argument can now proceed on the lines of the proof of theorem A10.1 to establish the existence of a limiting set and hence an infinite sequence of activity vectors that achieve initial consumption not less than $\bar{\boldsymbol{c}}_1 + \mu_0\bar{\boldsymbol{u}}$ and all subsequent consumption levels as on the original growth programme. Thus the programme is inefficient, contrary to assumption.

The argument has shown why economists have failed to obtain an exact characterization of efficiency for developments without an horizon in terms of the limit of the present value of final capital, and why, indeed, no such characterization is possible. In terms of the limiting form of the possibility frontier, efficiency has to do with the limiting height of the frontier to the left-hand side; while the limit of the value of capital (or more precisely the minimum possible limit) has to do with the limiting slope of the possibility frontier to the left-hand side. In some sense one is confronting here a classic double limit problem. The limit of the slope of the function is not the slope of the limiting function; indeed the former may be equal to minus infinity while the latter is equal to zero.

11

More on the Cambridge model: non-substitution theory

What the capitalist, and consequently also the political economist, see is that part of the paid labour per piece of commodity changes with the productivity of labour, and that the value of each piece also changes accordingly. What they do not see is that the same applies to unpaid labour contained in every piece of the commodity, and this is perceived so much less since the average profit actually is only accidentally determined by the unpaid labour absorbed in the sphere of the individual capitalist. It is only in such crude and meaningless form that we can glimpse that the value of commodities is determined by the labour contained in them.

K. MARX, *Capital*, vol. III, ch. 9

In ch. 6 we characterized the solution of the Cambridge model as proceeding in three distinct stages and we submitted the first stage to a close scrutiny. It is time now to do the same to the second stage. We are looking for conditions under which one may establish a unique relation between the rate of interest, the techniques of production and relative prices. Theorems on the conditions under which such a relation may be established have been extensively investigated by economists in recent years under the generic name of *non-substitution theorems*[1]. A non-substitution theorem is a result which shows that under certain specified conditions an economy will have one particular price structure, regardless of the pattern of final demand, this price structure corresponding to the costs of production of a particular set of activities. Our aim in the present investigation is to establish a fairly general result of this type without any attempt to treat the subject exhaustively. From his examination of the particular example the reader will be able to see what kinds of restrictions are necessary to any theorem of this type.

It is useful to consider first the simplest case. There is only one non-produced good in the economy, which we take to be labour time. Costs of production

---

[1] The literature is extensive, mainly in journal papers. The basic theorem on non-substitution was derived by Georgescu-Roegen (1951). This paper is included in Koopmans (1951). See also the paper by Arrow (1951) in the same volume. The idea that these results could be extended to cover a given interest rate, not necessarily equal to zero, has been 'in the air' for some time – see Sraffa (1960) and Samuelson (1959, 1961). Proofs are to be found in Mirrlees (1969) and Stiglitz (1970b).

are the sum of two components, direct labour costs and the costs of intermediate inputs, themselves produced goods. In general, there are many different methods of producing each good, requiring different amounts of labour time and other inputs to produce one unit of output. No durable goods are used for production, i.e. all material inputs are used up in the productive processes. Finally, the rate of interest is zero, so that there is no addition to materials costs on account of interest charged during the production period.

In these conditions it is intuitively plausible that prices should be equivalent to quantities of labour time embodied in the finished goods, for labour is the only ultimate cost, all other costs being reducible ultimately to labour costs. One might then postulate that it would be possible to find one method of producing each good such that all goods were then produced at minimum direct and indirect labour cost, and that these minimized labour costs would then determine uniquely the relative prices of all goods independently of demand. Intuition is here valid and the simplest non-substitution theorem makes the above argument precise. Notice that the result is not trivial for there is an unavoidable necessity to solve simultaneously for all minimized costs together – without knowing how coal and oil are to be produced one cannot know which method of producing electricity will minimize labour costs, but the minimizing techniques for producing coal and oil themselves depend upon the cost of electricity[2].

We do not attack the problem initially in terms of prices but by way of costs of production. These two coincide for any commodity that is produced, for profitable production requires that the value of output produced be at least as great as input costs, and there must in fact be equality of price and cost under competition. When, however, a commodity is not produced then the price–cost inequalities only impose an upper limit on the price. Hence, one case in which it would be incorrect to claim that prices will be uniquely determined by the technology is where some commodities are not produced at all. This has led theorists who have investigated the conditions for non-substitution theorems to consider very carefully when it can be guaranteed that all goods are produced and to limit their statements to such cases. We adopt a different approach here. We look first for unique *cost-of-production prices*. In other words, it is assumed that there is a quoted price for each good,

[2] The resultant costs correspond to what Marx called 'socially necessary labour time', the implication of the words 'socially necessary' being the same as 'minimized'. Compare his remark (1928, vol. I, part 1.1): 'As values, all commodities are only definite masses of congealed labour time.' To calculate these masses one needs to solve a programme like the one presented below.

whether it is produced or not. It is further assumed that this price corresponds to the minimum cost of producing that good (which will be a constant in the linear economy) given all the other prices. By investigating conditions under which there is a unique set of cost-of-production prices we are freed initially from the need to concern ourselves with the question of whether all goods will be produced, a question of some complexity, especially when we eventually introduce durable capital goods. It is then not difficult to show later that these cost-of-production prices are always possible equilibrium prices for the economy, although there may be other prices also consistent with equilibrium which differ only with regard to goods not produced in the equilibrium concerned.

To arrive at a non-substitution result it is clearly necessary to exclude joint production of the classic textbook variety. If there are just two goods in the economy, wool and mutton, which are produced jointly by shepherds (labour) alone, there can be no question of determining wool and mutton prices from the technological conditions pertaining to sheep farming. In this case, demand must necessarily be brought in to decree whether wool will be cheap or dear in relation to mutton. It is less obvious whether or not joint production of the notional variety, such as was used in ch. 9 to treat durable capital goods, must be excluded. We will return to that question.

Stated formally, the problem at issue is the following. There are n goods (indexed by $i = 1, \ldots, n$) and there are m_i known activities which produce the ith good as output. Labour time is good o. Let all activities be normalized so that they produce one unit of their respective outputs when run at unit level. The jth method of producing the ith good ($j = 1, \ldots, m_i$) is specified by the labour required for unit production, $\alpha_{ij} > 0$, and the vector of commodity requirements, $\boldsymbol{a}_{ij} \geqq \boldsymbol{0}$. The full 'family' of activities which produce the ith good can be summarized in an $n \times m_i$ matrix, $\boldsymbol{A}_i$, whose jth column is the vector $\boldsymbol{a}_{ij}$, and an m_i vector $\boldsymbol{a}_i^{\circ}$, whose jth component is α_{ij}. We are looking for an n vector of costs of production $\boldsymbol{p}$, which will satisfy the conditions

$$\boldsymbol{p} \cdot \boldsymbol{A}_i + \boldsymbol{a}_i^{\circ} \geqq \boldsymbol{p} \cdot \boldsymbol{E}_i \quad \text{and not} \quad \boldsymbol{p} \cdot \boldsymbol{A}_i + \boldsymbol{a}_i^{\circ} > \boldsymbol{p} \cdot \boldsymbol{E}_i \qquad (i = 1, \ldots, n), \quad (11.1)$$

where $\boldsymbol{E}_i$ is the $n \times m_i$ matrix with unit elements in the ith row and zeros elsewhere. The prices $\boldsymbol{p}$ are in labour units. We will show that there exists only one price vector $\boldsymbol{p}$ satisfying (11.1). For this we require one further and rather obvious assumption: that the economy specified by the matrices $\boldsymbol{A}_i$ is *productive*, by which is meant that the economy can produce a positive vector of outputs in excess of the commodity inputs required for this production to take place. Let $\boldsymbol{x}_i \geqq \boldsymbol{0}$ be an m_i vector of activity levels for the activities which produce the ith good and $\boldsymbol{e}_i$ an m_i vector, each of whose elements is 1.

Then the total gross production of the ith good is $\boldsymbol{x}_i \cdot \boldsymbol{e}_i$ and if the economy is productive there exist non-negative vectors $(\boldsymbol{x}_1, \ldots, \boldsymbol{x}_i, \ldots, \boldsymbol{x}_n)$ such that

$$\begin{bmatrix} \boldsymbol{x}_1 \cdot \boldsymbol{e}_1 \\ \vdots \\ \boldsymbol{x}_i \cdot \boldsymbol{e}_i \\ \vdots \\ \boldsymbol{x}_n \cdot \boldsymbol{e}_n \end{bmatrix} - \sum_{i=1}^{n} \boldsymbol{A}_i \cdot \boldsymbol{x}_i > \boldsymbol{0}. \tag{11.2}$$

Note an immediate implication of the condition (11.2): a productive economy can produce at least any positive net output vector provided that enough labour is available. To see this, simply increase all the $\boldsymbol{x}_i$ vectors proportionately until eventually the left-hand side of (11.2) dominates the positive vector concerned.

We first obtain production prices $\boldsymbol{p}$ for an economy which produces all the goods. The price vector $\boldsymbol{p}$ will be obtained, and shown to be unique, from the duality principle of linear programming[3]. We have already suggested that the prices can be regarded as minimized direct plus indirect labour requirements. Hence, it is natural to consider the problem of producing a positive net output vector at minimum total labour cost. Let $\boldsymbol{c} > \boldsymbol{0}$ be an arbitrary vector of net requirements. The problem in the form of a linear programme is as follows:

$$\text{minimize} \sum_{i=1}^{n} \boldsymbol{x}_i \cdot \boldsymbol{a}_i^{\circ} \quad \text{subject to} \begin{bmatrix} \boldsymbol{x}_1 \cdot \boldsymbol{e}_1 \\ \vdots \\ \boldsymbol{x}_i \cdot \boldsymbol{e}_i \\ \vdots \\ \boldsymbol{x}_n \cdot \boldsymbol{e}_n \end{bmatrix} - \sum_{i=1}^{n} \boldsymbol{A}_i \cdot \boldsymbol{x}_i \geqq \boldsymbol{c}, \tag{11.3}$$

and

$$\boldsymbol{x}_i \geqq \boldsymbol{0}, \quad i = 1, \ldots, n.$$

Or, in a more compact form, using the $\boldsymbol{E}_i$ notation,

$$\text{minimize} \sum_{i=1}^{n} \boldsymbol{x}_i \cdot \boldsymbol{a}_i^{\circ} \quad \text{subject to } [\boldsymbol{E}_1 - \boldsymbol{A}_1, \boldsymbol{E}_2 - \boldsymbol{A}_2, \ldots, \boldsymbol{E}_n - \boldsymbol{A}_n] \cdot \tilde{\boldsymbol{x}} \geqq \boldsymbol{c}, \tag{11.4}$$

and

$$\tilde{\boldsymbol{x}} \geqq \boldsymbol{0},$$

where $\tilde{\boldsymbol{x}}$ is the vector $(\boldsymbol{x}_1, \boldsymbol{x}_2, \ldots, \boldsymbol{x}_n)$, i.e. all the activity levels arranged in order. From (11.4) it is easily seen that the dual linear programme takes the form

$$\text{maximize } \boldsymbol{p} \cdot \boldsymbol{c} \quad \text{subject to}$$

$$\boldsymbol{p} \cdot [\boldsymbol{E}_1 - \boldsymbol{A}_1, \boldsymbol{E}_2 - \boldsymbol{A}_2, \ldots, \boldsymbol{E}_n - \boldsymbol{A}_n] \leqq (\boldsymbol{a}_1^{\circ}, \boldsymbol{a}_2^{\circ}, \ldots, \boldsymbol{a}_n^{\circ}), \tag{11.5}$$

---

[3] For a statement and derivation of this principle, see the mathematical appendix, theorem 16.6.

and

$$p \geqq 0.$$

It follows from the dual constraints that the vector p satisfies

$$p \cdot A_i + a_i^o \geqq p \cdot E_i \quad (i = 1, \ldots, n), \tag{11.6}$$

so that condition (i) of definition 9.1 is satisfied. Condition (ii) is obtained by noting that for each i there must be at least one positive element of the vector x_i, for otherwise positive production of the ith good would not take place, to say nothing of positive net production. So, by the duality principle, there is at least one activity which produces the ith good which is used in the solution to (11.4) and for which therefore the corresponding dual constraint is satisfied with equality. Thus one can rule out the possibility that

$$p \cdot A_i + a_i^o > p \cdot E_i \tag{11.7}$$

for some value of i. It follows that conditions (iii) and (iv) of definition 9.1 are satisfied.

Having established that there exist production prices, next bring in the *basis theorem*[4] to show that there exists a set of activities, just one productive technique for each good, such that any output vector c can be produced at minimum labour cost by use of these activities alone. The basis theorem states that a linear programme will always have a basic solution, defined as a solution in which the number of variables that take positive values in the solution does not exceed the number of constraints. In the present instance the theorem implies that it is never necessary for minimum labour cost to use two different methods for producing one of the goods, although it may not be non-optimal to do so. Again, this result is very much in harmony with intuition, which suggests that it should be possible to choose one of the (possibly many) minimum cost methods of producing any good and exclude all others.

The next step is to show that there is one basic set of activities which will do for optimal production of any final output vector c. Given any vector c, choose arbitrarily a basic solution to the programme (11.4). Notice that solutions to the programme have the property that all the programme constraints are exactly satisfied, for if there were a strict inequality in an optimal solution, corresponding to over-production of one of the goods beyond the minimum required level, then the level of one of the activities producing this good could be decreased, thereby saving labour, without violating any of the constraints. Corresponding to our basic solution we can find dual prices such that each of the chosen basic activities satisfies cost–price equality

[4] For a statement of this result, see the mathematical appendix, theorem 16.7.

as implied by these prices. Now, given another final demand vector, obtain a new solution using just the basic activities. This generates a new programme solution satisfying the programme constraints exactly. The old dual prices are still feasible for the dual, since the dual constraints are unaffected by a change in the vector $\boldsymbol{c}$. Furthermore, the value of the programme will be equal to the value of the dual, since in no case is there a strict inequality in the dual constraints for which the corresponding programme variable is positive. Thus the solution which has been derived is an optimal one.

It only remains to show that there is just one vector $\boldsymbol{p}$ which satisfies (11.5). For this linear programming commends itself. Aside from the fact that linear programming is an approach adopted frequently in the present work, a reason for dealing with the problem in this way is that the approach here yields results which are very amenable to economic interpretation.

Denote the minimum total labour time requirement necessary to produce a net output $\boldsymbol{c}$ by $L(\boldsymbol{c})$, where L is the value of the linear programme (11.4) regarded as a function of $\boldsymbol{c}$. As the price vector $\boldsymbol{p}$ has been obtained as the dual of this linear programme, it follows that $\boldsymbol{p}$ is unique if (11.5) can be shown to have a unique solution. One of the results of the mathematical appendix is that the dual programme has a unique solution if the function $L(\boldsymbol{c})$ is *differentiable*, and this is what we will establish. The line of argument is a very economic one; the prices are to be interpreted as marginal labour costs, including indirect labour, and the uniqueness of prices will follow from a demonstration that marginal labour costs are well defined. Herein lies the essence of the simple non-substitution theorem. It is not difficult to show that $L(\boldsymbol{c})$ is a differentiable function. Indeed, this follows almost immediately from two straightforward properties of L. Clearly L is homogeneous of degree 1, i.e.

$$L(\lambda \boldsymbol{c}) = \lambda L(\boldsymbol{c}) \tag{11.8}$$

for all $\boldsymbol{c}$ and all $\lambda > 0$. Also, it is readily established that L satisfies

$$L(\boldsymbol{c}_1 + \boldsymbol{c}_2) = L(\boldsymbol{c}_1) + L(\boldsymbol{c}_2), \tag{11.9}$$

where $\boldsymbol{c}_1$ and $\boldsymbol{c}_2$ are non-negative. Furthermore, defining $L(-\boldsymbol{c})$ to be $-L(\boldsymbol{c})$, one can show also that

$$L(\boldsymbol{c}_1 - \boldsymbol{c}_2) = L(\boldsymbol{c}_1) - L(\boldsymbol{c}_2). \tag{11.10}$$

These results follow immediately from the previous observation that one has only to find activity levels for the basic activities which produce a particular net output vector to produce that net output vector optimally. If therefore a basic activity vector (n basic activities at positive level) produces a net output vector $\boldsymbol{c}_1$ with labour requirement $L(\boldsymbol{c}_1)$; and a basic vector $\tilde{\boldsymbol{x}}_2$ produces a net output vector $\boldsymbol{c}_2$ with labour requirement $L(\boldsymbol{c}_2)$; then the basic vector $\tilde{\boldsymbol{x}}_1 + \tilde{\boldsymbol{x}}_2$ produces $\boldsymbol{c}_1 + \boldsymbol{c}_2$ with labour requirement $L(\boldsymbol{c}_1) + L(\boldsymbol{c}_2)$, and it necessarily does so optimally. Similarly, the basic vector $\tilde{\boldsymbol{x}}_1 - \tilde{\boldsymbol{x}}_2$ produces $\boldsymbol{c}_1 - \boldsymbol{c}_2$ with labour requirement $L(\boldsymbol{c}_1) - L(\boldsymbol{c}_2)$, again optimally[5]. Now consider the limit as $\theta \to 0$ of the ratio

$$[L(\boldsymbol{c} + \theta \cdot \boldsymbol{u}_i) - L(\boldsymbol{c})]/\theta, \tag{11.11}$$

where $\boldsymbol{u}_i$ is the vector whose ith element is 1 and all other elements are zeros. From (11.9) and (11.10), this ratio reduces to

$$[L(\boldsymbol{c}) + \theta L(\boldsymbol{u}_i) - L(\boldsymbol{c})]/\theta = L(\boldsymbol{u}_i). \tag{11.12}$$

Thus $L(\boldsymbol{c})$ is differentiable, and in fact the partial derivative with respect to c_i is simply $L(\boldsymbol{u}_i)$, which in this case must be equal to the ith dual variable of the programme (11.5) (mathematical appendix). So $L(\boldsymbol{c})$ is a linear function of the elements of $\boldsymbol{c}$, and not only must the prices in terms of labour be unique, but we have explicit expressions for the prices, i.e.

$$p_i = L(\boldsymbol{u}_i) \qquad (i = 1, \ldots, n). \tag{11.13}$$

From the economic point of view this is a satisfying result because it confirms the validity of the idea that prices will correspond to unique minimum direct plus indirect labour costs. $L(\boldsymbol{u}_i)$ is the minimum total labour cost of producing one unit of the ith good and all intermediate inputs including perhaps the ith good itself, necessary for this production to take place. Evidently $L(\boldsymbol{u}_i)$ is positive. The *simple non-substitution theorem* is now established.

We have arrived at the simple non-substitution theorem by way of reasoning that springs rather clearly from an economic approach to the problem, and the theorem that has been established may be given an 'economic' statement as follows.

---

[5] Here it must be shown that $\tilde{\boldsymbol{x}}_1 - \tilde{\boldsymbol{x}}_2$ is non-negative provided that $\boldsymbol{c}_1 - \boldsymbol{c}_2$ is positive, which is accomplished as follows. Suppose that $\boldsymbol{c}_1 - \boldsymbol{c}_2 > \boldsymbol{0}$ but that $\boldsymbol{z}_1 - \boldsymbol{z}_2 \ngeqq \boldsymbol{0}$, where the $\boldsymbol{z}$ vectors are activity levels for the basic activities. Let the matrix of input requirements for the basic activities be the square matrix $\boldsymbol{A}$. Since this is a productive system, there exists a $\boldsymbol{z}_0 \geqq \boldsymbol{0}$ such that $(\boldsymbol{I} - \boldsymbol{A})\boldsymbol{z}_0 > 0$. In fact, $\boldsymbol{z}_0 > 0$, for if $z_{0i} = 0$ the ith component of $(\boldsymbol{I} - \boldsymbol{A})\boldsymbol{z}_0$ cannot be positive. By assumption, $(\boldsymbol{I} - \boldsymbol{A})(\boldsymbol{z}_1 - \boldsymbol{z}_2) = \boldsymbol{c}_1 - \boldsymbol{c}_2$ and $\boldsymbol{z}_1 - \boldsymbol{z}_2$ has at least one negative component. Let $\theta = \max i[-(z_{1i} - z_{2i})/z_{0i}]$, say $\theta = -(z_{11} - z_{21})/z_{01}$. Now θ is positive and $\boldsymbol{z}_3 = \boldsymbol{z}_1 - \boldsymbol{z}_2 + \theta \boldsymbol{z}_0 > 0$, with $z_{31} = 0$, by construction. However,

$$\boldsymbol{z}_3 = \boldsymbol{z}_1 - \boldsymbol{z}_2 + \theta \boldsymbol{z}_0 > \boldsymbol{A}(\boldsymbol{z}_1 - \boldsymbol{z}_2) + \theta \boldsymbol{A} \boldsymbol{z}_0 = \boldsymbol{A} \boldsymbol{z}_3 \geqq \boldsymbol{0},$$

so that $z_{31} > (\boldsymbol{A}\boldsymbol{z}_3)_1 \geqslant 0$, contradicting $z_{31} = 0$ (Gale, 1960, p. 296).

Theorem 11.1(a). If the linear production model with no joint production defined by non-negative matrices A_i and positive vectors a_i° ($i = 1, \ldots, n$) is productive, in the sense that there exist non-negative vectors satisfying (11.2), then it has a unique cost of production price vector p, the ith component of which is the minimum total labour time, direct and indirect, required to produce one unit of the ith good.

It is evident, however, that theorem 11.1 is, from one point of view, just a mathematical theorem to which an economic interpretation has been given by way of the concepts of a linear production model and cost-of-production prices. For later use it is helpful to strip that mathematical theorem of this particular interpretation and look at it as just a formal mathematical result. Here it is:

Theorem 11.1(b). Let A_i ($i = 1, \ldots, n$) be non-negative matrices, each with n rows, and a_i° ($i = 1, \ldots, n$) a positive vector with as many components as A_i has columns. If there exist non-negative vectors ($x_1, x_2, \ldots, x_n$) such that

$$\begin{bmatrix} x_1 \cdot e_1 \\ \vdots \\ x_i \cdot e_i \\ \vdots \\ x_n \cdot e_n \end{bmatrix} - \sum_{i=1}^{n} A_i \cdot x_i > 0, \qquad (11.14)$$

then there exists a unique positive n vector p such that

$$p \cdot A_i + a_i^\circ \geqq p \cdot E_i \quad \text{and not} \quad p \cdot A_i + a_i^\circ > p \cdot E_i. \quad (i = 1, \ldots, n). \qquad (11.15)$$

The last theorem will be the mathematical key to all that follows.

The linear programme (11.4), by way of which the simple non-substitution theorem was obtained, specified a strictly positive net production vector c. Because c was positive, and because joint production was excluded by assumption, we were able to ascertain that the basic solution would require not less than n activities to be set at a positive level, one activity for each good, and there was therefore cost–price equality for each good. It is perhaps worth remarking that for this method one does not require that the economic system be *indecomposable*. To take an extreme example, the economy might be the union of two distinct technological systems which had no inputs or outputs in common, with the single exception of non-produced labour[6]. Just that

[6] In the language of Sraffa (1960) there might be no basic commodity.

common, but crucial, labour input serves to establish a unique relative price relationship between the two sub-economies. *A fortiori*, there is no need to assume that every good enters directly or indirectly into the production of every other. The assumption that $\boldsymbol{c}$ is positive is no more than an artifice designed to ensure that the prices that emerge are genuine cost-of-production prices. The assumption carries no implication that in fact $\boldsymbol{c}$ will be a positive vector in the growing economy. The conclusion of the argument is that the cost of production of glass slippers will be given uniquely by the technological possibilities, this regardless of whether anyone wants to wear them at that price.

The simple non-substitution theorem is not much help in the present investigation. It covers only the case in which the rate of interest is zero so that all costs are labour time plus unaugmented materials costs (to which one can add some forms of capital depreciation). A zero rate of interest will emerge from the Cambridge model, for example only if γ is zero, i.e. the special case of a classical stationary state. When γ is positive, a positive rate of interest will be implied, and this raises the question of whether the simple non-substitution theorem can be generalized to cover the case in which ρ is positive. When ρ is positive a further issue presents itself immediately; namely, whether the analysis can embrace durable capital goods. With a rate of interest in force, durable capital goods enter into costs of production in two distinct ways: through depreciation costs (as in the stationary state), and through the interest charges on the value of durable goods present while production takes place. So unless one can allow for durable capital goods, one cannot, when ρ is positive, include the case of perfectly durable capital goods, which are irrelevant in the stationary state because they do not influence costs of production.

It is clear what kind of result one might hope to obtain. There can be no question of establishing that prices correspond to direct plus indirect labour costs even if ρ is positive. The rate of interest will influence the structure of prices and these cannot be known then from the technology alone. Intuition, however, might advance the following hypothesis: as long as labour is the only non-produced input, costs of production should still be essentially direct plus indirect labour costs; but now the costs will be compounded at the rate of interest and will no longer be proportional simply to sums of congealed labour time. Nonetheless, the minimized compounded direct plus indirect labour cost for each commodity will still depend only upon technological possibilities *given the rate of interest*. Intuition is correct here, so far at least as it suggests that an extension of the simple case is possible. However, including a positive interest rate does more than merely compound labour costs – it also causes production costs to be influenced by the presence of fixed capital, even apart from depreciation costs. It is not immediately obvious how the compounded labour cost of the service of a fixed capital good is to be calculated; hence the idea that prices correspond to a weighted sum of direct and indirect labour costs runs into difficulties.

A result which states that under certain conditions each value of the rate of interest which is admissible implies a unique set of cost-of-production prices will be referred to as a *general non-substitution theorem*[7]. Obviously a general non-substitution theorem is a harder result to obtain than the simple non-substitution result, which is no more than a special case where the rate of interest is zero, hence all the restrictions that were required previously will again be necessary. In particular, joint production must again be excluded. Now the kind of joint production that mattered in the simple case was what one might call 'genuine joint production' (e.g. wool and mutton). But what about the type of joint production that was introduced in ch. 9 as a means of treating durable capital goods? If any joint production, no matter what its character, must be excluded, then there will be no non-substitution results for economies with durable capital goods. Here intuition suggests that it is only genuine joint production which will cause problems and intuition is not necessarily at fault. Yet the concept of a genuine joint production is not a precise one, and when it is clarified some cases to be excluded come to light which are not simply of the wool and mutton variety.

The reader will better keep his bearings if we next take a step rather than a leap. So we will go to the final result by way of an intermediate case. The simple non-substitution theorem is extended to allow a positive, but given, rate of interest; and the participation in production of perfectly durable fixed capital goods. However, what is not yet admitted is the transformation by production of fixed capital goods. Under this restriction, the capital stock that is employed to produce output is in no way used up. A little ingenuity suffices for the conclusion that, notwithstanding the foregoing assumption, there are certain cases in which depreciation of capital can still be brought into the present case – but these are rather special. Suppose that a stock of goods $\hat{\boldsymbol{b}}_{ij}$[8] is used to produce one unit of the ith good by the jth method, while the requirement of intermediate goods is $\hat{\boldsymbol{a}}_{ij}$. In the von Neumann format, which employs

[7] This is to be greatly preferred to Mirrlees' unfortunate terminology – dynamic non-substitution theorem. There is nothing dynamic about these results.

[8] The hat over the vector $\boldsymbol{b}_{ij}$ is included to remind the reader that this vector is not a column of the von Neumann $\boldsymbol{B}$ matrix. The relationship between the von Neumann notation and the current one is elucidated below.

a different notation, this is equivalent to a gross input requirement of $\hat{\boldsymbol{a}}_{ij} + \hat{\boldsymbol{b}}_{ij}$ (excluding the labour requirement from consideration), from which is obtained a gross output vector $\hat{\boldsymbol{b}}_{ij} + \boldsymbol{u}_i$.

Such a production process differs from the fully general von Neumann process in one respect only: *the quantity of only one good – in this case the ith good – is expanded by the productive process.* As long as this restriction is satisfied it is possible: (a) to associate productive processes with particular goods, and hence give some meaning to the idea that a certain process produces a particular good; and (b) to embrace any case in which the final capital vector is not greater than the initial capital vector. When part of the capital stock 'disappears' during production this can be included as part of the flow input requirements. Thus the transformation from the von Neumann format to the present one is accomplished as follows. Let the *j*th method of producing the *i*th good at unit level require a vector of gross inputs $\boldsymbol{a}_{ij}$ and produce a vector of gross outputs $\boldsymbol{b}_{ij}$. This is equivalent to requiring that a stock $\boldsymbol{b}_{ij} - \boldsymbol{u}_i$ be present, but not used up, during production, together with flow inputs $\boldsymbol{a}_{ij} - (\boldsymbol{b}_{ij} - \boldsymbol{u}_i)$ which are exhausted during production. This transformation can always be carried out provided that

$$\boldsymbol{a}_{ij} - (\boldsymbol{b}_{ij} - \boldsymbol{u}_i) \geqq \boldsymbol{0}, \tag{11.16}$$

as must be the case if only the *i*th good is expanded by this process.

The cases which can be included in the discussion without any extra trouble involve essentially the assumption of 'radioactive' decay of the capital stock. Under this assumption a certain proportion of each capital good used in any process depreciates (i.e. is no longer available after production is completed). The proportions concerned can vary from process to process and from good to good, when the only implication of the assumption is that the rates of decay be non-negative, so that no capital is expanded during production. This is a helpful way to look at the assumption because it shows that most realistic examples of capital depreciation have not so far been included, and indeed cannot be included as long as one maintains the restriction that there be no expansion of any capital good along with another output.

The point can be seen from an examination of the argument of ch. 9, where it was shown that the method of treating capital depreciation which allowed a wide class of cases to be covered involved the introduction into the analysis of many different sub-species of capital goods, including some purely notional ones. Typically then a productive activity involved the transformation of capital goods into goods of a different type, for example, more depreciated versions. The particular types available after production would be different from those used initially. Formally this is equivalent to the expansion of more than one type of good by an activity. An illustration is provided by the example of ch. 9, table 9.1, where activity 2 expands the quantity both of fish and of nets (2). Thus, the intermediate case now under consideration is a very special one, but a step in the right direction nonetheless.

The intermediate case is as follows. Just as in the simple case there are n goods and m_i activities which produce the ith good in excess of input requirements, which here include durable capital goods. An activity is normalized so that it produces one unit (gross) of the good that it produces when run at unit level. The jth method of producing the ith good ($j = 1, \ldots, m_i$) requires $\alpha_{ij} > 0$ units of labour per unit of gross output, a vector of intermediate requirements $\boldsymbol{a}_{ij} \geqq \boldsymbol{0}$ and a vector of capital requirements $\boldsymbol{k}_{ij} \geqq \boldsymbol{0}$ which will still be available after production has taken place. The 'family' of activities which produce the ith good can be summarized by an $n \times m_i$ matrix, $\boldsymbol{A}_i$, whose jth column is the vector $\boldsymbol{a}_{ij}$, an $n \times m_i$ matrix, $\boldsymbol{K}_i$, whose jth column is $\boldsymbol{k}_{ij}$, and an m_i vector of labour requirements $\boldsymbol{a}_i^0$, whose jth element is α_{ij}.[9]

The question at issue is whether in this system cost-of-production prices depend only upon the technical possibilities, as specified by $\boldsymbol{A}_i$, $\boldsymbol{K}_i$ and $\boldsymbol{a}_i^0$ ($i = 1, \ldots, n$), and the rate of interest ρ. Before proceeding further we must take at least some account of restrictions on the admissible values of ρ. An equilibrium model could seemingly give rise to any positive value of ρ. In the Cambridge model ρ can be as large as one pleases given appropriate values of γ and π. But not every value of ρ is consistent with the semi-stationary state – there is an upper limit on the value of ρ that is consistent with cost–price equalities. No discussion of cost-price equalities can proceed without taking this into account. Later it will emerge that we require a still more stringent upper limit on the value of ρ to ensure that the wage will purchase a subsistence basket. But this point can be put aside for the moment. Given that there is an upper limit on ρ, it is natural to ask whether the Cambridge-model equation $\rho = \gamma/\pi$ is in fact likely to yield a value consistent with the restriction. To answer this question one must take into account the fact that there is another restriction, this time on the values of γ that are consistent with semi-stationary growth. Let us take the last point first.

Suppose that we consider an economy for which the value of γ is very large. Since γ defines the rate of growth of the semi-stationary state, a very large

[9] This set-up is usually known as the dynamic Leontief system, after Leontief (1960). However, Leontief usually assumes that there is only one known method of producing each type of output – an unnecessary assumption in a theoretical investigation.

value will mean that the economy must grow very rapidly. Since γ could be as large as one likes to imagine, it seems that the economy might have to expand at an arbitrarily large rate. But will this prove possible? Obviously the answer is no. There is an upper limit on the rate at which the economy can grow, even if labour time were freely available on demand, and the assumptions concerning the semi-stationary state are mutually consistent only if γ does not exceed this value. Indeed, as will be seen later, γ must be less than the maximum technically feasible expansion rate. If this restriction is not satisfied there cannot be full employment of a labour force growing at rate γ. This is for the simple reason that the economy will be incapable of expanding the capital stock at a rate sufficiently large to equip the growing hoards of labour. Let the maximum expansion rate of which the economy is capable with free labour be γ^*. This is the growth rate which was introduced by von Neumann (1945–1946) in his famous paper[10]. It is now known that there can be a semi-stationary state with growth rate γ only if

$$\gamma \leqslant \gamma^*. \tag{11.17}$$

In fact, this restriction will have to be strengthened if the economy is to yield both a subsistence wage and capital accumulation at rate γ.

Return now to the upper limit on the value of ρ that is consistent with cost–price equality in the semi-stationary state. It is this: there is no possibility of obtaining cost-of-production prices expressed in terms of labour time unless ρ is less than γ^*. There could hardly be a more intuitively acceptable proposition. If one imagines labour to be a free good, then the whole of the

---

[10] Since that paper was published more elementary methods for proving the existence of a γ^* value have been discovered. Thus, given conditions that bound the expansion rate above, it is necessary to show that the least upper bound of proportional expansion rates is attainable. To this end, let $X(z_1, z_2)$, where z_1 and z_2 are non-negative vectors ($z_1 \neq 0$), be the function defined as follows:

$$X(z_1, z_2) = \min_i \,(z_{i2}/z_{i1}).$$

Now, given any activity vector denoted x, normalized so that its components sum to unity, consider the function $f(x)$ defined as

$$f(x) = X(\boldsymbol{B}\cdot x, \boldsymbol{A}\cdot x) - 1.$$

It is easy to show that f is a continuous function, bounded above by assumption. Because it is defined on a compact set, f has a maximum, i.e. there exists an x^* such that $f(x^*) \geqslant f(x)$ for each admissible x. $f(x^*)$ is the von Neumann expansion rate and x^* is an activity vector giving a structure of activity levels for which the economy attains the maximal expansion rate.

net addition to the stock of goods would be profit. This profit expressed as a percentage would then be equal to the rate at which the stock was expanded. A rate of profit larger than the greatest value which the expansion rate could reach is not therefore possible even if labour time were free. The point can be demonstrated formally as follows.

When a positive rate of interest is admitted the cost–price relations (11.1) have to be rewritten as

$$(1+\rho)\boldsymbol{p}\cdot\boldsymbol{A}_i + \rho\boldsymbol{p}\cdot\boldsymbol{K}_i + \boldsymbol{a}_i^{\mathrm{o}} \geqq \boldsymbol{p}\cdot\boldsymbol{E}_i$$

and not (11.18)

$$(1+\rho)\boldsymbol{p}\cdot\boldsymbol{A}_i + \rho\boldsymbol{p}\cdot\boldsymbol{K}_i + \boldsymbol{a}_i^{\mathrm{o}} > \boldsymbol{p}\cdot\boldsymbol{E}_i \qquad (i=1,\ldots,n).$$

Here the costs of (11.15) have been augmented by the inclusion of the interest on working capital ($\rho\boldsymbol{p}\cdot\boldsymbol{A}_i$) and on fixed capital ($\rho\boldsymbol{p}\cdot\boldsymbol{K}_i$). The prices are still in terms of labour, so that the case when labour is a free good is implicitly excluded.

Theorem 11.2. There exist cost-of-production prices satisfying (11.18) only if $\rho<\gamma^*$.

Proof. Suppose that a set of prices $\boldsymbol{p}$ satisfying (11.18) have been found where, contrary to the result to be proved, $\rho \geqslant \gamma^*$. It may happen that not all goods are produced on the path of economic expansion at the maximal rate. This possibility arises when the system is decomposable (i.e. not every good enters directly or indirectly into the production of every other). In this case, choose any minimal (i.e. not decomposable) set of goods which are produced on a path of maximal expansion. For this set, or for all goods as the case may be, choose any j such that

$$(1+\rho)\boldsymbol{p}\cdot\boldsymbol{a}_{ij} + \rho\boldsymbol{p}\cdot\boldsymbol{k}_{ij} + \alpha_{ij} = p_i. \tag{11.19}$$

One can imagine that the activities were so numbered that it happened that the j chosen was in each case 1. Let the matrix whose ith column is $\boldsymbol{a}_{i1}$ be $\bar{\boldsymbol{A}}$, the matrix whose ith column is $\boldsymbol{k}_{i1}$ be $\bar{\boldsymbol{K}}$ and the vector whose ith component is α_{i1} be $\bar{\boldsymbol{a}}^{\mathrm{o}}$. Then $\boldsymbol{p}$ satisfies

$$(1+\rho)\boldsymbol{p}\cdot\bar{\boldsymbol{A}} + \rho\boldsymbol{p}\cdot\bar{\boldsymbol{K}} + \bar{\boldsymbol{a}}^{\mathrm{o}} = \boldsymbol{p}. \tag{11.20}$$

Consider now the problem of finding a vector of activity levels such that there is maximal expansion of the economy, having no regard to labour supply, where only the first method for producing the ith good is to be used. Clearly there exists such a vector (call it $\bar{\boldsymbol{x}}$) and it satisfies

$$(1+\bar{\gamma})\bar{\boldsymbol{A}}\cdot\bar{\boldsymbol{x}}+\bar{\gamma}\bar{\boldsymbol{K}}\cdot\bar{\boldsymbol{x}}=\bar{\boldsymbol{x}}.^{11} \tag{11.21}$$

Multiplying both sides of (11.20) by $\bar{\boldsymbol{x}}$ and both sides of (11.21) by $\boldsymbol{p}$, one obtains

$$(1+\rho)\boldsymbol{p}\cdot\bar{\boldsymbol{A}}\cdot\bar{\boldsymbol{x}}+\rho\boldsymbol{p}\cdot\bar{\boldsymbol{K}}\cdot\bar{\boldsymbol{x}}+\bar{\boldsymbol{a}}^{\mathrm{o}}\cdot\bar{\boldsymbol{x}}=\boldsymbol{p}\cdot\bar{\boldsymbol{x}}$$

and (11.24)

$$(1+\bar{\gamma})\boldsymbol{p}\cdot\bar{\boldsymbol{A}}\cdot\bar{\boldsymbol{x}}+\gamma\boldsymbol{p}\cdot\bar{\boldsymbol{K}}\cdot\bar{\boldsymbol{x}}=\boldsymbol{p}\cdot\bar{\boldsymbol{x}},$$

from which

$$(\bar{\gamma}-\rho)[\boldsymbol{p}\cdot\bar{\boldsymbol{A}}\cdot\bar{\boldsymbol{x}}+\boldsymbol{p}\cdot\bar{\boldsymbol{K}}\cdot\bar{\boldsymbol{x}}]=\bar{\boldsymbol{a}}^{\mathrm{o}}\cdot\bar{\boldsymbol{x}}>0, \tag{11.25}$$

so that

$$\bar{\gamma}>\rho. \tag{11.26}$$

Notice that if the implicit assumption that labour time has a positive valuation were to be relaxed this would allow in the case $\bar{\gamma}=\rho$, but the same argument would do otherwise. Finally, it is immediate that $\bar{\gamma}\leqslant\gamma^*$, for the system cannot attain a greater expansion rate when constrained to use just n particular activities. Thus,

$$\rho<\bar{\gamma}\leqslant\gamma^*, \tag{11.27}$$

as required.

It would be nice to be able to go on to say now that the converse of theorem 11.2 is true, that we may establish unique cost-of-production prices provided

---

[11] $\bar{\gamma}$ is the von Neumann growth rate for this set of activities and $\bar{\boldsymbol{x}}$ is a vector of von Neumann activities. In the von Neumann format the input and output matrices would be, respectively, $\bar{\boldsymbol{A}}+\bar{\boldsymbol{K}}$ and $\bar{\boldsymbol{K}}+\boldsymbol{I}$. Since we want to confine attention still to productive systems it is assumed that $\bar{\gamma}>0$. It remains to be shown that there should be strict equality in (11.21), i.e. no good is over-produced on the maximal expansion path. Suppose not, i.e. there exists an $\boldsymbol{x}\geqq 0$ satisfying

$$(1+\bar{\gamma})\bar{\boldsymbol{A}}\cdot\boldsymbol{x}+\bar{\gamma}\bar{\boldsymbol{K}}\cdot\boldsymbol{x}\leqslant\boldsymbol{x}. \tag{11.22}$$

Decrease each component of $\boldsymbol{x}$ for which there is an inequality. For some suitably small decreases the inequalities are maintained. New inequalities are introduced for goods not previously over-produced and which are used to produce goods whose production has been curtailed. Since one is dealing here with a system in which there is no proper subset of goods which use only themselves as inputs, at least one new inequality must be introduced. Now repeat the process until there emerges an $\boldsymbol{x}$ satisfying

$$(1+\bar{\gamma})\bar{\boldsymbol{A}}\cdot\boldsymbol{x}+\bar{\gamma}\bar{\boldsymbol{K}}\cdot\boldsymbol{x}<\boldsymbol{x}. \tag{11.23}$$

Not more than n repetitions will be required. Evidently now, $\bar{\gamma}$ is not the maximal expansion rate, contrary to assumption.

only that $\rho < \gamma^*$. But that is not the case and the matter is altogether less neat than such a simple view would suggest. The complexities arise because not every economy expanding at its maximal rate produces every possible good. And if we are to treat of durable capital goods, then a recognition of that fact is imperative. So long as every good must be produced to allow positive net production we may argue as follows. Let $(\boldsymbol{x}_1^*, \boldsymbol{x}_2^*, \ldots, \boldsymbol{x}_n^*)$ be activity vectors corresponding to maximal expansion at rate γ^*. Then

$$\begin{bmatrix} \boldsymbol{x}_1^* \cdot \boldsymbol{e}_1 \\ \vdots \\ \boldsymbol{x}_i^* \cdot \boldsymbol{e}_i \\ \vdots \\ \boldsymbol{x}_n^* \cdot \boldsymbol{e}_n \end{bmatrix} - (1+\gamma^*) \sum_{i=1}^{n} \boldsymbol{A}_i \cdot \boldsymbol{x}_1^* - \gamma^* \sum_{i=1}^{n} \boldsymbol{K}_i \cdot \boldsymbol{x}_1^* \geqq \boldsymbol{0} \tag{11.28}$$

from the definition of semi-stationary expansion. If every good is produced we have

$$\sum_{i=1}^{n} \boldsymbol{A}_i \cdot \boldsymbol{x}_i^* + \sum_{i=1}^{n} \boldsymbol{K}_i \cdot \boldsymbol{x}_i^* > \boldsymbol{0} \qquad (i = 1, \ldots, n), \tag{11.29}$$

so that, for $\rho < \gamma^*$,

$$\begin{bmatrix} \boldsymbol{x}_1^* \cdot \boldsymbol{e}_1 \\ \vdots \\ \boldsymbol{x}_i^* \cdot \boldsymbol{e}_i \\ \vdots \\ \boldsymbol{x}_n^* \cdot \boldsymbol{e}_n \end{bmatrix} - (1+\rho) \sum_{i=1}^{n} \boldsymbol{A}_i \cdot \boldsymbol{x}_i^* - \rho \sum_{i=1}^{n} \boldsymbol{K}_i \cdot \boldsymbol{x}_i^* > \boldsymbol{0}. \tag{11.30}$$

A rearrangement of (11.30) is suggestive:

$$\begin{bmatrix} \boldsymbol{x}_i^* \cdot \boldsymbol{e}_1 \\ \vdots \\ \boldsymbol{x}_i^* \cdot \boldsymbol{e}_i \\ \vdots \\ \boldsymbol{x}_n^* \cdot \boldsymbol{e}_n \end{bmatrix} - \sum_{i=1}^{n} [(1+\rho)\boldsymbol{A}_i + \rho \boldsymbol{K}_i] \cdot \boldsymbol{x}_i^* > \boldsymbol{0}. \tag{11.31}$$

From (11.31) it may be seen that (11.14) of theorem 11.1(b) is satisfied, with the $\boldsymbol{A}_i$ replaced by $[(1+\rho)\boldsymbol{A}_i + \rho\boldsymbol{K}_i]$, by $\boldsymbol{x}_i = \boldsymbol{x}_i^*$. Hence, the requirement of theorem 11.1(b) that these should exist on $(\boldsymbol{x}_1, \boldsymbol{x}_2, \ldots, \boldsymbol{x}_n)$ such that

$$\begin{bmatrix} \boldsymbol{x}_1 \cdot \boldsymbol{e}_1 \\ \vdots \\ \boldsymbol{x}_i \cdot \boldsymbol{e}_i \\ \vdots \\ \boldsymbol{x}_n \cdot \boldsymbol{e}_n \end{bmatrix} - \sum_{i=1}^{n} [(1+\rho)\boldsymbol{A}_i + \rho \boldsymbol{K}_i] \cdot \boldsymbol{x}_i > \boldsymbol{0}. \tag{11.32}$$

may be satisfied.

It follows now from (11.32) that if the intermediate case is interpreted as the simple case with input-requirement matrices $[(1+\rho)\boldsymbol{A}_i+\rho\boldsymbol{B}_i]$ the resulting input-requirement matrices would be those of a productive system. Then the result of theorem 11.1(b) asserts that there exists one, and only one, vector $\boldsymbol{p}$ satisfying

$$\boldsymbol{p}\cdot[(1+\rho)\boldsymbol{A}_i+\rho\boldsymbol{K}_i]+\boldsymbol{a}_i^{\text{o}} \geqq \boldsymbol{p}\cdot\boldsymbol{E}_i$$

and not (11.33)

$$\boldsymbol{p}\cdot[(1+\rho)\boldsymbol{A}_i+\rho\boldsymbol{K}_i]+\boldsymbol{a}_i^{\text{o}} > \boldsymbol{p}\cdot\boldsymbol{E}_i \qquad (i=1,\ldots,n).$$

Hence, (11.18) has a unique solution. Hence, we have arrived at:

Theorem 11.3. If the input and output vectors of all the activities of the linear production model could be written in the form

$$\textit{input vector} = \boldsymbol{a}_{ij}+\boldsymbol{k}_{ij}$$

and

$$\textit{output vector} = \boldsymbol{k}_{ij}+\boldsymbol{e}_i, \tag{11.34}$$

with

$$\boldsymbol{a}_{ij} \geqq \boldsymbol{0} \quad \text{and} \quad \boldsymbol{k}_{ij} \geqq \boldsymbol{0} \qquad (j=1,\ldots,m_i;\, i=1,\ldots,n),$$

and if there exists a semi-stationary development, expanding at the maximal rate γ^*, *on which every good is produced, and if* $\rho<\gamma^*$, *then there exists a unique positive vector of cost-of-production prices satisfying (11.33).*

The theorem is unfortunately of limited interest since the assumption that every good is produced is too strong to be acceptable. That the assumption is needed is indicated by the following example.

Example 11.1. There are two produced goods in the economy, numbered 1 and 2. The activities are

$$\begin{aligned}&1 \text{ unit of labour time} \oplus 1 \text{ unit of good } 1 \ominus 2 \text{ units of good } 1,\\ &1 \text{ unit of labour time} \oplus 1 \text{ unit of good } 2 \ominus 3 \text{ units of good } 2.\end{aligned} \tag{11.35}$$

Evidently the maximal expansion rate is $\gamma^*=2$ using only the second activity. Hence, $\rho=1.5<\gamma^*$. However, cost-of-production prices do not exist for this system for $\rho=1.5$, for suppose that they did, and let p_i $(i=1,2)$ be the price in terms of labour time of good i. Then by definition we would have

$$1+2.5p_1=2p_1, \qquad 1+2.5p_2=3p_2 \tag{11.36}$$

and p_1 would have to be negative. We cannot get cost-of-production prices for this economy with a rate of interest as high as 1.5, although the economy can be in a semi-stationary state with production prices $p_1 = 1, p_2 = 2, \rho = 1.5$, $\omega = 1$ and $\gamma < 2$.

The example indicates that the idea of considering prices as cost-of-production prices falls down in certain cases. The conditions of equilibrium may demand that certain goods (which households must then not wish to consume) be priced below the cost of producing them. Notice that we are touching here upon a case where the solution procedure of the Cambridge model is not strictly applicable. Suppose we have the technology of example 11.1, the growth rate of labour is $\gamma = 1.0$ and π (the proportion of profits saved) is 0.75. The Cambridge-model equation gives us $\rho = \frac{4}{3}$. The costs of production of the two goods will be respectively

$$\text{good 1: } \omega + \tfrac{4}{3}p_1 > p_1, \qquad \text{good 2: } \omega + \tfrac{2}{3}p_2, \tag{11.37}$$

so that good 1 cannot be produced at a cost equal to, or less than, its price. Thus the only type of full-employment equilibrium that is admissible in this case is one for which only good 2 is produced. In this case there will be a surplus for consumption because activity 2 expands the stock of good 2 at a rate exceeding the growth rate. But is this type of equilibrium viable? Suppose that households only like to consume good 1? We are faced here with an issue involving demand conditions the specification of which cannot be relegated to the third step of the three-step solution procedure. Of course, the economy of the example does have an equilibrium, in which, however, the wage rate is zero, there being unemployed labour time, good 2 is a free good and $\rho = 1$ (the expansion rate of good 1).

One can go immediately from theorem 11.3 to a slightly more general version of the same result – the proof is parallel and is omitted – namely,

Theorem 11.4. If the input and output vectors of all the activities of the linear production model can be written in the form of (11.34), and if there exists a semi-stationary development expanding at rate γ^0, on which every good is produced, and if $\rho < \gamma^0$, then there exists a unique positive vector of cost-of-production prices satisfying (11.33).

So much for the formal demonstration of the non-substitution theorem for the intermediate case. The reader will ask himself what becomes of the interpretation of the prices as direct plus indirect labour requirements. Clearly this interpretation needs to be modified, for the linear programme to which the intermediate case gives rise involves the minimization of the labour required to produce an output vector $\boldsymbol{c}$, together with outputs sufficient to expand at rate ρ whatever stocks are required by the solution; an artefact with no very fruitful economic interpretation. In just one case, when there is no fixed capital, the modification is fairly straightforward – prices in this case do correspond to compounded labour costs[12] – but beyond that the notion of costs equal to compounded labour requirements is no longer valid[13].

The intermediate case is still a very restrictive one which hardly makes a significant contribution to the problem of obtaining non-substitution results for economies with capital depreciation. Capital depreciation typically involves the transformation of capital goods before they finally cease to have any economic use. The consequence of this, in the formal statement of technological relationships, is that joint production becomes a typical phenomenon. In the examination of the intermediate case it was seen that the simple non-substitution result may be generalized fairly readily so long as any individual productive activity brings about a net expansion of the quantity of only one good. But if a machine in mint condition is transformed by use into a used machine then, formally, the productive process uses labour, new machines and other inputs, to produce *jointly* outputs of used machines and the product itself in excess of the quantities available initially. The arguments that have been advanced so far fail in such a case.

Fortunately, the introduction of this particular type of 'joint production' does not necessarily invalidate the non-substitution result – but one must proceed with care. The transformation of capital goods does make a difference. There is a real possibility that bringing it into the analysis will introduce genuine joint production 'by the back door'.

An example will illustrate this last point. It is not uncommon for various goods, both consumers' goods and producers' goods, to be produced from discarded capital equipment. Suppose that the cheapest way of making

---

[12] If the matrix of input requirements for a basic set of activities in the solution to the labour minimizing programme is $\boldsymbol{A}$ and the vector of labour requirements is $\boldsymbol{a}_0$, then the unique goods price vector is $\boldsymbol{p} = \boldsymbol{a}_0'[\boldsymbol{I} - (1+\rho)\boldsymbol{A}]^{-1}$. It is known that

$$\boldsymbol{p} = \boldsymbol{a}_0[\boldsymbol{I} - (1+\rho)\boldsymbol{A}]^{-1} = \lim_{t\to\infty} \boldsymbol{a}_0[\boldsymbol{I} + (1+\rho)\boldsymbol{A} + (1+\rho)^2\boldsymbol{A}^2 + \cdots (1+\rho)^{t-1}\boldsymbol{A}^{t-1}]$$

which has the interpretation suggested. See Morishima (1964, pp. 21–22).

[13] Which is not to say that determined efforts to hang on to it will fail completely. The fixed capital goods could be regarded as yielding up a certain proportion of their compounded labour content which is then embodied in the total labour cost on top of depreciation charges. The proportion concerned must then be ρ, the rate of interest. 'It is only in such a crude and meaningless form that we can glimpse that the value of commodities is determined by the labour contained in them.'

sandals in a certain economy is to use worn and discarded motor tyres as an input. The effect of the use of old tyres in this manner is to make motor vehicles and cheap sandals joint products; not in the sense, of course, that there is a productive process in the economy which produces simultaneously cars and sandals; but in the sense, which is the one relevant to the present discussion, that the effect of the production and employment of a motor vehicle *over its whole lifetime* is to add to the net supply, first of the transport service provided by the vehicle and finally also to the supply of sandals. The example is not to be taken too seriously but it serves to make a point. It is clear that this type of case is going to undermine the non-substitution result, for there are various combinations of demand prices for transport services and sandals which would be consistent with the equality between the cost of production of a motor vehicle and the demand price for that vehicle.

What new feature was introduced by the case of the rubber sandals which caused it to be such a troublesome example? It was not the fact that motor vehicles deteriorated with use, even though that does bring in joint production of the notional variety. The feature of this example which leads to its destructive consequences for the non-substitution argument is that a capital good *moved from one sector to another* during its lifetime. The essential consequence of this was joint production, though not exactly the classic wool–mutton type, and non-substitution theorems depend critically upon the systematic exclusion of all kinds of 'genuine' joint production. Notice that it is only when the capital good which moves from one sector to another is not the same as a newly produced version that it makes any difference. It is for this reason that the intermediate case, which excluded the case of transformation of capital goods, was not forced to consider whether capital goods were mobile between sectors or not.

The final, and most general, non-substitution theorem is based on the assumption, which is virtually unavoidable, that the economy is divided into n sectors, one for each good, and that newly produced capital goods, once installed in one sector, put down the strongest roots, with the consequence that no capital good ever migrates from one sector to another[14]. That this assumption is indispensable is shown by the following example.

---

[14] Stiglitz (1970b) treats the consequences of capital migration, or the lack of it, extensively. His paper also covers some cases in which the cost-of-production prices are influenced by the rate of growth of the economy. This somewhat bizarre result comes about when there are productive techniques which employ old and new capital goods as joint inputs, in which case the optimal choice of technique depends upon the relative availability of the old and new versions, which is influenced in turn by the rate of growth of the economy. It seems that there are some cases where this would be a convincing specification. Thus, scrap steel may

Let there be two consumption goods, both produced from the same type of capital input. The consumption good denoted C(1) is produced only when the capital good is new; and the other, denoted C(2), only when it is old. An example, which is not entirely fanciful, would envisage a tree which first yields a crop and later the wood of the old tree is used to produce another product. Following this line of thought, let the capital good be called a 'tree'. The known productive activities are

$$\begin{aligned} &1 \text{ labour} && \ominus\ 1 \text{ new tree,} \\ &1 \text{ labour} \oplus 1 \text{ new tree} && \ominus\ 1 \text{ old tree} \oplus 1 \text{ unit of C(1),} \\ &1 \text{ labour} \oplus 1 \text{ old tree} && \ominus\ 1 \text{ unit of C(2).} \end{aligned} \tag{11.38}$$

Let ρ be the rate of interest, and the prices in terms of labour time of new trees, old trees, C(1) and C(2), respectively be π_1, π_2, π_3 and π_4. These prices are consistent with equality between input cost and output value if they satisfy

$$1 = \pi_1, \qquad 1 + (1+\rho)\pi_1 = \pi_2 + \pi_3, \qquad 1 + (1+\rho)\pi_2 = \pi_4. \tag{11.39}$$

Rearranging (11.39) one obtains

$$\pi_1 = 1, \qquad (1+\rho) = \pi_2 + \pi_3 - 1 = (\pi_4 - 1)/\pi_2. \tag{11.40}$$

It is clear that relations (11.40) do not uniquely determine the values of π_1 to π_4 given ρ. Thus, if $\rho = 0.5$, the following sets of values each satisfy (11.40):

$$\begin{aligned} &\pi_1 = 1, && \pi_2 = 0.5, && \pi_3 = 2.0, && \pi_4 = 1.75, \\ &\pi_1 = 1, && \pi_2 = 0.75, && \pi_3 = 1.75, && \pi_4 = 2.125. \end{aligned} \tag{11.41}$$

Demand conditions will have to declare whether the price ratio π_3/π_4 is: 8/7, as in the first line; 14/17 as in the second line; or another of the infinity of values consistent with (11.40). The conditions for a non-substitution theorem are not satisfied.

Once capital inputs are transformed during production it is no longer so natural to treat an activity as something which occupies just one week.

---

be used as an input to the production of new steel in which case a rapidly growing economy might have a higher relative price of steel. Or, to consider another example, suppose that equipment for generating electricity deteriorates with age with a consequent loss of efficiency (technical progress has a similar effect on relative costs). If demand fluctuates and the least efficient equipment is used only at times of peak demand, then the average cost of electricity will be lower in a rapidly growing economy, because the rate of utilization of high cost equipment will be lower. See also Nordhaus (1969 a, b).

When capital is committed to one sector over several weeks the relevant cost–revenue calculations look forward over as many weeks as is appropriate in the light of the durability of the investment concerned. So a more useful and natural specification of a productive activity would be in the following. Counting from the week when a new capital good is first committed to a particular sector, let the maximum number of weeks that must elapse until the capital good no longer yields any productive service be T. Then a particular investment and use of a capital good in the ith sector would be specified by

$$[\boldsymbol{a}_0^{ij};\boldsymbol{b}_1^{ij};\boldsymbol{a}_1^{ij};\boldsymbol{b}_2^{ij},\ldots,\boldsymbol{a}_{T-1}^{ij};\boldsymbol{b}_T^{ij}], \tag{11.42}$$

where $\boldsymbol{a}_t^{ij}$ is the vector of inputs required in week t of the life of the jth method of producing the ith good, and $\boldsymbol{b}_t^{ij}$ is the vector of outputs yielded in week t of the life of the jth method of producing the ith good.

Given the format (11.42) it is possible to include transformed but immobile capital goods by recognizing explicitly the existence of these goods only at the stage of initial investment. Suppose, for example, that it is the kth type of good that is invested to produce the ith good, by the jth method. Then $\boldsymbol{a}_0^{ij}$ would have a positive kth component corresponding to the amount of the kth good that has to be invested for this activity to be run at unit level. One week later the same type of capital good, but not the identical good, is available. Yet this 'joint output' is not included in the vector $\boldsymbol{b}_1^{ij}$ – nor are the various descendants of the kth good in later weeks listed explicitly as components of the vectors $\boldsymbol{b}_t^{ij}$. Equally, the part-worn capital goods are not recognized explicitly as inputs, i.e. components of the vectors $\boldsymbol{a}_t^{ij}$. Thus, in spite of capital transformation, one can adopt the assumption, which has the effect of excluding genuine joint production, that the vector $\boldsymbol{b}_t^{ij}-\boldsymbol{a}_t^{ij}$ $(t=1,\ldots,T)$ is non-positive, except for the ith component which may or may not be positive. The ith good is the only good whose supply is expanded by this activity at any time. Let the matrix whose jth column is $\boldsymbol{a}_t^{ij}$ be $\boldsymbol{A}_t^i$ and the matrix whose jth column is $\boldsymbol{b}_t^{ij}$ be $\boldsymbol{B}_t^i$.

What condition has to be satisfied for a system specified in the new format (11.42) to be productive? It is no longer adequate to require that it be possible to produce a positive vector of goods over and above input requirements for these goods, because many goods, i.e. part-worn capital goods, are now treated only in an implicit manner. However, the essential implication of the productivity assumption is that the system has a semi-stationary development with a positive growth rate in which every good is produced. It is this condition that will be assumed. The economy can expand at a positive rate indefinitely, having no regard to labour supply, if there exists a positive number γ and non-negative vectors of activity levels $\boldsymbol{x}_1, \boldsymbol{x}_2, \ldots, \boldsymbol{x}_n$, each of which has at least one positive component, and such that

$$\sum_{i=1}^{n}\sum_{t=1}^{T} \boldsymbol{B}_t^i \cdot \boldsymbol{x}\left(\frac{1}{1+\gamma}\right)^t \geqq \sum_{i=1}^{n}\sum_{t=1}^{T} \boldsymbol{A}_t^i \cdot \boldsymbol{x}_i\left(\frac{1}{1+\gamma}\right)^t. \tag{11.43}$$

So far, no account has been taken of labour requirements. Let the quantity of labour time required by the jth method for producing the ith good in the tth week be a_t^{ij} and the vector whose jth component is a_t^{ij} be $\boldsymbol{a}_{it}^{\mathrm{o}}$. Let the vector of goods prices in terms of present labour be $\boldsymbol{p}$ and ρ the rate of interest. Then $\boldsymbol{p}$ is a vector of cost-of-production prices if it satisfies

$$\sum_{t=0}^{T} \boldsymbol{p}\cdot\left(\frac{1}{1+\rho}\right)^t \boldsymbol{A}_t^i + \sum_{t=1}^{T} \boldsymbol{p}\cdot\left(\frac{1}{1+\rho}\right)^t \boldsymbol{B}_t^i + \sum_{t=0}^{T-1} \boldsymbol{a}_{it}^{\mathrm{o}}\left(\frac{1}{1+\rho}\right)^t \geqq \boldsymbol{0}$$

and not (11.44)

$$\sum_{t=0}^{T} \boldsymbol{p}\cdot\left(\frac{1}{1+\rho}\right)^t \boldsymbol{A}_t^i - \sum_{t=1}^{T} \boldsymbol{p}\cdot\left(\frac{1}{1+\rho}\right)^t \boldsymbol{B}_t^i + \sum_{t=0}^{T} \boldsymbol{a}_{it}^{\mathrm{o}}\left(\frac{1}{1+\rho}\right)^t > \boldsymbol{0} \qquad (i=1,\ldots,n)$$

which is the adaptation of (11.18) to the present case. Rearranging (11.44), one obtains for each $i=1,\ldots,n$

$$(1+\rho)\boldsymbol{p}\cdot\left[\sum_{t=0}^{T}\left(\frac{1}{1+\rho}\right)^{t+1} \boldsymbol{A}_t^i - \sum_{t=1}^{T}\left(\frac{1}{1+\rho}\right)^{t+1} \boldsymbol{B}_t^i\right] + \sum_{t=0}^{T} \boldsymbol{a}_{it}^{\mathrm{o}}\left(\frac{1}{1+\rho}\right)^t \geqq \boldsymbol{0}$$

and not (11.45)

$$(1+\rho)\boldsymbol{p}\cdot\left[\sum_{t=0}^{T}\left(\frac{1}{1+\rho}\right)^{t+1} \boldsymbol{A}_t^i - \sum_{t=1}^{T}\left(\frac{1}{1+\rho}\right)^{t+1} \boldsymbol{B}_t^i\right] + \sum_{t=0}^{T} \boldsymbol{a}_{it}^{\mathrm{o}}\left(\frac{1}{1+\rho}\right)^t > \boldsymbol{0}.$$

Compare this to (11.18) expressed in the form

$$(1+\rho)\boldsymbol{p}\cdot\left[\boldsymbol{A}_i + \left(\frac{\rho}{1+\rho}\right)\boldsymbol{B}_i - \left(\frac{1}{1+\rho}\right)\boldsymbol{E}_i\right] + \boldsymbol{a}_i^{\mathrm{o}} \geqq \boldsymbol{0}$$

and not (11.46)

$$(1+\rho)\boldsymbol{p}\cdot\left[\boldsymbol{A}_i + \left(\frac{\rho}{1+\rho}\right)\boldsymbol{B}_i - \left(\frac{1}{1+\rho}\right)\boldsymbol{E}_i\right] + \boldsymbol{a}_i^{\mathrm{o}} > \boldsymbol{0}.$$

In each case the form is basically

$$(1+\rho)\boldsymbol{p}\cdot[\boldsymbol{M}_i] + \boldsymbol{a}_i^{\mathrm{o}} \geqq \boldsymbol{0}$$

and not (11.47)

$$(1+\rho)\boldsymbol{p}\cdot[\boldsymbol{M}_i] + \boldsymbol{a}_i^{\mathrm{o}} > \boldsymbol{0},$$

where each column of $\boldsymbol{M}_i$ has negative components only in the ith row.

From theorem 11.1(a) it is known that there is a unique $\boldsymbol{p}$ which satisfies (11.47) provided that the matrices $(1+\rho)\boldsymbol{M}_i$ are the matrices of a productive system.

It may now be seen that the problem of establishing a non-substitution result for the final case, in which capital inputs may be transformed by production (provided that the 'heirs' of an original capital input are always associated with the production of the same good) bears a strong formal similarity to the intermediate case, in which capital goods could be depreciated but not transformed. However, the resemblance is not complete. To see why, suppose that (11.43) may be satisfied by a value of γ exceeding ρ and for $\boldsymbol{x}_i$ vectors, each of which has a positive component. This is equivalent to saying that the production system is capable, given sufficient labour time, of semi-stationary growth, with all original goods produced, at a rate exceeding ρ. However, what we need to apply theorem 11.1(a) is that there exist vectors $\boldsymbol{x}_i \geqq 0$ $(i = 1, \ldots, n)$ such that

$$\sum_{i=1}^{n} \boldsymbol{M}_i \cdot \boldsymbol{x}_i > \boldsymbol{0}, \tag{11.48}$$

which is equivalent to requiring that semi-stationary growth at rate ρ be possible with every good 'over-produced'. Now in every instance so far considered these two requirements have been equivalent, because the possibility of semi-stationary growth at rate γ with every good produced has implied *a fortiori* the possibility of semi-stationary growth, again with every good produced, at any rate less than γ. This is an elementary feature of the linear production model. However, in allowing in productive activities expressed as (11.42) we leave behind the linear production model of ch. 9 and in so doing allow of some new possibilities not encompassed by the linear production model. Among these possibilities is the bizarre occurrence of an economy which is capable of semi-stationary growth at a certain rate but not at every lower rate. The possibility of such a case is indicated by the following example.

Example 11.2. Let there be one good only (called 'stuff') and only one known productive activity. The activity, it will be seen, is rather a peculiar one. In the first week one unit of stuff is invested to start the activity. In the next week a yield of 11 units of stuff is forthcoming. In the third week 38 units of stuff must be invested (there is no option about this). Finally, in the fourth week, there is a yield of 40 units of stuff. Let $\Gamma = 1 + \gamma$ be the growth factor of the system. Growth at rate $\Gamma - 1$ is possible provided that the amount of stuff which is made available in each period is not less than the amount of stuff that is required to be invested. Suppose that the scale of the activity three weeks earlier was 1; then growth at rate $\Gamma - 1$ is possible if

$$-\Gamma^3 + 11\Gamma^2 - 38\Gamma + 40 \geqslant 0 \tag{11.49}$$

or

$$(5-\Gamma)(\Gamma-2)(\Gamma-4) \geqslant 0. \tag{11.50}$$

Hence, the system is capable of semi-stationary growth at a positive rate $\Gamma - 1$ if

$$1 < \Gamma \leqslant 2 \quad \text{or} \quad 3 \leqslant \Gamma \leqslant 4. \tag{11.51}$$

Of course, the manner in which this strange result has been achieved is perfectly transparent. The productive activity taking four weeks to complete is in reality two processes in sequence, each of which invests some output to obtain a greater return one week later. The rate of return on the first investment is 1000% – on the second it is $\frac{100}{19}$%. These two distinct investments are in a given relative proportion, the rate of investment in the second being 38 times as large as the rate of investment in the first. The result (11.50) can be understood in terms of the following account. If the rate of growth is zero, there is a surplus of output over investment requirements, because the sum of outputs is 51 while the sum of inputs is 39. At the other extreme, with rapid rates of growth, but $\Gamma < 4$, there is again a surplus. Here the first stage of the activity carries a predominant weight on account of the fact that the rapid rate of growth implies that most investments will be recent ones. In the middle range of growth rates, however, the surplus disappears. This is because the large second-week-after-investment requirements dominate the outputs of the first and fourth weeks. The key to this 'paradox' is the large requirement of 38 units. This is offset when growth is very slow by the still larger outputs of 40 units and it is dominated when growth is very rapid by the high productivity of the initial stage. In between semi-stationary growth is not possible.

It is evident that the example depends critically upon the assumption that the activity, in a Frankenstein-like manner, cannot be stopped once it is started. On pain of the unutterable, 38 units of stuff must be invested in week 3. Otherwise, one generates an alternative activity which simply invests one unit to obtain 11 units one week later and then stops, whereupon this new activity dominates the old one and growth is possible at any rate up to 1000% (i.e. $\Gamma = 11$).

Thus, while it is not entirely clear that the postulate would be justified – for not every example is as simple as, or shares the same character as, example

11.2 – we might be tempted to add an extra postulate to the effect that semi-stationary growth with every good produced at rate γ implies the possibility of semi-stationary growth, again with every good produced, at a rate less than γ. However, what we need to be able to apply theorem 11.1(b) is that (11.48) may be satisfied. For this we need specifically the possibility of semi-stationary growth at rate ρ with every good produced in excess of requirements. It is for this reason that the statement of the final non-substitution theorem takes a somewhat different shape from those that have gone before.

Theorem 11.5. Let each activity in a linear production model be expressible in the form of (11.42) with each component of $\boldsymbol{b}_t^{ij}$, *except for the ith, not greater than the corresponding component of* $\boldsymbol{a}_{t-1}^{ij}$, $(t = 1, \ldots, T)$. *Then, if the economy is capable of semi-stationary growth at rate* ρ, *with every type of new good produced in excess of input requirements, there exists a unique positive vector* $\boldsymbol{p}$ *satisfying (11.45).*

Proof. On reducing the system to the form of an intermediate case it is seen to be productive in that form so that earlier results apply.

Our investigation of the conditions under which the cost-of-production prices of an economy are determined independently of the structure of final demand, given only the rate of interest if this is positive, has been a lengthy one. It may be useful to summarize the main conditions that have emerged as underlying the non-substitution result. At the very core of every argument leading to such a result there lie three assumptions:

(1) There is only one non-produced good (labour).

(2) Constant returns to scale hold for all productive activities.

(3) There is no 'genuine' joint production.

The meaning of the word 'genuine' in condition (3) has been clarified by the foregoing discussion. It was seen that the existence of durable capital goods does not necessarily imply joint production in the relevant sense, but that the introduction of even this simple feature of reality may well cause trouble for the argument unless the capitals are either assumed to undergo no change during production (or to be made afterwards 'as good as new'), or if capitals were to be immobile between sectors.

Taken together these assumptions are extremely strong and exclude immediately many features of reality. In particular, the actual prices that rule in the world are greatly affected by the prices of many and various natural resources (land, minerals, etc.) to say nothing of decreasing costs. Yet *nothing less will do* as far as the non-substitution result is concerned. Without all these assumptions one is back to considering the solution of the equations which pertain to the state of an economy as one process which cannot be broken down in any meaningful manner into one or more separate steps. In particular, without all these assumptions, the designation even of cost-of-production prices must wait upon a full specification of the economic model and upon the preferences of households that will reflect themselves in the structure of demand.

It remains to give a little more justification for our concentration on cost-of-production prices. The claim was advanced above that these prices could always be the prices of any equilibrium semi-stationary state of an economy for which a non-substitution result could be established, although they might not be the only possible prices. If this proposition is not already obvious, consider a semi-stationary state in which the prices ruling do not all correspond to minimum production costs. Only one type of deviation is possible – one or more prices can be below the costs of production of the goods concerned – in which case, naturally, these goods will not be produced in the semi-stationary state. Now take any price less than the relevant cost of production and increase it until it is equal to the cost of production (which may itself be increasing if the good is used to produce itself; but the price must increase faster). There is no effect from the increase in the price, either on the side of production and choice of technique, or on the side of final demand. No productive activity comes into use which was not previously used, because production costs are either unaffected, or are raised, by a price increase. No productive activity ceases to be profitable which was previously profitable and which was used; for it follows from the fact that this good was not previously produced and that no productive activity which required it was used in the initial state. Finally, on the final demand side, a price increase cannot generate demand where none existed previously. An increase in price can increase demand for a good only through one or other kind of 'income effect'. There are two possibilities. A good might be an inferior good in the consumption of one or more individuals so that the income effect would work against the substitution effect (Hicks, 1946, pp. 32–37); but this cannot happen if the initial consumption of the good is zero as must be the case if the good is not produced, for then the income effect, be it perverse or otherwise, carries no weight. On the other hand, a change in the price of a final product may 'redistribute income' by requiring a change in factor prices and so disturb an equilibrium. But if the price of the good is below its cost of production, and the good is not produced, this last effect is nugatory.

It is fortunate that we have been able to establish that prices may be set equal to costs of production without disturbing equilibrium, for the interpretation of a price less than the cost of production of a good is not entirely clear. If the price is not the actual rate at which the good is traded for the *numeraire* and it is not a quotation of the price at which the good would be produced were there a demand, then what is it? It must be a price called out by an auctioneer. It is a pity to have to invoke the idea of an auctioneer, which was meant to be an idealization and not a description of reality, to have him set parametric prices for inactive markets and to set them below the cost of producing for those markets.

Does the non-substitution idea merit the attention that has been lavished upon it and the labour that must be applied to detail accurately the conditions that give rise to it? It is hard to resist the elegance of the conception, or to fail to feel some surprise and excitement that it generalizes as far as it does. However, surely some of the attraction of the construct lies in its seeming success in bypassing the 'circularity' of post-classical value theory, where everything in the economy must be resolved together and no price, or interest rate, has priority over any other. And some people have surmised in that circularity a problem, a mathematical indeterminacy, a theoretical deficiency. To any such the Cambridge model and the non-substitution theory that underlies the second step, may appear as the resolution of an enigma. But, of course, it is not the fault of non-substitution theory if such mistaken ideas are abroad.

12

The orthodox vision

As the quantity of stock to be lent at interest increases, the interest, or the price which must be paid for the use of that stock, necessarily diminishes, not only from those general causes which make the market price of things commonly diminish as their quantity increases, but from other causes which are peculiar to this particular case. As capitals increase in any country, the profits which can be made by employing them necessarily diminish.

ADAM SMITH, *The Wealth of Nations*

But I was commanded to believe; and yet it corresponded not with what had been established by calculations and my own sight, but was quite contrary.

ST. AUGUSTINE, *Confessions*

We consider an economy moving through time. The economy is characterized broadly by a tendency to saving, meaning that there is a willingness to forgo present consumption, or consumption in the near future, in order to raise consumption later on. We assume that the willingness to save is effective – the desired accumulation actually takes place. According to an ancient idea the accumulation of capital is accompanied by a continuous increase in consumption per capita, by a continuous decline in the rate of interest and by a continuous increase in the real wage rate. We refer to this idea as the *orthodox vision of capital accumulation* or, for short, as the *orthodox vision*.

At first sight it might seem that we have already disposed of the orthodox vision. In ch. 4 we devoted some space to the study of what was there called comparative statics of semi-stationary growth. From that study it emerged that only under very restrictive conditions could one conclude that 'more capital' must necessarily mean a lower rate of interest. Moreover, in ch. 8 we saw that it is perfectly possible for the ranking of stationary states by capital per head (there meaning the chain-index aggregate of capital) to differ from the ranking of stationary states by interest rate – the so-called 'capital reversal'. Then a 'movement' along the production function in the direction of more capital might take us to points corresponding to a higher value of the rate of interest. This is contrary to the orthodox vision. What further need have we of evidence?

If the reader reflects upon this question he will see that there remain some unresolved issues concerning the orthodox vision. The vision concerns what we will call *extended accumulation history*. By this term we will mean the description of the movement of an economy through time; and not just the comparison of some position it might be supposed to attain with some hypothetical initial position, having no regard to the process whereby the economy shifts itself from one state to another. The method of comparative statics by its nature ignores extended accumulation history. Now it might be objected that the orthodox vision was concerned specifically with comparative statics. And it might be adduced as evidence for this view that many economic theorists in the past (notably the Austrian school and Wicksell) have employed the method of comparative statics in an attempt to elucidate the process of capital accumulation through time. Yet it must be conceded that it is illegitimate to treat an economy unfolding an extended accumulation history as if it were passing sequentially through one semi-stationary state after another. There is no reason to believe that this is what such an economy will actually do, or even approximately do. Whenever we see economists in the past (or even today) making use of the method of comparative statics to say something about the process of capital accumulation we may safely assume that this is to be ascribed to primitive analytical technique, and not to a genuine interest in comparative statics and a lack of interest in the actual process of capital accumulation. Hence, if we are to evaluate the orthodox vision from a modern standpoint it behoves us to employ advanced analytical methods to confront directly extended accumulation histories.

An interesting example of a modern discussion of accumulation and comparative statics, and one which is perfectly explicit on the relation between the two, is to be found in the paper by Champernowne (1953–1954). The following passage is taken from that paper:

> Joan Robinson has pointed out that a rigorous discussion of the theory under conditions of steady increase in capital per head would be excessively complicated. However, the interest of a comparison of a sequence of stationary states is due to the presumption that this will give us a first approximation to a comparison of successive positions in a slow process of steady accumulation.

It must be said that this presumption is a very doubtful one. Furthermore, even if it were correct, it would leave unanswered an important question: namely, if the economy passes exactly or approximately through a sequence of stationary states, in what order will it pass through those states? Anyone tempted to answer that, provided that we are considering positive saving, it must pass through in the order of capital intensity as defined by a chain-index measure of capital should think again. The fact that a switch from one stationary state to another would involve an increase in capital per head if the economy could trade at the tie-point prices and make the switch all at once does not obviously imply that the process of changing from one state to the other in an extended accumulation history will involve net saving all along the route, or even on balance. The comparison of stationary states is a totally different exercise from the examination of an extended accumulation history that connects them[1]. Therefore, if we are to say anything at all about the latter topic, we must embark upon a new and independent investigation.

The *locus classicus* of the examination of an exact model of extended accumulation history is the paper on optimum growth by Ramsey (1928)[2]. This paper may be regarded not only as a pioneering venture in describing precisely accumulation through time, which it certainly is, but also as the very embodiment of the orthodox vision, because for the simple model considered by Ramsey the orthodox vision is completely validated. The model originally presented by Ramsey is so formulated that it does not fall into place as a special case of the linear production model. Hence, we will present a simple version of the Ramsey model more in accord with the assumptions adopted so far. The theory of optimal growth is a large area involving many models and problems. No attempt at a complete treatment is to be undertaken here. In fact, we are merely interested in the character of the solution to the model for the purpose of comparisons with the solutions to further models.

We assume that there is only one produced good, called 'stuff'. There are a finite number of linear activities each of which has the same general form. Thus, the ith activity ($i = 1, \ldots, M$) is

$$1 \text{ labour time} \oplus \alpha_i \text{ stuff} \ominus \beta_i \text{ stuff}. \tag{12.1}$$

---

[1] Thus, regretfully, one cannot accept Champernowne's (1953–1954) intriguing account of what will occur should capital accumulation take place in an economy subject to a 'capital reversal'. He writes:

'Suppose now, that instead of comparing stationary states, we are considering a sequence of states in time. If we conceive of the rise in food-wages and the accompanying fall in the rate of interest as being caused by a steady process of net investment, with all labour employed, it is interesting to consider what would happen next when a further rise in real wages and a fall in the rate of interest would make competitive only equipment with a lower productivity and employing *more* men per unit quantity, and thus requiring negative net investment. Presumably, the only way that investment would remain positive without a prolonged interval of disinvestment would be for food-wages to leap up and the rate of interest to leap down to levels where capital equipment even more productive than that in existence became competitive.'

[2] The massive revival of interest in this area during the 1960s gave rise to a literature so extensive that no attempt will be made here to cite references. A good selected bibliography is to be found in a companion volume to the present one, Hadley and Kemp (1971).

We may as well suppose that our schedule of activities has been sorted and that we are presented only with the efficient set. This means that for activities in the list

$$\alpha_i > \alpha_j \Rightarrow \beta_i > \beta_j \qquad (i, j = 1, \ldots, M). \tag{12.2}$$

Moreover, all the α_i coefficients are different. Finally, assume that the sorting of activities has eliminated all blended activities, i.e. no activity in the list is a convex combination of another pair in the list. Denote by $\boldsymbol{a}$ the M vector whose ith component is α_i, and by $\boldsymbol{b}$ the M vector whose ith component is β_i.

Stuff is consumable and the consumption of stuff in week t will be denoted $C_t (C_t \geqslant 0)$. For the sake of simplicity, which is what interests us here rather than generality, we suppose that one unit of labour time is available each week, no more and no less. We thus abstract from population growth and from the work-leisure decision and the disutility of effort[3]. Now whenever we refer to consumption we will be referring also to consumption per head. The utility to be had from a consumption of C_t in week t is $U(C_t)$, which does not depend directly on t and which is independent of consumption in other weeks. Both these are strong assumptions but both are helpful to our present purposes. U is a strictly concave differentiable function. Hence, the marginal utility of consumption declines as the level of consumption increases. The total utility, discounted, from a development which yields consumption $\{C_1, C_2, \ldots, C_t, \ldots\}$ is

$$\sum_{t=1}^{\infty} U(C_t)\left(\frac{1}{1+\sigma}\right)^{t-1}, \qquad \sigma > 0, \tag{12.3}$$

where σ is the constant rate at which future utility is discounted, *the degree of impatience*[4].

By imposing a positive degree of impatience we side-step, in the present context, all the awkward 'existence' problems to which Ramsey's theory gave rise. Thus, we must have

$$C_t \leqslant \max_i \beta_i = \beta^*, \tag{12.4}$$

because the level of consumption can never exceed the maximum gross output

[3] Ramsey (1928) did not abstract from the disutility of effort, but later writers have nearly always done so; largely no doubt because not much of extra interest emerges from allowing labour time to be a choice variable.

[4] Sometimes called, not very happily, the rate of time discount. There is an ambiguity in the use of that term. What σ measures is the rate at which future utilities are discounted, which will frequently not be the same as the rates at which consumptions are discounted.

of stuff producible. Thence

$$\sum_{t=1}^{\infty} U(C_t)\left(\frac{1}{1+\sigma}\right)^{t-1} \leqslant \sum_{t=1}^{\infty} U(\beta^*)\left(\frac{1}{1+\sigma}\right)^{t-1} = U(\beta^*)\frac{1+\sigma}{\sigma}, \tag{12.5}$$

so that the infinite sum (12.3) is bounded above. This is useful if, as it happens to be, we want to choose the development so as to maximize discounted utility.

Let the initial stock of stuff be K_0. Denote by $\boldsymbol{x}_t$ the M vector of activity levels for week t. The ith component of $\boldsymbol{x}_{it}$ $(i = 1, \ldots, M)$ will be x_{it}. Let $\boldsymbol{v}$ be an M vector each of whose elements is 1. Our version of the Ramsey problem takes the form:

choose $\{C_1, C_2, \ldots, C_t, \ldots\}$ so as to maximize

$$\sum_{t=1}^{\infty} U(C_t)\left(\frac{1}{1+\sigma}\right)^{t-1} \tag{12.6}$$

subject to

$$\boldsymbol{a}\cdot\boldsymbol{x}_t + C_t \leqslant \boldsymbol{b}\cdot\boldsymbol{x}_{t-1}, \qquad t = 2, 3, \ldots \tag{12.7}$$

$$\boldsymbol{a}\cdot\boldsymbol{x}_1 + C_1 \leqslant K_0, \tag{12.8}$$

$$\boldsymbol{v}\cdot\boldsymbol{x}_t \leqslant 1, \qquad t = 1, 2, \ldots \tag{12.9}$$

and

$$\boldsymbol{x}_t \geqq \boldsymbol{0}, \qquad C_t \geqslant 0, \qquad t = 1, 2, \ldots. \tag{12.10}$$

The programme (12.6)–(12.10) always has a solution and this solution is unique. That there exists a feasible sequence $\{C_1, C_2, \ldots, C_t, \ldots\}$ such that (12.6) attains its maximum is easily seen as follows. The value of (12.6) is a continuous function[5] of the sequence $\{C_1, C_2, \ldots, C_t, \ldots\}$, since U is a continuous function. However, conditions (12.7)–(12.10) confine $\{C_1, C_2, \ldots, C_t, \ldots\}$ to a compact set. Hence, (12.6) attains a maximum[6].

Because U is a strictly concave function the maximizing solution to (12.6)–(12.10) must be unique. For the sequences $\{C_1, \ldots, C_t, \ldots\}$ satisfying (12.7)–(12.10) form a convex set. Thus if two distinct consumption sequences were

[5] To define continuity relative to infinite sequences of the form $\{C_1, C_2, \ldots, C_t, \ldots\}$ choose as closed sets those induced by the following metric. The distance between $\{C_1, \ldots, C_t, \ldots\}$ and $\{C'_1, \ldots, C'_t, \ldots\}$ is the least upper bound of the set of real numbers $\{|C_1 - C'_1|, |C_2 - C'_2|, \ldots, |C_t - C'_t|, \ldots\}$. Since each C_t is bounded below by zero and above by β^* (see (12.4)) this least upper bound exists.

[6] Thus we dispose in the present simple case of the existence problem which forms such an important part of the theory of optimal growth. We want here to take avoiding action because the form of the solution and not the existence of the solution is our major concern.

both to maximize (12.6) a convex combination of these sequences would be feasible and would give rise to a larger value of (12.6). Hence, the two distinct sequences from which the convex combination was formed cannot be maximizing.

We apply a type of approach known as dynamic programming (Bellman, 1957). A necessary condition for a feasible sequence $\{C_1, C_2, \ldots, C_t, \ldots\}$ to solve the problem (12.6)–(12.10) is that the first T terms of that sequence should solve the problem of obtaining maximum discounted utility for the first T weeks subject to having at least the stock of stuff at the beginning of week $T+1$ as is provided by the supposed optimal solution. This is called by Bellman the *principle of optimality*. Formally, $\{C_1, C_2, \ldots, C_T\}$ must solve:

choose $\{C_1, C_2, \ldots, C_T\}$ so as to maximize

$$\sum_{t=1}^{T} U(C_t)\left(\frac{1}{1+\sigma}\right)^{t-1} \tag{12.11}$$

subject to

$$\boldsymbol{a}\cdot\boldsymbol{x}_t + C_t \leqslant \boldsymbol{b}\cdot\boldsymbol{x}_{t-1}, \qquad t = 2, 3, \ldots, T; \tag{12.12}$$

$$\boldsymbol{a}\cdot\boldsymbol{x}_1 + C_1 \leqslant K_0; \tag{12.13}$$

$$\boldsymbol{b}\cdot\boldsymbol{x}_T \geqslant K_{T+1}, \tag{12.14}$$

$$\boldsymbol{v}\cdot\boldsymbol{x}_t \leqslant 1, \qquad t = 1, \ldots, T \tag{12.15}$$

and

$$\boldsymbol{x}_t \geqq \boldsymbol{0}, \qquad C_t \geqslant 0, \qquad t = 1, \ldots, T, \tag{12.16}$$

where K_{T+1} is the stock of stuff made available at the start of week $T+1$ by the supposed optimal solution to (12.6)–(12.10).

The programme (12.11)–(12.16) gives rise to a Lagrangian form

$$\sum_{t=1}^{T} U(C_t)\left(\frac{1}{1+\sigma}\right)^{t-1} + \pi_1(K_0 - \boldsymbol{a}\cdot\boldsymbol{x}_1 - C_1) + \sum_{t=2}^{T} \pi_t(\boldsymbol{b}\cdot\boldsymbol{x}_{t-1} - \boldsymbol{a}\cdot\boldsymbol{x}_t - C_t)$$
$$+ \pi_{T+1}(\boldsymbol{b}\cdot\boldsymbol{x}_T - K_{T+1}) + \sum_{t=1}^{T} \omega_t(1 + \boldsymbol{v}\cdot\boldsymbol{x}_t). \tag{12.17}$$

Thence we may derive necessary conditions for a maximum. Denote by u_t the marginal utility of consumption in week t, i.e.

$$u_t = (\mathrm{d}U/\mathrm{d}C)_{C=C_t}. \tag{12.18}$$

Then, because (12.17) must be stationary with respect to the C_t values, we will have

$$u_t\left(\frac{1}{1+\sigma}\right)^{t-1} - \pi_t \leqslant 0 \quad \text{comp } C_t \geqslant 0, \qquad t = 1, \ldots, T. \tag{12.19}$$

If we assume that C_t will always be positive, as seems reasonable, we will have

$$u_t\left(\frac{1}{1+\sigma}\right)^{t-1} = \pi_t, \qquad t=1,\ldots,T. \tag{12.20}$$

The shadow prices π_t will measure the marginal contributions of consumption to discounted utility. Next, because (12.17) must be stationary with respect to the components of the activity vectors, we will have

$$\pi_{t+1}\boldsymbol{b} - \pi_t \boldsymbol{a} - \omega_t \boldsymbol{v} \leqq \boldsymbol{0} \quad \text{comp} \quad \boldsymbol{x}_t \geqq \boldsymbol{0}, \qquad t=1,\ldots,T. \tag{12.21}$$

Compare these conditions to (10.13) and (10.14) of ch. 10. It will be seen now that the development which solves (12.6)–(12.10) must be a production-price equilibrium with π_t the present value of stuff in week t and ω_t the present value of labour time in week t. The same π_t values must be the marginal contributions of consumption to discounted utility.

From (12.21) we may infer at once the following conclusion.

Theorem 12.1. Not more than two activities will be used in the course of one week.

Proof. Suppose, contrary to this assertion, that three activities are used in week t. Without loss of generality, let these activities be numbered 1, 2 and 3, and let $\alpha_1 > \alpha_2 > \alpha_3$. From (12.21) we have

$$\begin{aligned} &\pi_{t+1}\beta_1 - \pi_t\alpha_1 - \omega_t = 0, \qquad \pi_{t+1}\beta_2 - \pi_t\alpha_2 - \omega_t = 0, \\ &\pi_{t+1}\beta_3 - \pi_t\alpha_3 - \omega_t = 0. \end{aligned} \tag{12.22}$$

Let λ be chosen to satisfy

$$\lambda\alpha_1 + (1+\lambda)\alpha_3 = \alpha_2, \qquad 0 < \lambda < 1. \tag{12.23}$$

Now,

$$\pi_{t+1}[\lambda\beta_1 + (1-\lambda)\beta_3] - \pi_t[\lambda\alpha_1 + (1-\lambda)\alpha_3] - \omega_t = 0, \tag{12.24}$$

from (12.22). Hence,

$$\pi_{t+1}[\lambda\beta_1 + (1-\lambda)\beta_3] - \pi_t\alpha_2 - \omega_t = 0. \tag{12.25}$$

Thus,

$$\lambda\beta_1 + (1-\lambda)\beta_3 = \beta_2, \tag{12.26}$$

so that the activity numbered 2 is a blended activity, contrary to assumption.

Suppose for the sake of simplicity that $C_t > 0$, all t (we could choose U so that this condition would be satisfied automatically). Then (12.20) will apply for each t. Thence, we will obtain

$$\frac{u_{t+1}}{u_t}\left(\frac{1}{1+\sigma}\right)=\frac{\pi_{t+1}}{\pi_t}. \tag{12.27}$$

In week t at least one activity is used. Denote the coefficients of one such an activity by $\bar{\alpha}^t$ and $\bar{\beta}^t$. Let $\tilde{\alpha}$ and $\tilde{\beta}$ be the coefficients of alternative activities. Then, from (12.21),

$$\pi_{t+1}\bar{\beta}^t - \pi_t\bar{\alpha}^t - \omega_t = 0$$

and (12.28)

$$\pi_{t+1}\tilde{\beta} - \pi_t\tilde{\alpha} - \omega_t \leqslant 0.$$

Hence,

$$\pi_{t+1}(\tilde{\beta}-\bar{\beta}^t) - \pi_t(\tilde{\alpha}-\bar{\alpha}^t) \leqslant 0 \tag{12.29}$$

or

$$\left[\frac{\tilde{\beta}-\bar{\beta}^t}{\tilde{\alpha}-\bar{\alpha}^t}\right]_{(\tilde{\alpha}>\bar{\alpha}^t)} \leqslant \frac{\pi_t}{\pi_{t+1}} \leqslant \left[\frac{\tilde{\beta}-\bar{\beta}^t}{\tilde{\alpha}-\bar{\alpha}^t}\right]_{(\tilde{\alpha}<\bar{\alpha}^t)}. \tag{12.30}$$

Combining (12.27) and (12.30) we obtain

$$\left[\frac{\tilde{\beta}-\bar{\beta}^t}{\tilde{\alpha}-\bar{\alpha}^t}\right]_{(\tilde{\alpha}>\bar{\alpha}^t)} \leqslant \frac{u_t}{u_{t+1}}(1+\sigma) \leqslant \left[\frac{\tilde{\beta}-\bar{\beta}^t}{\tilde{\alpha}-\bar{\alpha}^t}\right]_{(\tilde{\alpha}<\bar{\alpha}^t)}. \tag{12.31}$$

Condition (12.31) is an important one to which a diagrammatic interpretation can be given. In fig. 12.1 the heavy lines show the graph of the function relating the maximum gross output of stuff that may be obtained, with employment not exceeding one unit, to the input of stuff available. This is the production function for the present case, but note that the output is gross and not net of the input. Let X be the input of stuff and Y the maximum feasible output. Then our function Φ is defined by

$$Y=\Phi(X)=\max_{\substack{\boldsymbol{v}\cdot\boldsymbol{x}\leqslant 1\\ \boldsymbol{a}\cdot\boldsymbol{x}\leqslant X}} \boldsymbol{b}\cdot\boldsymbol{x}. \tag{12.32}$$

Suppose that production in week t is confined to the use of the activity whose input–output coefficients (α_i, β_i) are represented by point E in fig. 12.1. Then the condition (12.31) is depicted. A tangent to the graph of the function with slope $(u_t/u_{t+1})(1+\sigma)$ must meet the graph at E. According to theorem 12.1 production may take place with two basic activities involved. In that case the point of production would be on one of the flats of the graph and the slope of this flat would have to equal $(u_t/u_{t+1})(1+\sigma)$. In fig. 12.1 we have marked

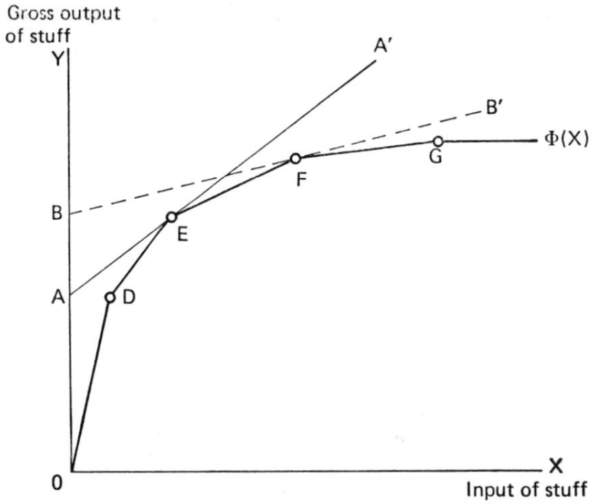

Fig. 12.1.

as a broken line a tangent to the graph of slope $(1+\sigma)$. Let $\mathscr{F}$ be the set of points on the graph of $\Phi(X)$ at which a supporting tangent line of gradient $(1+\sigma)$ meets the graph. It can be seen at once that if the point at which production takes place (E) is to the left of $\mathscr{F}$ (which may be a whole flat) then $u_t/u_{t+1} > 1$; while if E is to the right of $\mathscr{F}$ we must have $u_t/u_{t+1} < 1$. Since u_t is the marginal utility of consumption at t and since it is smaller the larger is C_t we reach an important conclusion which is stated as theorem 12.2.

Theorem 12.2. Either there exists a pure activity (α^*, β^*), *or there exists a pair of adjacent pure activities* (α^*, β^*) *and* $(\alpha^{**}, \beta^{**})$ *with* $\alpha^* < \alpha^{**}$, *such that if production involves the use of the activity* (α_t, β_t) *in week t, then*

$$C_{t+1} > C_t \quad \text{whenever } \alpha_t < \alpha^*$$

and (12.33)

$$C_{t+1} < C_t \quad \text{whenever } \alpha > \alpha^{**},$$

where 'α^{**}*' above is to be read '*α^**' if the condition is satisfied by the existence of one activity.*

From theorem 12.2 it may now be seen that the form of the solution to our version of the Ramsey problem is as follows. If the total quantity of stuff used for production is less than a certain critical value α^* then consumption will increase week by week as long as this situation pertains. It follows that the stock used for production must increase week by week, for the reader will readily convince himself that if consumption increases and the level of input of stuff does not increase, then it must fall and fall at an increasing rate. This will eventually make it impossible to satisfy the conditions for an optimal solution. Similarly, if consumption declines then the stock of stuff must decline, and this will occur whenever the stock of stuff used in production exceeds a certain critical value α^{**}, where $\alpha^{**} \geqslant \alpha^{*}$.

To tie up the loose ends of the argument we must note that we have not so far ruled out the possibility that the stock of stuff used in production will 'overshoot' $\mathscr{F}$, say starting below $\mathscr{F}$ but going above it. All that we have shown is that if this happens then consumption must first rise and then fall. However, we can now establish that the solution will not pass from one side of $\mathscr{F}$ to the other. In order to show the result we first establish another result which is of importance and interest in its own right.

The solution to (12.6)–(12.10) is unique and it depends, given the form of the problem, only on the parameter K_0. Hence, in particular, C_1 is a function of K_0. Moreover, the optimal development must be an optimal development starting in any week t and regarding the then available stock K_t as the initial endowment. Since the form of the problem is the same looking forward from week t as it is from week 1, the rate of consumption C_t must depend uniquely (and independently of t) on the stock K_t available for consumption and use as input. Denote this relationship by a function $C(K)$. Suppose that for $K = K^*$ there exists a value $C^* > 0$ such that

$$\begin{aligned}&\text{(i) } K^* - C^* \in \{X \mid \Phi(X) \in \mathscr{F}\};\\&\text{(ii) } \Phi(K^* - C^*) = K^*.\end{aligned} \tag{12.34}$$

That is, starting from $K_0 = K^*$ a stationary state is feasible with the production point located in $\mathscr{F}$. We may then show the following result.

Theorem 12.3. Let C^* and K^* satisfy (12.34). Then $C^* = C(K^*)$ and $\{C^*, C^*, \ldots, C^*, \ldots\}$ is the optimal development starting from $K_0 = K^*$.

Proof. Since $u(C_t) = u(C^*)$ all t for the stationary solution the prices for that solution $\{\pi_1^*, \pi_2^*, \ldots, \pi_t^*, \ldots\}$ satisfy

$$\pi_t^* = u(C^*)\left(\frac{1}{1+\sigma}\right)^{t-1}, \tag{12.35}$$

from (12.20). Hence, limit as $T \to \infty$ $\pi_T^* = 0$ and since $\boldsymbol{b} \cdot \boldsymbol{x}_T$ is bounded above by β^* it follows that condition (10.33) of ch. 10 is satisfied and this path has the property that it maximizes the present value of consumption. Suppose that there exists a consumption sequence, feasible starting from $K_0 = K^*$, and denoted $\{\tilde{C}_1, \tilde{C}_2, \ldots, \tilde{C}_t, \ldots\}$, such that

$$\sum_{t=1}^{\infty} U(\tilde{C}_t)\left(\frac{1}{1+\sigma}\right)^{t-1} > \sum_{t=1}^{\infty} U(C^*)\left(\frac{1}{1+\sigma}\right)^{t-1}. \tag{12.36}$$

Since U is a strictly concave function we have

$$R_t = u(C^*)(\tilde{C}_t - C^*) - [U(\tilde{C}_t) - U(C^*)] \geqslant 0, \tag{12.37}$$

and for $\tilde{C}_t \neq C^*$, $R_t > 0$. Hence, from (12.36) and (12.37),

$$\sum_{t=1}^{\infty} [U(\tilde{C}_t) - U(C^*)]\left(\frac{1}{1+\sigma}\right)^{t-1} = \sum_{t=1}^{\infty} [u(C^*)(\tilde{C}_t - C^*) - R_t]\left(\frac{1}{1+\sigma}\right)^{t-1} > 0. \tag{12.38}$$

It follows that

$$\sum_{t=1}^{\infty} [u(C^*)(\tilde{C}_t - C^*)]\left(\frac{1}{1+\sigma}\right)^{t-1} > \sum_{t=1}^{\infty} R_t\left(\frac{1}{1+\sigma}\right)^{t-1} > 0 \tag{12.39}$$

or

$$\sum_{t=1}^{\infty} u(C^*)(\tilde{C}_t - C^*)\left(\frac{1}{1+\sigma}\right)^{t-1} > 0. \tag{12.40}$$

The above implies, taking into account (12.20), that

$$\sum_{t=1}^{\infty} \pi_t^*(\tilde{C}_t - C^*) > 0, \tag{12.41}$$

which contradicts the present value maximizing property. This completes the proof.

We know now that stationary states in $\mathscr{F}$ are optimal developments in the sense that they provide solutions to the optimal growth problem (12.6)–(12.10). This is the particular result that we need here and now. However, the interested reader may care to note that the proof of theorem 12.3 works just as well where any development is concerned, not necessarily a stationary development in $\mathscr{F}$, to show that a development satisfying all the necessary conditions (12.19) and (12.21) will be an optimal development.

Let $\mathscr{F}$ comprise the line segment connecting (α_0, β_0) to (α^0, β^0) where these points may coincide. Where the points differ let $\alpha^0 > \alpha_0$. Take any point in $\mathscr{F}$ denoted $(\bar{\alpha}, \bar{\beta})$ to which there corresponds a stationary state consumption rate $\bar{C} = \bar{\beta} - \bar{\alpha}$. Now consider, for example, the development that crosses $\mathscr{F}$ from below. At the beginning of week t it has a stock less than β_0. At the beginning of week $t+1$ it has a stock greater than β^0. It must cross $\mathscr{F}$ in 'one hop' like this because we know that from a point in $\mathscr{F}$ the unique optimal development remains in $\mathscr{F}$ (theorem 12.3). Hence, given a larger stock, $\bar{\beta}$ in place of something less, at the start of week t, the optimal path ploughs back less into production, i.e. it not only consumes more from a larger stock but more than the increase in the stock. We will show that this is impossible.

Theorem 12.4. The function $C(K)$ relating optimal consumption to the available stock satisfies

$$[C(K_2) - C(K_1)]/(K_2 - K_1) < 1, \qquad K_2 \neq K_1. \tag{12.42}$$

The 'marginal' propensity to consume out of stock is less than 1.

Proof. The unique solution sequence $\{C_1, C_2, \ldots, C_t, \ldots\}$ depends, given the structure of the optimal growth problem, on K_0. Hence, the maximized value of discounted utility depends also upon K_0. We denote this relation by a function $V(K)$.

Obviously $V(K)$ is a non-decreasing function. It is also concave[7]. It is evident that the following equation is satisfied identically:

$$V(K) = U[C(K)] + \left(\frac{1}{1+\sigma}\right) V[\Phi\{K - C(K)\}]. \tag{12.43}$$

The valuation of a stock K is the utility of the immediate consumption to which it will give rise plus the discounted valuation of the stock that will arise from using the remainder as input. Since V and Φ are both concave functions, the second term in the right-hand side of (12.43) is a concave function of $K - C(K)$.[8] Because $V(K)$ is the maximized valuation of the stock K, and $C(K)$ the unique optimal consumption rate, it follows that any alteration in $C(K)$ would make the right-hand side of (12.43) smaller. Let $W(X) = V[\Phi(X)]$ and denote the left- and right-hand derivatives of W by, respectively, W'_{LH} and W'_{RH}. These derivatives exist because W is a concave function. For the right-hand side of (12.43) to be maximized by $C(K)$ we must have

$$W'_{\text{RH}}[K - C(K)] \leqslant u[C(K)] \leqslant W'_{\text{LH}}[K - C(K)]. \tag{12.44}$$

---

[7] Let $\{C_1^1, C_2^1, \ldots, C_t^1, \ldots\}$ be the solution starting from K_0^1, and let this sequence give the value $V(K_0^1)$ to (12.6). Let $\{C_1^2, C_2^2, \ldots, C_t^2, \ldots\}$ be the solution starting from K_0^2 and giving the value $V(K_0^2)$ to (12.6). Then

$$\{\lambda C_1^1 + (1-\lambda) C_1^2, \lambda C_2^1 + (1-\lambda) C_2^2, \ldots, \lambda C_t^1 + (1-\lambda) C_t^2, \ldots\}$$

is feasible starting from $\lambda K_0^1 + (1-\lambda) K_0^2$, for all λ such that $0 < \lambda < 1$ and gives to (12.6) a value at least as great as $\lambda V(K_0^1) + (1-\lambda) V(K_0^2)$ (because U is a concave function). Hence, the best feasible sequence starting from $\lambda K_0^1 + (1-\lambda) K_0^2$ must do at least as well.

[8] The reader might check the validity of this statement as an exercise.

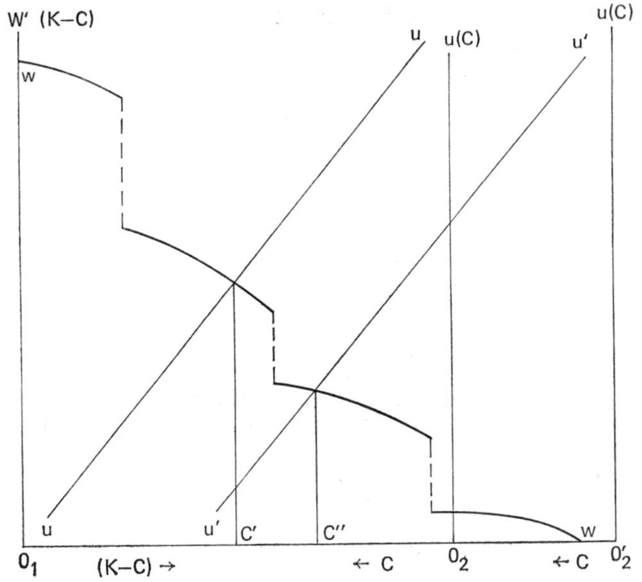

Fig. 12.2.

Our conclusion can be obtained immediately from the above condition and here fig. 12.2 is useful. For the time being consider only the box with base $0_1 0_2$ and ignore the region to the right of 0_2 and the curve marked *u′u′*. The distance between 0_1 and 0_2 is equal to *K*. Hence, a point on the line $0_1 0_2$ divides the total stock available between consumption *C* and input to production $K - C$. *C* is measured from 0_2 going leftwards. Hence, $u(C)$, the marginal utility of consumption, declines as one goes towards 0_1. The curvature of the $u(C)$ schedule is unclear and unimportant, depending as it does on the sign of the third derivative of the utility function. The schedule has therefore been depicted as a straight line *uu* for the sake of simplicity. The other curve *ww* depicts $W'[K - C]$. Where *W* is differentiable it is drawn as the continuous declining curve – the broken segments indicate corners in the function where left- and right-hand derivatives differ. Condition (12.44) is satisfied where the two curves, *ww* and *uu*, intersect. This is at $C = C'$.

Figure 12.2 may be used to evaluate the effect of an increase in *K*. To illustrate this simply shift the right-hand origin for *C* to the right so as to increase the distance $0_1 0_2$ to $0_1 0_2'$. The curve *uu* is carried to the right with its origin and becomes *u′u′*. Consumption increases from $0_2 C'$ to $0_2' C''$. The input to production increases from $0_1 C'$ to $0_1 C''$. It is clear that this is what will generally occur given the form of the curves. What is perfectly clear is that the increase in consumption cannot exceed the increase in stock $0_2 0_2'$. For that to happen the point of intersection between the curves would have to shift towards 0_1 and this cannot occur. Thus, or by an equivalent algebraic argument, we may derive from condition (12.44) the result of the theorem.

It only remains now to collect together the results that have been established and assess their consequences for the form of a Ramsey optimal development in our one-good model. It has been shown that if the initial stock K_0 allows a stationary development in $\mathscr{F}$ then this is the optimal development. If the initial stock falls short of that requirement then consumption and the gross output will both increase monotonically. If the initial stock exceeds that required for any stationary development in $\mathscr{F}$ then consumption and the gross output will both decline monotonically. It is clear now that all optimal developments tend to $\mathscr{F}$, for if this did not happen C_t would approach a limit not equal to the consumption rate of any stationary development in $\mathscr{F}$, the ratio $(u_t/u_{t+1})(1+\sigma)$ would tend to $(1+\sigma)$ and (12.31) would eventually be violated.

Consider now the implications for the development of prices. Suppose, for the sake of definiteness, that C_t and K_t are increasing over time towards $\mathscr{F}$ (i.e. we have optimal capital accumulation). Now an inspection of (12.30) immediately indicates that π_t/π_{t+1} will decline over time, so that $(\pi_t/\pi_{t+1}) - 1$ must decline. *The rate of interest falls as capital accumulation proceeds.* We know from the argument of ch. 8, of which we have here a special case, that as we move up the production function the wage rate (the intercept on the net output axis) will increase. Hence, here, in particular, we may conclude that *the wage rate in terms of current stuff rises as capital accumulation proceeds.* What we have here in short is a model for which the orthodox vision is completely valid.

Of course, from one point of view we need not be surprised that the orthodox vision is validated for this very simple model. It is a simple model and it is one which is devoid of paradoxical features in the context of comparative statics. However, it is worth taking note that the validation of the orthodox vision for this model has not been trivial, and it has occupied many pages, which pages include some quite intricate arguments. Usually the conclusion is arrived at more straightforwardly because the problem is formulated with a continuous and differentiable production function and in continuous time. In our period analysis, and starting from a finite set of linear activities, there is rather more arguing to be done. Nevertheless, there it is, optimal accumulation conforms fully to the orthodox vision.

Now the argument so far, lengthy as it has been, is no more than a prologue to the discussion of the wider question of the validity of the orthodox vision in the context of the general linear model of ch. 9. However, the reader will no doubt be grateful for the fact that he will be spared a discussion as lengthy, and possibly as tedious, as the argument above. We can dispose fairly briefly of the question of whether the orthodox vision is valid in the general linear production model. We will discover that the vision is not valid in the more general case. But it is invalid as much because it is inapplicable as because it is false. The simple vision of capital accumulation of which the Ramsey model provides a notable example is not a vision with which optimal capital accumulation is generally in accord, and it is not just that the vision is wrong, it is more than that. The vision incorporates a term which in general cannot be interpreted: the reference is to the rate of interest.

In generalizing the Ramsey model to treat of many goods let us hold to the assumption that only one good is consumed, and let it be good 1, the good represented by the first element of the commodity vectors. Let $\boldsymbol{u}^1$ be a vector with first element 1 and all other elements zero. The general problem of optimal growth takes the following form:

choose $\{C_1, C_2, \ldots, C_t, \ldots\}$ so as to maximize

$$\sum_{t=1}^{\infty} U(C_t)\left(\frac{1}{1+\sigma}\right)^{t-1} \tag{12.45}$$

subject to

$$\boldsymbol{A}\cdot\boldsymbol{x}_t + \boldsymbol{u}^1 C_t \leqq \boldsymbol{B}\cdot\boldsymbol{x}_{t-1}, \qquad t = 2, 3, \ldots \tag{12.46}$$

$$\boldsymbol{A}\cdot\boldsymbol{x}_1 + \boldsymbol{u}^1 C_1 \leqq \boldsymbol{k}_0, \tag{12.47}$$

$$\boldsymbol{v}\cdot\boldsymbol{x}_t \leqslant 1, \qquad t = 1, 2, \ldots \tag{12.48}$$

and

$$\boldsymbol{x}_t \geqq \boldsymbol{0}, \qquad C_t \geqslant 0. \tag{12.49}$$

Compare this formulation to (12.6)–(12.10) which will be seen to be a special case.

We may now proceed as before, and briefly since the approach is now familiar, to derive necessary conditions for a solution to (12.45)–(12.49). Again, applying the Bellman principle of optimality, we seek to maximize a Lagrangian form

$$\begin{aligned}\sum_{t=1}^{T} U(C_t)\left(\frac{1}{1+\sigma}\right)^{t-1} &+ \boldsymbol{p}_1\cdot\{\boldsymbol{k}_0 - \boldsymbol{A}\cdot\boldsymbol{x}_1 - \boldsymbol{u}^1 C_1\} \\ &+ \sum_{t=2}^{T} \boldsymbol{p}_t\cdot\{\boldsymbol{B}\cdot\boldsymbol{x}_{t=1} - \boldsymbol{A}\cdot\boldsymbol{x}_t - \boldsymbol{u}^1 C_t\} \\ &+ \boldsymbol{p}_{T+1}\cdot\{\boldsymbol{B}\cdot\boldsymbol{x}_T - \boldsymbol{k}_{T+1}\} + \sum_{t=1}^{T} \omega_t(1 - \boldsymbol{v}\cdot\boldsymbol{x}_t).\end{aligned} \tag{12.50}$$

Hence, we obtain the following necessary conditions for a solution, denoting by π_t the first element of the vector $\boldsymbol{p}_t$:

$$u_t\left(\frac{1}{1+\sigma}\right)^{t-1} - \pi_t \leqslant 0 \quad \text{comp} \quad C_t \geqslant 0, \qquad t = 1,\ldots,T; \tag{12.51}$$

$$\boldsymbol{p}_{t+1}\cdot\boldsymbol{B} - \boldsymbol{p}_t\cdot\boldsymbol{A} - \omega_t\boldsymbol{v} \leqq \boldsymbol{0} \quad \text{comp} \quad \boldsymbol{x}_t \geqq \boldsymbol{0}, \qquad t = 1,\ldots,T. \tag{12.52}$$

Compare these results to (12.20) and (12.21). It will be seen that the conclusion is clear and the same. A development which solves (12.45)–(12.49) must be a production price equilibrium with the present price of consumption in week t equal to the marginal contribution of consumption to discounted utility in week t.

We may now ask under what conditions and to what extent an optimal development for the problem (12.45)–(12.49) satisfies the description of capital accumulation which is the orthodox vision. There are two difficulties in the way of providing a clear and decisive response to this question. In the first place, as we have had reason to remark and underline above, the rate of interest is not a legitimate concept outside the particular and special conditions of semi-stationary growth with a constant-rate-of-interest price system. The orthodox vision includes the statement that the rate of interest will decline as capital accumulation proceeds. Strictly, in the present case, that statement cannot be interpreted. We have a whole structure of interest rates, even in one week, not a single rate of interest. Which rate of interest should decline to validate the orthodox vision? The question is otiose. One might seize upon the own-rate of interest of the consumption good, taking advantage of the fact that we happen to have taken a problem with a single consumption good. Is this the rate of interest that should decline? What meaning can one attach to such a question? All that one can reasonably say with regard to the rate of interest is that as a description of an optimal development in a model with the technology of ch. 9 the orthodox vision fails to make sense.

A second difficulty stands in the way of elucidating the question of whether the orthodox vision has any validity for the problem to hand. Consider the orthodox vision as excluding certain 'paradoxical' or 'irregular' features (it is hard to find a wholly satisfactory substitute for the words in quotes). The reference is to such possibilities as the time path of consumption not proving to be monotonic, or to a period during which capital per head in constant prices declines, being followed by a period during which capital per head rises. Now the existence of apparently parallel features in the study of comparative dynamics is wholly irrelevant to the question of how, or when, or with what likelihood, such features will arise in the case of extended accumulation histories of an optimal type. The questions are unconnected: the answer to one gives no guidance at all as to the answer to the other[9]. It may by now be unnecessary to argue the point that comparative dynamics is not extended accumulation history. However, the difference can be underlined forcefully by the consideration of a particular point. Suppose that we could show, as we were able to do in the case of the simple Ramsey model, that the optimal growth problem (12.45)–(12.49) had a unique solution depending only upon the vector of initial endowments $\boldsymbol{k}_0$.[10] Then we could express consumption and the activity vector as functions of the total available stock $\boldsymbol{k}$ as

$$C = C(\boldsymbol{k}) \quad \text{and} \quad \boldsymbol{x} = \boldsymbol{x}(\boldsymbol{k}). \tag{12.53}$$

Suppose that the rate of interest really were a proxy for time as Champernowne suggested. Consider the phenomenon of double switching with which we became acquainted in ch. 8, and again in ch. 10. Where this phenomenon manifests itself a certain state of the economy corresponds to a particular value of the rate of interest: it vanishes when the rate of interest is higher only to reappear (the exact same state) when the rate of interest is higher still. Could it happen in an extended accumulation history, optimal in the sense of Ramsey, that the economy would reach a particular state, that later it would have left this state, but later still it would have returned to it? Well, suppose that we have just such an outcome. Let the initial state be one in which the vector of available resources is $\bar{\boldsymbol{k}}$. Let the week for which we begin our tale be week 1. In imagining that the economy might come 'full circle' back to the original state we are imagining that there might exist some T so that the following conditions would be satisfied:

$$\begin{aligned} \boldsymbol{k}_2 &= \boldsymbol{B}\cdot\boldsymbol{x}(\bar{\boldsymbol{k}}_1), \\ \boldsymbol{k}_3 &= \boldsymbol{B}\cdot\boldsymbol{x}(\boldsymbol{k}_2), \\ &\cdots \\ \boldsymbol{k}_T &= \boldsymbol{B}\cdot\boldsymbol{x}(\boldsymbol{k}_{T-1}), \end{aligned} \tag{12.54}$$

and

$$\bar{\boldsymbol{k}}_1 = \boldsymbol{k}_T. \tag{12.55}$$

---

[9] This point has been made well, at length, and with several interesting examples (although none of them being a case of our problem) by Stiglitz (1973).

[10] The conditions for this are a little stronger than they are in the case of the one-good model because the linear technology may allow an assortment of activity vectors all to prove equally acceptable. This was easily ruled out in the one-good model by our assumptions concerning the sorting of activities. However, the assumption for the general model, while by no means vacuous, is quite a reasonable one.

If this is the case then we know the character of the optimal solution at once. A solution is fully defined by its activity vectors and here these would comprise the infinite sequence

$$\{x(\bar{k}_1), x(k_2), \ldots, x(k_{T-1}); x(\bar{k}_1), x(k_2), \ldots, x(k_{T-1}); \ldots; \\ x(\bar{k}_1), x(k_2), \ldots, x(k_{T-1}); \ldots\}. \tag{12.56}$$

The solution is an oscillatory one. It continues indefinitely to go through a sequence of steps, like a ballroom dancer, which carry it from a starting position through one turn and another back eventually to the same position – and then off again through the same routine. Now this is to all intents and purposes a stationary solution. Not, of course, exactly as we have defined stationarity because our definition required that the events of each week be essentially a repetition of the events of every other. However, it is a small change to say that the events of a sequence of $T-1$ weeks should be repeated in each following block of $T-1$ weeks. What better illustration could there be of the difference between comparative dynamics and extended accumulation history. That which in the latter context is seemingly closely analogous to double switching turns out after all to be virtually a stationary outcome!

Can we have an optimal solution of the character of (12.56)? Well why should we not if the initial conditions dictate one? It is not difficult to concoct technologies and suitable initial conditions that will enforce an oscillatory solution in the sense that they will allow of no other stationary outcome. But the character of such cases differs completely from the character of double-switching examples. The technology that enforces oscillation may exclude double switching in comparative dynamics: the technology that allows double switching may have no oscillatory Ramsey solutions.

It would be tediously repetitious now to go through the same type of discussion with regard to the direction of movement of consumption or capital per head. The reader will see already clearly in his mind's eye how the argument must unroll. Is it possible, for example, that consumption will rise, then fall, then rise again? Yes, of course, it is possible. Indeed, we have already inspected an example where consumption can increase in no other way (example 10.3 of ch. 10). That example would serve again to show that there can be no theorem which states that consumption will increase (or decrease) monotonically on a development optimal in the sense that it solves the general Ramsey problem (12.45)–(12.49). Yet from one point of view the example cited is an unfortunate one because it is of the double-switching type. It would be perilous to try to forge a link between the existence of double switching and the time pattern of changes in consumption in an extended accumulation history. This is what Solow attempted to do and we hope to have shown in ch. 10 that the connection cannot, in general, be established.

Let not the intricacies of the foregoing argument obscure what should be a clear and compelling message. Capital accumulation does not necessarily conform to the orthodox vision. It follows therefore that the vision is misleading. But it is important to grasp clearly where and how it misleads. Bear in mind that a hypothesis is not refuted because something contrary to it can be depicted on a blackboard. It is in failing to note that point that the discussion of these matters by economic theorists has fallen down so badly. Did the law of demand cease to have any importance when the theory of the Giffen good was expounded? No, the problem with the orthodox vision is rather different. Hence, the evaluation of it does not come down to deciding whether certain examples are likely to be found in practice. What emerges instead is that a simple one-good model is wholly misleading in the picture that it gives of extended accumulation history, say in the manner of Ramsey. It is misleading because it allows of an unambiguous notion of the rate of interest, and in general this is not allowed to us[11]. It is misleading because it suggests a pattern of accumulation which we know will not usually be realized. However, the situation is not correctly described by saying that the simple one-good model is misleading on account of the fact that it is free from the paradoxes (or whatever) of comparative dynamics so that a production function across stationary states may be constructed. Nothing could be more misleading than that statement. The examples are legion in which an 'unparadoxical' technology allows of the construction of a perfectly usual production function across stationary states. Yet the extended accumulation history under that same technology may not accord with the pattern suggested by the simple Ramsey model with regard to the way in which consumption and capital (measured by a chain index) move over time. In the very same case 'the rate of interest' may fail to conform to the pattern of the Ramsey model in the most drastic manner of all – by failing to exist.

---

[11] Notice the contrast with comparative dynamics which, as we have emphasized, is a distinct and unlike area. There the concept of 'the rate of interest' was a slippery one but recourse to it could be defended by appeal to the result of the appendix to ch. 4. Here no parallel result can be cited to justify our confining attention to constant-rate-of-interest price systems. Relative prices will typically change from week to week and there is no escaping this possibility.

Part V

INVESTMENT AND THE SHORT RUN

13

Investment

In the present chapter I shall study in some detail the obstructive influence of ignorance. A flowing stream of resources is continually coming into being and struggling, so far as avoidable costs of movement allow of this, to distribute itself away from points of relatively low returns towards points of relatively high returns. Success in this struggle is interfered with by imperfect knowledge on the part of those in whose hands the power to direct the various branches of the stream resides.

A. C. Pigou, *The Economics of Welfare*

In the intertemporal economy of ch. 3 investment was seen to be entailed by a solution to the problem with which each firm in that economy was confronted: the maximization of the present value of net production. In a full and certain knowledge of the technical possibilities open to it and, because a complete system of present-value prices was quoted to it, free from any uncertainty about market situations, the firm could find a plan and put it into effect just as a comparable firm would in the atemporal economy. Of course, that model does not serve to represent reality and that is not its purpose. Where the simple model of an intertemporal economy with all the forward markets functioning can prove useful is as a point of departure, as a guide to which concepts are central and fundamental and which peripheral, and as a reminder that time and capital make an important difference precisely because and only because the system of forward markets postulated in chapter 3 are not in fact extant.

While it is true that investment is entailed by an intertemporal production plan such a plan, if presented most conveniently, does not make investment explicit. Let the firms taken together choose a production plan characterized by the sequence of activity vectors

$$\{x_1, x_2, \ldots, x_T\}. \tag{13.1}$$

Here we are once again assuming, as in ch. 3, a finite number of weeks. What rates of investment, one for each week, are entailed by the above plan? This is in part a question of accounting conventions and as such is as well dealt with at the aggregate level, taking the activities of all firms together. Since we know that all the firms in a competitive economy may be treated as one firm with a production set equal to the sum of individual firms' production sets (see above, p. 68), there is in fact no loss of generality in dealing only with the complete productive system.

At the commencement of week t the stock of produced goods is $\boldsymbol{b}_t$, and we know that this stock is divided between consumption $\boldsymbol{c}_t$ and demands of productive activities not met by non-produced inputs. If the total input vector is $\boldsymbol{a}_t$ then $\boldsymbol{a}_t - z_t$ is the vector of non-produced inputs. We are here assuming that nothing is produced in excess and disposed of but, because when we come to use prices to value the various items such goods will have no value, the assumption is harmless. Hence, we have

$$\boldsymbol{b}_t \quad = \quad \boldsymbol{c}_t \quad - \quad z_t \quad + \quad \boldsymbol{a}_t, \tag{13.2}$$

gross output for week t	consumption for week t	use of non-produced resources in week t	inputs to production for week t

$$t = 2, \ldots, T.$$

We may present the same information slightly differently as

$$\{\boldsymbol{b}_t - \boldsymbol{a}_{t-1} + z_{t-1}\} \quad = \quad \boldsymbol{c}_t \quad + \quad \{\boldsymbol{a}_t - z_t\} - \{\boldsymbol{a}_{t-1} - z_{t-1}\}. \tag{13.3}$$

net output of produced goods for week t	consumption for week t	use of produced inputs in week t over and above those used in week $t-1$

Since we would expect and demand for any week that

$$\text{net output} = \text{consumption} + \text{net investment}, \tag{13.4}$$

we see that we have a vector of net investments for each week, and that it is just what a careful consideration of the question would lead us to expect, i.e.

$$\{\boldsymbol{a}_t - z_t\} - \{\boldsymbol{a}_{t-1} - z_{t-1}\} \quad \text{in week } t. \tag{13.5}$$

Naturally the present value of net investment is the product of the vector (13.5) and $\boldsymbol{p}_t$.

The above derivations are suggestive of an important conclusion. From the point of view of the theory of production investment is a rather derivative concept. It is something which is entailed by the choice of a sequence of activity vectors. And even the entailment is an indirect one, for the activity vectors entail most directly demands for inputs. It is from these by subtracting out the use of non-produced inputs that we may calculate net investment, as a vector or as an aggregate present value, through (13.5).

One might conclude then that, at least for the intertemporal model of ch. 3, the theory of investment is a straightforward application of static production theory, generalized in the manner with which we are now familiar to include the passage of time. In short, the rate of investment (actually the rate of net investment in each particular commodity) might be attributed to much the same influences as would explain the current production of mushrooms in a static economy, or an economy of the intertemporal type; namely, price-guided maximization of profits. Now it is evident that the prices which a firm faces may not uniquely determine[1] its plan of action. This is as true in the intertemporal economy as it is in the static economy. There may be distinct plans each of which is maximally profitable and we will shortly consider the consequences of this fact. For the time being, however, we will put aside this possibility and suppose that the plan which maximizes profit is always unique, although we must realize in so doing that the linear economy is excluded from consideration.

Now it so happens that even a cursory examination of the literature will show that few writers on the subject of the theory of investment are minded to think about the matter in the light of the foregoing considerations[2]. For this fact there is more than one explanation. Not infrequently theorists have in mind constructs which cannot be encompassed within the boundaries of the intertemporal model as it stands. In particular, it is quite usual to assume that the individual firm is constrained as to the output it can sell or the inputs it can buy, so that production decisions are not simply those which would be dictated by profit maximization if the firm could buy and sell as much or as little as it wanted. The numerous 'accelerator' models of one kind or another belong to this category. Less frequently uncertainty is explicitly allowed for.

However, in many cases the cause of the divergence of an investment theory from that implicit in the intertemporal equilibrium model must be sought elsewhere. Very often the cause will be found to be one or another version of the idea that one requires two somewhat separable components to construct an investment model – a theory of the 'desired' or 'target' capital holding and a theory of the rate of 'adjustment' towards the target. To say that there is no warrant whatsoever for this idea and that it must be dismissed as simply fallacious would be to exaggerate. Nevertheless, we will argue that the idea is extremely dubious and that there is really no call for this, as it happens complicating, tendency in the theory of investment.

We have argued, basing our case it is true on the intertemporal equilibrium model, that the demand for capital (i.e. the choice of the vector $(\boldsymbol{a}_t - \boldsymbol{z}_t)$) might

---

[1] Recall the particular sense in which this term is used throughout the present volume. See above, pp. 33–34

[2] For a concise survey of the literature to which reference is made the reader may consult Junankar (1972).

be derived from a model of profit-maximizing production planning. We have shown that rates of net investment, real or in value terms, may be derived from the capital demands by the simple process of taking first differences[3]. Hence, a theory of the demand for capital is a theory of (the demand for) investment. However, not everyone agrees. Thus Haavelmo (1960, pp. 215–216) has written:

> We have tried, by adoption of the most hard-boiled assumptions, to discover whether there is room for a positive rate of capital accumulation within the traditional framework of general equilibrium analysis. We have tried to show that the answer to this question is in the affirmative. But we hope, also, to have convinced the reader that this answer is not reached simply by a traditional supply–demand scheme, equating the 'demand for investment' to the supply of a flow of new capital goods. The 'demand' in this case is for a *stock* of capital, whereas the supply is a flow. In this dimensional difference between the demand and the supply side lies the main problem of an equilibrium theory of investment.

Or again later:

> What we would reject is the naive reasoning that there is a 'demand schedule' for investment which would be derived from a classical scheme of producers' behaviour in maximizing profit. The demand for *investment* cannot simply be derived from the demand for *capital*.

It is clear that the 'demand for capital' in the above quoted passage is a completely different kind of demand from the 'demand for investment'. The latter is what producers taken singly or together would actually purchase were they able to do so (i.e. if disequilibrium of markets did not forbid them to make desired purchases). The 'demand for capital', on the other hand, is not the same kind of demand at all. It turns out on examination to be a target towards which there is a long-run tendency, or towards which there would be a long-run tendency if everything stood still. In view of the differences in meaning the use of the same term in the two closely adjacent contexts is unfortunate. As will by now be clear the revealed immediate demand for capital does imply a demand for investment by way of an identity. The question is why we should bother with notions of 'target' or 'desired' capital stocks, which look suspiciously like hangovers from a rather static analysis, when all that we need is actual capital holdings[4].

Our argument applies especially to the theoretical framework that has been erected by the 'adjustment-cost school'[5]. Broadly, these writers have argued that certain 'costs' associated with change are to be invoked to explain the

---

[3] Were the model formulated in continuous time these would be time derivatives.

[4] In rejecting Haavelmo's conclusion in the quoted passages we are not wishing to suggest that his argument taken as a whole is worthless. Rather, his is an important book full of sharp observations and insights.

[5] The literature is large. The reader might consult Brechling (1975), Eisner and Strotz (1963), Gould (1968), Haavelmo (1960) and Treadway (1969).

gradual alteration of capital inputs to accommodate to different output levels. The intention is to provide a theoretical foundation (meaning an explanation in terms of *equilibrium* theory) of the 'flexible' or 'lagged' accelerator. We may best explain what is going on here by comparing a general intertemporal production possibility set, such as emerges from the mechanical generalization of the atemporal equilibrium model to form the intertemporal model, with the particular technology of the linear production model of ch. 9. A general production possibility set would pertain to the complete sequence of input vectors $(\boldsymbol{a}_t)$ and output vectors $(\boldsymbol{b}_t)$:

$$\{\boldsymbol{a}_1; \boldsymbol{b}_2, \boldsymbol{a}_2; \boldsymbol{b}_3, \boldsymbol{a}_3; \ldots, \boldsymbol{a}_T; \boldsymbol{b}_{T+1}\}. \tag{13.6}$$

In the case of the linear production model, however, we can test for the feasibility of a plan such as (13.6) by testing separately and independently whether each of the transformations $\boldsymbol{a}_t \ominus \boldsymbol{b}_{t+1}$ $(t = 1, \ldots, T)$ is feasible. The writers whose work we are discussing would not like this feature of the linear production model. In particular, they would declare that if $\boldsymbol{a}_t$ is different from $\boldsymbol{a}_{t-1}$ the possibilities for $\boldsymbol{b}_t$ will be less bountiful because the change from $\boldsymbol{a}_{t-1}$ to $\boldsymbol{a}_t$ will impose some adjustment costs. This is the idea of adjustment costs expressed in terms of the type of production model with which we have been concerned. However, the models presented by the writers to whose work we have referred are highly aggregated – hence simpler than the ones now discussed. Also, but unimportantly, they are formulated in terms of continuous time.

Now it need not be underlined that there is more generality in expressing production possibilities in terms of a sequence of separate and independent constraints on the vector triples $\{\boldsymbol{a}_{t-1}, \boldsymbol{a}_t, \boldsymbol{b}_{t+1}\}$ than there is in expressing them similarly in terms of constraints on the vector couples $\{\boldsymbol{a}_t, \boldsymbol{b}_{t+1}\}$. However, both approaches are less than fully general and the hop from one to the other is hardly a revolutionary leap. Nevertheless, there is a particular consequence of the generalization which merits our drawing the reader's attention to it.

To be sure of obtaining a unique maximizing choice given prices one needs strict convexity of the production set, and hence one cannot allow constant returns to scale. Let $\mathscr{S}$ be the set of feasible triples $\{\boldsymbol{a}_{t-1}, \boldsymbol{a}_t, \boldsymbol{b}_t\}$. One may consistently assume

$$\{(\boldsymbol{a}, \boldsymbol{b}) \mid (\boldsymbol{a}, \boldsymbol{a}, \boldsymbol{b}) \in \mathscr{S}\} \tag{13.7}$$

to be a cone without implying that

$$\{(\boldsymbol{a}, \boldsymbol{b}) \mid (\boldsymbol{a}_0, \boldsymbol{a}, \boldsymbol{b}) \in \mathscr{S}\} \tag{13.8}$$

is a cone. In other words, one may have long-run constant returns to scale, with no costs of adjustment, but diminishing returns in the short run on account of costs of adjustment.

From the point of view of theory this is not interesting and not important. It is perfectly obvious that one may derive definite production choices if one assumes the intertemporal production set to be strictly convex. The adjustment cost idea is a kind of story that one can tell to convince someone that this strict convexity is not in conflict with one kind of presumption at least for constant returns where that presumption is valid. However, ultimately one either has constant returns or one does not. If not there are certain theoretical possibilities open which are otherwise closed. In that case one might as well forget about constant returns. There is nothing to be said in favour of regarding the choices that are made when the production couples are constrained to lie in

$$\{(\boldsymbol{a}_t, \boldsymbol{b}_{t+1}) \mid (\boldsymbol{a}_{t-1}, \boldsymbol{a}_t, \boldsymbol{b}_{t+1}) \in \mathscr{S}\} \tag{13.9}$$

as adjustments towards the choices that would be made in the counterfactual situation in which production couples were constrained to lie in

$$\{(\boldsymbol{a}_t, \boldsymbol{b}_{t+1}) \mid (\boldsymbol{a}_t, \boldsymbol{a}_t, \boldsymbol{b}_{t+1}) \in \mathscr{S}\}. \tag{13.10}$$

All this may be wildly unfair to the adjustment cost idea. It was, after all, largely with empirical applications in mind that the construct came to be formulated and what to the theorist is mundane may be of considerable interest to the econometrician. Furthermore, some adjustment theories embody the idea of disequilibrium, or the idea that optimization is only partially achieved, or the notion that the plans that would be put into effect were the producer able to transact freely at the prices which he faces cannot immediately be put into effect because of the way in which markets operate. All these ideas are potentially of the greatest significance, but they demand close and detailed analysis and this they frequently do not receive from those who invoke them. Moreover, the trend is against these interpretations and towards models in which the process of adjustment is 'optimized' so that we have a full value-maximizing solution to a problem formulated by grafting an allowance for adjustment costs onto an otherwise plain and highly aggregated constant-returns technology. It would seem that the case for clinging to a hypothetical target towards which adjustment takes place is weakest precisely when full optimization along an adjustment path is assumed.

The model put forward by Jorgenson (1967)[6] has affinities with the intertemporal equilibrium model where the production possibility set is strictly convex. However, the differences are as notable as the similarities. In contrast

---

[6] The model is published in a conference volume along with discussion of it by Tobin, Griliches and Miller.

to the great generality of the intertemporal production model the production function example on which Jorgenson bases his argument is peculiarly special. However, a more general version of the argument could be produced in which there would be many capital inputs and these would be modified as a consequence of production activity. Such a generalization would not undermine the conclusion that in the conditions of intertemporal equilibrium (this is not at all how Jorgenson puts it) it would be necessary for the firm to look only one week ahead[7]. We can derive that by noting that in the case of the linear production model (or even in a more general version of it in which there are non-linear or interdependent activities) in week t the firm transforms a vector of inputs $\boldsymbol{a}_t$ into a vector of outputs $\boldsymbol{b}_t$. The present value of the profit that it makes is the sum of the values of these transformations, i.e.

$$\sum_{t=1}^{\infty} (\boldsymbol{p}_{t+1} \cdot \boldsymbol{b}_{t+1} - \boldsymbol{p}_t \cdot \boldsymbol{a}_t). \tag{13.11}$$

The intertemporal production set constrains the choices of the couples $(\boldsymbol{a}_t, \boldsymbol{b}_{t+1})$. If it does so in such a way that the constraints on $(\boldsymbol{a}_t, \boldsymbol{b}_{t+1})$ are independent of the transformations in weeks other than week t then evidently the maximization of the infinite sum (13.11) is achieved by the separate and independent maximization of the component terms.

$$\boldsymbol{p}_{t+1} \cdot \boldsymbol{b}_{t+1} - \boldsymbol{p}_t \cdot \boldsymbol{a}_t \qquad (t = 1, 2, \ldots). \tag{13.12}$$

This is the general form of a conclusion at which Jorgenson arrives for his special case. However, the problem with his argument is not so much that he confines attention to a special case: it is useful to have it shown even for a special case that the position that Haavelmo has adopted is more than a little shaky. The problem with Jorgenson's theory is that he has failed to elect either statics or dynamics, so that his theory is an uncomfortable amalgam of the two. Thus he wants to show how 'the demand for investment goods as a function of the rate of interest' may be derived. We need hardly reiterate the point that there is no justification for elevating the idea of a single rate of interest to such a central place in the theory of capital accumulation. If one assumes, as Jorgenson does, that the firm's production set is strictly convex then its choice of a production plan, and hence the sequence of its investment choices, will depend uniquely upon the sequence of present-value prices with which it is confronted. Here is a set of investment functions which are strictly analogous to static supply functions. It were better if one allowed this simple but fundamental conclusion to hold the stage alone, but Jorgenson is not satisfied with it. The reason is not far to seek.

---

[7] In the words of Arrow the firm can make use of a 'myopic decision rule'. See Arrow (1968), particularly section I and references cited therein.

In the case of stationary conditions with invariant relative prices and a constant rate of interest Jorgenson's firm, given his assumption of strict convexity of the production set, will have a unique maximizing production plan and this plan will be the same for each successive week. In these conditions then the firm will not invest at all, i.e. it will not add to the capital stock of the previous week. Hence, for any value of the rate of interest, and given stationary conditions, the rate of investment is identically zero. All this is quite natural and as it should be given the assumptions. However, regarded as the demand for investment as a function of the rate of interest the derived relation is disappointing! So, of course, this is not the investment function that Jorgenson has in mind. What he does is to assume stationary conditions at the outset, those corresponding to a rate of interest ρ_0. Then the rate of interest changes to another value, call it ρ_1, *relative prices of all inputs and outputs in each subsequent week remaining the same as they would have been had this alteration not come about*, and one derives the subsequent history of the firm's production plan, which typically will embody investment, be it positive or negative. Thus what is obtained is a sequence of investment values which depend upon three parameters. These are *two* values of the rate of interest, ρ_0 and ρ_1, and also a price vector of relative prices. We have then an 'investment function', strictly a family of investment functions, one for each subsequent week, with three arguments including two values of the rate of interest.

All these arguments in the investment function may seem rather many, but in fact they are very few. If one considers that what is derived is a sequence of vectors of capital holdings then, by analogy with the static theory, one would expect to need a sequence of price vectors of the same dimension as the number of goods. And indeed this is what Jorgenson has obtained for himself, but in a very special and particular manner. The parameter ρ_0 is not genuinely in the function as a price variable – it serves to define initial conditions on the capital vector. Let the vector of relative prices be $\boldsymbol{p}_0$. Then the intertemporal price system is defined by the infinite sequence

$$\boldsymbol{p}_0, \left(\frac{1}{1+\rho_1}\right)\boldsymbol{p}_0, \left(\frac{1}{1+\rho_1}\right)^2 \boldsymbol{p}_0, \ldots, \left(\frac{1}{1+\rho_1}\right)^t \boldsymbol{p}_0, \ldots \tag{13.13}$$

Thus, the theory of investment at which Jorgenson arrives is a description of the investment of a profit-maximizing firm facing a semi-stationary price system but starting from initial conditions inappropriate to a stationary solution at those prices. It is not obvious which succinct phrase would best describe this theory. But it is obvious that the phrase is not 'the neoclassical theory of investment'.

The foregoing remarks are concerned with abstract economic theory. It is, however, the case that Jorgenson regards this model, in which there is no uncertainty about future developments of prices and technology, as directly and immediately applicable to reality in the form of econometric investigation. We can offer no explanation for this fact.

Jorgenson's theory of investment is a rather idiosyncratic one with regard to several of its details. But probably the most significant departure that he has made from the usual assumptions of the mainstream contemporary pure theory is that he is quite happy to abandon the assumption that the individual firm is subject to constant returns to scale. Moreover, his abandonment of the assumption is a wholehearted one; in this he is unlike the adjustment cost theorists whose thinking, as we have seen, is dominated by the constant returns postulate, although formally their models do not accord with that postulate. In assuming strict convexity Jorgenson also parts company, apparently, with the majority of writers on the theory of economic growth. The reference is to the authors of the so-called 'neoclassical' growth models. The terminology is perhaps not entirely appropriate but the term will be used because it is so familiar. One unhappy consequence of its adoption is that the impression might be given that the problems to be discussed arise only in these growth models and that a writer who would repudiate the term 'neoclassical' has provided a solution to them. This is very far from being the case.

It is hard to be definite about the views of the neoclassical growth theorists because these writers have very frequently given scant consideration to the firm, or indeed to any individual micro unit, in the construction of their models. A neglect of these considerations gives rise inevitably to ambiguities. If we know, for example, that the aggregate production set of the economy exhibits constant returns this may be because each firm in the economy produces under constant returns, or it may be because the number of firms is itself variable. However, the former possibility seems the more plausible, not least because a variable number of firms would not give rise to a linear aggregate production set unless each firm was vanishingly small relative to the size of the economy. What one can be definite about is this: the assumption by growth theorists of constant returns to scale, combined with their predilection for semi-stationary growth, has the consequence that they have no theory of investment as such. This is not to say that the rate of investment is indeterminate, it is rather to claim that what determines it is more than just investment decisions by firms.

Let us establish some terminology. A set of relations pertaining to the equilibrium of an economy may or may not give unique values of the variables (i.e. there may be one equilibrium or many), but even if the equilibrium is unique the fact that a particular variable can only take one value may be a consequence of uniquely determined decisions by the individual micro units of the model or it may be a consequence of aggregate balancing relations in the model. Thus, a model may contain one or more variables with the following property: the variable concerned could take some other value without violating any conditions of the system pertaining to the behaviour of individual decision-makers. Naturally, such a change would typically involve the violation of an aggregate balancing relation (e.g. a market clearing condition) and so be inconsistent with the maintenance of equilibrium, but the variable is not, as it were, held in place by prices and other decision parameters. Such a variable will be called here an *accommodating variable*.

Examples of accommodating variables in economic theory are legion and include the following: levels of production of goods in Ricardo's international trade model when one of the countries does not specialize; the number of firms (i.e. the scale of the industry) in long-run Marshallian equilibrium; and output and consumption plans in the most refined general equilibrium models which work in terms of excess demand correspondences. The notion of an accommodating variable is important to the present discussion because it, or its opposite, underlies the definition of an *investment function*. A growth model will be said to contain an *investment function* if the aggregate level of investment is not an accommodating variable. In that case investment levels of producers must be uniquely determined by the values of variables known to them, for example, own technology and profits, prices, interest rates, etc.[8] To put the matter differently, a model owns an investment function if there is contained within it a microeconomic explanation of the rate of investment as the sum of determinate investment decisions by individual firms.

Macroeconomic growth models are commonly presented without reference to the behaviour of micro units[9]. Thus one meets assumptions such as: a constant proportion of output is saved. In the case of savings assumptions, however, it is typically quite easy to find a set of assumptions about the behaviour of micro units which imply the macro behaviour assumed; although such assumptions will have to be fierce enough, naturally, to allow aggregation.

---

[8] Notice that the usage proposed above is narrower than the usage which denotes by the words 'investment function' any functional relationship pertaining to investment. The investment function must give a value to the absolute level of investment, not merely specify or constrain the character of the investment (e.g. choice of technique). Therefore Kaldor's use of the term in his paper with Mirrlees (1962, section 16) is not the present one.

[9] There are many exceptions of course. To cite one example there is Uzawa (1969). The main references to the growth models which are under discussion are Solow (1956), Swan (1956) and Meade (1961). These are all highly aggregated models but that is not the source of the difficulties to which attention is directed here.

If every income receiver in the economy saves the same given proportion of his income, then the economy does likewise. If all owners of capital save all their income from capital, and all labour income is spent on consumption, then the economy spends all wages and saves all profits. Furthermore, the individuals concerned would not be willing to save any other amount, apart from the amount that they do save, unless they were faced by different income receipts, or a different array of prices. In short, saving is not an accommodating variable in the macroeconomic growth models. Where investment is concerned the position is apparently different. It is assumed that there are constant returns to scale. Saving and investment decisions are taken independently by uncoordinated decision units, but they might be consistent with each other in a special case, the equilibrium growth path. Along that equilibrium growth path the rate of investment is an accommodating variable. The competitive firms with constant returns-to-scale technology, borrowing in perfect capital markets, invest at some particular rate, but would be just as happy to invest at another rate. As long as the production plan chosen by the firm is a maximally profitable plan then so is the identical plan at a different scale. Hence, the firms travel the equilibrium path in a neutral equilibrium with the price system providing them with no incentive to do other than they do do, but equally providing them with no disincentive to follow another path. This, of course, is the situation which holds whenever an accommodating variable is included in the equilibrium of a model. Indeed, the same state of affairs arises with respect to output levels when producers having available constant returns-to-scale activities produce positive outputs in equilibrium[10].

It should be noted in passing that the account given above is not substantially altered if the typical firm has a U-shaped cost curve. In this case the scale of each firm will become determinate, and this will no longer be an accommodating variable, but the number of firms in the industry will then become an important variable and this will be, under competitive conditions, an accommodating variable just like firm size. The basic issues now under discussion would thus reappear in only a slightly different guise.

The fact that investment is an accommodating variable in the neoclassical model is what underlies the claim which one meets sometimes that saving governs investment in the neoclassical model. This claim as it stands is a little unfortunate because it could, like Say's law, mean a number of things. Furthermore, the authors of these models have clearly felt that saving and

---

[10] This point is very familiar in linear programming theory, where the dual prices sort activities into those that might be used and those that are not used, but do not determine activity levels.

investment decisions are taken independently. It is therefore likely that if their models are at fault the fault lies in not determining the level of investment at all. It is important to be clear about these matters because otherwise two quite distinct issues can get muddled in together. It is possible that discontent with the neoclassical growth model arises from a feeling that the 'vision' of the process of economic growth incorporated in the model is an incomplete or misleading one because it assigns so little a role to producers[11]. Firms have no utility functions and the lack of any forward-looking behaviour, except under certainty, precludes the operation of the 'animal spirits' of investors which are embodied in their reactions to investment opportunities with uncertain outcomes[12]. These are obviously important issues, but they are logically separate from the immediate concern of the present discussion which has to do with the determination of investment given the economic environment assumed.

If one assumes full-employment growth equilibrium in a one-good neoclassical model then an equation of the form

$$\mathrm{d}K(t)/\mathrm{d}t = sY(t) \tag{13.14}$$

must be satisfied and the analysis can proceed from there. We are assuming here the most aggregated model of all, and continuous time, to facilitate comparison with familiar models, but these are not essential points.

This is what most writers have actually done; there has been little analysis of how a price system might bring about such an equilibrium development. An exception is Solow (1956) who long ago provided a rather sketchy account of how prices and price changes might play a role, which account, however, is probably incorrect and certainly very incomplete. He writes (1956, pp. 78–79) as follows:

> From another point of view, however, we can ask what kind of market behaviour will cause the model economy to follow the path of equilibrium growth. In this direction it has already been assumed that both the growing labour force and the existing capital stock are thrown on the market inelastically, with the real wage and the real rental of capital adjusting instantaneously so as to clear the market.

It is a most remarkable fact, and a commentary in itself on the way in which the theory of economic growth has developed since Solow's pioneering paper, that there has been no subsequent discussion of this particular process of adjustment to equilibrium. The process that Solow had in mind included the 'instantaneous' adjustment of real factor prices to equal full-employment

---

[11] On the notion of the 'vision' of an economic model see Schumpeter (1954; pp. 41–43, 892–893).

[12] On the point that 'animal spirits' are to do with reactions to uncertainty, see Keynes (1936, pp. 161–162) and Kahn (1959).

marginal products. There are two points to be made about this idea. One is that it is not clear what process is here described, i.e. it is not obvious what has been added to the assumption of full employment of resources by bringing in prices. The other point is that however this adjustment process might be assumed to operate it is very important for the coherence of the neoclassical model that it should not occur. We consider each point in turn.

It is supposed that the word 'instantaneously' is not to be taken quite literally; for if prices adjust instantaneously we cannot discuss how they adjust, in which case it is hard to see how introducing such prices has added anything to the tale. If, however, the motion of the invisible hand is slower, but still very rapid relative to the rate of change of capital stock, then we may be able to see how it operates. One could usefully, from this point of view, rewrite the model in a discrete time period form and imagine that the adjustment process operates during a few hours of one day in a Hicksian week. The important point, for the analysis, is that the process is a *tâtonnement*, i.e. no capital or labour is hired at disequilibrium prices.

One might formalize the adjustment process as follows. Denote inputs of two factors by X_1 and X_2, and supplies available by $\bar{X}_1$ and $\bar{X}_2$. $F(X_1, X_2)$ is output, where F is a linear homogeneous function. Let F_1 and F_2 be partial derivatives (marginal products) with respect to X_1 and X_2 respectively, and let W_1 and W_2 be the input prices. A dot over a variable denotes its time rate of change, i.e. $\dot{X}$ is $\mathrm{d}X/\mathrm{d}t$. Finally, α_1 and α_2 are adjustment rate parameters; the corresponding parameters for $\dot{W}_1$ and $\dot{W}_2$ are set equal to one by choice of input units.

$$\begin{aligned} &\dot{X}_1 = \alpha_1(F_1 - W_1), \qquad \dot{W}_1 = X_1 - \bar{X}_1, \\ &\dot{X}_2 = \alpha_2(F_2 - W_2), \qquad \dot{W}_2 = X_2 - \bar{X}_2, \\ &\alpha_1 > 0, \qquad \alpha_2 > 0. \end{aligned} \tag{13.15}$$

Obviously all variables should be constrained to be non-negative, but that is not important to the present discussion[13]. The adjustment process (13.15) cannot be shown to converge to its stationary solution

$$[X_1 = \bar{X}_1;\, X_2 = \bar{X}_2;\, W_1 = F_1(\bar{X}_1, \bar{X}_2);\, W_2 = F_2(\bar{X}_1, \bar{X}_2)];$$

---

[13] Readers familiar with the literature on decentralized economic planning will recognize that this process reduces, when $\alpha_1 = \alpha_2 = 1$, to the gradient method for finding a saddle point for the Lagrangian form

$$F(X_1, X_2) + W_1(\bar{X}_1 - X_1) + W_2(\bar{X}_2 - X_2),$$

which form arises from the problem

$$\max F(X_1, X_2) \quad \text{subject to } X_1 \leqslant \bar{X}_1 \quad \text{and} \quad X_2 \leqslant \bar{X}_2.$$

These readers will already anticipate the outcome of the present analysis. See Arrow and Hurwicz (1960).

indefinite oscillation is a possible outcome. Analysis of system (13.15) in its general form is rather difficult and complicated, and will not be attempted here. The point presently at issue can be illustrated by the consideration of a particular example for which the analysis is tractable:

$$F(X_1, X_2) = X_1^{\theta} X_2^{1-\theta}, \qquad \alpha_1 = \alpha_2 = 1. \tag{13.16}$$

The adjustment coefficients are all equal to one and the production function is Cobb–Douglas.

The Jacobian of the system (13.15) when $\alpha_1 = \alpha_2 = 1$ is

$$\begin{bmatrix} F_{11} & F_{12} & -1 & 0 \\ F_{21} & F_{22} & 0 & -1 \\ 1 & 0 & 0 & 0 \\ 0 & 1 & 0 & 0 \end{bmatrix}, \tag{13.17}$$

where

$$F_{ij} = \partial^2 F / \partial X_i \, \partial X_j.$$

This gives rise to a characteristic equation:

$$\lambda^4 - (F_{11} + F_{22})\lambda^3 + (2 + F_{11}F_{22} - F_{12}F_{21})\lambda^2 - (F_{11} + F_{22}) + 1 = 0. \tag{13.18}$$

Let $F_{11} + F_{22} = Q < 0$, and note that in the Cobb–Douglas case, $F_{11}F_{22} - F_{12}F_{21} = 0$. Then (13.18) can be written

$$\lambda^4 - Q\lambda^3 + 2\lambda^2 - Q\lambda + 1 = 0 \tag{13.19}$$

or

$$(\lambda^2 - Q\lambda + 1)(\lambda + i)(\lambda - i) = 0. \tag{13.20}$$

So two characteristic roots are given by $\lambda = \pm i$. The nature of the remaining two roots depends upon whether $-Q \lesseqgtr 2$. If $-Q < 2$ there are two further complex roots,

$$\lambda = Q/2 \pm i\left(1 - \frac{Q^2}{4}\right)^{1/2},$$

with negative real parts. If $-Q \geqslant 2$ there are two real roots which satisfy $\lambda_1 + \lambda_2 = Q < 0$ and $\lambda_1 \lambda_2 = 1$, so that both are negative. The result then is that the characteristic roots of (13.17) will have two real parts equal to zero and two negative real parts. Hence, there will usually be neutral oscillation neither converging nor diverging, for a *linear system* with matrix (13.17). Now this, of course, does not indicate that (13.15) is not stable under conditions (13.16) because it is precisely in the case that the real part of a characteristic root for the linear approximation is zero that the analysis of the linear approximation is not telling us what we need to know about local stability. However, an example indicates that stability cannot, in general, be established.

Example 13.1. In the system (13.15) and (13.16) let $\bar{X}_1 = \bar{X}_2 = 1$, and $\theta = 0.5$. Let $X_1(0) = X_2(0)$ and $W_1(0) = W_2(0)$. Notice that for all $t > 0$ we must have $X_1(t) = X_2(t)$ and $W_1(t) = W_2(t)$, by symmetry. Thus, for all t, $F_1 = F_2 = 0.5$ and the system is equivalent to the following system with

$$X_1(t) = X_2(t) = X(t) \quad \text{and} \quad W_1(t) + W_2(t) = 2W_1(t) = W(t).$$

$$\dot{X} = 1 - W, \qquad \dot{W} = X - 1, \tag{13.21}$$

which gives simple harmonic motion with undamped oscillation.

Is this a special case which could only arise by chance initial conditions? Notice that the case arises when relative quantities and relative factor prices are appropriate to the stationary solution but absolute magnitudes are wrong. There is then no further tendency to convergence. Thus stability will be obtained if, starting from arbitrary initial conditions, and excluding the above particular case, absolute magnitudes converge faster than relative magnitudes.

Regardless of what is generally true of the behaviour of the system (13.15), enough has been said to suggest that the question of whether the prices of factors 'thrown onto the market inelastically' can properly be assumed continuously equal to marginal products requires a fair amount of discussion, and that it is not obvious that an account of continuous full-employment equilibrium involving prices of inputs can be given which has any explanatory value with regard to the full-employment assumption. It should be clear that the source of the difficulties lies in the absence of demand functions for inputs which follows from the constant-returns assumption. Under this assumption factor inputs are accommodating variables, though their ratios are not, and prices sustain absolute levels of inputs only in the sense that they provide no incentive (but also no disincentive) to movement away from equilibrium.

There is another ground for scepticism about whether the assumption of the instantaneous adjustment of prices to full-employment marginal products enriches the neoclassical account of capital accumulation. While the discussion above was unavoidably complicated, this next point is more straightforward. If the real rental of capital were to adjust instantaneously to the marginal product of fully employed capital, however that might come about, then the neoclassical model would be devoid of any mechanism whereby saving and investment could be brought into equality. The own-rate of return or marginal product of the capital-consumption good[14] is uniquely determined at full employment if the production function is smooth. But investment is not determined by this rate, being, as has been remarked above, an accommodating variable. So saving can equal investment only by the purest chance, and if the two are unequal there is no price to respond. One can, of course, introduce another rate of interest to respond to differences between planned saving and planned investment, say the rate of return on bonds denominated in a unit of account. But either this will make no difference (because deviations between this rate and the own-rate of return to capital will be neutralized by appropriate expectations about the rate of change of the price of capital in terms of unit of account)[15], or changes in this rate of interest will destroy the equilibrium in the markets for inputs (because the condition that individuals be indifferent between holding claims to output and bonds will be invalidated). To put it simply, the rate of interest cannot regulate both K and $\dot{K}$, and if it is regulating the former (as Solow's account suggests) then the latter is unregulated[16].

It is worth pursuing now the analogy between the rate of investment in a macroeconomic growth model and the level of output of producers with constant-returns-to-scale processes. The two cases pose rather similar problems. It is obvious that competitive producers cannot be assumed to instantaneously maximize profits, except in the special case of equilibrium, when they control linear processes. For there might exist no maximum *ex-ante* profit level under these assumptions. And even if the problem of indefinitely large desired output levels were removed by placing bounds on production levels, there would still remain a chronic tendency to instability. The standard method of treating this problem in stability analysis is to give profit maximization a dynamic formulation, assuming that output increases or decreases at a rate proportional to marginal (i.e. in this case, average) net profitability. This idea has already been put forward by Walras (1954, pp. 243–254). A similar

---

[14] The discussion here assumes a one-sector version of the neoclassical model. But the problem under discussion does not disappear when the number of sectors is increased.

[15] See Solow (1956, pp. 80–82) for a demonstration of how this could happen for equilibrium paths.

[16] In the case of a two-sector model, full employment of inputs does not determine the rate of interest uniquely anyway; one needs demand conditions as well. But this just leads to a different form of the same question. Suppose that the 'momentary equilibrium' of a neoclassical two-sector model is unique. Is not investment then fixed at a unique value by the *tâtonnement* which establishes momentary equilibrium, and does not investment then cease to be an accommodating variable? The point which this question misses is that the discussions in the literature assume that saving is demand for the capital good (see, for example, Hahn (1965)), thus either begging the question of savings–investment equality or adopting a solution which is also available in a one-sector model, i.e. assuming that saving and investment decisions are not independent.

treatment is possible for investment. We may assume, in other words, that the level of investment is given initially by the initial conditions and that the subsequent history of this magnitude is determined by a function giving the rate of change of investment in terms of relevant variables. But, of course, there is no clear and obvious way of deciding whether this dynamic formulation should be applied to investment itself, or to the capital stock. It is hard to know *a priori* what should adjust when profit is not momentarily maximized. If, for example, the capital stock is adjusted, then the model yields an investment function, and investment ceases to be an accommodating variable, not because the arbitrariness associated with the scale of firms has disappeared, but because, while the firms have no unique desired stock of capital there is a unique rate at which, taken together, they are willing to change the capital stock that they hold. We then arrive at a description of investment which sees it as in part a sluggish adjustment of the capital stock to the appropriate level. This, of course, is exactly the account to which the adjustment-cost school has taken exception.

The difficulties with which we are confronted here, and which present themselves at every turn, derive from ambiguities as to what equilibrium analysis is about, to which reference has been made already and at length in ch. 2. As was there made clear, the fact that an equilibrium exists provides no guarantee that it will be attained. If we assume that it is attained then it may well be that producers, for example, must collectively act in a particular way, say by investing according to the requirements of the equilibrium state. However, that would not explain why they would collectively choose that particular action as opposed to some other if the alternative would be equally profitable. One might suppose that some stable adjustment process would bring it about that individual actions would together conform to the requirements of overall equilibrium. But we have seen enough by now to know that no such presumption exists, and particularly not in the present case, when certain decision variables are from the point of view of equilibrium analysis accommodating variables.

Where the architects of neoclassical growth models have left themselves open to the charge of determining investment from saving is in specifying models in which it is only the overall requirement of an equilibrium, which dictates that saving and investment totals shall be in accord, that assigns to the level of investment that value which it will take. Of course, there is no necessity for this. We can equally well assume that firms have strictly convex production sets whereupon, at the micro level, the investment decisions would derive from the maximization of the present value of profit in parallel with the case of static production theory. For the whole economy investment would be derived simultaneously, along with saving, and prices and interest rates, as part of the general equilibrium.

The questions concerning the theory of investment which have been the preoccupation of the present chapter until this point will probably not be felt by the reader to be easy ones. To have made any progress at all in their resolution, and it is hoped that some progress has been made, might seem to be a considerable achievement. Yet from one point of view the argument so far has amounted to little more than 'shadow boxing'. We have been concerned solely with investment in an equilibrium of the intertemporal economy. It is for this reason that we have been able to refer repeatedly to the analogy with static production theory; for it is to that case that the analogy is applicable. Many of the issues that make the theory of investment a peculiarly interesting and challenging subject of study arise precisely because it is not in the context of a full intertemporal equilibrium that actual investment decisions are taken. Unless some progress can be made in elucidating the theory of investment as it applies to decisions taken in the clouds of uncertainty that in actuality obscure the forward vision of an investor, then the task will be for the most part uncompleted.

Fortunately, it is not impossible to throw some light on investment in the state of temporary equilibrium, which state approximates to reality better than the full intertemporal equilibrium. However, the problem is an intricate one which gives rise to numerous issues. These for the most part are hard to resolve. Moreover, it so happens that there has been scarcely any work on the theory of investment in conditions of uncertainty concerning prices, except for very special cases. Hence, even a superficial discussion of the problem must break new ground and could very easily become extremely lengthy. To avoid this outcome we will confine the argument to some highly simplified examples and merely take note of the problems that would be encountered in a more general investigation.

As has been remarked already, if forward markets do not exist and do not provide the firm with quotations of present-value prices for future goods, then that firm has no choice but to take a view about how prices will develop. As we have seen in ch. 3 this amounts at least to taking a view about relative prices of goods for which no forward markets operate in terms of the good or goods for which forward trading is possible. There is a possibility of even greater complications if the firm is disinclined to take the structure of own rates of interest embodied in the forward prices of a good for which forward trading is possible at their face value. Recall that there will in due course be possibilities for forward trading aside from those provided by the forward markets that operate in the current week. Let the current week be week 1, and consider forward sales or purchases of a good to be delivered in weeks 2 and 3, the present prices for these deliveries in terms of the good itself being respectively $\Pi_2(1)$ and $\Pi_3(1)$. In week 2 it will again be possible to trade forward commitments to provide this good in week 3 at a price then to be determined, $\Pi_3(2)$.

In the case in point an actor accepts forward prices at their face value if, being desirous of acquiring command over the good in week 3, he supposes that he can do no better than to purchase it forward in week 1 at the price $\Pi_3(1)$. An alternative method of acquiring the good in week 3 is to buy it forward for delivery in week 2 in the anticipation of selling it at once to finance a forward purchase of the same good for delivery in week 3. This last method will prove to be superior to a straightforward initial purchase for delivery in week 3 if it should turn out that

$$\Pi_3(1) > \Pi_3(2)\,\Pi_2(1). \tag{13.22}$$

The belief in the possibility that the indirect method (13.22) of purchasing the good forward for delivery in week 3 may prove to be the better method can lead to the firm taking speculative positions in its forward trading. Obviously, this observation applies more generally than to just the simple case that was chosen for the sake of illustration. Also, it points to an added complication which should ideally be taken into account in the theory of investment.

The problems involved in elucidating investment under uncertainty can be arranged under three headings, each of which takes the form of a question:

(1) What is the objective of the firm, i.e. what does it aim to maximize?

(2) What are the constraints under which it operates?

(3) Can the solution to the problem of maximizing the objective designated by the answer to (1), subject to the constraints as designated by the answer to (2), be characterized in any way that assists an understanding of the nature of such solutions?

Consider firstly the question of the objective of the firm. An immediate issue is whether the firm pursues its own objectives or those of others. This issue is especially critical in the present context because in the absence of some forward markets there will be divergent price expectations. Hence, even if the firm were to pursue maximum profits, and even supposing that an unambiguous meaning could be given to profit, there would still remain the question as to which price expectations would be used to evaluate prospective profits. As will be clear already from the discussion of the issue in ch. 3 we adhere firmly to the view that the firm should be regarded as being an independent entity, having its own price expectations, and acting according to them. We will not depart here from that viewpoint.

The matter of the objective of the firm can be elucidated by considering briefly in turn several different cases. Firstly, there is the intertemporal economy with all the forward markets in operation. There the firm has a clear and simple incentive to maximize the present value of its intertemporal production plan. The analogy to the static production theory is complete. By choosing the production plan with the greatest present value the firm maximizes its ability, or the ability of those who own it, to secure resources at no matter what time. Secondly, there is the case of temporary equilibrium where the firm thinks that it knows for sure what relative prices will be in future weeks. In this case, so far as the objective of the firm is involved, it is just the same as in the intertemporal economy. The firm does not confront a full system of forward markets, but on its own view it is as if it did. At least this is the case so long as the firm can transact freely in the forward markets that do exist. Thirdly, there is the most important case where not only is the future development of prices uncertain, but also the firm is aware of this uncertainty.

The recognition that uncertainty is subjective as well as objective[17] brings with it several problems. To focus attention on the objective of the firm imagine that the firm must choose a production plan once and for all, and that it will not be able to alter its choice, even partially, in the light of subsequent developments. Of course, the assumption is not a reasonable one, and is certainly not in accord with the production relations of the linear economy. There the only decision which the firm has to make is that concerning the current activity vector. It is not bound in any way to commit itself in advance concerning later activity vectors. Then, realizing that the future is uncertain, it will only arrive at tentative decisions about the activity vectors of future weeks. It goes without saying that this feature is not peculiar to the linear economy, although that is an extreme example, but is a much more general aspect of intertemporal production decisions. The implication is that usually the only definite choice which the firm makes is that concerning its current production activities. This choice is made with later production activities in view but does not amount to a definite commitment regarding these activities.

There is a rather important distinction here between the formal structure of production decisions in the atemporal economy and that which arises in the case of an intertemporal production plan. That distinction is obscured in the intertemporal economy with its full complement of forward markets but it emerges clearly when we consider temporary equilibrium. Naturally, time makes an essential difference and imposes upon the production decision a

[17] There is objective uncertainty if the future is unpredictable. There is subjective uncertainty if actors feel the future to be uncertain and act accordingly.

wholly distinctive structure if that decision decomposes into an ordered sequence of sub-decisions, be they independent or interdependent. When we come shortly to examine the question of characterizing a solution to the problem of investment under uncertainty it will be essential to take into account the sequential nature of the decisions. But for the time being set aside this aspect of the matter.

We imagine then that the production decision is a once-for-all choice of an intertemporal production plan:

$$\{\boldsymbol{a}_1; \boldsymbol{b}_2, \boldsymbol{a}_2; \ldots; \boldsymbol{b}_T, \boldsymbol{a}_T; \boldsymbol{b}_{T+1}\}. \tag{13.23}$$

To put this plan into effect the firm will have to engage in some forward transactions. At the start, for example, if we suppose that it has no resources to hand, it must purchase the input vector $\boldsymbol{a}_1$ at a cost $\boldsymbol{p}_1 \cdot \boldsymbol{a}_1$. To finance this outlay there must be one or more forward sales. To put it another way, the firm must borrow to finance its purchase of inputs. Under conditions of uncertainty it may be that the firm cannot be sure of its ability to honour an obligation to deliver in accordance with its forward sales. If the outcome for prices is a very unfortunate one the revenue from the sales that it will make may be insufficient to provide for the commitments into which the firm has entered in its forward contracting. There is the possibility here that the firm will be forced into bankruptcy. What matters of course is the profitability of the complete plan (13.23). If the firm is temporarily short of revenue to meet a commitment it can always sell a forward commitment for a later week and so gain the revenue needed to comply with its obligation.

We have assumed that the firm chooses a complete plan (13.23) at the outset. As prices unfold that plan is translated into a sequence of net revenues, positive or negative, in terms of the *numeraire*, i.e.

$$-\boldsymbol{p}_1 \cdot \boldsymbol{a}_1, \boldsymbol{p}_2 \cdot (\boldsymbol{b}_2 - \boldsymbol{a}_2), \boldsymbol{p}_3 \cdot (\boldsymbol{b}_3 - \boldsymbol{a}_3), \ldots, \boldsymbol{p}_T \cdot (\boldsymbol{b}_T - \boldsymbol{a}_T), \boldsymbol{p}_{T+1} \cdot \boldsymbol{b}_{T+1}, \tag{13.24}$$

where $\boldsymbol{p}_t$ $(t = 1, \ldots, T+1)$ is the vector of relative prices that will actually come to be.

Even after the plan has been chosen, from among those feasible for the firm, the sequence (13.24) is, and is perceived by the firm to be, a stochastic sequence. This is because the prices are stochastic variables. The terms of the sequence (13.24) would indicate the net revenue, positive or negative, accruing to the firm in the weeks 1 to $T+1$ if it did no more than carry out the production plan. However, the firm can make use of forward trading in the *numeraire* good 1 to transfer net revenue from one week to another. It will normally do this in such a manner as to convert deficit weeks into weeks of surplus or balance. If it could transact just as it liked in the forward markets for good 1 the firm could choose any sequence of numbers, positive or negative, $\{\alpha_1, \alpha_2, \ldots, \alpha_T, \alpha_{T+1}\}$, being the forward purchases of good 1, to satisfy

$$\sum_{t=1}^{T+1} \Pi_t \alpha_t \leqslant 0, \tag{13.25}$$

where Π_t is the present cost of a forward purchase of one unit of good 1 for delivery in week t in terms of good 1 in week 1. Hence, such a series of forward transactions would convert the net revenue sequence to

$$\alpha_1 - \boldsymbol{p}_1 \cdot \boldsymbol{a}_1, \alpha_2 + \boldsymbol{p}_2 \cdot (\boldsymbol{b}_2 - \boldsymbol{a}_2), \ldots, \alpha_T + \boldsymbol{p}_T \cdot (\boldsymbol{b}_T - \boldsymbol{a}_T), \alpha_{T+1} + \boldsymbol{p}_{T+1} \cdot \boldsymbol{b}_{T+1}. \tag{13.26}$$

To put the matter more exactly, (13.26) is the sequence that would come into effect if the relative prices were to take the values $\{\boldsymbol{p}_1, \boldsymbol{p}_2, \ldots, \boldsymbol{p}_{T+1}\}$ and the firm were to engage in no further forward transactions in good 1. But, of course, this is not what will typically occur. As the sequence of net revenue outcomes unfolds itself so the firm will discover that the forward transactions which it has undertaken are no longer the most appropriate ones and further transactions will be undertaken to correct the discrepancy. By that time the structure of forward prices for the remaining weeks may well be different from that which was implicit in the original forward prices $\{1, \Pi_2, \ldots, \Pi_{T+1}\}$.

What we have here is a problem which fundamentally and inescapably belongs to the theory of capital. There is no analogue in static production theory, or indeed in its close relative intertemporal equilibrium theory, for the present type of maximization in which the initial choice is, and is seen by the decision-maker to be, the prelude to a series of further decisions. We have avoided this aspect of the matter with regard to the production decision itself by assuming, quite arbitrarily and not in accord with previous assumptions, that the production decision is a once-for-all decision from which the firm cannot retreat. But this does not give us even a determinate stochastic sequence of net revenues because there remains the possibility of subsequent transactions in forward markets. When one really gets down to doing capital theory its problems are indeed formidable!

So what will the firm maximize? To start with let us put aside some important issues which, however, are not particularly germane to the present discussion. Clearly the firm faces a problem of choice under uncertainty, so one must begin with some assumptions concerning how such choices may be characterized. It is known (Savage, 1954) that under some not too unreasonable assumptions consistent choice of actions under uncertainty implies the existence of a utility function defined over outcomes, and a subjective probability distribution defined over those outcomes, such that the action chosen is one that maximizes the mathematical expectation of utility. It is very far from clear that human beings faced with complicated choices under uncertainty do act consistently, indeed there is evidence to the contrary. But this has not deterred economic theorists from relying almost exclusively on the assumption that they do. Of course, it is not easy to choose an alternative assumption, for which one should it be? We have no contribution to offer on this important question, except that incidentally in discussing investment decisions under uncertainty we will present an example of how complicated these choices can be, and this may lead one to wonder how people can be supposed to choose consistently in a context in which it is difficult even to write down formally the problem that they face. We will follow the usual practice, however, in supposing that where a choice under uncertainty is con rned the firm will choose so as to maximize the expected value of the utilit of the net revenue stream.

If the firm could only trade in the for ard markets once and for all at the outset, in parallel with the assumption hat we are making concerning the production decision, the matter would e straightforward. The firm would choose a production plan $\{a_1 : b_2, a_2; \ldots; b_T, a_T; b_{T+1}\}$ and forward purchases of good 1 $\{\alpha_1, \ldots, \alpha_{T+1}\}$ so as to maximize

$$\mathsf{E}\{U[\alpha_1 - a_1 \cdot p_1, \alpha_2 + p_2 \cdot (b_2 - a_2), \ldots, \alpha_{T+1} + p_{T+1} \cdot b_{T+1}]\}$$

subject to

$$\{a_1; b_2, a_2; \ldots; b_T, a_T; b_{T+1}\} \in \mathscr{S} \tag{13.27}$$

and

$$\sum_{t=1}^{T+1} \Pi_t \alpha_t \leqslant 0,$$

where E stands for the mathematical expectation of the random variable enclosed between the following braces $\{\ldots\}$. So far so good, but of course the assumptions are peculiarly fierce.

To get a feel for a less restricted case consider that the firm has only to choose current input and output vectors and that it may trade repeatedly in the forward markets for good 1. However, we suppose that the firm believes that the structure of own rates of interest in terms of good 1 will remain unaltered. Hence, it has no incentive to speculate in its forward transactions. Suppose further, an important assumption for simplicity in presentation, that the relative price vectors p_t are independently distributed and that the firm does not anticipate the possibility that its subjective probability distributions concerning these price vectors will alter in the future. These assumptions are to be justified only by the simplicity that they bring with them: they are surely not reasonable.

We show that there exists a function relating the mathematical expectation of the final outcome to the initial choices made by the firm. The demonstration is by means of mathematical induction.

Theorem 13.1. Let the firm choose part of the production plan, i.e. the vector couple $(\boldsymbol{a}_1, \boldsymbol{b}_2)$, *and an initial sequence of forward trades* $\{\alpha_1, \ldots, \alpha_{T+1}\}$, *on the assumption that it will subsequently make optimal decisions concerning later production choices and forward trades. Then there exists a function* $V^1(\boldsymbol{a}_1, \boldsymbol{b}_2; \alpha_1, \ldots, \alpha_{T+1})$ *relating the maximized mathematical expectation of the utility of the net revenue sequence to these choice variables.*

Proof. We show that if there exists a function V^t relating the mathematical expectation of the outcome to the choices at week t, to the previous choices, and to the prices that have come to be, then there exists a similar function for week $t-1$. We further note that V^T clearly exists since in the case of decisions in one week, with only the outcome in the following week mattering, there is no problem. Indeed, the formulation is a special case ($T=1$) of (13.27). Then the existence of V^1 follows by mathematical induction.

To start with let us examine the function V^t which exists by assumption. Its arguments are all the production decisions that have been made up to week $t-1$, that is $\{\boldsymbol{a}_1; \boldsymbol{b}_2, \boldsymbol{a}_2, \ldots, \boldsymbol{b}_t\}$; all the forward trades that have already been entered into and which have been discharged or must now be discharged; and all prices which have so far realized themselves. From this data the sequence of net revenues to date can be calculated. On the assumption that relative forward prices are unchanged forward commitments to buy or sell good 1 can be cancelled out by opposing transactions, so these are not relevant. Let α_s^t be the net purchase of good 1 that was obtained in week s ($s = 1, \ldots, t$).

Let

$$\tilde{\mathscr{S}}^t = \{(\boldsymbol{x}, \boldsymbol{y}) \mid \exists (\boldsymbol{a}_t; \boldsymbol{b}_{t+1}, \ldots, \boldsymbol{b}_{T+1})$$

such that

$$(\boldsymbol{a}_1; \boldsymbol{b}_2, \boldsymbol{a}_2; \ldots; \boldsymbol{b}_{t-1}, \boldsymbol{x}; \boldsymbol{y}, \boldsymbol{a}_t; \boldsymbol{b}_{t+1}, \ldots, \boldsymbol{b}_{T+1}) \in \mathscr{S}\}. \tag{13.28}$$

Now we can write V^{t-1} explicitly as

$$V^{t-1}\{\boldsymbol{a}_1; \boldsymbol{b}_2, \boldsymbol{a}_2; \ldots; \boldsymbol{b}_{t-1} | \alpha_1^{t-1}, \ldots, \alpha_{t-1}^{t-1} | \boldsymbol{p}_1, \boldsymbol{p}_2, \ldots, \boldsymbol{p}_{t-1}\}$$
$$= \max_{\substack{\boldsymbol{a}_{t-1}, \boldsymbol{b}_t, \alpha_t^t \\ \text{ST}: (\boldsymbol{a}_{t+1}, \boldsymbol{b}_t) \in \tilde{\mathscr{S}}^t}} \exists \{V^t(\boldsymbol{a}_1; \boldsymbol{b}_2, \boldsymbol{a}_2, \ldots, \boldsymbol{b}_t | \alpha_1^{t-1}, \ldots, \alpha_{t-1}^{t-1}, \alpha_t^t | \boldsymbol{p}_1, \ldots, \boldsymbol{p}_{t-1}, \boldsymbol{p}_t)\}. \tag{13.29}$$

Hence, V^{t-1} is well defined, so that V^1 exists by the induction argument, as required.

We see from theorem 13.1 that it is possible under certain assumptions, and in spite of the complexity of an investment decision under uncertainty, to state that the firm will maximize a particular function of its choice variables. Of course, the argument depends upon the maximization of expected utility, and we have added some additional and quite restrictive assumptions, notably those concerning subjective expectations on prices. Some of these assumptions might be relaxed but it will prove more fruitful now to turn our attention elsewhere.

The reader will have taken note that we have been assuming a general intertemporal production set. In the case of the linear economy the production set constrains separately and independently the individual production couples $(\boldsymbol{a}_t, \boldsymbol{b}_{t+1})$. Moreover, we have previously assumed all goods, even the notional goods of ch. 9, to be priced in competitive markets. Under these assumptions we will arrive, of course, at the conclusion that, even in conditions of temporary equilibrium, the firm need look no more than one week ahead in its production planning. All that will concern it will be the value of its gross output less the cost of inputs in the following week. It can if it wishes sell everything it has, including part used capital goods, and start again. The thrust of these remarks is to underline again the point that the linear economy is not entirely realistic. It is thus appropriate that we have gone beyond it in the present chapter.

The discussion of the objective pursued by the firm has been a lengthy one. Fortunately, the remaining points, concerning constraints on the firm's choices and the character of the solution to the investment problem, can be disposed of quite briefly.

In referring to constraints on the firm's choices we do not of course have in mind the production set, about which enough has already been said. The meaning of the constraints imposed on the firm by the production set is clear. The status of these constraints is unambiguous. Apart from purely budgetary constraints we have not so far taken into account any constraints on the firm's choices aside from those imposed by the production set. As a consequence we have been supposing that the firm can trade as it likes, including trading as it likes in forward markets. We are not going to dispense with the assumption here, but it is worth taking note that it is a very unnatural assumption. We have noted the possibility of bankruptcy if the firm is unfortunate; we have been assuming that the firm has its own private expectations concerning the probabilities that prices will develop in one way or another. One might expect in these circumstances that the capital market would impose its own demands on the firm. It would prove impossible, for example, for a firm likely to be profitable only on its own highly eccentric price expectations to have its forward commitments accepted by a market which was highly sceptical about its prospects.

To put the point differently, we have assumed a perfect capital market and discussed investment in that context. It seems, however, that there could not be a perfect capital market in conditions of temporary equilibrium. The commitments of different firms are far from homogeneous: they cannot be perfect substitutes one for another.

Finally, we may ask to what extent we have been able to provide a characterization of the investment decision as the constrained solution to a maximization problem. At first sight it seems that we have done so. We have the function $V^1(\boldsymbol{a}_1, \boldsymbol{b}_2, \alpha_2^2)$ and the reduced production set $\tilde{\mathcal{S}}^1$. Hence the choice of $(\boldsymbol{a}_1, \boldsymbol{b}_2)$ may be seen as solving

$$\max V^1(\boldsymbol{a}_1, \boldsymbol{b}_2, \alpha_2^2) \quad \text{subject to } (\boldsymbol{a}_1, \boldsymbol{b}_2) \in \tilde{\mathcal{S}}^1. \tag{13.30}$$

Formally, this is equivalent to an ordinary maximization problem. However, the similarity is in fact rather illusory. The point is that a great deal of data on the problem has been dissolved into the function V^1. That function depends, for example, on the form of the full production set $\mathcal{S}$. Hence, as a preference relation it is highly derived. And it hides within itself all the intricacies of the investment decision, under uncertainty, as it has been described. It is doubtful whether it is possible to picture that decision in all its complexities in the mind's eye and to get a clear grasp of it. For this very reason it may be doubted whether the firm in fact chooses investment so as to maximize the expected utility of the outcome.

14

The structure of interest rates

Taking these things together, it still appears that the forward market for loans (like the forward market for commodities) may be expected to have a constitutional weakness on one side, a weakness which offers an opportunity for speculation. If no extra return is offered for long lending, most people (and institutions) would prefer to lend short, at least in the sense that they would prefer to hold their money on deposit in some way or other. But this situation would leave a large excess of demands to borrow long which would not be met.

J. R. HICKS, *Value and Capital* (1946, ch. XI)

The question with which we will be concerned in this chapter is one which has been posed only in recent times and for which it is difficult to discover historical antecedents. For centuries men have asked why interest is paid, whether it should be regulated or prohibited, what makes the rate of interest high here but low there. But always it is *the rate of interest* which stands in need of an explanation. Of course, it is inescapable that there is more than one rate of interest. Always and everywhere the rate of interest charged for loans for which the risk of default is great has been higher than the rate for a safe loan secured by a desirable and negotiable asset. However, that obvious fact can readily be interpreted as the addition of a risk premium to the ruling rate of interest, so that the observer may hold to the view that fundamentally there is only one rate of interest while recognizing that in reality not every loan will cost the exact same rate. Or consider the, again inescapable, fact that the rate of interest is high in time of war when the borrowing requirements of prince or republic are very large. Again, such an obvious observation does not unseat the rate of interest from its place as the dominant concept. The rate is seen as high at times, low at other times, while yet remaining at any one time a single rate.

The time may come when the theory of capital will rebel and throw off once and for all the government of its investigations by the concept of a single interest rate, but that time is not yet here. Indeed, many recent developments have served to enshrine the rate of interest more and more firmly at the centre of the conceptual apparatus of the theory. While theorists have become increasingly aware that there is no rigorous justification for the aggregation of capital, as would be required by a production function, there has not been a parallel growth in awareness that the use of a single rate of return to summarize a stream of returns is quite simply an illegitimate aggregation of the shadow prices that may be associated with an intertemporal possibility set (see above, pp. 229–224).

For Keynes the idea of the marginal product of capital was an abhorrent one because, as he put it (1936, p. 138), it involved '...difficulties as to the definition of the physical unit of capital, which I believe to be both insoluble and unnecessary.' However, the difficulties of definition turn out to be unnecessary because in their place is substituted the *marginal efficiency of capital*, defined by Keynes (1936, p. 135) as '...that rate of discount which would make the present value of the series of annuities given by the returns expected from the capital asset during its life just equal to its supply price.' In this way the yield of an investment in a particular asset is specified by one summary number. Of course, the sleight of hand is all too apparent. Given the *set* of present-value prices at which the yield on an asset just discounts to its cost attention is confined within that set to geometric progressions and if, as Keynes expected, only one such is to be found, the constant of the series provides one summary number. The assertion in the final sentence of the footnote in which Keynes indicates an awareness of the peculiarly special character of this approach is, unfortunately, false (1936, p. 137):

> For the sake of simplicity of statement I have slurred the point that we are dealing with complexes of rates of interest and discount corresponding to the different lengths of time which will elapse before the various prospective returns from the asset are realised. But it is not difficult to re-state the argument so as to cover the point.

Far from it being true that it is not difficult to restate the argument so as to cover the point, it is in fact simply not possible to do so. Only in the special case to which Keynes confined his attention can one hope to obtain an unambiguous definition of the marginal efficiency of capital independently of rates of interest. And even in the special case there is no guarantee that the ambiguity will be absent because, as has already been remarked, the polynomial (10.45) may have multiple roots.

Economic theory has made do for a long time with one rate of interest because economic theory has for a very long time been concerned mainly, if not exclusively, with stationary states or semi-stationary growth. Then, as we have seen (in the appendix to ch. 4) there can be a constant-rate-of-interest price system and provided that the theorist steers clear of such problems as elucidating the nature of 'double switching' no difficulties arise. However, we must now concern ourselves, albeit briefly, with the short run and in that case there can be no valid appeal to a result on the existence of a constant-rate-of-interest price system which applies only to semi-stationary growth paths.

The problem of the structure of interest rates presents itself clearly and unavoidably in the context of a temporary equilibrium. We have seen how a temporary equilibrium in which forward trading is possible only in terms of one good – let it be good 1 to be referred to as *money* – will be characterized by a series of forward prices for that good, i.e.

$$(\Pi_1), \Pi_2, \Pi_3, \ldots, \Pi_T. \tag{14.1}$$

Here we have included the present price of good 1, Π_1. These prices may be translated into a series of interest rates according to the now familiar transformation

$$\left(\frac{\Pi_1}{\Pi_2} - 1\right), \left(\frac{\Pi_1}{\Pi_3} - 1\right), \ldots, \left(\frac{\Pi_1}{\Pi_T} - 1\right). \tag{14.2}$$

To facilitate comparisons we may express these rates as weekly equivalent rates, i.e.

$$\left(\frac{\Pi_1}{\Pi_2}\right) - 1, \left(\frac{\Pi_1}{\Pi_3}\right)^{1/2} - 1, \left(\frac{\Pi_1}{\Pi_4}\right)^{1/3} - 1, \ldots, \left(\frac{\Pi_1}{\Pi_T}\right)^{1/(T-1)} - 1. \tag{14.3}$$

We will refer to (14.3) as the *yield series*[1].

In the case of a constant rate of interest all the terms in the series (14.3) will be the same. There are two further special cases which deserve to be covered by terminology. If (14.3) were monotonically increasing, which would mean that the cost of borrowing long was uniformly higher in terms of the implicit average weekly interest rate than borrowing short, we would say that the term structure is *Hicksian*[2]. If on the contrary the series (14.3) were monotonically decreasing we would say that the term structure is *anti-Hicksian*. Notice that these categories do not exhaust all the possibilities. The series (14.3) may not be monotonic, in which case it will be neither Hicksian nor anti-Hicksian. When the yield series is a sequence of constants the term structure is *flat*. A flat yield series is at once Hicksian and anti-Hicksian.

Now it is obvious that, for temporary equilibrium, the case of a constant interest rate, i.e. a flat term structure, is incredibly special and most unlikely to occur in practice. Indeed, in principle the term structure might be anything one cared to imagine. Recall that in specifying a temporary equilibrium (and taking for simplicity the case where relative price expectations are definite

---

[1] The idea is the same as the *yield curve*, cf. Meiselman (1965, p. 3).

[2] The reference is to the argument of Hicks (1946, ch. XI), from which the quotation at the head of this chapter is taken.

values) one may choose at will not merely technology and preferences, but also price expectations, initial conditions, etc.

Suppose that good 1 is money, the role of which is to act as the medium for intertemporal transactions. Then future money is not desired for itself, but for what it will buy. What it is expected to buy depends upon the anticipations of other prices in terms of money. Hence, one may take a temporary equilibrium and adjust it in the following manner. Let the original expected prices in terms of money for week t ($t = 2, \ldots, T$) for actor i be

$$\begin{bmatrix} 1 \\ \hat{\pi}^i_{2t} \\ \hat{\pi}^i_{3t} \\ \vdots \\ \hat{\pi}^i_{nt} \end{bmatrix}, \qquad t = 2, \ldots, T \tag{14.4}$$

and the present values of money for weeks 2 to T be

$$\Pi_2, \Pi_3, \ldots, \Pi_T. \tag{14.5}$$

Assume throughout that actors accept whatever interest rates an equilibrium throws up, i.e. there is no 'speculation'. Now substitute for the price expectations (14.4) the following price expectations:

$$\begin{bmatrix} 1 \\ \left(\dfrac{1}{1+\sigma_t}\right)^{t-1} \hat{\pi}^i_{2t} \\ \left(\dfrac{1}{1+\sigma_t}\right)^{t-1} \hat{\pi}^i_{3t} \\ \vdots \\ \left(\dfrac{1}{1+\sigma_t}\right)^{t-1} \hat{\pi}^i_{nt} \end{bmatrix}, \qquad t = 2, \ldots, T, \tag{14.6}$$

where the series $\sigma_2, \sigma_3, \ldots, \sigma_T$ comprises positive strictly monotonically increasing terms. The reader may confirm that, were money merely a unit of account to which there corresponded no physical entity, there would exist a new temporary equilibrium identical with regard to real variables, with the same price vector for week 1, and a new present-value-of-money series

$$\Pi_2(1+\sigma_2), \Pi_3(1+\sigma_3)^2, \ldots, \Pi_T(1+\sigma_T)^{T-1}. \tag{14.7}$$

The equilibrium is to all intents and purposes the very same equilibrium. The only difference is that the expectation that money prices will be lower, and to an increasing extent, in future weeks is compensated by a fall in interest rates, which fall is more and more marked the further into the future that we go. If the original present-value prices of money in (14.5) corresponded to a flat yield series we will now have an anti-Hicksian yield series.

Now evidently money is not just a unit of account and one cannot offset the influence of inflationary or deflationary expectations in such a simple manner just by changing interest rates. However, what the discussion has served to show is the crucial importance of expectations in influencing the term structure of interest rates. It will hardly prove possible to say anything definite about what the yield series will be without in some way delimiting the expectations which our actors might hold.

The conclusion is reinforced if we turn to consider the possibility that our actors might adopt speculative positions with regard to futures transactions in money. In week 1 the futures markets offer to an actor the opportunity to trade present money for future money at various dates at prices

$$\Pi_1^{(1)}, \Pi_2^{(1)}, \ldots, \Pi_T^{(1)}. \tag{14.8}$$

In week 2 there will be again an opportunity for forward trading at prices not yet known to the actors:

$$\Pi_2^{(2)}, \Pi_3^{(2)}, \ldots, \Pi_T^{(2)}. \tag{14.9}$$

Again in week 3 there will be prices

$$\Pi_3^{(3)}, \Pi_4^{(3)}, \ldots, \Pi_T^{(3)} \tag{14.10}$$

and so on.

An actor will be said to be a *non-speculator* if he behaves as if he expected for certain that for each t_1 and t_2, and for each s_1 and s_2 ($s_2 > s_1 \geqslant t_2 > t_1$) the following condition would be satisfied:

$$\Pi_{s_1}^{(t_1)}/\Pi_{s_2}^{(t_1)} = \Pi_{s_1}^{(t_2)}/\Pi_{s_2}^{(t_2)}. \tag{14.11}$$

By this it is meant that his actions in the extant markets would not be altered by an infallible revelation that (14.11) will be satisfied. If an actor is a non-speculator he takes the yield series which he faces in week 1 at its face value, i.e. he does not allow for the possibility that the yields for futures transactions which are implicit in the current yield series will not be the yields that will in due course be realized. If an actor is not a non-speculator we refer to him as a *speculator*.

The terms *speculator* and *non-speculator* have been chosen for want of better alternatives but may carry overtones which are not wholly appropriate to the exact definition that has been adopted. However, the terms are not wholly out of place. A speculator is someone who buys something which he does not himself require in the hope of selling it later and thereby gaining. An example of such behaviour is forward purchases and sales of money which the actor does not intend to allow to translate themselves as they stand into net debits or credits for the various subsequent weeks. Rather he intends to transact again later in future money so as to offset some of the commitments which for the time being he has entered into.

Consider as an example a simple case. An actor desires to use part of the revenue that will come to him in week 1 to augment his command over resources in week 3, i.e. he wants to save part of his week 1 wealth with the intention of spending in week 3. The direct and straightforward manner of achieving that end is to purchase money forward for delivery in week 3, which is equivalent to buying a bond of two weeks term to maturity. If the requirement for week 3 money is 1.0 unit the cost in week 1 is $\Pi_3^{(1)}$, which is equivalent to a rate of interest return per week equal to

$$(1/\Pi_3^{(1)})^{1/2} - 1. \tag{14.12}$$

But there is another way of pursuing the same end and it may do better for our actor, although it has to be admitted that it may do worse for him. Instead of purchasing week 3 money forward he can instead purchase week 2 money forward with the intention of using that same week 2 money to purchase week 3 money forward. The cost of buying one unit of money for delivery in week 3 by this method cannot be known for certain in week 1 for it depends upon the presently unknown value $\Pi_3^{(2)}$. It will eventually turn out to be

$$\Pi_2^{(1)}\,\Pi_3^{(2)} \tag{14.13}$$

or

$$\left\{\frac{1}{\Pi_2^{(1)}}\,\frac{1}{\Pi_3^{(2)}}\right\}^{1/2} - 1, \tag{14.14}$$

expressed as a rate of interest return per week. This is an unknown in week 1 because $\Pi_3^{(2)}$ is not revealed at that time. It will eventually turn out to have been better to choose the indirect route if

$$\left\{\frac{1}{\Pi_2^{(1)}}\,\frac{1}{\Pi_3^{(2)}}\right\}^{1/2} > \left\{\frac{1}{\Pi_3^{(1)}}\right\}^{1/2}, \tag{14.15}$$

which, of course, stands in contradiction to (14.11).

Why would an actor choose the indirect route in preference to the direct one? The answer is implicit in the possibility of which (14.15) is an illustration. He may get a better return to his saving by lending short and then lending again than he would by lending long. However, assuming that it is in week 3 that he definitely wants to expend his saving then by choosing the indirect route to adding to his purchasing power in that week he incurs a risk, which he might otherwise have avoided, namely that he is no longer certain at the outset what he will eventually realize in week 3. An actor who is averse to facing risk will not lightly expose himself to the uncertainty that the indirect method necessarily involves. If he does so it will be because he hopes to gain. In other words, if faced with the choice of M units of money in week 3 with certainty, or a probability distribution for money in week 3 given by $P(\mu)$, where μM is the amount of money, $P(\mu)$ the probability of obtaining μM and

$$P(\mu) = Q[\Pi_3^{(1)}/\Pi_2^{(1)})\mu]\,(\Pi_3^{(1)}/\Pi_2^{(1)}\mu^2), \tag{14.16}$$

where $Q(\sigma)$ is the probability distribution of $\Pi_3^{(2)}$, however derived[3], the actor prefers to chance his luck on the outcome of the lottery defined by (14.16). Voluntarily undertaking risk through financial transactions in the hope of gaining thereby is not unreasonably called speculation, which is why the term is not wholly inappropriate.

The point which the above example has served to make clear is in fact quite general. As long as there is a complete system of forward markets for money an actor is enabled, by matching his forward sales or purchases of money in week 1 to his intended savings or dissavings in the various weeks, to avoid all uncertainty with regard to what his saving will yield, and his borrowing cost, in future weeks. It does not follow, of course, that an actor can rid himself of all uncertainty simply by trading in forward money. He does not know for certain the relative price vectors $\boldsymbol{p}_2, \boldsymbol{p}_3, \ldots, \boldsymbol{p}_T$ and he may realize that he cannot be sure of these values. According to the outcome for those vectors his plan, unless he has been peculiarly fortunate in his guesses, will need to be altered and the result will be more forward trading in money. Hence, a non-speculator is not someone who does all his forward trading in money in week 1 and never again trades. It is someone whose actions in week 1 with regard to forward trades in money are not governed in part by a belief that the yield series does not reflect the returns to saving and the costs of borrowing for later weeks that will eventually come about.

Naturally the example that was chosen for the sake of illustration was a very special one, while the point that an actor may gear his trading in future money to his beliefs concerning likely future movements in interest rates is quite general. The minimum number of weeks needed to make the point is of course three, otherwise there is no opportunity to trade later on a second occasion. However, the point is just as valid if there are many weeks to come.

[3] Q could simply be the subjective probability distribution. On decisions and subjective probability, see above, pp. 322–323.

Also, it is not generally the case, as it was in the example, that a speculator chooses to lend shorter than his planned saving period. He can just as well, according to his beliefs, choose to use his savings in week 1 to buy say a claim to money in week 3 although he intends to translate his saving into expenditure as soon as week 2. When week 2 arrives he can borrow (i.e. sell money forward for delivery in week 3) and the money that he collects in week 3 will enable him, all being well, to deliver money in week 3 as promised. If he is fortunate he will have more eventually than a direct transaction would have given him. As is to be expected there is again an avoidable uncertainty in the indirect transaction in that the actor cannot know for sure what he will end up with.

So far we have been discussing only the mildest form of speculation, that which is appended to transactions which would take place anyway in one form or another. We have looked at the case where an actor wants to save for a certain period of time but chooses to buy a longer-dated security (or a shorter-dated security) than corresponds to that period. In so doing he speculates on the terms for loans improving in favour of lenders or going in favour of borrowers. An analogy to international trade may help to underline the point. The most common form which speculation on exchange-rate changes takes is the so-called 'leads and lags'. This involves firms or people who are going to need to buy or sell foreign exchange, as a result, say, of export or import transactions, choosing the exact timing of the sale or purchase of foreign exchange so as to make a gain, or avoid a loss, consequent upon the movement in the exchange rate. Yet there are other cases where foreign exchange is bought or sold for no other reason beyond the hope of a speculative gain. And the same is true of forward transactions in money. If an actor really believes firmly that the yield series will move in some particular manner, then why should he speculate only to the extent of adjusting his own 'genuine' intertemporal transactions? If the forward market for money is open to him, why should he not buy and sell in it to an unlimited extent to reap the gains which his beliefs tell him are there for the taking? There is a technical problem here for the existence of temporary equilibrium which admits of various solutions. The problem is that the excess demand functions will not be well defined if an actor wishes to trade forward for present money to an indefinite extent. The problem is resolved most simply by not allowing such free access to futures markets for money as will allow unbounded trading. This is not merely an assumption of convenience, it makes good economic sense. No capital market is so 'perfect' that an actor can trade in it to any desired extent no matter how far his beliefs diverge from those of other actors. Alternatively, suppose that beliefs concerning the future of the yield series are not held with perfect confidence. Then the fear of losses will tend to deter excessive speculative trading in future money.

It may now be observed that widespread beliefs or expectations concerning the future of the yield series, so long as these amount to more than mere acceptance of whatever the present series happens to be, will themselves carry implications for what form that series will presently take. An example will illustrate the point. Suppose that it is very generally believed that the prices of long-dated securities are temporarily exceptionally high. To be specific, consider an absurdly stylized example. Suppose that the yield series expressed in weekly equivalent interest rates in percentage terms stands at

$$\begin{array}{ccccc} 2 & 3 & 4 & & T \\ 5.0, & 10.0, & 10.0, & \ldots, & 10.0, \end{array} \tag{14.17}$$

while actors for the most part are only willing to attach considerable probabilities to a yield series for week 2 not very dissimilar to

$$\begin{array}{cccc} 3 & 4 & \ldots & T \\ 5.0 & 5.0 & & 5.0. \end{array} \tag{14.18}$$

It must follow that there are powerful forces being exerted to move the latter part of the yield series (14.17) towards (14.18). For lenders who are saving for more than one week will certainly prefer the direct approach, purchasing money for forward delivery two or more weeks ahead, and thereby getting high rates of return which they do not expect to be obtainable next week. Borrowers, on the other hand, will prefer to sell money for forward delivery only one week forward, even if their borrowing needs will persist for more than one week, in the expectation of 'rolling over' the loans more cheaply in week 2. The tendency then will be for borrowing to dominate the short (week 2 money for forward delivery) market and for lending to predominate in the longer markets. As a consequence, the short rate will tend to rise and longer rates to fall and the yield series from week 2 on will move towards (14.18).

There is a general tendency then for the structure of interest rates, or the yield series, to reflect what actors expect it to be. Here we are assuming a general widely held expectation. Obviously if the expectations of individual actors are quite divergent, without any concentration around a particular pattern of expectations, the influence of expectations cancel out, leaving only the general equilibrium forces of supply and demand to determine what will be the yield series. There is a view according to which expectations are the paramount influence on the yield series and this view forms the starting point of the empirical investigations of Meiselman (1965) under the name of the *expectations hypothesis*.

Meiselman undertook a path-breaking piece of work and to do it justice a discussion would have to be lengthy. This is not the place for a complete evaluation of the work, particularly of the empirical testing of the model. However, it is important for us to consider Meiselman's theoretical model of the term structure, partly because it is influential and partly because an examination of it turns out to be an excellent way of elucidating the relations between expectations, speculation and the term structure.

We have seen that if expectations are sufficiently firm and uniform they will tend to be reflected in the yield series. If the yield series is to reflect expectations then risk aversion must be weak enough not to deter the actors from speculating. If risk aversion is very strong the trades that actors undertake will largely reflect the time form of their plans to draw on wealth or add to it. The question is, to what extent are forward purchases and sales of money of different terms – i.e. for different weeks – good substitutes for each other? If an actor does not wish to consume all his net value in week 1 he must buy money for forward delivery. If he is risk averse, money for delivery in one week is not a close substitute for money to be delivered in another week. If he is not very risk averse all forms of saving are close substitutes in his preferences, and he will choose that one which is 'cheapest' (i.e. offers the prospect of the highest return) according to his expectations. Similar considerations apply to borrowers, those who sell money for forward delivery. Where risk aversion is strong the balance of supply and demand in each forward market will determine the forward price in that market. As in the case of many goods, the supplies and demands in any forward market will depend upon all prices and interest rates. But it is only through this usual type of interdependence that the markets will be interrelated. The price of money for forward delivery in 10 weeks will have to balance the demand and supply for money for delivery in 10 weeks, and both these demands and supplies are specific to that particular good. In this case we say that money markets are *segmented*, and we call the hypothesis that they are segmented the *segmentation hypothesis*.

The expectations hypothesis states that money markets are dominated by speculator actors who will switch purchases and sales from one forward market to another according to the expected profitability of such transfers. Hence, the balance of direct non-speculative supply and demand for an individual market becomes unimportant and expectations govern the term structure.

Plainly, the expectations hypothesis is at variance with the argument proposed by Hicks in the quotation at the head of this chapter. Hicks is claiming that on average those who wish to sell money forward (i.e. to borrow) wish to do so for a longer term than those who wish to buy money forward (i.e. to lend). If the markets for forward money are segmented the yield series will have to increase – to take the Hicksian form – to encourage some borrowers to borrow short, or some lenders to lend long, against the inclinations that they would have were the yield series flat. Hicks' argument therefore raises two separate questions, both of which are ultimately empirical questions:

(a) Which is the more valid model, the expectations hypothesis or the market segmentation hypothesis?

(b) Are lenders in general averse to lending long and borrowers to borrowing short?

An argument is sometimes advanced with reference to the second question which is importantly wrong. It is claimed that lenders prefer to lend short because by so doing they avoid *capital risk*. Consider an actor who wants to use part of his purchasing power for week 1 to buy money for forward delivery in a later week. If he buys money for forward delivery next week, week 2, he knows for certain what he will get in week 2 – his contract tells him how much is due to him. But if he buys money for forward delivery in a later week, say week 3, he does not know what the present value of that claim will be in week 2. The value of one unit of money to be delivered in week 3 will be $\Pi_3^{(2)}$ in week 2, but that value is not known for certain in week 1.

When it is put like this it becomes rather transparently obvious what is wrong with the argument. It is undeniable that a short loan avoids capital risk (i.e. uncertainty about the value of the claim in the near future) but in so doing it incurs what might be called *income risk*[4] (i.e. uncertainty about the value of this claim, or subsequent claims purchased by reinvesting the proceeds, in the distant future).

To assume that the average lender is anxious above all to avoid capital risk and that he regards income risk to be a secondary consideration is to beg an important question. Indeed one could imagine a world in which money markets would be dominated on the lending side by widows, averse to risk concerning money income, and desiring to buy long-dated gilts, and on the side of borrowers dominated by businesses desiring mainly to borrow for short-term capital requirements, and preferring short loans. Such a world would be characterized by an anti-Hicksian yield series. Hence, the validity of the vision to which the quotation from Hicks gives expression depends on the validity of the market segmentation hypothesis, and also on the validity of the view that with a flat

---

[4] The term *income risk* is appropriate for the following reason. An actor who wanted to arrange to consume wealth over a period of many weeks and desired to avoid risk concerning the money value of his rate of consumption would buy money for forward delivery in the series of subsequent weeks. This is equivalent to buying a long-dated bond with weekly coupon payments. The value of the bond in week 2 is uncertain but the stream of money payments that will come from it (the income aspect) is not.

The actor is none other than Mrs. Robinson's widow (or orphan); see Robinson (1960), Kahn (1972) and Stiglitz (1970a).

yield series lenders would predominate in the short end of the market and borrowers in the long end. Both views have been challenged. With regard to the second view Meiselman (1965, pp. 14–15) writes:

> Hicks' analytical conclusions do not follow from his assumptions of risk aversion. Lenders face the same uncertainty as borrowers and can, if they so prefer, also hedge against the consequences of interest rate fluctuations. The hedging mechanism for borrowers and lenders is identical and involves matching the expected payments streams of assets, and liabilities. Contrary to Hicks' assertion, there are many institutions which appear to be hedgers in some degree and which have strong preferences for holding long-term assets. Among them are life insurance companies, and pension, endowment, and trust funds. Taken together they hold more financial assets than commercial banks and other institutions which appear to prefer holding short-term assets to hedge their short-term liabilities against some of the consequences of interest rate shifts.

Furthermore, the expectations hypothesis is itself a challenge to the market-segmentation hypothesis. If the expectations hypothesis is valid actors switch from one time pattern of forward sales or purchases of money to another, or speculators do it for them, so freely that it is the pattern of expectations that governs the term structure, not the balance of supplies and demands for long- and short-term credit.

As Meiselman makes very clear the expectations hypothesis as it stands has no empirical content. The reason is obvious. Unless some way can be found of measuring expectations the claim that the pattern of interest rates reflects these expectations is at once uninformative and unfalsifiable. Meiselman finds an ingenious way of giving empirical content to the hypothesis, one which rewards him with impressive statistical results. However, viewed from the position of a theorist, the approach is decidedly perplexing. The idea is to measure not expectations, but changes in expectations. Specifically the 'substantive hypothesis' is that 'forward short-term rates change on the basis of errors made in forecasting the current short-term rate' (Meiselman, 1965, pp. 14–15).

Consider the series of present values of future money that hold in three successive weeks 0, 1, 2. These are

$$\begin{array}{l} \Pi_0^{(0)}, \Pi_1^{(0)}, \Pi_2^{(0)}, \ldots, \Pi_T^{(0)}, \\ \qquad \Pi_1^{(1)}, \Pi_2^{(1)}, \ldots, \Pi_T^{(1)}, \\ \qquad\qquad \Pi_2^{(2)}, \ldots, \Pi_T^{(2)}. \end{array} \tag{14.19}$$

In week 0 there was implicit in the price series a forward rate of return for lending week 1 money for one week. Suppose an actor would like to arrange such a transaction in week 0: specifically he would like to lend out \$1 in week 1 to be repaid in week 2. He first sells forward week 1 money to the value \$1. For this he obtains $\$\Pi_1^{(0)}$ in week 0 money, which money he uses to buy week 2 money forward, obtaining a claim to $\$(\Pi_1^{(0)}/\Pi_2^{(0)})$. His saving will be for one week only, from week 1 to week 2, for he has committed no resources of his own in week 0. The rate of return will be

$$(\Pi_1^{(0)}/\Pi_2^{(0)}) - 1. \tag{14.20}$$

If the expectations hypothesis is valid, (14.20) gives the expectation in the money market of the one-week, or short, rate of interest that will rule in week 1.

However, when week 1 dawns a new series is established and our actors discover that the short rate of interest is in fact

$$(\Pi_1^{(1)}/\Pi_2^{(1)}) - 1, \tag{14.21}$$

which in general will differ from (14.20). The hypothesis is that these 'forecasting errors' concerning the short rate govern movements in forward short rates.

$$\left(\frac{\Pi_{t-1}^{(2)}}{\Pi_t^{(2)}}\right) - \left(\frac{\Pi_{t-1}^{(1)}}{\Pi_t^{(1)}}\right) = h\left[\frac{\Pi_1^{(1)}}{\Pi_2^{(1)}} - \frac{\Pi_1^{(0)}}{\Pi_2^{(0)}}\right], \qquad t = 3, 4, \ldots, T, \tag{14.22}$$

where $h[x]$ is an increasing function with $h[0] = 0$. What the hypothesis states is that the yield series will adjust from week to week so that errors in forecasting the short rate will lead to sympathetic movements in the implicit forward short rates that are embodied in the yield series and which, if the expectations hypothesis is to be credited, are the short rates which the actors expect to rule in the future.

The claim then is that it is expectations that govern the term structure and that changes in expectations are due to unanticipated errors in forecasting the short rate. *The autonomous element in this account is the short rate itself.* The fluctuations in supply and demand for loanable funds can move that rate in any manner whatsoever. What then happens to other rates is a reflection of these movements in expectations. The movements in all other rates apart from the short rate are endogenous.

From the theoretical point of view it is far from clear why the short rate should be elevated to such a regal position. In two separate regards it is given an extremely special role to play. Firstly, the whole structure of interest rates is arranged as a sequence of short rates and implicit forward short rates. Unanticipated movements in current short rates govern expectations of future short rates. One might say that long interest rates as such are faded out of the picture – they remain only as ghostly averages of short rates. If one is talking of the psychology of expectations it is hard to say dogmatically that it cannot be so. Yet from the theoretical point of view this approach is quite arbitrary, which is not to say that it is not correct in fact. Secondly, and more critically, it is very difficult to understand why it should only be movements in the short rate which are autonomous. This is not the only money market that is active, hence not the only money market that is liable to be disturbed by shifts in supply and demand for funds. Of course, if it really were the case that expectations were quite rigid and the market in no way segmented then a shift in the balance of supply and demand in a long market would spill into the short market – the only market where actors would 'accept' a movement in the rate of interest. However, it is not Meiselman's view, for he is proposing precisely a scheme for adjustment of expectations: he does not hold them to be completely rigid.

The discussion of Meiselman's theory has not covered his empirical investigations. It might be argued that the foregoing theoretical arguments are irrelevant to the status of a theory that has acquitted itself well in the empirical arena. We do not share this view of the relation between theory and econometrics. Moreover, it has not been shown that the model performs better than alternative models, for example those which would adjust expectations concerning long rates directly.

There remains a question of considerable importance to which reference must be made. In ch. 3 we sketched an argument showing that there will always exist a configuration of prices, for current goods and for good 1 futures, such that the economy is in temporary equilibrium. At that point it was assumed that our actors accepted the term structure and derived their actions on the assumption that forward rates of interest implicit in it would be the rates in due course realized. That is, the actors were assumed to be non-speculators and they accepted the yield series at its face value. There is no reason for this assumption and it is not at all a natural one. But what happens to the existence of temporary equilibrium if our actors speculate? The question is highlighted by our recent consideration of the expectations hypothesis. For we know that in the extreme case the term structure might be dictated solely by expectations and hence unable to adapt itself to the requirements of equilibrium. What would be the consequences of this state of affairs?

It turns out that speculation and the expectations hypothesis do raise some difficulties for the existence of temporary equilibrium. However, these are more technical difficulties than a fundamental undermining of the idea of temporary equilibrium. We know that the critical features for which we must look, if the existence argument is to proceed as it did before, are that excess demand functions are well defined and continuous. We have noted already that speculation might lead to unbounded excess demand functions for money futures. However, quite plausible restrictions can rule this out.

There may also be discontinuities. As an example, consider the following type of case. An actor confidently expects a particular yield series to be realized in due course. If the yield series announced by the money markets is different from his firm expectation he nevertheless expects just the same yield series to result eventually. If the yield series announced by the market is exactly the one he expects, his trades in future money will reveal just the time form of his net excess demands for money in future weeks. However, most yield series, however close to his expectations, will cause him to respond quite differently, for example by buying no forward money for a certain week at all, but planning an indirect purchase of that money instead. Excess demands for future money exhibit discontinuities.

The obvious way around this difficulty, and one which is again economically plausible, is to require that expectations are not held with such total confidence. In that case an actor will be neither a 'bull' nor a 'bear' and switch sharply from the 'bull ring' to the 'bear ring' when interest rates change ever so slightly (Tobin, 1957–1958).

The reader will be anticipating where our discussion is to lead us. Technical difficulties aside, speculation does not as such interfere with the existence of temporary equilibrium. So long as it may be plausibly assumed that excess demand functions for future money are well defined and continuous, which properties are not fundamentally in conflict with the assumption of speculation, the argument for the existence of temporary equilibrium goes through just as before.

This conclusion is important for certain discussions in macroeconomic theory. Many people have maintained that the reason why 'classical' economic theory was unable to elucidate the phenomenon of involuntary unemployment of labour was that it ignored the uncertainty of the future and the resulting, and inescapable, dependence of current market conditions on subjective, and possibly irrational, expectations. It is true that classical economic theory ignored these problems and that the classical stationary state is a device well designed to ensure that they are ignored. It is not the case, however, that simply bringing these factors into consideration will produce a theory of unemployment. Formally, this is because these factors do not necessarily interfere with the existence of temporary equilibrium – and a temporary equilibrium necessarily has no involuntary unemployment.

That speculation in security markets is not by itself the cause of unemployment is a view implicit in Keynes (1936). Keynes was at pains to argue against the classical (more accurately the neoclassical) view that the labour market is just like any other market in which the price responds to supply and demand just like any other price. Instead he claimed that the supply of labour is related to the money wage as well as to the real wage. It is this feature in conjunction with speculation and uncertainty that gives rise to the distinctly Keynesian conclusions[5].

It should not be forgotten that temporary equilibrium is of very doubtful descriptive value. To show that an equilibrium exists is not to show that it will be attained. This is especially the case where temporary equilibrium is concerned. For does it not take time to attain equilibrium? And by the time that it would have been attained will not time have slipped by and taken us already into the disequilibrium of the next week? However, economic theorists have been understandingly reluctant to follow this line of reasoning to the complete abandonment of equilibrium concepts. In so far as they retain an interest in equilibrium, and in the weakest form of equilibrium, which is temporary equilibrium, it is important to know that speculation and the expectations hypothesis do not necessarily destroy that construct.

---

[5] The point was argued long ago, but in terms of a model which was unhappily vague about the futures markets and the term structure, by Modigliani (1944). It seems that the opposite view is held by Leijonhufvud (1968) (see, in particular, p. 340). Unfortunately the argument of the latter writer is so loose that it is impossible to say for sure where he parts company with our temporary equilibrium model. See Bliss (1974).

Part VI

CONCLUSION

15

Disputations

'Very good, your majesty', replied that man, and in obedience to the rajah gathered together all the blind men, took them with him to the rajah and said: 'Your majesty, all the blind men of Savatthi are now assembled.'
'Then, my good man, show these blind men an elephant.'
'Very good, your majesty', said the man, and did as he was told, saying, 'O ye blind, such as this is an elephant!'
And to one man he presented the head of the elephant, to another the ear, to another a tusk, the trunk, the foot, back, tail and tuft of the tail, saying to each one that that was the elephant.
Now, brethren, that man having presented the elephant to the blind men, came to the rajah and said, 'Your majesty, the elephant has been presented to the blind men. Do what is your will.'
Thereupon, brethren, that rajah went up to the blind men and said to each, 'Have you studied the elephant?'
'Yes, your majesty.'
'Then tell me your conclusions about him.'
Thereupon those who had been presented with the head answered, 'Your majesty, an elephant is just like a pot.' And those who had only observed the ear replied, 'An elephant is just like a winnowing-basket.' Those who had been presented with the tusk said it was a plough-share. Those who knew only the trunk said it was a plough. 'The body', said they, 'is a granary: the foot, a pillar: the back, a mortar: its tail, a pestle: the tuft of the tail just a besom.' Then they began to quarrel, shouting, 'Yes it is! No it isn't! An elephant is not that! Yes it's like that!' and so on, till they came to fisticuffs about the matter.

Sayings of the BHUDDHA, Udana, vi. 4

The theory of capital is notorious for controversy and can even be presented, in the style of a 'western', as a battle between opposing parties (see, for example, Harcourt (1972)). In the foregoing chapters, however, there has been rather little explicit controversy, although several arguments have been mounted which would be fiercely contested by many practitioners of the art. Naturally, where such questions as the status of marginal concepts in capital theory, or the validity of the production function concept, are concerned a strongly controversial element is involved and the reader will not have missed the flavour of it there and elsewhere. However, in many cases our argument has proceeded at a tangent to the main lines of the familiar debates. For this there is a simple reason, namely that the starting point has not been a usual one.

We have looked upon the theory of capital not as some quite separate section of economic theory, only tenuously related to the rest, but rather as an extension of equilibrium theory and production theory to take into account the role of time. This is a programme which others have seen themselves as undertaking, but their pursuit of its logic has not been wholehearted enough. In fact, the implications of the exercise are very radical. We have discovered, for example, that the rate of interest must be dethroned from its unquestioned place as one of the central concepts of the theory. In its place must be substituted an intertemporal price system. Again, comparing global aggregation procedures in the case of the theory of capital with the problem that arises in static production theory, we have not concluded that the aggregation of capital is peculiarly difficult – our conclusion was the opposite. And lastly the so-called problems with marginal concepts in the theory of capital are seen to have exact analogues in static production theory, and arise only from a great over-estimate of what marginal theory can ever achieve.

However, all this concerns technical questions and a consideration of technical questions alone will never reveal why the theory of capital is such hotly contested territory. Everyone understands that there is a strongly ideological element to the debates, but the element is an elusive one.

Consider the following beliefs. 'No meaning can be attached to the idea of "capital" regarded as an aggregate and none to the "marginal product of capital". The distribution of income should be seen as something determined prior to the determination of prices, just as the classical economists saw it, and not simultaneously in a "general equilibrium".' These beliefs could be adhered to just as comfortably by a romantic conservative as by a raging radical. Equally consider this view. 'The wages on which the livelihood of men and women depend are the outcome of a competitive process in which employers with no interest beyond their own profit decide how many hands to employ in the same way as they decide on how much inert land to use.' Is that an apologetic for competitive capitalism? No doubt a great deal could be said, and has been said, in answer to the last question.

However, to see the debates as political wrangles between conservatives and radicals masquerading as economic theory is importantly to misunderstand what is at the bottom of the contentious character of the subject. Beyond doubt there are many causes of disagreement and incivility. The subject is a difficult one; famous schools replete with proud economists are involved; there are faces to be saved, traditions to be vindicated, men to be cut down to size. Each of these explanations contains a germ of truth but none of them is likely to be underestimated. What may easily be underestimated is the importance of Marx and the Marxist tradition, something which is more specific than general radicalism and dislike of capitalism.

The construction of a theory of capital inescapably involves an evaluation of the economic theory of Marx. There was a time when this was perfectly obvious. Böhm-Bawerk constructed his theory of capital as an alternative to the one proposed by Marx, and in this he was not untypical of his time. Marx was perhaps the first architect of a full-blown theory of capital and the evaluation of his theory, whether positively or negatively, became a major concern of later writers.

Today the importance of Marxism in generating the heat that is characteristic of controversy concerning the theory of capital is obscured by several factors. Firstly, until recently at least, and even today on numerous occasions, the controversy includes no explicit reference to Marx or Marxist ideas from either side of the debate. Secondly, only a few of the participants are actually Marxists and of those some are not at all orthodox in their views. Finally, some of the debates (for example the one concerning Solow's views on the rate of return) are concerned with questions on which established Marxist theory has scarcely any purchase.

The importance of Marxism should not be exaggerated. There are some independent influences at work which owe nothing to Marx. Keynes, for example, happened to believe that the marginal product of capital involved insoluble problems of definition[1] and that moreover it was as a concept unnecessary. This view could be traced back to Marshall and beyond without ever reaching Marx. The view as we have seen is neither wholly correct nor wholly incorrect. On a reasonable guess, we have here the main source of the distinctively 'Cambridge' obsession with the problems of aggregate concepts in the theory of capital and the detestation of the production function[2].

There is, however, little danger that the importance of Marxist ideas in fuelling controversy in the theory of capital will be exaggerated. The current tendency is to overlook this factor. Yet when it is overlooked the strongly ideological overtones which attach to seemingly technical debates – on questions for which no sensible man, however sure in his views, would burn at the stake – must be unintelligible. Consider two hypothetical individuals, each with a set of beliefs concerning the theory of capital. Mr. A believes that the rate of profit is determined by the long-run rate of growth divided by the

---

[1] See above, p. 328.

[2] The reader should be clear that to show that an idea is derivative is neither to devalue it nor to enhance its value.

propensity to save out of capitalist income. Mr. B believes that the rate of profit is determined by the marginal product of capital. We have learnt a good deal about these ideas in the foregoing pages. We know that Mr. A might even be right, although if his formula is more than the rehearsal of an uninformative identity the economy must conform to some drastic simplifying assumptions. Mr. B is surely not right if he means by 'determined by' more than 'can be calculated from', although understood in that somewhat hollow sense, and assuming that the marginal product of capital is well defined, what he claims cannot be faulted.

But as far as our present concerns go, by what conceivable process of logical deduction could we derive the conclusion that Mr. B must view the capitalist economic system in a more favourable light than does Mr. A? Naturally, if the appeal be to logical deduction, there is no possibility of making any such inference. Mr. B might deeply detest an economic system based on the pursuit of individual gain. He might hold to the view that there is a fundamental obligation on each and every individual to devote himself to the benefit of his fellow men without thought to personal gain. He might hold it to be an outrage that other men do not behave as he believes they should. As long, however, as he recognizes that they do not so behave he can believe what he believes without any question of inconsistency arising. Mr. A, on the other hand, might take a very benign view of the capitalist system. He might hold the pursuit of individual gain to be a thoroughly healthy activity and believe that men have an inalienable right to what they thereby acquire by way of wealth or income. Those who fare badly he might believe to get their just deserts. One may agree or disagree, but one cannot show the belief to be in contradiction to the theory of the rate of profit to which Mr. A adheres.

It is likely that many people, while agreeing with the claim that ideological evaluations of capitalism cannot be logically inferred from simple theories of capital, would want to point out that one set of beliefs and another set can be connected in more than one manner. Thus, for example, if a man believes in the Newtonian theory of gravitation and also that the mass of the Sun is very large relative to that of the Earth, he ought to believe that the Earth describes an elliptical orbit around the Sun. This is not a case of two sets of beliefs that happen to be associated for whatever reason – one set of beliefs logically implies the other. Let us consider, however, a contrasting example. If someone believes that every man should make a pilgrimage to Mecca at least once in his lifetime we are fairly safe in assuming that he also believes that the meat of the pig should not be eaten. But the confidence with which we would infer the second belief from the first is not founded in any way on a logical implication. There is no logical contradiction in believing that the pilgrimage to Mecca is required while at the same time holding that the meat of the pig must be eaten every day.

In the latter example the connection between the two beliefs is an historical one, not as in the first case a logical implication. Both beliefs are associated with the Muslim religion, in fact the belief that a pilgrimage to Mecca is obligatory virtually identifies the man as an adherent of the Muslim faith. It is surely the case that many statistical associations between one belief and another are to be explained by historical and social factors, not by the occurrence that one belief is logically implied by the other. Certainly the task of anyone who wants to elucidate the nature of the ideological component of the theory of capital includes the analysis of relations between adherence to one kind of model or another and political stances. This is something that Harcourt fails to do when he writes (1972, pp. 12–13):

> One must add that there are ideological reasons as well. These are harder to document, indeed, by their very nature, can only reflect impressions obtained from reading the literature and talking to the participants in the present debate. Nor do I mean that ideologies necessarily affect either logic or theorems. Rather they affect the topics discussed, the manner of discussion, the assumptions chosen, the factors included or left out or inadequately stressed in arguments, comments and models, and attitudes shown, sympathetic or hostile, to past and contemporary economists' works and views. It is my strong impression that if one were to be told whether an economist was fundamentally sympathetic or hostile to basic capitalist institutions, especially private property and the related rights to income streams, or whether he were a hawk or a dove in his views on the Vietnam War, one could predict with a considerable degree of accuracy both his general approach in economic theory and which side he would be in the present controversies[3].

The worrying point about Harcourt's argument is not that he may be wrong to claim the correlation that he thinks he has observed between adherence to a simple neoclassical view of the theory of capital and a lack of sympathy for left political positions. There probably is such a correlation. But it is incumbent on a social scientist to ask and investigate why a correlation exists. Some correlations are spurious – they do not indicate any direct causal connection between the correlated variables. The remark is by no means a hair-splitting one. To take just one example, there are undoubtedly correlations between nationality and adherence to theoretical systems. This reflects the great importance of teaching and tradition in moulding ideas. Equally there are correlations between nationality and political stance. Americans in

---

[3] Of the numerous subsidiary issues to which this passage gives rise one at least deserves a brief remark. Why are ideological positions so hard to document? Why does the questionnaire approach usually adopted by social scientists fail in this case? It is not clear why it should be so. Of course, it is not much use asking on a questionnaire: Are you fundamentally sympathetic or hostile to basic capitalist institutions, especially private property and the related rights to income streams?

general are not noted for a 'fundamental hostility to basic capitalist institutions', although where intellectuals are concerned this may be changing. It is very important that we be alert to the possibility of spurious correlations between ideology and the choice of a simple capital model precisely because there is no direct logical connection to be made. Hence, the discussion of this question by Harcourt is altogether too facile. The demonstration of correlations between theory and ideology does not show that the capital theory debates are in any real sense about ideology.

Nevertheless, there is an indirect connection and it is founded in history – specifically in the history of economic thought. The models which are today dubbed 'neoclassical' do genuinely owe a great deal to that tradition of economics which has been called, perhaps not fortunately, the neoclassical school. The critical feature which connects the modern 'neoclassicals' to the tradition of Cournot, Jevons, Marshall, Menger, Walras and Wicksell, to name but a few writers, and these of quite disparate views, is the belief that the distribution of income is the outcome of market processes the operation of which is not prior to the determination of prices, but which operate along with the determination of prices. To characterize the neoclassical writers by their adherence to this viewpoint is a gross simplification, for not all the writers whom we recognize as in some sense 'neoclassical' arrived at this view. But if one were to use the benefit of hindsight to say where marginal ideas (not the essence of the theory, although many thought it was, but a very crucial tool in the development of the theory) were taking economics it was in the direction of the model of simultaneous determination of incomes and prices.

That was away from the classical view, if again one may grossly simplify, which is why Schumpeter is right to point out (1954, p. 919) that the term 'neoclassical' is a gross misnomer. The classical idea that income distribution is in some sense prior to prices of commodities was submerged by the growth of neoclassical ideas but it did not die. It lived on in the Marxist tradition.

Now is it not the case that the neoclassical writers were apologists for capitalism? Did not economics take a step to the right with the growth of these ideas? These are questions which will spring to the lips of many readers. They do not, however, admit of very simple answers. On the one hand, it is not the case that the economists we usually call neoclassical were in general politically reactionary when compared to their classical predecessors. On the other hand, the vindication of the institution of capitalism was a major concern for them where it had not been one for the English classical political economists. But what is the reason for this? One reason is obvious but may yet be overlooked. The mid-nineteenth century had seen an enormous growth and development of socialist ideology, notably Marxism, and in Britain the radical–liberal tradition. Hence, the institution of capitalism was intellectually under attack on a scale unknown at the beginning of the century. The apologetic element in neoclassical economics is to a large extent the reaction to these new intellectual forces.

This brings us back to the earlier remarks. What is true of socialist ideology is true even more of Marxism. The ideological composition of the neoclassical writers after 1870 necessarily reflects the operation of a selective principle – *whatever else they were they were not Marxists.* Moreover, Marxism was too important to be ignored. Hence, it is no surprise to discover that some of them regarded it as an important part of their task to refute Marxian claims. The refutation of Marxian claims, and apologetics for capitalism and the distribution of income that it throws up, are by no means necessarily the same thing. But they very easily become confounded one with the other[4]. Just as Marx with his theory of exploitation meant to call into question the distribution of income under capitalism so Clark thought that the marginal productivity theory vindicated it. In either case one must note a serious failure to delimit facts and values and to examine the interconnections between them. But note also a likely corollary: attempts to erect an alternative theoretical system to that of Marx will certainly be seen by Marxists as apologetics for capitalism and may well be seen in the same light by those who erect them.

On balance then it looks as though one must reject the view that says that the disputants who do battle in the theory of capital are really engaged in disputes about whether capitalism is an admirable form of social organization, and whether the distribution of income that it throws up is a good one. More plausibly they are engaged, for the most part, just as they seem to be engaged, in rather dry technical arguments. However, these arguments necessarily impinge upon the question of the validity of Marxian economic theory. Marxian economic theory by its nature is part of a larger system, and is seen by the orthodox adherents to that system to be inseparable from it. Hence, there is no call to be surprised that highly technical discussions can trigger strong ideological feelings.

As has been noted many of those who feel that neoclassical theory is apologetics for capitalism are not themselves Marxists. However, since many people are influenced by Marxist ideas who are not themselves Marxists it is not clear that this point invalidates what has been claimed.

The model that has figured in the foregoing chapters is not the 'neoclassical'

---

[4] A good example is the manner in which the argument for the *efficiency* of a competitive market system became confounded with the demonstration of the supposed *optimality* of such a system – quite a different matter.

model as many people will understand that term. Outside ch. 8, and a brief example or two, the notion of a production function with aggregate capital as one of its arguments, to some the hallmark of neoclassical theory, has not figured at all. Moreover, marginal ideas feature in the model as quite subsidiary to the important properties of that model. The *equilibrium theory of capital* would be a more natural title – but let it not be forgotten that we have examined more than one kind of equilibrium. Nevertheless, the model is much closer to neoclassical theory than it is to one version at least of Marxist theory in the following regard. It does not show the distribution of income to be the outcome of a uni-directional chain of causes starting from the rate of exploitation. It shows the distribution of income to be the outcome of the balancing of a large number of mutually interacting forces. In so depicting the determination of the distribution of income the model may be accurate or misleading. The reader will have to make up his own mind which, and he would be ill-advised to do so without reading other works than this one.

It is a serious disadvantage of the equilibrium theory that it is a complicated model devoid of simple general results. As such it is perhaps not very practical and even its adherents may have recourse to simpler models (such as the partial equilibrium model) to assist with answering concrete questions. Its advantage, on the other hand, is that it is flexible and can be adapted to answer all kinds of questions and to take into account institutional factors of many kinds. Where the justification of the distribution of income is concerned it is, of course, impotent, although it can be employed by people with all kinds of different values, and even to choose policies to improve the distribution of income. It is apologetic only if all alternatives to the Marxian system are apologetic – for it is an alternative to the Marxian system.

Mathematical appendix

In this mathematical appendix a number of definitions and results, to which reference has been made above, will be stated. In most cases proofs will be provided. There is no intention to provide a coverage beyond the needs of the present volume and the reader broadly interested in the mathematics which is particularly applicable to economics should look elsewhere; see in particular, Intriligator (1971) and Lancaster (1968).

While, however, it is not our aim to duplicate the work of specialized texts on mathematical economics, we have not avoided dealing with matters which may be found in other places. There are several reasons for including such material. First, where something may be briefly and simply disposed of it is useful to have it close to hand. Second, even where a result is readily available in another place the proof here offered may be different from the usual ones in some significant way. An instance of this is the theory of linear programming and the duality theorem where the proofs provided in mathematical texts are not as intuitive from the economic point of view as the proof given below. Third, there is one result in this appendix (theorem 16.9) which, while it is by no means unobvious, has not apparently been stated and proved before.

1. Sets and convex sets

We consider *subsets* of the vector space[1] R^n which we will refer to as *sets*. If the vector $\boldsymbol{x}$ is contained in the set $\mathcal{Q}$ we write '$\boldsymbol{x} \in \mathcal{Q}$'. A particular example of a subset of R^n is the ε *neighbourhood* of $\boldsymbol{x}$, denoted $\mathcal{N}_\varepsilon(\boldsymbol{x})$, and defined as

$$\mathcal{N}_\varepsilon(\boldsymbol{x}) = \{\boldsymbol{y} \mid (\boldsymbol{x} - \boldsymbol{y})^2 < \varepsilon\}. \qquad (16.1)$$

The vector $\boldsymbol{x}$ is said to be in the *interior* of $\mathcal{Q}$ (denoted int $\mathcal{Q}$) if there exists a scalar $\mu > 0$ such that for all $\varepsilon < \mu, \mathcal{N}_\varepsilon(\boldsymbol{x}) \subset \mathcal{Q}$. If $\boldsymbol{x}$ is a vector each of whose

[1] For the concept of a vector space and for algebraic operations involving vectors, see Halmos (1958).

neighbourhoods contains vectors $\in \mathcal{Q}$, and also vectors $\notin \mathcal{Q}$, $\boldsymbol{x}$ is said to be in the *boundary of* $\mathcal{Q}$ (denoted bnd $\mathcal{Q}$).

Definition 16.1. The set $\mathcal{Q}$ is said to be *convex* if for all $\boldsymbol{x}_1 \in \mathcal{Q}$ and $\boldsymbol{x}_2 \in \mathcal{Q}$, and for all λ such that $0 < \lambda < 1$, we have

$$\lambda \boldsymbol{x}_1 + (1-\lambda)\boldsymbol{x}_2 \in \mathcal{Q}. \tag{16.2}$$

If all convex combinations of the form of (16.2) for $0 < \lambda < 1$ are in int $\mathcal{Q}$ we say that $\mathcal{Q}$ is *strictly* convex.

Definition 16.2. The set $\mathcal{Q}$ is said to be a *cone* if for all $\boldsymbol{x} \in \mathcal{Q}$ and $\lambda > 0$, $\lambda \boldsymbol{x} \in \mathcal{Q}$.

Definition 16.3. The *convex sum* of two sets $\mathcal{Q}_1$ and $\mathcal{Q}_2$ is the set

$$\{\boldsymbol{x} | \boldsymbol{x} = \lambda \boldsymbol{x}^1 + (1-\lambda)\boldsymbol{x}^2, 0 \leqslant \lambda \leqslant 1, \boldsymbol{x}^2 \in \mathcal{Q}_1 \text{ and } \boldsymbol{x}^2 \in \mathcal{Q}_2\}. \tag{16.3}$$

Definition 16.4. A set $\mathcal{H}$ is a *hyperplane* if there exists a vector $\boldsymbol{a}^0$ and a scalar α_0 such that $\boldsymbol{x} \in \mathcal{H}$ if and only if $\boldsymbol{a}^0 \cdot \boldsymbol{x} = \alpha_0$.

Definition 16.5. Let $\mathcal{Q}$ be a subset of R^n. Let $\boldsymbol{x}^0$ be a point in the boundary of $\mathcal{Q}$. The hyperplane defined by $\boldsymbol{a}$ and passing through $\boldsymbol{x}^0$ (i.e. the set of all $\boldsymbol{x}$ such that $\boldsymbol{a} \cdot \boldsymbol{x} = \boldsymbol{a} \cdot \boldsymbol{x}^0$) is said to *support* $\mathcal{Q}$ at $\boldsymbol{x}^0$ if

$$\boldsymbol{a} \cdot \boldsymbol{x} < \boldsymbol{a} \cdot \boldsymbol{x}^0 \Rightarrow \boldsymbol{x} \notin \mathcal{Q}. \tag{16.4}$$

We have now prepared the ground for the statement of a most important result.

Theorem 16.1. Let $\mathcal{Q}$ be a convex set, and let $\boldsymbol{x}^0$ be a point in the boundary of $\mathcal{Q}$. Then there exists a hyperplane which supports $\mathcal{Q}$ at $\boldsymbol{x}^0$.

Proof. The proof is omitted. An elegant and none too difficult proof is to be found in Karlin (1959, vol. I, appendix A).

2. Concave functions

Definition 16.6. Let $f(\boldsymbol{x})$ be a real-valued function of the vector $\boldsymbol{x}$ defined on a convex set. f is said to be *concave* if

$$f[\lambda \boldsymbol{x}^1 + (1-\lambda)\boldsymbol{x}^2] \geqslant \lambda f(\boldsymbol{x}^1) + (1-\lambda) f(\boldsymbol{x}^2), \qquad 0 < \lambda < 1. \tag{16.5}$$

If the inequality of (16.4) is satisfied strictly f is *strictly concave.*

The following result on concave functions proves useful[2].

Theorem 16.2. Let $f(\mu)$ be a concave function of the real number μ, defined on a closed interval I. Consider a sequence of points of I $(\mu_1, \mu_2, \ldots, \mu_k, \ldots)$ such that limit as $k \to \infty$ of $\mu_k = \mu_0$. Then:

(i) f is continuous on the interior of I;

(ii) $\mu_k > \mu_0$ all k, implies either that

$$\lim_{k\to\infty} [f(\mu_k) - f(\mu_0)]/(\mu_k - \mu_0),$$

denoted $f'_+(\mu_0)$, exists; or that limit is '$+\infty$';

(iii) $\mu_k < \mu_0$ all k, implies either that

$$\lim_{k\to\infty} [f(\mu_k) - f(\mu_0)]/(\mu_k - \mu_0),$$

denoted $f'_-(\mu_0)$, exists or that limit is '$-\infty$';

(iv) the or case in both (ii) and (iii) can only be realized at an endpoint of I;

(v) $f'_+(\mu_0) \leqslant f'_-(\mu_0)$ for μ_0 in the interior of I.

Proof. Notice first that (ii) and (iii) together imply (i). For suppose that f is not continuous at μ_0 interior to I. Then there exists a sequence in I whose limit is μ_0 such that $f(\mu_k)$ does not tend to $f(\mu_0)$. Furthermore, we can choose the sequence μ_k either greater than or less than μ_0 (for if a function is continuous above and below μ_0, tending in each case to the same limit, then it is continuous at μ_0). But then, as $k \to \infty$,

$$[f(\mu_k) - f(\mu_0)]/(\mu_k - \mu_0) \to \text{'}\pm\infty\text{'}$$

at an interior point of I. Notice that continuity at the endpoints of I is not implied by concavity as can be seen from the following concave function on the unit interval:

$$f(0) = 0, \qquad f(\mu) = 1, \qquad f(1) = 0, \qquad 0 < \mu < 1. \tag{16.6}$$

Here f is concave but not continuous.

We show (ii); an analogous argument taking account of sign changes establishes (iii).

Confine attention to monotonically decreasing sequences μ_k since this suffices. Then

$$\mu_0 < \mu_k \leqslant \mu_{k+1} \tag{16.7}$$

---

[2] For this and many other results on convexity and concave functions the reader may consult Eggleston (1963).

and

$$\mu_k = \lambda_k \mu_0 + (1-\lambda_k)\mu_{k-1} \quad \text{for some } \lambda_k, \qquad 0 \leqslant \lambda_k < 1; \tag{16.8}$$

and

$$\mu_k - \mu_0 = (1-\lambda_k)[\mu_{k-1} - \mu_0]. \tag{16.9}$$

Now, since f is concave,

$$f(\mu_k) \geqslant \lambda f(\mu_0) + (1-\lambda_k) f(\mu_{k-1}), \tag{16.10}$$

so that

$$f(\mu_k) - f(\mu_0) \geqslant (1-\lambda_k)[f(\mu_{k-1}) - f(\mu_0)]. \tag{16.11}$$

Dividing (16.11) by (16.9) one obtains

$$\frac{f(\mu_k) - f(\mu_0)}{\mu_k - \mu_0} \geqslant \frac{f(\mu_{k-1}) - f(\mu_0)}{\mu_{k-1} - \mu_0}, \tag{16.12}$$

so that these ratios increase monotonically with k. A sequence which increases monotonically either has a limit, or increases without limit, so that the first part of (ii) is established.

Now suppose that μ^- and μ^+ are two values such that $\mu^- < \mu_0 < \mu^+$. Then there exists a λ between zero and 1 such that

$$\mu_0 = \lambda\mu^- + (1-\lambda)\mu^+ \tag{16.13}$$

or

$$-\lambda(\mu^- - \mu_0) = (1-\lambda)[\mu^+ - \mu_0]. \tag{16.14}$$

Then, by concavity of f,

$$f(\mu_0) \geqslant \lambda f(\mu^-) + (1-\lambda) f(\mu^+) \tag{16.15}$$

so that

$$-\lambda[f(\mu^-) - f(\mu_0)] \geqslant (1-\lambda)[f(\mu^+) - f(\mu_0)]. \tag{16.16}$$

From (16.14) and (16.16),

$$\frac{f(\mu^-) - f(\mu_0)}{\mu^- - \mu_0} \geqslant \frac{f(\mu^+) - f(\mu_0)}{\mu^+ - \mu_0}. \tag{16.17}$$

This last inequality holds when we take limits so that

$$f'_-(\mu_0) \geqslant f'_+(\mu_0), \tag{16.18}$$

as required.

It only remains to note that (16.17) rules out the possibility of $f'_- =$ '$+\infty$' ($f'_+ =$ '$-\infty$') except at an endpoint, since at an interior point of I the sequence of ratios $[f(\mu_k)-f(\mu_0)]/(\mu_k-\mu_0)$ is bounded above (below) by any ratio of the same form evaluated at $\mu_k<\mu_0$ $(\mu_k>\mu_0)$. The proof of theorem 16.2 is complete.

3. Non-linear programming

Let $f(\boldsymbol{x})$ and $g^j(\boldsymbol{x})$ $(j=1,\ldots,m)$ be continuous functions of the vector $\boldsymbol{x}$. Then the following problem is a *programme*:

$$\max_{\boldsymbol{x}} f(\boldsymbol{x}); \qquad \text{ST}: g^j(\boldsymbol{x}) \geqslant 0 \qquad (j=1,\ldots,m); \qquad \boldsymbol{x} \geqq \boldsymbol{0}.^3 \tag{16.19}$$

If f and g^j $(j=1,\ldots,m)$ are concave functions the programme is a *concave programme*. If the functions f and g^j $(j=1,\ldots,m)$ are linear functions the programme is a *linear programme*. A linear programme may be written concisely as

$$\max_{\boldsymbol{x}} \boldsymbol{a}\cdot\boldsymbol{x}, \qquad \text{ST}: \boldsymbol{B}\cdot\boldsymbol{x} \leqq \boldsymbol{c}, \qquad \boldsymbol{x} \geqq \boldsymbol{0}, \tag{16.20}$$

where $\boldsymbol{B}$ is a matrix with m rows. This is a special case of (16.19) with $f(\boldsymbol{x})=\boldsymbol{a}\cdot\boldsymbol{x}$, and $g^j(\boldsymbol{x})=c_j-\boldsymbol{b}^j\cdot\boldsymbol{x}$, where c_j is the jth element of the vector $\boldsymbol{c}$ and $\boldsymbol{b}^j$ is the jth row of $\boldsymbol{B}$. We will devote the next section to a discussion of this special case.

Let $\boldsymbol{x}$ and $\boldsymbol{y}$ be two vectors. Then $\mathrm{d}(\boldsymbol{x},\boldsymbol{y})$ is defined to be $[(\boldsymbol{x}-\boldsymbol{y})\cdot(\boldsymbol{x}-\boldsymbol{y})]^{1/2}$, i.e. $\mathrm{d}(\boldsymbol{x},\boldsymbol{y})$ is the Euclidean distance between $\boldsymbol{x}$ and $\boldsymbol{y}$.

Definition 16.7. Let $f(\boldsymbol{x})$ be a real-valued function defined for all $\boldsymbol{x}\in\mathscr{C}$ and let $\boldsymbol{x}^0$ be a point of $\mathscr{C}$. Then f will be said to have *bounded steepness in* $\mathscr{C}$ at $\boldsymbol{x}^0$ if there exists a scalar $\alpha_{\boldsymbol{x}^0}$ such that

$$[f(\boldsymbol{x})-f(\boldsymbol{x}^0)]/\mathrm{d}(\boldsymbol{x},\boldsymbol{x}^0) \leqslant \alpha_{\boldsymbol{x}^0} \quad \text{for } \boldsymbol{x}\in\mathscr{C}. \tag{16.21}$$

Let (16.19) be a concave programme which has a solution and let the function $V(\boldsymbol{z})$ be defined as follows:

$$V(\boldsymbol{z}) = \max_{\boldsymbol{x}} f(\boldsymbol{x}); \qquad \text{ST}: g^j(\boldsymbol{x}) \geqslant z_j \qquad (j=1,\ldots,m); \qquad \boldsymbol{x} \geqq \boldsymbol{0}. \tag{16.22}$$

V is defined for all $\boldsymbol{z}$ such that the programme (16.22) has a solution, i.e. for all $\boldsymbol{z}\in\mathscr{C}$. Clearly $\boldsymbol{0}\in\mathscr{C}$ since with $\boldsymbol{z}=\boldsymbol{0}$ (16.22) reduces to (16.19).

---

[3] 'max $\boldsymbol{x}$' means that $\boldsymbol{x}$ is to be chosen so as to maximize the value of $f(\boldsymbol{x})$. 'ST' is short for 'subject to' and means that $\boldsymbol{x}$ must be chosen so as to satisfy each of the conditions that follow.

Theorem 16.3 (Kuhn and Tucker)[4]. *If V defined for feasible $\mathbf{z}$ has bounded steepness at $\mathbf{0}$ there exists a non-negative m vector $\mathbf{p}^*$ such that the Lagrangian form*

$$f(x) + \sum_{j=1}^{m} p_j^* g^j(x) \tag{16.23}$$

is maximized for $\mathbf{x}$ non-negative by choosing $\mathbf{x} = \mathbf{x}^*$.

Proof. Consider the set $\mathscr{S}$ defined as follows:

$$\mathscr{S} = \{(\gamma, z) | \exists\, \mathbf{x} \geqq \mathbf{0}, g^j(x) \geqslant z_j (j = 1, \ldots, m);\ f(x) \geqslant \gamma\}. \tag{16.24}$$

$\mathscr{S}$ is the set of all feasible pairs of constraining vectors and the value of the programme. Next, note the following properties of $\mathscr{S}$ (detailed proofs are exercises):

(1) $\mathscr{S}$ is closed,
(2) $\mathscr{S}$ is convex, (16.25)
(3) $[V(z), z]$ is in the boundary of $\mathscr{S}$.

Given the conditions (16.25), theorem 16.1 may be applied to declare that there exists a supporting hyperplane to $\mathscr{S}$ at $[V(\mathbf{0}), \mathbf{0}]$. That is, there exists an $(m+1)$ vector, with elements $(\pi_0; \pi_1, \ldots, \pi_m)$ such that

$$\pi_0 \gamma + \sum_{j=1}^{m} \pi_j z_j < \pi_0 V(\mathbf{0}) \Rightarrow (\gamma; z_1, z_2, \ldots, z_m) \notin \mathscr{S}. \tag{16.26}$$

The π values may be signed from the following considerations. Firstly, notice that $\pi_j \leqslant 0, j = 1, \ldots, m$. For suppose that, for some j, $\pi_j > 0$. Clearly $[V(\mathbf{0}), \mathbf{0}] \in \mathscr{S}$ implies that $[V(\mathbf{0}), z'] \in \mathscr{S}$ for any $z' \leqq \mathbf{0}$. Hence, we may choose z' equal to $\mathbf{0}$ except for the jth element which will be negative. Then

$$\pi_0 V(\mathbf{0}) + \sum_{j=1}^{m} \pi_j z_j' < \pi_0 V(\mathbf{0}), \tag{16.27}$$

notwithstanding the fact that $[V(\mathbf{0}), z'] \in \mathscr{S}$, so that $(\pi_0; \pi_1, \ldots, \pi_m)$ does not define a supporting hyperplane, contrary to assumption. Secondly, notice that $\pi_0 < 0$. For suppose $\pi_0 \geqslant 0$. We take the two particular possibilities in turn. Consider $\pi_0 > 0$. Evidently this is impossible, for the definition of $\mathscr{S}$ only constrains the choice of the first element of a constituent vector by the

---

[4] This is only one of the theorems proved by Kuhn and Tucker (1951), and it is not even necessarily the most important. However, for our present purposes it is the one that is required. The theorem is not exactly that proved by Kuhn and Tucker. It is in fact an amalgam of two of their results; moreover, they impose a different regularity condition from the bounded steepness condition. The latter condition is due to Gale (1967).

inequality $f(x) \geqslant \gamma$. Hence, γ may be chosen as small as desired. Then (16.26) could be satisfied trivially with $(\gamma; \tilde{z}_1, \ldots, \tilde{z}_m)$ a point in $\mathscr{S}$. It would only be necessary to assign to γ a smaller value than $V(\mathbf{0})$. Consider now the possibility that we might have $\pi_0 = 0$. There is nothing to rule out that possibility, but if it arises choose another supporting hyperplane with $\pi_0 \neq 0$. It is only necessary to show that this is always possible. Since the function $V(\mathbf{z})$ has bounded steepness at $\mathbf{z} = \mathbf{0}$ there exists a scalar α^0 such that (16.21) is satisfied. Hence, in particular there exists an α^0 such that for any scalar λ,

$$[V(-\lambda \mathbf{u}) - V(\mathbf{0})]/\sqrt{m}\lambda \leqslant \alpha^0, \tag{16.28}$$

where $\mathbf{u}$ is the m vector each of whose elements is 1. From (16.28) it follows that the ray $\mathscr{R}$ defined as

$$\mathscr{R} = [V(\mathbf{0}), \mathbf{0}] + \lambda[\alpha^0\sqrt{m}, -\mathbf{u}] \tag{16.29}$$

does not intersect the interior of $\mathscr{S}$. Form the convex sum of $\mathscr{R}$ and $\mathscr{S}$. Then the points of $\mathscr{R}$ are in the boundary of this set which is itself a convex set. Then from theorem 16.1 there exists a supporting hyperplane to the convex sum at $[V(\mathbf{0}), \mathbf{0}]$ and this hyperplane must contain $\mathscr{R}$. It must also support $\mathscr{S}$, which is a subset of the convex sum. However, clearly this hyperplane cannot be defined by a vector the first element of which is zero, for then it would not contain $\mathscr{R}$. It follows that we may choose a supporting hyperplane such that $\pi_0 \neq 0$.

We will now show that

$$\mathbf{p}^* = \begin{bmatrix} \dfrac{\pi_1}{\pi_0} \\ \dfrac{\pi_2}{\pi_0} \\ \vdots \\ \dfrac{\pi_m}{\pi_0} \end{bmatrix} \tag{16.30}$$

satisfies the requirement of the theorem. Suppose that this is not the case. Then there exists $\mathbf{x}^0 \geqq \mathbf{0}$ such that

$$f(\mathbf{x}^0) + \sum_{j=1}^{m} \frac{\pi^j}{\pi_0} g^j(\mathbf{x}^0) > f(\mathbf{x}^*) + \sum_{j=1}^{m} \frac{\pi^j}{\pi_0} g^j(\mathbf{x}^*). \tag{16.31}$$

Hence, since $\pi_0 < 0$,

$$\pi_0 f(\mathbf{x}^0) + \sum_{j=1}^{m} \pi^j g^j(\mathbf{x}^0) < \pi_0 f(\mathbf{x}^*) + \sum_{j=1}^{m} \pi^j g^j(\mathbf{x}^*) \tag{16.32}$$

or

$$\pi_0 f(\boldsymbol{x}^0) + \sum_{j=1}^{m} \pi^j g^j(\boldsymbol{x}^0) < \pi_0 V(\mathbf{0}) + \sum_{j=1}^{m} \pi^j z_j, \tag{16.33}$$

since

$$f(\boldsymbol{x}^*) = V(\mathbf{0}) \quad \text{and} \quad \pi^j z_j \geqslant \pi^j g^j(\boldsymbol{x}^*). \tag{16.34}$$

However,

$$[f(\boldsymbol{x}^0); g^1(\boldsymbol{x}^0), g^2(\boldsymbol{x}^0), \ldots, g^m(\boldsymbol{x}^0)]$$

is a point of $\mathscr{S}$ by the definition of that set. Hence, taking into account (16.32), $(\pi_0, \pi_1, \ldots, \pi_m)$ cannot define a supporting hyperplane, contrary to assumption.

Finally, notice that $\pi^j/\pi_0 \geqslant 0$ all j so that the vector defined by (16.30) is non-negative, as required. The proof of theorem 16.3 is now complete.

To understand the important role played by the assumption of bounded steepness consider the following example.

Example 16.1. The programme is as follows:

$$\max \mu, \qquad \text{ST}: -\mu^2 \geqslant 0, \qquad \mu \geqslant 0. \tag{16.35}$$

The solution is $\mu = 0$ (there is no other feasible solution). The Lagrangian form is

$$\mu - \pi\mu^2. \tag{16.36}$$

However, (16.36) can be made positive by choice of some positive μ for each value of π however large. Hence, there exists no value of π for which $\mu = 0$ maximizes (16.36).

If we assume, as we have not so far assumed, that the functions f and g^j are differentiable we can derive a further result.

Theorem 16.4. Let the programme (16.19) be characterized by differentiable functions. Let $\boldsymbol{x}^*$ be an n vector, the solution to the programme, and $\boldsymbol{p}^*$ a vector satisfying the conditions of theorem 16.3. Then the following conditions are satisfied:

$$f_i(\boldsymbol{x}^*) + \sum_{j=1}^{m} p_j^* g_i^j(\boldsymbol{x}^*) \leqslant 0 \quad \text{comp} \quad x_i^* \geqslant 0 \qquad (i = 1, \ldots, n);^5 \tag{16.37}$$

[5] The term 'comp' means that at least one of the inequalities between which it appears is satisfied strictly. More generally, where vectors are involved, '$\boldsymbol{z}^1 \geqq \mathbf{0}$ comp $\boldsymbol{z}^2 \geqq \mathbf{0}$' means that $\boldsymbol{z}^1 \cdot \boldsymbol{z}^2 = 0$.

where $f_i(\boldsymbol{x}^*) = \partial f/\partial x^i$ *evaluated at* $\boldsymbol{x} = \boldsymbol{x}^*$, *and* $g_i^j(\boldsymbol{x}^*) = \partial g^j/\partial x^i$ *evaluated at* $\boldsymbol{x} = \boldsymbol{x}^*$. *We will also have*

$$g^j(\boldsymbol{x}^*) \geqslant 0 \quad \text{comp} \quad p_j^* \geqslant 0.^6 \tag{16.38}$$

Proof. Let $\bar{\boldsymbol{x}}'$ be any vector with the property that $\bar{x}_i' = 0$ whenever $x_i^* = 0$. Since (16.23) is maximized by $\boldsymbol{x} = \boldsymbol{x}^*$ we must have

$$f(\boldsymbol{x}^* + \theta\bar{\boldsymbol{x}}') + \sum_{j=1}^{m} p_j^* g^j(\boldsymbol{x}^* + \theta\bar{\boldsymbol{x}}') \tag{16.39}$$

maximized by $\theta = 0$, since $\boldsymbol{x}^* + \theta\boldsymbol{x}' \geqq \boldsymbol{0}$ for θ sufficiently small. Thus we must have

$$\sum_{i=1}^{n} f_i(\boldsymbol{x}^*)\,\bar{x}_i' + \sum_{j=1}^{m}\sum_{i=1}^{n} p_j^* g_i^j(\boldsymbol{x}^*)\bar{x}_i' = 0 \tag{16.40}$$

or

$$\sum_{i=1}^{n}\left[f_i(\boldsymbol{x}^*) + \sum_{j=1}^{m} p_j^* g_i^j(\boldsymbol{x}^*)\right]\bar{x}_i' = 0. \tag{16.41}$$

Hence, whenever $\bar{x}_i'$ is not zero by definition, i.e. whenever $x_i^* \neq 0$, we must have

$$f_i(\boldsymbol{x}^*) + \sum_{j=1}^{m} p_j^* g_i^j(\boldsymbol{x}^*) = 0, \tag{16.42}$$

for otherwise (16.41) could not be satisfied for arbitrary $\bar{x}_i'$.

Next, choose $\bar{\boldsymbol{x}}^2$ such that $\bar{x}_1^2 > 0$ for some i such that $x_1^* = 0$, $\bar{x}_i^2 = 0$ otherwise. For positive θ, $\boldsymbol{x}^* + \theta\bar{\boldsymbol{x}}^2$ is non-negative. Hence, since (16.23) is maximized, we must have

$$f(\boldsymbol{x}^* + \theta\bar{\boldsymbol{x}}^2) - f(\boldsymbol{x}^*) + \sum_{j=1}^{m} p_j^*[g^j(\boldsymbol{x}^* + \theta\bar{\boldsymbol{x}}^2) - g^j(\boldsymbol{x}^*)] \leqslant 0. \tag{16.43}$$

Hence,

$$\frac{f(\boldsymbol{x}^* + \theta\bar{\boldsymbol{x}}^2) - f(\boldsymbol{x}^*)}{\theta} + \sum_{j=1}^{m} p_j^*\left[\frac{g^j(\boldsymbol{x}^* + \theta\bar{\boldsymbol{x}}^2) - g^j(\boldsymbol{x}^*)}{\theta}\right] \leqslant 0. \tag{16.44}$$

Taking the limit as $\theta \to 0$ we obtain

$$f_i(\boldsymbol{x}^*)\,\bar{x}_1^2 + \sum_{j=1}^{m} p_j^* g_i^j(\boldsymbol{x}^*)\,\bar{x}_1^2 \leqslant 0. \tag{16.45}$$

Thus,

$$f_i(\boldsymbol{x}^*) + \sum_{j=1}^{m} p_j^* g_i^j(\boldsymbol{x}^*) \leqslant 0, \tag{16.46}$$

---

[6] Kuhn and Tucker (1951) show that a vector $\boldsymbol{p}^*$ exists such that (16.37) and (16.38) are satisfied even without a restriction of the argument to concave programming. Of course, concavity is definitely required to obtain theorem 16.3.

for this value of i for which $x_i^* = 0$. But the same argument applies to any i for which $x_i^* = 0$. Hence, for all such i we have (16.45). Thus, taking into account this last result, together with (16.42), we have shown (16.47), as required.

Lastly note that (16.36) must be satisfied by construction. If one of the programme constraints is non-binding this implies that the same programme value would be attained with a larger constant attaching to that constraint. But then (16.32) could be violated since the π_j in that case would be negative. The proof of the theorem is complete.

4. Linear programming

Associated with the *linear programme*

$$\max_{\boldsymbol{x}} \boldsymbol{a}\cdot\boldsymbol{x}, \qquad \text{ST}: \boldsymbol{B}\cdot\boldsymbol{x} \leqq \boldsymbol{c}, \qquad \boldsymbol{x} \geqq \boldsymbol{0} \tag{16.47}$$

is another linear programme, the *dual linear programme*

$$\min_{\boldsymbol{p}} \boldsymbol{p}\cdot\boldsymbol{c}, \qquad \text{ST}: \boldsymbol{p}\cdot\boldsymbol{B} \geqq \boldsymbol{a}, \qquad \boldsymbol{p} \geqq \boldsymbol{0}. \tag{16.48}$$

Since we have

$$\boldsymbol{p}\cdot\boldsymbol{B} \geqq \boldsymbol{a} \quad \text{and} \quad \boldsymbol{x} \geqq \boldsymbol{0}, \tag{16.49}$$

we obtain

$$\boldsymbol{p}\cdot\boldsymbol{B}\cdot\boldsymbol{x} \geqslant \boldsymbol{a}\cdot\boldsymbol{x}. \tag{16.50}$$

Similarly, since

$$\boldsymbol{B}\cdot\boldsymbol{x} \leqq \boldsymbol{c} \quad \text{and} \quad \boldsymbol{p} \geqq \boldsymbol{0}, \tag{16.51}$$

we obtain

$$\boldsymbol{p}\cdot\boldsymbol{B}\cdot\boldsymbol{x} \leqslant \boldsymbol{p}\cdot\boldsymbol{c}. \tag{16.52}$$

Hence, we have, from (16.50) and (16.52),

$$\boldsymbol{a}\cdot\boldsymbol{x} \leqslant \boldsymbol{p}\cdot\boldsymbol{c} \tag{16.53}$$

for all feasible programme and dual vectors. Hence, if we can find $\boldsymbol{x}^*$ and $\boldsymbol{p}^*$ such that

$$\boldsymbol{a}\cdot\boldsymbol{x}^* = \boldsymbol{p}^*\cdot\boldsymbol{c}, \tag{16.54}$$

we will have obtained solutions to the programme and the dual.

Theorem 16.5[7]. *In the case of a linear programme which has a solution the function $V(z)$ as defined by (16.22) always has bounded steepness.*

Proof. Where a linear programme is concerned the definition of $V(z)$ is

$$V(z) = \max_{\boldsymbol{x}} \boldsymbol{a}\cdot\boldsymbol{x}, \qquad \text{ST}: \boldsymbol{c} - \boldsymbol{B}\cdot\boldsymbol{x} \geqq \boldsymbol{z}, \qquad \boldsymbol{x} \geqq \boldsymbol{0}. \tag{16.55}$$

Let $\boldsymbol{x}^*(0)$ satisfy (16.55) when $\boldsymbol{z} = \boldsymbol{0}$. Since $f(\boldsymbol{x}) = \boldsymbol{a}\cdot\boldsymbol{x}$ has bounded steepness it suffices to show that the maximum of $\boldsymbol{a}\cdot\boldsymbol{x}$ may be achieved with an $\boldsymbol{x}$ which varies continuously with $\boldsymbol{z}$. Moreover, if $\boldsymbol{x}$ can be shown to vary continuously with respect to each component of $\boldsymbol{z}$ taken alone then it varies continuously with respect to $\boldsymbol{z}$, as required. Hence, we need consider only a variation in the first component of $\boldsymbol{z}$, z_1.

We first provide a rule for picking from among the possible multiplicity of solutions to (16.55) a unique value $\boldsymbol{x}$. If there is more than one solution apply the following *lexicographic choice routine*. Choose $\boldsymbol{x}$ such that $(x_1^* - x_1)^2$ is a minimum. If a multiplicity of values of $\boldsymbol{x}$ conform to this requirement, choose from among them $\boldsymbol{x}$ such that $(x_2^* - x_2)^2$ is a minimum. If a multiplicity of values of $\boldsymbol{x}$ conform to this requirement, choose from among them $\boldsymbol{x}$ such that $(x_3^* - x_3)^2$ is a minimum, and so on. Denote this unique solution $\boldsymbol{x}^*(z_1)$.

Suppose that solutions chosen according to the lexicographic choice routine do not vary continuously with z_1. Then for some value of z_1, which we can take to be $z_1 = 0$ without loss of generality, there is a value $\delta > 0$ such that for z_1 of arbitrarily small absolute value, $\mathrm{d}[\boldsymbol{x}^*(z_1), \boldsymbol{x}^*(0)] > \delta$. However, $V(\boldsymbol{z})$ is clearly continuous since if $\boldsymbol{c} - \boldsymbol{B}\cdot\boldsymbol{x}^1 \geqq \boldsymbol{z}^1$ and $\mathrm{d}(\boldsymbol{z}^1, \boldsymbol{z}^2)$ is sufficiently small, there exists an $\boldsymbol{x}^2$ such that $\boldsymbol{c} - \boldsymbol{B}\cdot\boldsymbol{x}^2 \geqq \boldsymbol{z}^2$. Hence, we are forced to the conclusion that an arbitrarily small variation in z_1, away from $z_1 = 0$, would take $\boldsymbol{x}^*(z_1)$ to a hyperplane, $\boldsymbol{a}\cdot\boldsymbol{x} =$ constant, arbitrarily close to $\boldsymbol{a}\cdot\boldsymbol{x} = V(0)$ (in the sense that the constant would be arbitrarily close to $V(0)$), but there would have to be a discrete movement along a hyperplane with slope $\boldsymbol{a}$. For this to happen the set

$$\{\boldsymbol{x} \mid c_2 - \boldsymbol{b}^2\cdot\boldsymbol{x} \geqslant 0;\ c_3 - \boldsymbol{b}^3\cdot\boldsymbol{x} \geqslant 0;\ \ldots;\ c_m - \boldsymbol{b}^m\cdot\boldsymbol{x} \geqslant 0\}, \tag{16.56}$$

---

[7] This theorem is a little intricate and the necessity of providing a proof of it could be avoided by proving theorem 16.6 directly (i.e. not going to linear programming via non-linear programming) which it is perfectly possible to do. However, it is hoped that the present approach is more enlightening in that it shows exactly why linear programming is straightforward when compared to non-linear programming. The reader may skip the proof if he wishes to do so bearing in mind that it is only important in a particular type of boundary case. If $\pi_0 = 0$ and $\boldsymbol{z}$ may be chosen with all coefficients smaller (16.26) can be violated. Hence, it is only where not all constraints may be tightened without making the programme infeasible that it is necessary to invoke bounded steepness.

would have to have a discontinuous frontier, whereas in fact its frontier is continuous. The proof of the theorem is complete.

The following theorem may now be stated without any substantial extra proof since it embodies for the most part results at which we have by now arrived.

Theorem 16.6 (the duality theorem). If and only if the linear programme (16.47) has a solution then so does the dual linear programme (16.48) and for these solutions the value of programme and dual programme are equal. The following complementary slackness conditions are satisfied:

$$\boldsymbol{B}\cdot\boldsymbol{x} \leqq \boldsymbol{c} \quad \text{comp} \quad \boldsymbol{p} \geqq \boldsymbol{0}, \tag{16.57}$$

$$\boldsymbol{p}\cdot\boldsymbol{B} \geqq \boldsymbol{a} \quad \text{comp} \quad \boldsymbol{x} \geqq \boldsymbol{0}. \tag{16.58}$$

Proof. Since (16.47) is a special case of (16.19), and one which we know to satisfy the bounded steepness condition, there exists a vector $\boldsymbol{p}$ satisfying the requirements of theorem 16.3. Since all the functions in (16.47) are differentiable, theorem 16.4 applies, from which we have

$$\boldsymbol{a} \leqq \boldsymbol{p}^*\cdot\boldsymbol{B} \quad \text{comp} \quad \boldsymbol{x}^* \geqq \boldsymbol{0} \tag{16.59}$$

and

$$\boldsymbol{c} \geqq \boldsymbol{B}\cdot\boldsymbol{x}^* \quad \text{comp} \quad \boldsymbol{p}^* \geqq \boldsymbol{0}, \tag{16.60}$$

in conformity with (16.57) and (16.58). Hence, we have

$$\boldsymbol{a}\cdot\boldsymbol{x}^* = \boldsymbol{p}^*\cdot\boldsymbol{B}\cdot\boldsymbol{x}^* = \boldsymbol{p}^*\cdot\boldsymbol{c}, \tag{16.61}$$

as required.

Theorem 16.7 (the basis theorem). Let the linear programme (16.47) involve the choice of an n vector $\boldsymbol{x}$ *subject to m linear constraints. Then there exists a solution for which at most m components of* $\boldsymbol{x}^*$ *are positive.*

Proof. We show that if a solution vector $\boldsymbol{x}^*$ has more than m positive components it is possible to produce another solution vector with one less positive component. Suppose, without loss of generality, that the first $m+k$ components of $\boldsymbol{x}^*$ are positive. Let $\boldsymbol{b}^i$ be the ith column of the matrix $\boldsymbol{B}$. Then the vectors $\boldsymbol{b}^1, \boldsymbol{b}^2, \ldots, \boldsymbol{b}^{m+k}$ are not linearly independent. Let

$$\boldsymbol{b}^{m+k} = \sum_{i=1}^{m+k-1} \mu_i \boldsymbol{b}^i. \tag{16.62}$$

Now decrease x_{m+k} as follows. Let $\bar{x}_{m+k} = x^*_{m+k} - \theta$ and $\bar{x}_i = x^*_i + \theta\mu_i$. By construction $\boldsymbol{B}\cdot\boldsymbol{x}$ is independent of θ. Thus, as θ increases we still obtain feasible solutions, so that the value of $\boldsymbol{a}\cdot\boldsymbol{x}$ must also be independent of θ. Eventually some $\boldsymbol{x}$ value will become equal to zero, and we will have obtained an optimal solution with one less positive value in $\boldsymbol{x}$. The result follows.

Theorem 16.8. There can be a solution to the dual linear programme (16.48) with the jth component of $\boldsymbol{p}^*$ *taking the value* p^*_j *only if*

$$(\partial V/\partial c_j)^- \geqslant p^*_j \geqslant (\partial V/\partial c_j)^+. \tag{16.63}$$

Proof. We show that (16.63) holds for $j = 1$, from which it follows by symmetry that it holds for all j. Denote by $V(\lambda)$ the function $V(c_1 + \lambda, c_2, c_3, \ldots, c_m)$. Then the derivative of $V(\lambda)$ is the first partial derivative of V. By the duality theorem we have

$$V(\lambda) - V(0) = \boldsymbol{p}^*_\lambda\cdot\boldsymbol{c} + \lambda p^*_{1\lambda} - \boldsymbol{p}^*_0\cdot\boldsymbol{c}, \tag{16.64}$$

where $\boldsymbol{p}^*_\lambda$ is a solution to the dual linear programme when the constant vector is

$$\begin{bmatrix} c_1 + \lambda \\ c_2 \\ \vdots \\ c_m \end{bmatrix}.$$

$p^*_{1\lambda}$ is the first component of $\boldsymbol{p}^*_\lambda$ and $\boldsymbol{p}^*_0$ is a solution to the dual when the constant vector is $\boldsymbol{c}$ ($\lambda = 0$). Since $\boldsymbol{c}$ has no effect on the dual constraints, both $\boldsymbol{p}^*_\lambda$ and $\boldsymbol{p}^*_0$ are feasible for the constraints of the dual of the linear programme constrained by $\boldsymbol{c}$. Hence, since $\boldsymbol{p}^*_\lambda$ minimizes $\boldsymbol{p}\cdot\boldsymbol{c} + \lambda p_{1\lambda}$, we have

$$\boldsymbol{p}^*_0\cdot\boldsymbol{c} + \lambda p^*_1 \geqslant \boldsymbol{p}^*_\lambda\cdot\boldsymbol{c} + \lambda p^*_{1\lambda}. \tag{16.65}$$

Combining (16.64) and (16.65) gives

$$V(\lambda) - V(0) \leqslant p^*_1. \tag{16.66}$$

Hence,

$$\underset{\lambda<0}{\frac{V(\lambda) - V(0)}{\lambda}} \geqslant p^*_1 \geqslant \underset{\lambda>0}{\frac{V(\lambda) - V(0)}{\lambda}}. \tag{16.67}$$

Taking limits in (16.67) as $\lambda \to 0$, and noting from the observation that $V(\lambda)$ is a concave function, and theorem 16.2, that these limits exist, we obtain the required result.

Finally, we show that it is possible to choose any value in the closed interval whose endpoints are the right- and left-hand partial derivates of $V(\mathbf{c})$, and that a solution to the dual linear programme (16.41) may be obtained, such that the particular shadow price for the corresponding constraint will take that value.

Theorem 16.9. If $\bar{p}_1$ *is such that*

$$(\partial V/\partial c_1)^- \geqslant \bar{p}_1 \geqslant (\partial V/\partial c_1)^+ \tag{16.68}$$

then there exists a solution $\mathbf{p}^*$ *to the dual linear programme such that* $p_1^* = \bar{p}_1$.

Proof. Consider the ray $\mathscr{R}$ defined as

$$\mathscr{R} = \{\mathbf{y} \in R^{n+1} | \mathbf{y} = [V(\mathbf{c}), \mathbf{c}] + \lambda(\bar{p}_1; 1, 0, \ldots, 0)\}. \tag{16.69}$$

$\mathscr{R}$ is a ray passing through $[V(\mathbf{c}), \mathbf{c}]$. Furthermore, this ray supports $\mathscr{S}$ at $[V(\mathbf{c}), \mathbf{c}]$ by the concavity of $V(c_1)$ and the fact that $\bar{p}_1$ lies between the derivative limits $(\partial V/\partial c_1)^-$ and $(\partial V/\partial c_1)^+$. Now let $\mathscr{Q}$ be the convex sum of $\mathscr{R}$ and $\mathscr{S}$. $[V(\mathbf{c}), \mathbf{c}]$ is in the boundary of $\mathscr{Q}$ since the ray $\mathscr{R}$ supports $\mathscr{S}$. Hence, there exists a supporting hyperplane to $\mathscr{Q}$ at $[V(\mathbf{c}), \mathbf{c}]$, and this hyperplane must also support $\mathscr{R}$ and $\mathscr{S}$ alone, since these are subsets of $\mathscr{Q}$. But a vector can only support $\mathscr{R}$ if its first two components, after normalization, are 1 and $\bar{p}_1$. On the other hand, since this vector is supporting $\mathscr{S}$ it must provide a solution to the dual linear programme. Hence, there exists a solution to the dual linear programme with the first shadow price taking the value $\bar{p}_1$, as required.

References

Arrow, K. J. (1951). Alternative proof of the substitution theorem for Leontief models in the general case. In: Koopmans, T. C. (Ed.) *Activity Analysis of Production and Allocation* (New York: Wiley) ch. IX.

Arrow, K. J. (1968). Optimal capital policy with irreversible investment. In: Wolfe, J. N. (Ed.) *Value, Capital and Growth* (Edinburgh: Edinburgh University Press) 1–19.

Arrow, K. J. and Hahn, F. H. (1971). *General Competitive Analysis* (Mathematical Economics Texts, 6) (San Francisco: Holden-Day).

Arrow, K. J. and Hurwicz, L. (1960). Decentralization and computation in resource allocation. In: Pfouts, R. W. (Ed.) *Essays in Economics and Econometrics* (North Carolina University School of Business Administration, Studies in Economics and Business Administration) (Chapel Hill: University of North Carolina Press).

Bellman, R. E. (1957). *Dynamic Programming* (Princeton: Princeton University Press).

Black, J. (1962) The technical progress function and the production function. *Economica*, **XXIX**, May, 166–170.

Bliss, C. J. (1968). On putty clay. *Review of Economic Studies*, **35**, 105–132.

Bliss, C. J. (1974). The reappraisal of Keynes' economics: an appraisal. In: *Proceedings of the Annual Meeting of the AUTE* (Manchester: Basil Blackwell).

Brechling, F. P. (1975). *Investment and Employment Decisions* (Manchester: Manchester University Press).

Burmeister, E. (1974). A synthesis of the neo-Austrian and alternative approaches to capital theory. *Journal of Economic Literature*, **XII**, 413–456.

Champernowne, D. G. (1953–1954). The production function and the theory of capital: a comment. *Review of Economic Studies*, **21**, 112–135.

Cobb, C. W. and Douglas, P. H. (1928). A theory of production. *American Economic Review Papers and Proceedings*, **XVIII**, March, 139–165.

Cournot, A. A. (1897). *Researches into the Mathematical Principles of the Theory of Wealth* (New York: Macmillan).

Debreu, G. (1959). *Theory of Value: An Axiomatic Analysis of Economic Equilibrium* (Cowles Foundation for Research in Economics at Yale University, Monograph 17) (New York: Wiley).

Divisia, F. (1925). L'indice monétaire et la théorie de la monnaie. *Revue d'Economie Politique*, 39e Année, nos. 4, 5, 6, Juillet–Août, Septembre–Octobre, Novembre–Decembre, 842–861, 980–1008, 1121–1151.

Divisia, F. (1928). *Economiqué Rationnelle* (Paris: Gaston Doin).

Dobb, M. (1970). The Sraffa system and critique of the neo-classical theory of distribution. *De Economist*, **118**, July–August, 347–362.

Dorfman, R., Samuelson, P. and Solow, R. (1958). *Linear Programming and Economic Analysis* (New York: McGraw-Hill).

Eggleston, H. G. (1963). *Convexity* (Cambridge Tracts in Mathematics and Mathematical Physics, No. 47) (Cambridge: Cambridge University Press).

Eisner, R. and Strotz, R. (1963). Determinants of Business Investment. Research Study Two. In: *Impacts of Monetary Policy* (prepared for the Commission on Money and Credit) (Englewood Cliffs, N.J.: Prentice-Hall).

Fenchel, W. (1953). Convex cones, sets and functions. Princeton University, Department of Mathematics. September.

Fisher, F. M. (1965). Embodied technical change and the existence of an aggregate capital stock. *Review of Economic Studies*, **22**, 263–288.

Fisher, F. M. (1972). On price adjustment without an auctioneer. *Review of Economic Studies*, **39**, 1–15.

Friedman, M. (1957). *A Theory of the Consumption Function* (National Bureau of Economic Research, No. 63) (Princeton: Princeton University Press).

Friedman, M. (1969). *The Optimum Quantity of Money and Other Essays* (Chicago: Aldine).

Gale, D. (1960). *The Theory of Linear Economic Models* (New York: McGraw-Hill).

Gale, D. (1967). A geometric duality theorem with economic applications. *Review of Economic Studies*, **34**, 19–24.

Garegnani, P. (1970). Heterogeneous capital, the production function and the theory of distribution. *Review of Economic Studies*, **37**, 407–436.

Georgescu-Roegen, N. (1951). Some properties of a generalized Leontief model. In: Koopmans, T. C. (Ed.) *Activity Analysis of Production and Allocation* (New York: Wiley).

Goodwin, R. M. (1970). *Elementary Economics from the Higher Standpoint* (Cambridge: Cambridge University Press).

Gorman, W. M. (1959). Separable utility and aggregation. *Econometrica*, **27**, July, 469–481.

Gorman, W. M. (1968). Measuring the quantities of fixed factors. In: Wolfe, J. N. (Ed.) *Value, Capital and Growth* (Edinburgh: Edinburgh University Press).

Gould, J. P. (1968). Adjustment costs in the theory of the firm. *Review of Economic Studies*, **35**, 47–56.

Green, H. A. J. (1964). *Aggregation in Economic Analysis: An Introductory Survey* (Princeton: Princeton University Press).

Haavelmo, T. (1960). *A Study in the Theory of Investment* (Studies in Economics of the Economics Research Centre of the University of Chicago) (Chicago) 215–216.

Hadley, G. and Kemp, M. C. (1971). *Variational Methods in Economics* (Advanced Textbooks in Economics, vol. 1) (Amsterdam: Elsevier).

Hahn, F. H. (1965). On two sector growth models. *Review of Economic Studies*, **32**, 339–346.

Hahn, F. H. and Matthews, R. C. O. (1964). The theory of economic growth: a survey. *Economic Journal*, **LXXIV**, December, 779–902.

Halmos, P. R. (1958). Finite-dimensional vector spaces (University Series in Undergraduate Mathematics) (Princeton).

Harcourt, G. C. (1972). *Some Cambridge Controversies in the Theory of Capital* (Cambridge: Cambridge University Press).

Hicks, J. R. (1932). *The Theory of Wages* (London: Macmillan).

Hicks, J. R. (1946). *Value and Capital. An Inquiry into Some Fundamental Principles of Economic Theory* (Oxford: Clarendon Press) second edn.

Hicks, J. R. (1965). *Capital and Growth* (Oxford: Clarendon Press).

Hicks, J. R. (1973). *Capital and Time. A Neo-Austrian Theory* (Oxford: Clarendon Press).

Intriligator, M. D. (1971). *Mathematical Optimization and Economic Theory* (Series in Mathematical Economics) (Englewood Cliffs, N.J.: Prentice-Hall).

Jevons, W. S. (1911). *The Theory of Political Economy* (London: Macmillan) fourth edn.

Jorgenson, D. W. (1967). The theory of investment behaviour. In: Ferber, R. (Ed.) *Determinants of Investment Behaviour*. A conference of the Universities–National Bureau Committee for Economic Research (Universities National Bureau Conference Series, 18) (New York: Columbia University Press).

Jorgenson, D. W. and Griliches, Z. (1967). The explanation of productivity change. *Review of Economic Studies*, **34**, 249–283.

Junankar, P. N. (1972). *Investment: Theories and Evidence* (Macmillan Studies in Economics) (London: Macmillan).

Kahn, R. F. (1959). Exercises in the analysis of growth. *Oxford Economic Papers*, **11**, June, 143–156.

Kahn, R. F. (1972). Some notes on liquidity preference. In: *Selected Essays on Employment and Growth* (Cambridge: Cambridge University Press).

Kaldor, N. (1955–1956). Alternative theories of distribution. *Review of Economic Studies*, **23**, 83–100.

Kaldor, N. (1957). A model of economic growth. *Economic Journal*, **LXVII**, December, 591–624.

Kaldor, N. (1961). Capital accumulation and economic growth. In: Lutz, F. A. and Hague, D. C. (Eds.) *The Theory of Capital*. Proceedings of an International Economic Association Conference (London: Macmillan).

Kaldor, N. (1966a). *Causes of the Slow Rate of Economic Growth of the United Kingdom: An Inaugural Lecture* (Cambridge: Cambridge University Press).

Kaldor, N. (1966b). Marginal productivity and the macro-economic theories of distribution. *Review of Economic Studies*, **33**, 309–319.

Kaldor, N. and Mirrlees, J. A. (1962). A new model of economic growth. *Review of Economic Studies*, **29**, 174–192.

Karlin, S. (1959). *Mathematical Methods and Theory in Games, Programming and Economics* (London: Pergamon) Vol. 1.

Keynes, J. M. (1936). *The General Theory of Employment, Interest and Money* (London: Macmillan).

Klein, L. R. (1946). Macroeconomics and the theory of rational behaviour. *Econometrica*, **14**, April, 93–108.

Knight, F. H. (1921). *Risk, Uncertainty and Profit* (Boston: Houghton Mifflin).

Koopmans, T. C. (Ed.) (1951). *Activity Analysis of Production and Allocation*. Proceedings of a conference (Cowles Foundation Monographs, 13) (New York: Wiley).

Koopmans, T. C. (1957). *Three Essays on the State of Economic Science* (New York: McGraw-Hill).

Kuhn, H. W. and Tucker, A. W. (1951). Nonlinear programming. In: Neyman, J. (Ed.) *Proceedings of the second Berkeley Symposium on Mathematical Statistics and Probability* (Berkeley and Los Angeles: University of California Press).

Kurz, M. (1969). Tightness and substitution in the theory of capital. *Journal of Economic Theory*, **1**, 244–272.

Lancaster, K. (1968). *Mathematical Economics* (Macmillan Series in Economics) (New York: Macmillan).

Leijonhufvud, A. (1968). *Keynesian Economics and the Economics of Keynes: A study in Monetary Theory* (New York: Oxford University Press).

Leontief, W. W. (1936). Implicit theorizing: a methodological criticism of the neo-Cambridge school. *Quarterly Journal of Economics*, **LI**, November, 337–351.

Leontief, W. W. (1947). Introduction to a theory of the internal structure of functional relationships. *Econometrica*, **15**, October, 361–373.

Leontief, W. W. (1960). *The Structure of American Economy* (New York: Oxford University Press).

McFadden, D. (1967). The evaluation of development programmes. *Review of Economic Studies*, **34**, 25–50.

Machlup, F. (1963). On the meaning of the marginal product. In: Miller, M. H. (Ed.) *Essays on Economic Semantics* (Englewood Cliffs, N.J.: Prentice-Hall).

Malinvaud, E. (1953). Capital accumulation and the efficient allocation of resources. In: Arrow, K. J. and Scitovsky, T. (Eds.) *Readings in Welfare Economics* (London: Allen & Unwin).

Malinvaud, E. (1960–1961). The analogy between atemporal and intertemporal theories of resource allocation. *Review of Economic Studies*, **XXVII**, 143–160.
Marshall, A. (1920). *Principles of Economics* (London: Macmillan) eighth edn.
Marx, K. (1928). *Capital* (translated from fourth German edition by E. & C. Paul) (London: Allen & Unwin).
Meade, J. E. (1952). External economies and diseconomies in a competitive situation. *Economic Journal*, **LXII**, March, 54–67.
Meade, J. E. (1961). *A Neoclassical Theory of Economic Growth* (London: Allen).
Meade, J. E. (1965). *The Stationary Economy* (Principles of Political Economy, vol. I) (London: Allen and Unwin).
Meade, J. E. (1968). *The Growing Economy* (Principles of Political Economy, vol. 2) (London: Allen and Unwin).
Meiselman, D. (1965). *The Term Structure of Interest Rates* (Ford Foundation Doctoral Dissertation Series).
Mirrlees, J. A. (1969). The dynamic nonsubstitution theorem. *Review of Economic Studies*, **36**, 67–76.
Modigliani, F. (1944). Liquidity preference and the theory of interest and money. *Econometrica*, **12**, 45–88.
Modigliani, F. and Brumberg, R. (1970). Lifetime income and the savings ratio. In: Keiser, N. F. (Ed.) *Readings in Macroeconomics: Theory, Evidence and Policy* (Englewood Cliffs, N.J.: Prentice-Hall) ch. 8.
Morishima, M. (1961). An historical note on Professor Sono's theory of separability. *International Economic Review*, **2**, September, 272–275.
Morishima, M. (1964). *Equilibrium, Stability and Growth. A Multi-sectoral Analysis* (Oxford: Clarendon Press).
Morishima, M. (1969). *Theory of Economic Growth* (Oxford: Clarendon Press).
Nataf, A. (1948). Sur la possibilité de la construction de certains macromodèls. *Econometrica*, **16**, July, 232–244.
Neumann, J. von (1945–1946). A model of general economic equilibrium. *Review of Economic Studies*, **13**, 1–9.
Nordhaus, W. D. (1969a). Theory of innovation. An economic theory of technological change. *The American Economic Review Papers and Proceedings*, **LIX**, May, 18–28.
Nordhaus, W. D. (1969b). *Invention, Growth and Welfare: A Theoretical Treatment of Technological Change* (Cambridge, Mass.: Harvard University Press).
Pasinetti, L. L. (1962). Rate of profit and income distribution in relation to the rate of economic growth. *Review of Economic Studies*, **29**, 267–279.
Pasinetti, L. L. (1969). Switches of technique and the 'rate of return' in capital theory. *Economic Journal*, **LXXIX**, September, 508–531.
Patinkin, D. (1965). *Money, Interest and Prices: An Integration of Monetary and Value Theory* (New York: Harper and Row) second edn.
Pearce, I. F. (1970). *International Trade* (University of Southampton Economics Series) (London: Macmillan).
Quirk, J. and Saposnik, R. (1968). *Introduction to General Equilibrium Theory and Welfare Economics* (New York: McGraw-Hill).
Ramsey, F. P. (1928). A mathematical theory of saving. *Economic Journal*, **XXXVIII**, December, 543–559.
Ricardo, D. (1953). *Principles of Political Economy*, vol. 1 of *The Works and Correspondence of David Ricardo*. Eds.: Sraffa, P. with the collaboration of Dobb, M. H. (10 volumes) (Royal Economic Society) (Cambridge: Cambridge University Press).
Robertson, D. H. (1950). Wage grumbles. *Reading in the Theory of Income Distribution* (American Economic Association) (London: Allen and Unwin).
Robinson, J. V. (1934). What is perfect competition? *Quarterly Journal of Economics*, **XLIX**, November, 104–120.

Robinson, J. V. (1953–1954). The production function and the theory of capital. *Review of Economic Studies*, **21**, 81–106.
Robinson, J. V. (1956). *The Accumulation of Capital* (London: Macmillan).
Robinson, J. V. (1960). The rate of interest. In: *Collected Essays* (Oxford: Basil Blackwell) vol. II, 246–265.
Robinson, J. V. (1962). *Essays in the Theory of Economic Growth* (London: Macmillan).
Robinson, J. V. (1970). Capital theory up to date. *Canadian Journal of Economics*, **III**, 390–417.
Robinson, J. V. (1971). *Economic Heresies: Some Old-Fashioned Questions in Economic Theory* (London: Basic Books).
Samuelson, P. A. (1947). *Foundations of Economic Analysis* (Harvard Economic Studies, vol. 80) (Cambridge, Mass.: Harvard University Press).
Samuelson, P. A. (1959). A modern treatment of the Ricardian economy: capital and interest aspects of the pricing process. *Quarterly Journal of Economics*, **LXXIII**, February and May, 217–231.
Samuelson, P. A. (1961). A new theorem on nonsubstitution. *Money, Growth and Methodology*. Published in honour of Johan Akerman (Lund Social Science Studies, vol. 28) (Lund: C. W. K. Gleerup) 407–423.
Samuelson, P. A. (1966). An exact consumption–loan model of interest with or without the social contrivance of money. In: Stiglitz, J. E. (Ed.) *The Collected Scientific Papers of P. A. Samuelson* (Cambridge, Mass.: M.I.T. Press) vol. I, ch. 21.
Samuelson, P. A. (1967). *Economics: An Introductory Analysis* (New York: McGraw-Hill) seventh edn.
Savage, L. J. (1954). *The Foundations of Statistics* (New York: Wiley).
Schumpeter, J. A. (1954). *History of Economic Analysis*. Ed. from manuscript by Schumpeter, E. B. (London: Allen and Unwin).
Simmons, G. F. (1963). *Introduction to Topology and Modern Analysis* (New York: McGraw-Hill).
Solow, R. M. (1955–1956). The production function and the theory of capital. *Review of Economic Studies*, **23**, 101–108.
Solow, R. M. (1956). A contribution to the theory of economic growth. *Quarterly Journal of Economics*, **70**, February, 65–94.
Solow, R. M. (1963). *Capital Theory and the Rate of Return* (Professor Dr. F. De Vries Lectures, 1963) (Amsterdam: North-Holland).
Solow, R. M. (1967). The interest rate and transition between techniques. In: Feinstein, C. H. (Ed.) *Socialism, Capitalism and Economic Growth, Essays presented to Maurice Dobb* (Cambridge: Cambridge University Press) 30–39.
Sraffa, P. (1960). *Production of Commodities by Means of Commodities. Prelude to a Critique of Economic Theory* (Cambridge: Cambridge University Press).
Stiglitz, J. E. (1969). A re-examination of the Modigliani–Miller theorem. *American Economic Review*, **59** (5) December, 784–793.
Stiglitz, J. E. (1970a). A consumption-orientated theory of the demand for financial assets and the term structure of interest rates. *Review of Economic Studies*, **37**, 321–351.
Stiglitz, J. E. (1970b) Non-substitution theorems with durable capital goods. *Review of Economic Studies*, **37**, 543–553.
Stiglitz, J. E. (1973). Recurrence of techniques in a dynamic economy. In: Mirrlees, J. A. and Stern, N. H. (Eds.) *Models of Economic Growth* (London: Macmillan) 138–161.
Swan, T. W. (1956). Economic growth and capital accumulation. *Economic Record*, **XXXII**, November, 334–361.
Taussig, F. W. (1939). *Principles of Economics* (New York: Macmillan) fourth edn.
Theil, H. (1954). *Linear Aggregation of Economic Relations* (Contributions to Economic Analysis, 7) (Amsterdam: North Holland).

Tobin, J. (1957–1958). Liquidity preference as behavior towards risk. *Review of Economic Studies*, **25**, 65–86.

Treadway, A. B. (1969). On rational entrepreneurial behavior and the demand for investment. *Review of Economic Studies*, **36**, 227–239.

Uzawa, H. (1969). Time preference and the Penrose effect in a two-class model of economic growth. *Journal of Political Economy*, **77** (4, part II) July–August, 628–652.

Viner, J. (1931). Cost curves and supply curves. *Zeitschrift für Nationalökonomie*, **3**, September, 23–46.

Viner, J. (1937). *Studies in the Theory of International Trade* (London: Allen and Unwin).

Walras, L. (1954). *Elements of Pure Economics or the Theory of Social Wealth* (London: Allen and Unwin).

Weizsäcker, C. C. von (1971). *Steady State Capital Theory*. Lecture Notes in Operations Research and Mathematical Systems (Economics, Computer Science, Information and Control), No. 54, Beckermann, M. and Künzi, H. P. (Eds.) (Berlin, Heidelberg, New York: Springer-Verlag).

Wicksell, K. (1934). *Lectures on Political Economy* (London: Routledge) vol. I.

Wicksell, K. (1954). *Value, Capital and Rent* (London: Allen and Unwin).

Wicksell, K. (1958). *Selected Papers on Economic Theory*. Ed. by Lindahl, E. (London: Allen and Unwin).

INDEX